bs
6.10.04

LIBR

SMALL FIRMS IN TOURISM: INTERNATIONAL PERSPECTIVES

ADVANCES IN TOURISM RESEARCH

Series Editor: Professor Stephen J. Page
University of Stirling, UK
s.j.page@stir.ac.uk

Advances in Tourism Research series publishes monographs and edited volumes that comprise state-of-the-art research findings, written and edited by leading researchers working in the wider field of tourism studies. The series has been designed to provide a cutting edge focus for researchers interested in tourism, particularly the management issues now facing decision makers, policy analysts and the public sector. The audience is much wider than just academics and each book seeks to make a significant contribution to the literature in the field of study by not only reviewing the state of knowledge relating to each topic but also questioning some of the prevailing assumptions and research paradigms which currently exist in tourism research. The series also aims to provide a platform for further studies in each area by highlighting key research agendas which will stimulate further debate and interest in the expanding area of tourism research. The series is always willing to consider new ideas for innovative and scholarly books, inquiries should be made directly to the Series Editor.

Published:

LUMSDON & PAGE
Tourism and Transport: Issues and Agenda for the New Millennium

KERR
Tourism Public Policy and the Strategic Management of Failure

WILKS & PAGE
Managing Tourist Health and Safety in the New Millenium

BAUM & LUNDTORP
Seasonality in Tourism

ASHWORTH & TUNBRIDGE
The Tourist-Historic City: Retrospect and Prospect of Managing the Heritage City

RYAN & PAGE
Tourism Management: Towards the New Millennium

SONG & WITT
Tourism Demand Modelling and Forecasting: Modern Econometric Approaches

TEO, CHANG & HO
Interconnected Worlds: Tourism in Southeast Asia

Related Elsevier Journals — sample copies available on request

Journal of Air Transport Management
Annals of Tourism Research
International Journal of Hospitality Management
International Journal of Intercultural Relations
Tourism Management
World Development

SMALL FIRMS IN TOURISM: INTERNATIONAL PERSPECTIVES

EDITED BY

RHODRI THOMAS

Centre for Tourism Management, Leeds Metropolitan University, UK

2004

ELSEVIER

Amsterdam – Boston – Heidelberg – London – New York – Oxford
Paris – San Diego – San Francisco – Singapore – Sydney – Tokyo

ELSEVIER B.V.	ELSEVIER Inc.	**ELSEVIER Ltd**	ELSEVIER Ltd
Sara Burgerhartstraat 25	525 B Street, Suite 1900	**The Boulevard, Langford**	84 Theobalds Road
P.O. Box 211,	San Diego,	**Lane Kidlington,**	London
1000 AE Amsterdam	CA 92101-4495	**Oxford OX5 1GB**	WC1X 8RR
The Netherlands	USA	**UK**	UK

First edition 2004

Library of Congress Cataloging in Publication Data
A catalog record is available from the Library of Congress.

British Library Cataloguing in Publication Data
A catalogue record is available from the British Library.

ISBN: 0-08-044132-7

⊗The paper used in this publication meets the requirements of ANSI/NISO Z39.48-1992 (Permanence of Paper). Printed in The Netherlands.

Contents

Contributors

Marcjanna M. Augustyn   Department of Leisure, Tourism and Hospitality, University of Wolverhampton, England

Jack Carlsen   Cutrin Sustainable Tourism Center, Curtin University of Technology, Australia

Daniel Felsenstein   Department of Geography, Hebrew University of Jerusalem, Israel

Aliza Fleischer   Department of Agricultural Economics and Management, Hebrew University of Jerusalem, Israel

William C. Gartner   Tourism Center, University of Minnesota, USA

C. Michael Hall   Department of Tourism, University of Otago, New Zealand

Colin Johnson   Department of Hospitality Management, San Jose State University, USA

Donna Keen   Department of Tourism, University of Otago, New Zealand

Raija Komppula   Department of Business and Economics, University of Joensuu, Finland

Eric Laws   Aberdeen Business School, The Robert Gordon University, Scotland

Paul A. Lynch   School of Business and Enterprise, Queen Margaret University College, Edinburgh, Scotland

Harry Matlay   The Business School, University of Central England

Alison Morrison   The Scottish Tourism Research Unit, University of Strathclyde, Glasgow, Scotland

Andrew Mungall   Lausanne Institute for Hospitality Research, Switzerland

Nigel D. Morpeth   Centre for Tourism Management, Leeds Metropolitan University, England

Christian M. Rogerson	School of Geography, Archaeology and Environmental Studies, University of Witwatersrand, South Africa
Kristy Rusher	Tourism Central Otago, New Zealand
Michael Schaper	School of Management, Curtin University of Technology, Australia
Noel Scott	Department of Tourism and Leisure Management, University of Queensland, Australia
Myra Shackley	Centre for Tourism and Visitor Management, Nottingham Business School, Nottingham Trent University, UK and Visiting Professor, Centre for Tourism Management, Leeds Metropolitan University, England
Gareth Shaw	Department of Geography, University of Exeter, England
Rivanda Meira Teixeira	Universidada Federal de Sergipe, Brazil
Rhodri Thomas	Centre for Tourism Management, Leeds Metropolitan University, England
Hazel Tucker	Department of Tourism, University of Otago, New Zealand
Stephen Wanhill	School of Service Industries, Bournemouth University and Centre for Regional and Tourism Research, Bornholm, Denmark
Allan M. Williams	Department of Geography, University of Exeter, England

Preface

This book provides a varied collection of recent research relating to small businesses in tourism. In doing so it reflects the eclecticism of interest and method associated with this under-researched and under-theorised area of investigation. Topics range from the potential contribution of small firms to achieving social or economic goals to understanding more about business performance and growth. As is common in tourism research, disciplinary boundaries are routinely transgressed in the interests of gaining greater illumination.

The book is intended primarily for those engaged in tourism research relating to small businesses, public policy and community development. It will also be of interest to final year undergraduate and postgraduate students of tourism, and those studying small businesses more generally. Reflective policy-makers will also find much of interest.

The volume brings together highly experienced academics with others who are new to research. Insights from a variety of countries are offered, sometimes as a result of direct collaboration between authors initiated specifically for this book. Because chapters overlap in different ways — for example by theme, national setting, methodology — they are not organised into groups. Instead, the Introduction provides an overview of the contributions, and begins to draw out their collective significance. It also offers the beginnings of a longer term research agenda.

I am grateful to Stephen Page for suggesting and promoting the idea of creating this book from the small business conference held at Leeds in September 2002. In the event, fewer than half the chapters started out as conference papers with the remainder arising from special invitation. Naturally, I am especially grateful to the contributors for participating in this project. I have thoroughly enjoyed working with such capable and enthusiastic academics.

I should also take this opportunity to thank colleagues at Leeds, and elsewhere, for providing a stimulating academic climate and a network of free advice and support (sometimes I suspect unwittingly), notably: Warwick Clifton, Andrew Eaglen, Xavier Font, Linda Glover, Vicky Harris, David Hind, Stephanie Jameson, Conrad Lashley, Guy Lincoln, Jonathan Long, Paul Lynch, Agata Maccarrone-Eaglen, Alison Morrison, Nigel Morpeth, David Parsons, Annemarie Piso, Nia Thomas, Huw Thomas, David Ward, and Emma Wood. In addition, I thank Jane Marsh for her consistently faultless administrative assistance and Rachel Hayden for her help with the index.

Rhodri Thomas
Editor

Chapter 1

International Perspectives on Small Firms in Tourism: A Synthesis

Rhodri Thomas

Introduction

There has been a flourishing of interest in a variety of issues relating to small businesses in tourism over recent years. This has resulted in the organisation of international conferences dedicated to the theme, the creation of formal research networks and there have been a number of books and articles published. Yet, this area of inquiry is vastly under-researched; though some may protest, the depth of our knowledge of the dynamics of smaller enterprises in tourism and how they articulate with the economy and society remains relatively shallow. There is, however, room for optimism. The chapters that follow provide valuable access to understanding some key issues. Though the research focus of particular chapters and the methods of investigation vary according to the interests of commentators, and they undertake work in different national settings, some common themes begin to emerge. As is explored more towards the end of this chapter, the contributions to this volume help provide insights into owner-manager motivations and business practices, and their potential contribution to social and economic development goals. Some conventional wisdom is undermined by the insights afforded in this book.

It is important to point out that Chapter authors do not adopt a single definition of "small firm." In part, this reflects the lack of academic consensus (for a review see Thomas 2000) and the fact that official definitions — usually expressed in numerical terms — also vary between countries. For consistency of presentation, contributors tend to use the term "small firm" but define its usage as appropriate.

Although the collection of papers is eclectic, readers would be mistaken if they equated this with a lack of coherence. Most of the chapters are predicated on an interest in policy interventions where, for example, small firms in tourism may contribute to regional competitiveness, regeneration or sustainability. Other commentators are driven more by an interest in evaluating business practices with a view to informing business policy at the level of the firm. These appear in the final stages of the book.

Economic and Social Policy Goals

The first substantive chapter, by Rogerson, examines small business development in the context of developing countries, taking the case of South Africa. If there is limited research and theorising on small tourism businesses in general, there is still less available to support Rogerson's endeavours. His contribution in starting to open this field is, therefore, especially welcome.

The location of the study in South Africa is interesting because of official concerns not only to use tourism as a means of economic development but also because small business development is seen as a means of achieving particular social goals, namely black economic empowerment (currently some 95% of tourism businesses are owned by whites).

Drawing on contrasting literatures, he develops a framework for examining the promotion of small business development in South African tourism that is comprised of four elements. Briefly, he notes the need to recognise how smaller enterprises are currently marginalised by the domination of large (and often foreign owned) enterprises; to paraphrase, they are left to scratch around for the crumbs from the table of their wealthier counterparts. Secondly, he draws our attention to the literature on new or alternative tourism, suggesting that such niche offerings relating to say social or cultural tourism may provide more fruitful opportunities for small scale enterprise development than mass (Fordist) tourism. The third strand of the literature he uses relates to that written about the role small firms play in poverty alleviation, especially by considering the articulation of the informal with the formal economy; lessons may be learnt by policy-makers (notably in providing smaller enterprises with access to markets). This theme is developed when Rogerson examines what policy-makers might learn from the literature that has explored "business linkages," notably those relating to the supply chain. In essence, the argument is that during the early stages of development there is a role for the state in encouraging foreign firms to use local suppliers.

The themes identified above are examined in the context of post-apartheid interventions in tourism and small business development. Although it is too early to offer a full assessment — and there is too little research evidence — Rogerson provides a broadly sanguine interpretation of events. There are clearly obstacles to be overcome; the discrimination and inequalities inherited by the post-apartheid regime will not be countered quickly. However, it seems that the measures taken thus far recognise many of the issues raised by the literatures reviewed, and are likely to make a positive contribution to development.

Gartner's (Chapter 3) explores some of the themes raised by Rogerson. More specifically, his interest is in using notions of dependency — relating the concept to relations between countries and, in turn, small and large enterprises — to examine small business behaviour. His starting point is to construct a framework of selective key issues: population growth, consumption centre development, public involvement, technology. The framework is then used to organise an investigation into small tourism firms in Ghana's Central Region.

The discussion provides a fascinating insight, especially for those familiar only with small business research in advanced capitalist economies. Amongst other things, it emphasises the importance of recognising the cultural dimension. By way of illustration, this case study shows that there are contrasting attitudes to public sector interventions. Further, in many instances, business owners may commonly consult priests or priestesses for advice on business decisions which, presumably, is in sharp contrast with "western economies."

There are, however, also similarities that should not be overlooked: dependence on family labour amongst the smallest firms, low demand for and utilisation of skills, and a suggestion that many small firms engage in informal economic activity.

Wanhill (Chapter 4) also considers the role of the state in promoting entrepreneurship and sustaining small business development, though his work is located in the advanced capitalist economies of the European Union (EU). In doing so, he draws attention to how resources allocated to regional development via tourism initiatives have increased over the recent past. These resources have, in turn, impacted upon numerous small firms because of their preponderance in the sector.

Wanhill makes the case for state intervention in tourism by pointing to various market failures. This is refreshing because in other contexts far too many commentators make assumptions about the desirability of particular forms of intervention based on weak theoretical or empirical foundations (for a critique see Thomas 1998).

The initial focus of Wanhill's chapter is on the nature and potential impact of various forms of investment incentives, from mechanisms to reduce capital or operating costs to schemes that provide security for funds borrowed by SMEs. Although he is broadly supportive of investment incentives, he argues that a wider programme of intervention is required that goes beyond financial considerations to include ways of upgrading standards, improving communication and distribution channels, and enhancing the level of market intelligence available for small firms. He makes an interesting case which will need to be tested in light of the complexity of drivers that influence the decision-making of small business owners and owner-managers.

Fleischer & Felsenstein (in Chapter 5) examine empirically the extent to which public sector investment made in small business support services that relate specifically to tourism enterprises can be justified in terms of their short-run impact on output and employment. The data used for their analysis are gathered from participants in programmes that operated in Israel in the early to mid-1990s.

Their starting point is to model output and employment responses to capital assistance, the focus of their attention. As they suggest, although there is an expectation that output would increase for firms receiving capital assistance, the impact on employment may be less predictable. With assistance, labour becomes more expensive compared with capital so may result in a substitution of capital for labour. However, if output increases substantially, the net result may be an increased demand for labour. It is possible, therefore, for employment generation to increase or decrease as a result of capital assistance.

The authors' reading of the data suggests that a public sector subsidy has a disproportionate impact on employment in small tourism firms compared with other sectors, though they do not observe significant differences relating to output. The explanation for this, they argue, is linked with the labour intensity of tourism firms and seasonality. The latter encourages small tourism firms to invest in technology that has few cost implications for fluctuations in demand, using changes to the numbers of workers as the main means of adjustment.

Official aspirations to enhance the competitiveness of the tourism sector forms the backdrop to Hall & Rusher's examination of the entrepreneurial characteristics and business practices of bed and breakfast accommodation providers in New Zealand (Chapter 6). As elsewhere, public policy-makers recognise that if interventions concerned with shaping business practices — particularly with those that impact so significantly on the tourist experience — are to be effective, they must "touch" small firms, given their numerical preponderance.

Hall & Rusher's study focuses mainly on operators that employ few, if any, beyond the immediate family. Drawing on data gathered from a comprehensive questionnaire survey, the authors provide a fascinating profile of the attitudes and business practices of bed and breakfast operators in New Zealand's upper North Island. Their findings confirm some aspects of existing research — for example that lifestyle factors permeate decision-making — but also challenge others — for example gender divisions in the operation of micro-businesses, and the importance of profit and "professionalism" in operations to owner-managers. What emerged clearly from this research was the sense that lifestyle goals can be seen as strategic business objectives, consistently (informally) evaluated in the light of commercial considerations (which are clearly required for survival). As the authors point out, a failure to recognise — indeed to understand more fully — the complexity of objectives and circumstances is unlikely to yield public policies that will influence change.

Shaw & Williams (Chapter 7) also focus on small business owners. Their starting point is to provide a systematic review of the literature on entrepreneurship in tourism and the motivations of small business owners in the sector. Not surprisingly, much of the discussion focuses on notions of "lifestyle." Although use of the term varies, at its heart is the idea that non-economic factors — such as the desire for autonomy or wishing to live in a particular area — play an important part in explaining the reason why many individuals establish small businesses in tourism. Further, it helps illuminate why certain decisions are taken and not others (notably those relating to investment and growth). Readers may recall the contributors' highly influential study of small firms in Cornwall (Williams *et al.* 1989) which found that such businesses were as much about consumption as production.

Shaw & Williams — like Hall & Rusher — are alert to the dangers of oversimplification and point out that lifestyle motivations clearly influence behaviour but need to be read alongside the economic (or financial) motives that apply simultaneously. The chapter concentrates on discussing the findings of a recent study of "surf tourism" entrepreneurs in Cornwall. The research suggests that lifestyle factors, linked with surfing, the surfing community and the attractiveness of the area are important to entrepreneurs. However, they also identify a prominent business development orientation that appears to be more important than elsewhere in tourism. As the authors point out, these findings contrast both with their earlier work in Cornwall (where small business owners were often semi-retired) and with the ethically driven lifestyle entrepreneurs associated with New Zealand backpacking (Ateljevic & Doorne 2000). Although more research is required, it seems that the way of running a business by lifestyle entrepreneurs varies by place and sector of activity, with their sometimes distinctive lifestyle norms.

Rural Development

The next four chapters — Komppula (Chapter 8), Keen (Chapter 9), Scott & Laws (Chapter 10), and Hall (Chapter 11) — examine the role of small businesses in contributing to change in rural locations. The first of these focuses on a question that has challenged policy-makers with an interest in regional development for some time, namely how to stimulate and support rural business development in tourism. Komppula starts her examination by drawing attention to the contrasting aspirations of small business owners alluded to above, noting not only lifestyle motivations as a factor that potentially stifles business growth of the type exhorted by officials, but also factors such as lack of capability or skills to manage growth within particular enterprises.

Komppula provides a systematic, yet succinct, review of the literature on small business "success," "growth" and "performance" (terms that are usually rather vaguely defined and used inconsistently between authors), drawing out aspects that relate particularly to issues of owner-manager agency. The insights offered in her chapter emerge from empirical work undertaken in Finland that comprised a set of almost one hundred and eighty structured interviews with rural tourism entrepreneurs, followed by semi-structured in-depth interviews with an additional smaller sample of business owners from the North Korelia region of Eastern Finland.

Building on the work of those that have for some time sought to construct ways of understanding notions of "success" that include non-financial criteria, Komppula develops a more comprehensive conceptualisation that takes account of a variety of what she terms "quality" aspects: quality of life, quality of service and quality of product. These "interests," she argues, guide the decision-making of small business owners. The challenge for public policy-makers is to develop strategies for intervention that are consistent with *public* goals yet resonate with the *private* interests of small business operators.

Keen's (Chapter 9) research suggests that for some operators in some rural communities, the social benefits of running a tourism business — including a sense of contribution to the maintenance of "community" — were important factors in continuing with operations that were financially of marginal importance. These were positive reasons from people that might operate other financially more secure operations; they *chose* to continue with tourism enterprises. Keen examines this phenomenon via notions of social and community entrepreneurship, paying attention to how such "movers and shakers" may influence the development of tourism in particular locations.

Her research is based on a case study of Maniototo, Southern New Zealand, a rural area with a population of fewer than 1,000 people dispersed between a network of villages. Keen documents the growth of tourism in the area from a very low base to its current position; one in which the local economy (and apparently community) has been revitalised. Keen ascribes significance to the pivotal actions of one individual who — *inter alia* — organised community activities to raise funds and, in turn, investments to facilitate tourism. Although ultimately benefitting from a private tourism venture, the main point of interest here is that her actions went considerably beyond what might be expected of someone only interested in financial gain.

This rich vein of potential research is also explored by Scott & Laws in Chapter 10. They examine the articulation of community, small business interests and tourism development by tracing the emergence of commercial whale watching — niche markets — in two case locations: Hervey Bay and Byron Bay, both on the east coast of Australia. The cases are interesting because in the former, small firms have developed the market successfully but were prevented from doing so in the latter.

Scott & Laws begin to explain this contrast in terms that relate to considerations of agency — a particularly dynamic entrepreneur in Hervey Bay whose business ideas were imitated by others — and "structural" factors, such as the availability of, or an ability to set in place, supplier networks. They also draw attention to how the values of key stakeholders have a bearing on development. Thus, in Byron Bay, although entrepreneurs had identified a market opportunity, they were prevented from exploiting it by Cape Byron Trust who controlled access to the beach and chose not to issue many licences for fear of environmental damage. Scott & Laws' contribution highlights the importance of examining power relations in tourism policy-making. Clearly in the case of Byron Bay, small enterprises were unable to influence the policy-making process and were unable to mobilise political support.

In Chapter 11 Hall examines what might at this stage loosely be called business networks in the context of wine and food tourism. His interest is to examine such associations in terms of rural economic development in New Zealand. As he points out early in his chapter, in some places — such as Australia and the European Union — the state has expended considerable energy and imagination in seeking to facilitate various forms of co-operative behaviour amongst firms in particular locations and/or sectors. In New Zealand, by contrast, the precipitation of innovative arrangements in this regard has, it appears, been as a result of highly motivated and capable individuals that have utilised their social capital to initiate change within particular areas. Hall's chapter examines this and several other conditions that also appear to obtain where local collaboration between firms operates to the mutual economic benefit of participants.

Hall's starting point is to note that regional economic development is successful where areas can change effectively from declining industries to new ones. In essence, that requires a process of utilising local intangible assets such as brands, talent and small business networking. More precisely, his analysis of networks is set within a framework of economic clusters, where a cluster is defined as a "geographically bounded concentration of interdependent businesses with active channels for business transactions, dialogue and communications, and that collectively shares common opportunities and threats" (from Rosenfield 1997: 10).

Following an examination of three case studies of leading wine regions in New Zealand — Central Otago, Hawkes Bay and Marlborough — Hall advocates a route for increasing the effectiveness of clusters and networks' contribution to regional competitiveness, suggesting that the stronger the networking characteristics the higher the degree of regional competitiveness. Without denying the potential value of studies that have concentrated on financial aspects of small business performance, Hall effectively opens the assessment of determinants of competitiveness to include intangible elements such as the value of trust between the various agents and knowledge transfer between network members.

Non-Economic Policy Goals and Settings

The focus of attention changes from Chapter 12 to a consideration of wider policy contexts. First, Lynch & Tucker examine the appropriateness of quality grading and assurance schemes as they relate to small accommodation enterprises that have a home dimension; what the authors refer to as "commercial homes." Commercial homes are characterised by the high level of personal interaction between the hosts and guests. The chapter draws on and develops research that has until now been undertaken separately by each author in the context of their national settings, Scotland and New Zealand respectively. Their work represents a valuable example of the additional insights that become available from international comparative research.

The core of their work undermines those that suggest a fit between official grading schemes — often developed with conceptions of large enterprises in mind — and the very small "home-based" firms in question. If this were ever a marginal issue for policy-makers, those days have gone given the growth in numbers of tourists that use such accommodation units in both countries.

Following a discussion of the nature of possible host and guest relationships, the authors provide a summary of some of the recent debates surrounding quality assurance schemes in the two countries. Not surprisingly, the grading systems vary. However, in both cases — and this is probably generalisable internationally — there is an emphasis on the physical aspects of provision and on the various services offered. As is pointed out, the models may fit hotels but hardly resonate with commercial homes. As a consequence, Lynch & Tucker propose an alternative system of grading that captures the notion of a private home as the benchmark. In doing so, they argue that grading needs to emphasise the relationship between guest and hosts; information that is most likely to be gleaned meaningfully from guests themselves rather than inspectors. Adoption of a more fluid system of grading that drew attention to the qualities (or otherwise) alluded to by guests would avoid the inappropriately standardised approaches that currently prevail.

Schaper & Carlsen's contribution (Chapter 13) examines the environmental performance of small tourism firms in Western Australia. They begin by noting the main arguments in favour of encouraging sustainable business practices, and the manner in which this might be achieved. The emphasis of the discussion is on the environmental (or "green") aspects of sustainability. The authors then provide a review of recent research into the environmental practices of smaller tourism enterprises, paying particular attention to identification of the barriers to improved environmental performance.

One of the key issues is the dissonance between the attitudes of smaller firms and their subsequent actions; as they point out, attitudes are not necessarily good indicators of practice. In this context, Schaper & Carlsen suggest an agenda for action that involves: providing green business advice; working with industry associations; starting with achievable targets; advocating tourism educators to encourage engagement with the issues; building support networks, and recognising best practice. As the authors readily acknowledge, the efficacy of these is not assured because of the weak evidence base. Hence their advocacy of a new research agenda during the concluding stage of their chapter.

Morpeth (Chapter 14) also examines the role small firms play in the promotion of sustainable tourism. More specifically, he examines the issue in the context of cycle tourism within a U.K. national park, the Lake District. His central concern is to understand more about the extent to which very small (micro) enterprises in the accommodation sector are responsive to the hospitality needs of cycle tourists and whether provision arises from a wider concern with sustainability.

His review of existing studies and a small scale research project enables Morpeth to point out that small firms are certainly not environmentally benign, or necessarily any more receptive to the idea of altering business practices to reduce environmental impacts than any others category of enterprise. However, he suggests that those operating in some sub-sectors — in his case cycle tourism — may be more likely to operate their business in a manner that takes account of environmental considerations, though the evidence is mixed.

Following an international review of the main characteristics of religious tourism, Shackley (Chapter 15) examines retreat houses as a form of small tourism business, concentrating in particular on the British context. A "retreat house" is defined in her chapter as "a small firm that provides catered accommodation and spiritual input for guests in search of peace and quiet, whether or not this is associated with a religious or monastic experience" (p. 228). Apparently, the main features of such houses vary between countries. In the U.K. and Western Europe, for example, retreat houses tend to be rural or at least set in quiet gardens, provide opportunities for (optional) worship, offer simple but good quality food and have high levels of repeat business. As a consequence, marketing costs are low. By contrast, North American houses often provide far longer "retreats" (a term that is itself difficult to pin down) in motel-style accommodation.

The picture Shackley paints of the (sub-) sector is both novel and fascinating. Although there are similarities with other small firms in tourism — enterprises often operate at the margins of financial survival and may have idiosyncratic management — there are also important differences that warrant separate analysis from the purely commercial sector. In particular, Shackley estimates that some 60% of retreat houses are registered with the Charity Commission, they tend not to be owner-managed (the owners may be a religious community) and are often particularly sensitive to the importance of sustainable tourism, unlike small tourism firms in general (Dewhurst & Thomas 2003). Perhaps Shackley's main contribution by writing this chapter is to alert researchers to the existence of the sub-sector and to begin the process of baseline data gathering.

Small Business Management and Growth

The remaining chapters are all concerned with matters that relate to enhancing the performance of small firms. Drawing on data gathered from more than fifty interviews in Glasgow, Scotland, and Aracaju, Brazil, Morrison & Teixeira examine factors that influence the performance of small firms in tourism (Chapter 16). The framework for their assessment rests on the premise that factors influencing firm performance comprise a blend of structural factors — the business environment within which an enterprise operates — as well as issues of agency, notably the skills, capabilities and resources of the owner-manager. In this they are consistent with others that have examined small business growth (for example Storey 1996) and those that have taken a broader interpretation of "business performance" (for example Dewhurst & Horobin 1998).

The conspicuously different operating environments that are discussed fully in this chapter clearly *condition* market responses; for example, the stable demand in Glasgow does not require operators to devise flexible tariffs — including selling rooms by the hour when demand is low — as in Aracaju. However, the authors also find significant similarities of outlook and behaviour among the owner-managers interviewed. Few anticipate growth, some because of perceived resource and (personal) capacity constraints, whereas others are reluctant to engage in the trade-off between growth and other quality of life indicators.

In Chapter 17, Augustyn is concerned with those tourism SMEs that aspire to grow. In doing so, she implicitly rejects the need for a specific and separate approach to assessing strategic management within SMEs. Instead, she takes a resource-based view (RBV) of strategy, arguing that it is as appropriate a conceptualisation for smaller as for larger enterprises. Her position is likely to be less contentious than it otherwise might be because of her focus on growth-orientated businesses only, rather than the small business community as a whole.

Augustyn is persuasive in arguing that the two major routes to effective resource utilisation and performance are "resource leverage" (seeking less resource intensive means of achieving goals), and building "organisational capability platforms" (those, sometimes intangible, organisationally specific competences). Her application of these concepts in two detailed, yet exploratory studies, is instructive; it suggests ways in which those aspiring to grow might learn from others and, inevitably, points to new avenues of investigation. In terms of the former, she argues for example that the growth experienced by the case study enterprises could be explained in part by reference to the distinctive capability platforms developed to enable further movement on their growth trajectory.

Mungall & Johnson examine internationalisation among tourism SMEs in Switzerland (Chapter 18). Their chapter begins with an assessment of the literature on internationalisation with a view to developing indicators of internationalisation that are appropriate for the tourism context. This results in a number of factors being identified that are then investigated empirically. Broadly, internationalisation is examined from three different perspectives: foreign customers as a share of total turnover; foreign goods and services as suppliers; and the importance of foreign partnerships in marketing activities. The research reported in the chapter is based on a questionnaire survey of hotels and other tourism businesses. The findings suggest to the authors a relatively low level of internationalisation among tourism SMEs in Switzerland. Perhaps predictably, they find greater evidence of internationalisation amongst those located in urban areas (notably Geneva and Zurich), and they tend to be larger enterprises. Although the case is not made explicitly, the assessment is predicated on the notion that the more internationalised an enterprise is, the more likely it is to prosper. They note in conclusion that as competition intensifies, more enterprises may need to seek competitive advantage by co-operating with others, nationally or internationally.

As the title of final chapter suggests — Small tourism firms in e-Europe: definitional, conceptual and contextual considerations — Matlay explores a range of issues relating to the use of Information and Communications Technology (ICT) by small tourism firms in relation to e-commerce. He sets his review in the context of the tourism sector in Europe. Particular attention is drawn to the potentially contrasting experiences of those operating in Central and Eastern Europe with those located in Western Europe. Although differences should not be under-stated, Matlay highlights the significance of many similarities, such as the fragmentation of the sectors, the growth of ICT and public policies that claim to be supportive of entrepreneurship. Although not examined critically in detail, they provide a valuable background for Matlay's closer examination of shifts toward e-commerce in tourism.

In explaining the growth of e-commerce — and its forecast expansion — Matlay draws attention to several inter-related contributory factors. Briefly, these encompass the reduced costs yet increased reliability, capability and capacity of technology that is available to even modest businesses, and, critically, households. Such conditions not only enable innovative smaller enterprises to gain access to wider markets, but have also resulted in less dynamic enterprises adopting at least some aspects of technology-based business practice. However, Matlay also notes several barriers to the adoption of e-commerce among small tourism firms, the most notable being the skill shortages in ICT-related skills required to service e-commerce development within the sector.

Conclusion

The preceding discussion has demonstrated several things. First, that there are factors that distinguish the *study of* small firms in tourism from small firms in other sectors. Certainly there are areas of investigation that will be of common interest, probably most notably relating to job creation and economic development, and the impact of management interventions, such as training or marketing, on business performance. Further, academics from a variety of disciplines have taken an interest in, say, the part smaller firms might play in social policy goals or sustainable development, and the influence of owner-manager motivations on how small businesses are organised. However, as the chapters in this volume have shown, the impact of small firms on the tourist experience — i.e. their part in the overall consumption of places — coupled with particular kinds of lifestyle considerations, and the fact that many businesses in the accommodation sector share their homes with guests, tends to raise issues that justify small firms in tourism as an distinctive unit of analysis. Clearly, the point should not be exaggerated.

The book has also highlighted the *emergent* nature of research in this area. There is little international agreement even on basic issues such as how to define small firms, how to count them or how to distinguish *tourism* enterprises from others. Evidently there is a need to address these matters, though — arguably — they are not the most stimulating of potential research topics!

Collectively, the chapters presented in this book have added to our understanding of a variety of issues. The final part of this chapter attempts to briefly signpost some of these and offers an indicative research agenda.

- *Lifestyle motivations predominate in the tourism sector but "lifestyle" needs to be conceptualised in a manner that recognises the influence of sub-sector (see for example Shaw & Williams; and also hinted at by Morpeth), national cultures (for example Gartner; Morrison & Teixeira), location (for example Rogerson) and domestic circumstances (for example Hall & Rusher; Komppula).* Lifestyle may simply mean wanting to live somewhere that is desirable, with a modest level of income, driven by a particular social outlook (see Keen; Schaper & Carlsen; Shackley). However, it can also imply a desire to generate a "good" standard of living, operating a "professionally" organised business but within a particular set of "lifestyle" activities (Hall & Rusher; Shaw & Williams). Engaging in research that produces a clearer picture of lifestyle categories and their articulation with the economy must be an essential element of future research.

- *An examination of the behaviour of the smallest of firms without appreciating the role of informal economic activity will generate only a partial understanding of their dynamics.* This observation applies as much in developed capitalist economies as elsewhere (see for example Gartner; Hall & Rusher; Morrison & Teixeira; Rogerson) though its manifestation will vary. Although such research is fraught with methodological difficulties (Piso *et al.* 2002; Williams & Thomas 1996), rising to the challenge is likely to yield rewarding insights.

- *That the organisation of small enterprises in tourism is typically delineated by gender is contested (compare Hall & Rusher with Morrison & Teixeira).* Clearly, further detailed research is required.

- *Growth-oriented small firms can enhance business performance by adopting particular business practices (see for example Augustyn; Matlay; Mungall & Johnson) but the influence of such behaviours is circumscribed by particular contexts (Hall; Morrison & Teixeira).* There is a strong vein of research on innovation and entrepreneurship in the small business literature and some in tourism (for a review see Morrison *et al.* 1999). The veracity of assertions about the nature of entrepreneurial firms and the utility of various management techniques for small firms in tourism will inevitably form an important part of future research programmes.

- *Research reported in this book points to the potentially positive outcomes of policy measures directed at small firms in tourism (see for example Fleischer & Felsenstein; Rogerson; Wanhill). However, there is also evidence of the inappropriateness of particular measures for at least some categories of firm (Lynch & Tucker).* Projects that seek to inform public policy by connecting more effectively the heterogeneity of the enterprises and their particular contexts with creative and clearly articulated policy goals, are likely to be valued by users of academic research.

- *Small firms engage with the policy-making process in different ways in different settings. Contributions to this volume (for example Hall; Keen; Scott & Laws) have shown that smaller enterprises can — under certain conditions — influence tourism policy outcomes.* Although there has been a growth in official intervention that impacts upon small tourism businesses, there has been little examination of how small firms engage with — or are excluded from — policy formulation. Research that seeks to analyse their role in policy-making, as opposed to seeking policy prescriptions, would add a complimentary dimension to existing policy studies.

References

Ateljevic, I., & Doorne, S. (2000). Staying within the fence: Lifestyle entrepreneurship in tourism. *Journal of Sustainable Tourism, 8*(5), 378–392.

Dewhurst, H., & Thomas, R. (2003). Encouraging sustainable business practices in a non-regulatory environment: A case study of small tourism firms in a U.K. National Park. *Journal of Sustainable Tourism, 11*(4).

Dewhurst, P., & Horobin, H. (1998). Small business owners. In: R. Thomas (Ed.), *The management of small tourism and hospitality firms* (pp. 19–38). London: Cassell.

Morrison, A., Rimmington, M., & Williams, C. (1999). *Entrepreneurship in the hospitality, tourism and leisure industries.* Oxford: Butterworth-Heinemann.

Piso, A., Thomas, R., Uwamungu, B., & Johnson, C. (2002). Informal employment in small firms: A comparative study of the tourism sectors in Switzerland and the United Kingdom. International Conference: Small Firms in the Tourism and Hospitality Sectors. Leeds (September).

Rosenfield, S. A. (1997). Bringing business clusters into the mainstream of economic development. *European Planning Studies, 5*(1), 3–23.

Storey, D. J. (1996). *Understanding the small business sector.* London: Routledge.

Thomas, R. (1998). Small firms and the state. In: R. Thomas (Ed.), *The management of small tourism and hospitality firms* (pp. 78–97). London: Cassell.

Thomas, R. (2000). Small firms in the tourism industry: Some conceptual issues. *International Journal of Tourism Research, 2*(6), 345–353.

Williams, A. M., Shaw, G., & Greenwood, J. (1989). From tourist to tourism entrepreneur, from consumption to production: Evidence from Cornwall, England. *Environment and Planning, A21,* 1639–1653.

Williams, C. C., & Thomas, R. (1996). Paid informal work in the Leeds hospitality industry: Unregulated or regulated work? In: G. Haughton, & C. C. Williams (Eds), *Corporate city? Partnership, participation and partition in urban development in Leeds* (pp. 171–183). Aldershot: Avebury.

Chapter 2

Tourism, Small Firm Development and Empowerment in Post-Apartheid South Africa

Christian M. Rogerson

Introduction

During the past two decades a considerable amount of research has been undertaken on issues surrounding the impacts of tourism in the developing world, in particular assessing the contribution that the sector can make to economic development (Ashley *et al.* 2001; Brohman 1996; Harrison 1992, 1994; Sharpley & Telfer 2002; Sinclair 1998; Sinclair & Stabler 1998). Nevertheless, it remains true, as pointed out by Lea (1988), that the extent to which tourism "can actually promote business activity in a Third World country has not received much attention." To borrow a recent analogy used in discussing tourism small firms research in the developed North, the field of tourism small business development in the South is *terra incognita* (Page *et al.* 1999). Questions concerning entrepreneurship and small firm development occupy only a relatively minor role in the volumes of writing produced on tourism in the developing countries of Africa, Latin America and Asia developing world (Gartner 1999; Hampton 2001; Kirsten & Rogerson 2002; Rogerson 2001a). In this chapter the aim is to contribute to this undeveloped literature by investigating the problems and opportunities for the development of small firms in the tourism economy of South Africa, as an example of developing world tourism.

It can be argued that for studies on tourism small firm development, the South African case is of particular interest for several reasons, not least the recent global focus on the country with the hosting during 2002 of the World Summit on Sustainable Development. South Africa's highly visible role as a symbol of peaceful democratic transition with the potential to create racial harmony functions as a powerful generic tool for international tourism. Tourism is widely acknowledged as a strategic priority and potentially one of the economic drivers for South Africa in the 21st century (Lewis 2001; Rogerson 2002a; World Travel and Tourism Council 1998, 2002). The tourism sector is recognized as important in South African development planning in terms of its potential role as one of the few sectors that can be employment-intensive and create new jobs through the stimulation of what is officially called in South Africa, the small, medium and micro-enterprise (SMME) economy (South Africa 1996, 2000).[1] In research conducted by the WTTC (1998, 2002) it is estimated that by 2010 more than 174,000 new jobs can be directly created and a total of 516,000 employment opportunities can be generated, directly and indirectly, across the broader South African travel and tourism economy; of this projected employment growth linked to travel and tourism in South Africa, the majority of these new jobs are anticipated to be found within the SMME economy.

The South African case of tourism small firm development is distinctive, in certain respects, within the developing world. More especially, it is distinguished by the commitments made by post-1994 democratic government to introduce new national policy frameworks and institutions designed to support the SMME economy as a whole because of its potential contributions towards meeting the objectives of post-apartheid reconstruction. In particular, a high priority is attached by national government to achieving the objectives of transformation and of "black economic empowerment" in South African tourism. Currently, the tourism economy of South Africa is estimated to be 95% in the ownership of whites and on several occasions the Minister of Tourism and Environmental Affairs has drawn attention to the "lilywhite complexion" of the ownership structure of South African tourism. After one notable tourism gathering (Indaba) which was held at Durban in May 2000, the Minister identified the major problem in the South African tourist industry as that it "was unrepresentative of the country's population" and reportedly said that "as one walked through the isles of Indaba, there was a striking reality that the South African tourism industry is just too white" (DEAT 2000a: 1). Whilst black economic economic empowerment is being achieved partly through equity shares granted in existing large travel and tourism enterprise (Letsema Consulting 1999; The Cluster Consortium 1999), the promotion of black ownership of small tourism enterprises is a fundamental element of national government initiatives for the wider transformation of the South African economy (Letsema Consulting and Infonomics SA 2002).

Against this background and of a suite of emerging new policy initiatives designed to encourage black-owned small enterprises as part of restructuring patterns of ownership in the South African tourism industry, this paper examines the existing constraints and support needs of these emerging enterprises in the context of the challenges of economic empowerment of the country's historically disadvantaged communities. The paper is organized in terms of three uneven sections of material. First, the South African case is situated within a review of existing relevant research on tourism, entrepreneurship and small firm development in the developing world. Second, the shifting policy frameworks impacting upon tourism and especially of small enterprise development in South Africa are elaborated. Finally, the major findings are presented of local research on the opportunities, constraints and support needs of the emerging black owned small firm economy of post-apartheid South Africa.

Tourism Entrepreneurship and Small Firm Development in the Developing World

The benefits of developing small firms in tourism have been argued by several writers (Dahles 1998; Rodenburg 1980; Wanhill 2000). In particular, within a developing world context, it is suggested that the economic objectives of increased earnings, foreign exchange, investment, job opportunities as well as the minimization of adverse social and cultural effects are not best promoted through inward investment and large tourism enterprise. Instead, the advantages of developing local small tourism firms are stressed (Telfer 2002; Wanhill 2000). Notwithstanding this recognition of the importance of tourism small firms for economic development across the developing world, only a limited range of studies have been pursued directly on tourism entrepreneurship and enterprise development (Gartner 1999; Kirsten & Rogerson 2002; Rogerson 2001a). Within the existing literature on issues surrounding tourism entrepreneurship and enterprise development in the developing world, however, there are several important and different themes that are highlighted which serve as a context to investigating the South African case.

Large Firm Dominance, Small Enterprise Marginality

From a political economy perspective there is an important set of works which contextualise the dominance of large business enterprises in the tourism economies of the developing world and relate large enterprise domination to small firm marginalization or exclusion in tourism. It is argued that foreign domination and external dependency "seriously reduce tourism's potential for generating broadly based growth, as well as the net financial advantages that the industry brings to developing economies" (Brohman 1996: 54–55). Common concerns relate to the development of the so-termed "plantation tourism landscape" in the Caribbean (Weaver 1988) and of the widespread phenomenon of "enclave tourism" (Freitag 1994; Oppermann 1993) both of which fail to articulate linkages with local communities and produce situations of opulence and privilege, often enclosed by a sea of poverty (Britton 1982, 1983; Oppermann 1993). The growth of small firms in the tourism sector is severely constrained by these existing power relationships and the domination of large enterprises (Britton 1982, 1983). Overall, small locally owned tourism firms are essentially "left to scratch around for any crumbs" that might fall from the table which is dominated by large enterprise (Harrison 1994: 242).

Within the conventional mass tourism model of the industry, therefore, the experience across the developing world is thus of only limited space available for the growth and functioning of small tourism firms (Ashley *et al.* 2000; Britton 1983, 1987a, b; Rajotte 1987). Therefore, Britton (1982, 1983) concluded that if national governments of developing countries wish to ensure more widespread benefits from tourism, "then the organization of the tourist industry, and the distribution of power within their own countries, requires consideration" (Britton 1982: 355).

New or Alternative Tourism

Since 1980 the concepts of alternative or new tourism have received considerable attention (Mowforth & Munt 1998; Weaver 1991, 1995, 1998). Such "new tourism," Mowforth & Munt (1998) contend tends to be post-Fordist in how it is produced, that is it is small-scale often niche tourism. Ecotourism and cultural tourism are often viewed as typical examples of this new form of tourism which is regarded as manifesting major organizational differences from that of conventional tourism. Across the developing world, it is argued that such alternative tourism forms might be promoted to foster greater levels of community participation in tourism planning, a more equitable distribution of the costs and benefits of tourism, and more culturally appropriate and environmentally sustainable forms of tourism (Fennell 1999; Weaver 1991). Of special importance here is the acknowledgement that "new tourism" is associated with small-scale tourism and of high levels of small firm participation (Hampton 2001; Mowforth & Munt 1998). Such indigenous small firms in new tourism might be either under individual ownership or in small community-owned establishments (Hampton 2001; Kamsma & Bras 2000).

It is argued sometimes that the defining characteristics of "new tourism" are in direct contrast to those of mass tourism (Brohman 1996). For example alternative tourism forms, such as ecotourism developments, are stylised as small scale, locally owned with low import leakages and with a higher proportion of profits remaining in the local economy (Ranck 1987; Weaver 1998). By promoting new or alternative tourism therefore, the growth prospects for small firms are seen as more promising than under conventional mass tourism (see Hamzah 1997). Nevertheless, detailed examination of the experience of alternative tourism casts doubts on this line of analysis (Weaver 1998). In the absence of formalized planning or government intervention, the possibilities for local communities to benefit from business opportunities linked to alternative tourism may be reduced severely (Campbell 1999; Kirsten & Rogerson 2002).

Small Enterprises and Poverty Alleviation

A third group of writings that relate to tourism small firm development concerns the role of informal tourism enterprises and associated questions of poverty alleviation. It is recognised that in developing countries informal tourism enterprises occupy the bottom rung in the entrepreneurship ladder. Several studies disclose that the sellers or suppliers of handicraft goods, street guides, or the providers of petty transport services, including rickshaws or small boats, are marginal to but simultaneously dependent upon the dominant larger tourism enterprises (see Britton 1982; Crick 1992; Dahles 1998; Timothy & Wall 1997; Wahnschafft 1982). For the majority of such informal tourism enterprises, the prospects for graduation to more established small enterprises are extremely limited (Britton 1992; Oppermann 1993; Telfer 2002; Timothy & Wall 1997). In many cases this is further constrained by government hostility towards informal enterprise; for example, Dahles (2000: 154) notes that the Indonesian government "does not regard micro entrepreneurs as a force for economic development, in general, nor in tourism development in particular."

In the wave of new "pro-poor tourism" writings, however, informal tourism enterprises, are shown to assume a critical role in the livelihoods of poor communities and in the alleviation of poverty. Especially in rural areas of the developing world small firms linked to formal sector tourism may be extremely important in terms of their livelihood impacts (Ashley *et al.* 2001; Shah & Gupta 2000). Roe *et al.* (2002) stress that many people participate in tourism through small enterprises, including selling drinks, food and crafts; supplying cultural services — such as dance or music shows; or supplying inputs to accommodation facilities, such as locally produced food or building material. Although often either neglected by governments in tourism planning or viewed as a "nuisance" and subject to official harassment, the role of informal and micro-enterprises is accorded considerable focus in initiatives for developing a "pro-poor" tourism agenda (Ashley *et al*. 2000, 2001; Goodwin 1998, 2000; Shah & Gupta 2000). Overall, it is contended that the informal tourism sector "is where opportunities for small-scale enterprise or labour by the poor are maximised" (Ashley *et al*. 2000: 3). Improving the access of local entrepreneurs to tourism markets is therefore a critical element for poverty elimination (Ashley *et al*. 2000, 2001; Goodwin 1998).

Business Linkages

The development of business linkages between large established tourism enterprises and small, local firms through outsourcing, subcontracting or other linkage arrangements, is viewed an important means to upgrade the tourism small firm, including informal enterprise. Business linkages enable small firms run by indigenous or local entrepreneurs "to participate in the dynamic segments of a growing market economy" (Grierson & Mead 1996: 1). Outsourcing opportunities in tourism are identified in a host of activities, including food supply, handicrafts, laundry, furniture production, transport services, guiding and so forth.

A small number of research studies examine the organic development of business linkages in tourism between large and small firms (Alila & McCormick 1999; McCormick & Atieno 1998; Telfer & Wall 2000). In Kenya one-third of tourism firms were found to subcontract out some portion of their business (Alila & McCormick 1999). Large tour operators were particularly active in terms of subcontracting transport, security, and specialised tours, such as air or balloon safaris. Moreover, Kenya's leading hotels source 95% of their furniture from local manufacturers (Schneider 1999). Overall, it is argued that in order to enable domestic small firms in Kenya to take advantages of linkage opportunities "certain interventions by government and/or private sector organisations may be necessary" (Alila & McCormick 1999: xl). In particular, policies are required to improve their access to capital from financial institutions as well as to facilitate marketing, training, skills and technology acquisition. In Indonesia, support to local small food producers is required in order to increase backward economic linkages from resort developments (Telfer & Wall 2000).

The need for support interventions is a theme which is further reinforced in research which focusses on active intervention programmes designed to encourage business linkages between tourism enterprises. From research conducted on active intervention programmes operating in both Indonesia (Telfer & Wall 1996, 2000) and Zimbabwe (Grierson & Mead 1996, 1998) it is evident that a number of basic components must be in place for successful linkages: opportunities, information, capacity and capital. First, in terms of opportunities, the buyer must be able to recognize profitable opportunities to engage in linkage activities and have ways to determine when it is in their interest to enter into long-term contracts. Second, information is essential for successful business linkages. Potential partners must know who the potential suppliers are and who are the potential buyers for a particular good or service. The third and fourth building blocks for successful business linkages relate to issues of capacity and capital. It is critical that the enterprises engaged in supplying the good or service must have the capacity to fulfil its obligations, to meet the client's requirements in

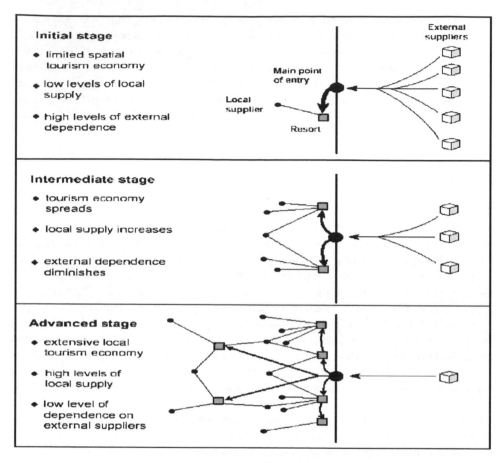

Figure 1: Models of business linkages and tourism. (*Source:* Modified after Williams 1998)

terms of quantity, quality and timeliness. In addition, it is vital that financing be mobilised in order to enable businesses to take advantage of available opportunities (Grierson & Mead 1996, 1998). The mentoring of small firms involved in tourism business linkage arrangements is a further ingredient for success (Grierson & Mead 1998; Telfer & Wall 1996).

Lastly, it is useful to note that there have been certain attempts to model the development of tourism entrepreneurship and business linkages in a developing world context (Figure 1). The mechanisms by which tourism development may galvanize new small firm development or business linkages are recognised as complex (Williams 1998: 90). In a simplified form they are captured in a three stage model of entrepreneurial development (Shaw & Williams 1998). In the initial stage, local provision to a new hotel/tourism complex is limited and the tourism industry is highly dependent upon overseas suppliers. This situation is common either because the local agricultural system cannot meet the rapid increase in demand or because the hotel is foreign-owned, and has a corporate policy of not using local produce.

In the second or intermediate stage the numbers of tourism businesses increase and become more geographically spread, profits filter more widely into the local economy and existing or newly formed enterprises start to supply the hotel. Accordingly, as these local business linkages evolve, levels of foreign ownership and dependence are reduced (Williams 1998: 90). Within the advanced or mature stage of the model, a situation is reached whereby "a broadly based local tourism economy has been formed with developed patterns of local supply and minimal dependence on foreign suppliers" (Williams 1998: 90). A factor of critical importance for achieving this degree of integration is the role of government intervention. The limited linkages that exist in the initial stages can be addressed through programmes to enhance local entrepreneurial processes and deal with a situation of poor entrepreneurial skills.

South Africa — Shifting Policy Frameworks for Small Enterprise Development and Tourism

The international body of tourism literature provides a useful foundation for interrogating tourism and small firm development (SMME) in South Africa. In particular, the developing world literature highlights the many constraints faced by small firms in tourism as a result of the dominance of large enterprises in the mass tourism industry. Unless deliberate policy interventions are made by government to counter the power of large enterprises and/or to foster positive linkages with small firms, the best prospects for small enterprise development appear to lie in the arena of new tourism, including cultural and ecotourism. Important potential intervention roles for government — training, entrepreneurial promotion and controlling the pace of tourism expansion — are highlighted. Finally, the rich literature on pro-poor tourism offers critical insights on the importance of supporting the small firm tourism economy, and more especially of informal tourism enterprises, for achieving the objective of poverty reduction through enhanced livelihood opportunities for poor communities.

Since 1994 new policy frameworks have been put in place to guide the development of the country's small enterprise economy (SMME) in post-apartheid South Africa as well as for changing the direction of the tourism economy. These two frameworks must be taken together with the commitment to transformation as providing the overarching policy and institutional context for tourism small firm development in contemporary South Africa.

New Frameworks for Small Firm Development

Since 1994 South Africa has confronted the dual challenges of re-integration into the global economy as well as positioning itself to realise the high expectations associated with the new democratic order. Accordingly, in order to attain the objectives of economic growth through competitiveness on the one hand and employment generation and income redistribution on the other, increased policy attention focuses on the promotion of the country's small, medium and micro-enterprise (SMME) economy (Berry *et al.* 2002). A radical policy break has occurred from the apartheid period when the SMME economy was either largely neglected by policy-makers or, in the case of black-owned firms, actively discouraged by an arsenal of repressive measures (Rogerson 1999). In the changed policy environment of the 1990s, promotion of the SMME economy began to be linked to a range of new optimistic policy objectives, including poverty alleviation, job creation and enhancement of national economic growth. Indeed, since 1995 one of the major thrusts of the national Department of Trade and Industry (DTI) "has been the restructuring, design and establishment of a new and sustainable institutional framework" (Dorfling 2001: 101). At the base of this new approach to small firm development is the 1995 White Paper on Small Business (Rogerson 1999).

The White Paper set forth several policy goals (South Africa 1995: 15–16). The primary goal was stated as "to create an enabling environment" in terms of national, regional and local policy frameworks for SMME development. In addition to this basic objective, several more specific policy objectives were identified. First, it was "to facilitate the greater equalisation of income, wealth and economic opportunities" which is inseparable from "a strengthening of the labour-absorptive process in the micro-enterprise and survivalist segments, the redressing of discrimination with respect to blacks as well as women's access to economic opportunities and power, and the facilitation of growth in black and small enterprises in rural areas." Second, it was to create long-term jobs which demands policy interventions designed to upgrade human resource skills and to strengthen the use of appropriate modern technologies. Third, it was the goal of stimulating economic growth through addressing the obstacles and constraints that prevent SMMEs from contributing to overall growth. Fourth, was the policy objective of strengthening the cohesion between SMMEs to overcome their isolation or "loneliness" by facilitating the networking of small firms in an endeavour to build collective efficiency, to address development obstacles and to take up opportunities. The fifth objective was to level the playing fields both between large enterprises and SMMEs and between rural and urban businesses. Finally, the White Paper targeted the goal of enhancing the capacity of small firms to comply with the challenges of globalisation and an internationally competitive economy (South Africa 1995).

The White Paper essentially centred around a number of specific strategic considerations. The first was attaining broad-based legitimacy for the government's new SMME strategy which represented a marked change from the apartheid era. A second critical issue was that of addressing the apartheid legacy of the disempowerment of black business. The final and critical strategic issue was that of establishing a set of new national institutions to support, coordinate and monitor the process. At the heart of national government's SMME support programmes were the policy interventions introduced by the new institutions and structures which were set up to implement the national SMME strategy. The key actors were Ntsika Enterprise Promotion Agency, which was responsible for non-financial or business development services, and Khula Enterprise Finance which functions as a wholesale finance institution supporting a range of retail finance intermediaries which would deal directly with the SMME entrepreneurs themselves. Support was focussed on improved and decentralised access to information, training, markets, finance and technology, improvements in business infrastructure and the market environment, and the strengthening of networks between enterprises. Essentially, the institutional support network that was created through the White Paper to nurture the sustainability of South Africa's SMME economy was organised primarily around Ntsika and Khula and included a number of new innovations. A critical component of the support strategy was the establishment of a set of decentralized or localised support service centres, which became styled as local business service centres or LBSCs. The LBSCs were to provide a variety of real and appropriate services to SMMEs and represented the flagship support programme of Ntsika. Other important support initiatives related to support for training, business linkages and improving the supply of finance and credit to small entrepreneurs (Rogerson 1999).

New Frameworks for Tourism

Since 1994 new policy frameworks have evolved also to support the development of the tourism sector (Rogerson 2002a). Most significant is the 1996 *White Paper on The Development and Promotion of Tourism in South Africa* (South Africa 1996) and the 1998 *Tourism in GEAR* strategy document (South Africa 1998). The *White Paper* on Tourism and the *Tourism in GEAR* strategy link to furnish the key policy foundations for developing the tourism industry in post-apartheid South Africa. A number of subsequent policy documents elaborate critical dimensions of the new national tourism policy framework, (South Africa 1999; Department of Environmental Affairs and Tourism [DEAT] 2000a, b), especially concerning transformation issues and black economic empowerment (DEAT 2001).

The *White Paper on the Development and Promotion of Tourism* is the core of South Africa's new tourism policy. It identifies tourism as a priority for national economic development and major stimulus for achieving objectives of the government's macro-economic strategy. Several key constraints are seen as limiting the effectiveness of the tourism industry to play a more meaningful role in the national economy. The major constraints relate, *inter alia*, to the fact that tourism has been inadequately resourced and funded by government; the short-sightedness of the private sector towards the nature of the South African tourism product; the limited integration of local communities and previously neglected groups into tourism; inadequate or absence of tourism training, education and awareness; inadequate protection of the environment through environmental management; poor level of service standards within the industry; lack of infrastructure in rural areas; the lack of appropriate institutional structures; and, the immediate problem of violence, crime and the security of tourists (South Africa 1996).

The *White Paper* aims to chart a path towards changing the tourism industry in South Africa and offers proposals to unblock constraints within the context of objectives for reconstruction (Rogerson 2002a). In terms of planning, "the concept of 'Responsible Tourism' emerges as the most appropriate concept for the development of tourism in South Africa" (South Africa 1996: 19). Six key guiding principles were put forward towards developing responsible tourism in post-apartheid South Africa:

* tourism will be private sector driven;
* government will provide the enabling framework for the industry to flourish;
* effective community involvement will form the basis of tourism growth;
* tourism development will be underpinned by sustainable environmental practices;
* tourism development is dependent on the establishment of cooperation and close partnerships among key stakeholders; and

• tourism will be used as a development tool for the empowerment of previously neglected communities and should particularly focus on the empowerment of women in such communities (South Africa 1996: 23).

Building upon the foundations provided by the *White Paper*, the Department of Environmental Affairs and Tourism document, *Tourism in GEAR* aims to create a framework for implementing these policies, particularly within the context of the GEAR macroeconomic strategy (South Africa 1998). This document is of particular interest as in initial post-apartheid economic planning, tourism was something of an afterthought and was omitted entirely from the GEAR framework (Page 1999). The discovery of tourism's potential as an economic driver is based on several features, *inter alia*, the comparative advantages of South Africa's natural and cultural resources; the fact that South Africa's tourism attractions complement global trends towards alternative tourism; the ability of tourism to attract substantial private sector investment as well as to accommodate SMME development; the employment-intensive nature of tourism; its potential catalytic role for major infrastructural investment; its ability to stimulate linkages with other production sectors (jewellery, curios); and, its value as an export earner (South Africa 1998). Overall, the vision is "to develop the tourism sector as a national priority in a sustainable and acceptable manner so that it will significantly contribute to the improvement of the quality of life of every South African" (South Africa 1998: 4).

Taken together the *White Paper* on Tourism and the *Tourism in GEAR* document signal the need for a collaborative approach within which "tourism should be led by government and driven by the private sector, and be community-based and labour-conscious" (South Africa 1999: 1). As a policy and strategic leader for the tourism industry, among the most critical roles for national government is that of seeking "to rectify historical industry imbalances, resulting from a discriminatory political system by promoting tourism entrepreneurship, human resources development, equity and ownership among disadvantaged individuals and communities" (South Africa 1999: 1). Transformation is a critical problem facing the tourism economy and requires expanding the involvement of South Africa's historically disadvantaged black populations (Letsema Consulting and Infonomics SA 2002). As mentioned earlier, the South African tourism economy is overwhelmingly dominated by white entrepreneurs. For example, the guest house accommodation sector well-illustrates this domination; of an estimated 5,000 guest houses operating in South Africa in 2002, only 60 are black-owned firms. An urgent challenge confronting the South African tourism industry is that of "changing the nature of the South African tourism industry from one that is predominantly white-owned to one that is increasingly owned equitably by the majority of South Africans" (DEAT 2000b: 1).

Towards meeting the objectives for transformation, the South African government, through DEAT, has prepared preliminary guidelines for a transformation strategy (DEAT 2001). Moreover, in a historic document signed in 2001 the Tourism Business Council of South Africa (TBCSA), the representative organization of private sector tourism, issued a charter of empowerment and transformation which represents a commitment to the objectives of furthering black economic empowerment in tourism. The charter acknowledges that two main challenges currently face the tourism industry in South Africa, namely the imperative to become more globally competitive and to include in the mainstream economy "the formerly disadvantaged" (TBCSA 2001). The Charter states that: "We believe that these two challenges are fundamentally linked. For our industry to thrive and grow we commit to do both" (TBCSA 2001). The development of small firms in South African tourism is thus an integral element of broader objectives for transformation in the economy as a whole.

Small Firms in South African Tourism — Opportunities and Constraints

Prior to the 1994 democratic transition, development issues, including issues of enterprise development, did not feature prominently on the agenda of South African tourism researchers. Throughout the apartheid period the linkages of tourism to economic development largely went overlooked by South African tourism scholars. With the challenges of post-apartheid reconstruction, since 1994 development issues have gravitated to the forefront of local tourism research. In terms of recent tourism writings, the major research priorities have centred upon assessments of the contribution that tourism can make to the objectives for post-apartheid reconstruction (Rogerson 2002a). In this section, we provide a review of the debates concerning the challenges, opportunities and constraints on small firm development in the tourism economy of post-apartheid South Africa.

Challenges and Debates

The critical challenge faced in South Africa's tourism small firm economy is the limited involvement of previously disadvantaged individuals or black entrepreneurs. In investigations conducted during the early 1990s, it was disclosed that the major barriers to emerging tourism firms relate to a complex set of issues surrounding factors of tourist supply, industry segmentation and restructuring, development infrastructure, access to markets, and the legal and regulatory environment (Ellis 1994: iv; Ellis & Joubert 1996). With the watershed change of national government in 1994 much optimism was expressed as to the new potential for galvanizing SMMEs in tourism (South Africa 1996, 1998). None the less, it is clear that: "Democratic changes notwithstanding, this (apartheid) inheritance leaves multiple backlogs that have to be addressed in order to create space for black entry into tourism" (Mathfield 2000: 30).

Core backlog issues include the limited savings and continuing difficulties that face black entrepreneurs in securing access to finance from conventional financial institutions, which regard the tourism sector as high-risk (Ellis & Joubert 1996; Saayman & Saayman 1998). The question of access to finance for emerging tourism entrepreneurs is identified as of paramount concern (DEAT 2001). One recent report on empowerment concluded that "access to finance remains the single biggest constraint on increased black ownership in the tourism industry" (Letsema Consulting and Infonomics SA 2002: 12). Limited or inadequate training and education is a further generic challenge that confronts black entrepreneurs; in one study of black tourism entrepreneurs in rural Mpumalanga, close to Kruger National Park, it was disclosed that one-third of the sample had only a primary school level of education and 88% had no formal skills or qualifications (Rogerson & Sithole 2001: 154). Overall, it has been shown that the poor levels of education and training in South Africa's black pop-ulation does not equip them to effectively compete in what is an increasingly "knowledge-based" tourism industry (Hughes & Vaughan 2000; Rogerson 2002b). Further, access to new or established tourism markets is limited for black entrepreneurs by existing business network domination by established (white) entrepreneurs (Ellis & Joubert 1996). Another constraint, however, that is disclosed in recent research, relates to the levels of awareness by black entrepreneurs of tourism opportunities with at least one study showing a perception that tourism was "not attractive" to black owned companies (Letsema Consulting and Infonomics SA 2002: 12).

In rural areas the fundamental constraints of limited infrastructure, poor transport and absence of basic services also must be recognized (Rogerson 2002a, b). Moreover, across both urban and rural areas black incorporation into tourism also has to contend with the narrow outlook and "the myopia of racial and class bias in the established industry" (Mathfield 2000: 30). Indeed, it is argued that despite a significantly improved policy en-vironment post-1994, for several reasons black entrepreneurship "is beset with historically established inequalities and discrimination that will not be easily overcome" (Mathfield 2000: 30). Finally, the Cluster Consortium attributes the lagging nature of tourism entrepreneurship in South Africa, in large measure, to the fact that "Governmentally based entrepreneurial support programs are virtually non-existent; what programs do exist are poorly advertised, and take so long to implement that they are of little value" (The Cluster Consortium 1999: III–10).

Against these critical commentaries it must be acknowledged that since 1994 a number of government-led programmes have been innovated to supported emerging black small firms in the tourism economy. The various policy measures that have been introduced by national government to support black economic empowerment or "making the markets work for the poor" are seen by some observers as going "well beyond what is pursued in most other countries in tourism" (Ashley & Ntshona 2002: 1). Several analysts go a step further and suggest that South Africa currently is emerging as an international leader and innovator in developing the practices and applications of pro-poor tourism (Ashley & Roe 2002; Roe & Urquhart 2001). Among the most significant of government initiatives are those involving programmes, *inter alia*, to support the tourism industry as a whole, to develop new tourism products favourable to black entrepreneurs, to initiate new support initiatives for both community based tourism as well as individual entrepreneurship, and to foster linkages between existing large or established tourism enterprises and emerging small firms.

New Initiatives — Opportunities and Progress

Although several important initiatives introduced to advance black economic empowerment through the support of either the SMME institutional apparatus and of programmes of the Department of Environmental Affairs and Tourism some of the most significant are indirect interventions to open new opportunities. In particular, these concern infrastructural improvements and the making of a new "enabling environment" for tourism expansion as a whole. One critical factor blocking any ownership transformation of the tourism economy is the lack of essential infrastructure which has been an undoubted block on tourism entrepreneurship in many areas of both urban and more especially rural South Africa. The provision of infrastructure as a means to "debottleneck" investment opportunities in areas of tourism potential was a critical element of the South Africa's Spatial Development Initiatives (SDI) programme, especially in the Lubombo and Wild Coast SDIs, in which tourism is the lead economic sector (Rogerson 2001b). With improvements in infrastructure in the Wild Coast area, in the form of road improvements, expansion of electricity provision, and telecommunications upgrading, new opportunities are opened for rural tourism enterprises in this scenically spectacular but relatively undeveloped part of South Africa (Ashley & Ntshona 2002; Bourgouin 2002). Overall, the SDI programme was committed heavily to empowerment objectives, promoting new entrepreneurship and maximizing the impact of large investments for emerging small firms through programmes of procurement, linkages and outsourcing (De Beer & Elliffe 1997; Rogerson 1998, 2001b).

Another national government initiative that is changing the business environment for tourism entrepreneurs is the improvement of targeted infrastructure in so-termed "priority areas for tourism infrastructure investment" or "PATIIs." Such areas have been defined across South Africa as those with high potential for upgrading existing tourism development or for new planned tourism product developments, albeit hindered by a weak infrastructural base (DEAT 2000b: 7). Although the majority of these PATIIs are situated in rural areas, a number are located in the country's major metropolitan areas. For example, Soweto is identified as one of the PATIIs in urban South Africa with infrastructural improvements seen as one key to unlocking tourism potential. Overall, alongside the SDIs the network of PATIIs is to function as an important vehicle for changing the tourism economy, achieving a greater geographical dispersal of tourists and tourism business opportunities across South Africa, not least for emerging black entrepreneurs (Rogerson 2002a).

A critical set of initiatives which forge potential new opportunities for black entrepreneurship are those relating to the promotion of new forms of niche tourism in South Africa. The most significant of these "new" tourism products that are opening up specific opportunities for black entrepreneurs relate to indigenous cultural villages, township tourism, cross-border or regional tourism and ecotourism. The work of Jansen van Veuren (2001, 2003) shows that the expansion of cultural villages, as an element of cultural tourism in South Africa, has offered a host of new business opportunities for black entrepreneurs variously in the form of the building and operation of such enterprises as well as in a suite of linked opportunities concerning handicrafts, the selling of cultural performances, music, or indigenous food. Township tourism is another avenue for business opportunities with international interest in the political history of the democratic struggle opening opportunities in Soweto as well as other South African urban townships. The core opportunities relate to tour guiding, transport and tours, the provision of food and liquor as well as crafts. In urban areas, cross-border or regional tourism is potentially another significant avenue for emergent black tourism entrepreneurship. In Johannesburg, for example, proposals have been developed for "an African retailing Mecca" targeted at tourism shoppers from other parts of sub-Saharan Africa, a development project which it is envisioned will have considerable multiplier effects for black small firm development in tourism. Finally, ecotourism is viewed optimistically as offering major new potential for rural tourism small business development (Fakir 1999; Stavrou 1999). Opportunities are targeted in terms of a host of activities that include the running of small accommodation facilities, tour guiding, construction, supply of food as well as local services, including laundry and security services.

Community-based tourism receives a strong focus in the tourism *White Paper* as the organizational form of tourism which is considered most appropriate for potentially incorporating black communities into the mainstream of economic development. The reasons are that community-based tourism is viewed as labour-intensive, employs a vast range of skills, but not necessarily of a high order, and creates multiple opportunities for SMME entrepreneurship. The *White Paper* identifies a large number of examples of the kinds of opportunities for community involvement, such as operators of infrastructure (guest houses, taxis); services (guides, bookings); and, suppliers (production and sale of craft, construction and maintenance). Examples of so-called community based tourism initiatives include programmes for developing "township tourism" in localities such as Soweto, Inanda (Durban) or Khayelitsha (Cape Town) and of several rural community-based eco-tourism initiatives (Hughes & Vaughan 2000; Ndlovu & Rogerson 2003).

National government views further support and development of community-based tourism initiatives as essential to ensure that tourism contributes towards the goals of responsible tourism in South Africa (Spenceley *et al.* 2002). Community-based tourism initiatives are seen as especially important for achieving the optimistic targets for new employment creation through small business development and expansion. Nevertheless, from a number of existing investigations, it is apparent that community-based tourism in South Africa faces a number of difficulties that need to be overcome in order that its full potential be realised (Leballo 2001; SAFIRE 2002). First, many communities often have a limited understanding and awareness of tourism and often develop products that are not appropriately designed, marketed or managed (see Ndlovu 2002; Rogerson & Sithole 2001). Second, there is considerable degree of unreliability in standards of community-based facilities that creates unacceptable risks for the private sector in linking tourists to such community-based tourism initiatives. Third, there is lack of capacity and skills in communities for tourism business and enterprise management (Mafisa 2001; Ndlovu 2002). Linked to this problem is that communities generally have no idea about marketing. Finally, community-based tourism ventures are often at risk because of insecure community rights of tenure, particularly as regards access to land and natural resources (Leballo 2001; SAFIRE 2002). Despite the introduction of several initiatives to promote community-based tourism in South Africa, it was sadly observed in a policy document produced by the Department of Environmental Affairs and Tourism (DEAT) that "there has not been any significant progress in this area even after our democratisation of 1994" (DEAT 2000a: 1).

The promotion of individual entrepreneurship in tourism and of new SMME opportunities in tourism projects is a further core issue of policy concern. Since 1999 there has occurred a flurry of activity within the Department of Environmental Affairs and Tourism with new supply-side proposals put forward for supporting individual SMMEs in tourism. These include proposals for a "Tourism SMME 'first-stop-shop' " which would provide basic business information and products and refer clients to expert advice on a needs basis. In recognition of the need for supporting SMMEs within tourism, DEAT is developing the Tourism Enterprise Programme (TEP) which aims at increasing the economic participation of previously disadvantaged individuals (DEAT & DTI 2002). The TEP is an integrated support package comprising training, market linkages, mentorship assistance and access to affordable finance. The approach, being developed with other key role players such as the Development Bank of Southern Africa, Business Trust, Ntsika and Khula, aims to "supplement the existing base of entrepreneurial support with sector specific tools" as well as to ensure a focus upon the specific needs of the industry (DEAT 2000b: 6). Another initiative to support SMME development is that afforded under the International Tourism Marketing Assistance Scheme, which targets assistance mainly at previously disadvantaged tourism product owners to enable them to market their products overseas (DEAT & DTI 2002). Overall, a number of new financing packages have been launched designed to assist small firms in tourism (DEAT & DTI 2002).

The role of the private sector in transformation is another important theme in contemporary South Africa. The proponents of responsible tourism advocate that the private sector tourism enterprises should seek to maximize their involvement in local economics through expanding linkages with local enterprises and seeking to promote local of goods and services (Spenceley *et al.* 2002). In the case of casino tourism enterprises a programme of affirmative procurement of certain goods and services has been developed in order to advance more rapidly the development of black-owned and operated tourism small businesses (Rogerson 2003). Moreover, wherever possible mentorship linkages or relationships between large enterprises and emerging small firms are encouraged (Kirsten & Rogerson 2002). Overall, in terms of attaining further empowerment targets in tourism, DEAT concedes that the extended development of linkages between large and small enterprises in the tourism industry "is critical" to the success of transformation (Pillay 2000: 5). The importance of extending affirmative procurement practices to favour black-owned tourism firms is reiterated in several recent debates and official documents concerning transformation and economic empowerment (DEAT 2001; Letsema Consulting and Infonomics SA 2002).

The findings of recent research on tourism and business linkages point to a number of constraints that need to be overcome before black entrepreneurs are able to fully take advantage of business linkage opportunities (Kirsten & Rogerson 2002). Amongst the most important problems that need to be addressed through government support are improving access and awareness of entrepreneurs to finance, training and advice facilities. It is argued that for the immediate future the greatest opportunities for black entrepreneurs may be in what is termed the wider travel and tourism economy, incorporating elements of manufacturing, construction and service activities that are linked to tourism projects in both their construction and operational phases of operation rather than in the areas of accommodation and transport and travel provision (Kirsten & Rogerson 2002).

Conclusion

The South African case represents a contribution to the sparse literature which discusses the prospects for small firm development in tourism within a developing world context. It is clear from the foregoing analysis that there are a number of marked differences in the issues of small firm development in the South as compared to debates in the North (cf. Page *et al.* 1999; Shaw & Williams 1998). Of special interest in the South African context is the adoption of radical new policy frameworks both for SMME development and for tourism which are geared to overcome the apartheid legacy of black entrepreneurial exclusion from the tourism industry. Under the umbrella of transformation and empowerment, since 1994 it is evident that a number of important and innovative pro-poor initiatives have been launched in South Africa to support both emerging growth-oriented small firms as well as the group of survivalist informal sector enterprises. The progress of these initiatives must be assessed on a long-term basis in relation to the enormous challenges that need to be addressed for expanding black entrepreneurship and small firm development in tourism. In final analysis, the South African experience potentially may offer certain lessons for other developing countries in terms of the promotion of small firm development in the tourism economy.

Note

1. Officially, the South African SMME economy is divided into three sets of enterprises: (1) survivalist enterprises of the informal economy; (2) a segment of growth-oriented micro-enterprise; and (3) the formal SME (small and medium-size) economy which is presently dominated by established white-owned enterprise. The group of survivalist enterprises and the micro-enterprise economy form the emergent SMME economy, which is dominated by members of South Africa's historically disadvantaged communities (see Rogerson 1999). Government policy and support programmes for SMME development in South Africa pay special attention to the emergent SMME economy.

Acknowledgments

The financial support of the National Research Foundation, Pretoria, for my research on small firm development in South African tourism is gratefully acknowledged.

References

Alila, P. O., & McCormick, D. (1999). *Firm linkages in Kenya's tourism sector*. Discussion Paper No. 297, Institute for Development Studies, University of Nairobi, Nairobi.

Ashley, C., Boyd, C., & Goodwin, H. (2000). *Pro-poor tourism: Putting poverty at the heart of the tourism agenda*. London: Natural Resource Perspectives No. 61, Overseas Development Institute.

Ashley, C., & Ntshona, Z. (2002). Transforming roles but not reality? Private sector and community involvement in tourism and forestry development on the wild coast. Sustainable Livelihoods in Southern Africa Wild Resources Theme Research Briefing, Overseas Development Institute, London.

Ashley, C., & Roe, D. (2002). Making tourism work for the poor: Strategies and challenges in Southern Africa. *Development Southern Africa*, 19, 61–82.

Ashley, C., Roe, D., & Goodwin, H. (2001). *Pro-poor tourism strategies: Making tourism work for the poor: A review of experience*. London: Pro-Poor Research Report No. 1, Overseas Development Institute.

Berry, A., von Blottnitz, M., Cassim, R., Kesper, A., Rajaratnam, B., & van Seventer, D. E. (2002). *The economics of SMMEs in South Africa*. Unpublished draft paper for Trade and Industrial Policy Secretariat, Johannesburg, available at http://www.tips.org.za

Bourgouin, F. (2002). Information communication technologies and the potential for rural tourism SMME development: The case of the wild coast. *Development Southern Africa, 19,* 191–212.

Britton, S. G. (1982). The political economy of tourism in the third world. *Annals of Tourism Research, 9,* 331–358.

Britton, S. G. (1983). *Tourism and underdevelopment in Fiji.* Canberra: Development Studies Centre Monograph, No. 31, Australian National University.

Britton, S. G. (1987a). Tourism in Pacific-Island states: Constraints and opportunities. In: S. Britton, & W. C. Clarke (Eds), *Ambiguous alternative: Tourism in small developing countries* (pp. 113–139). Suva: University of South Pacific.

Britton, S. G. (1987b). Tourism in small developing countries. In: S. Britton, & W. C. Clarke (Eds), *Ambiguous alternative: Tourism in small developing countries* (pp. 167–194). Suva: University of South Pacific.

Brohman, J. (1996). New directions in tourism for third world development. *Annals of Tourism Research, 23,* 48–70.

Campbell, L. M. (1999). Ecotourism in rural developing communities. *Annals of Tourism Research, 26,* 534–553.

Crick, M. (1992). Life in the informal sector: Street guides in Kandy, Sri Lanka. In: D. Harrison (Ed.), *Tourism and the less developed countries* (pp. 135–147). Chichester: Wiley.

Dahles, H. (1998). Tourism, government policy and petty entrepreneurs. *South East Asian Research, 6,* 73–98.

Dahles, H. (2000). Tourism, small enterprises and community development. In: G. Richards, & D. Hall (Eds), *Tourism and sustainable development* (pp. 154–169). London: Routledge.

De Beer, G., & Elliffe, S. (1997). *Tourism development and the empowerment of local communities.* Cape Town: Working Paper No. 11, Development Policy Research Unit Industrial Strategy Project Phase Two, University of Cape Town.

DEAT (Department of Environmental Affairs and Tourism) (2000a). *Transforming the South African tourism industry.* Unpublished Report, Department of Environmental Affairs and Tourism, Pretoria.

DEAT (Department of Environmental Affairs and Tourism) (2000b). *Unblocking delivery on tourism strategy by government departments.* Pretoria. Department of Environmental Affairs and Tourism.

DEAT & DTI (Department of Environmental Affairs and Department of Trade and Industry) (2002). *Support programmes for tourism businesses handbook.* Pretoria: DEAT & DTI.

Dorfling, T. (2001). *Enhancing small, medium and micro enterprise support provision: The case of Port Elizabeth, South Africa.* Unpublished MA dissertation, University of the Witwatersrand, Johannesburg.

Ellis, S. (1994). *An investigation into barriers facing emerging small, micro and medium enterprises in the South African tourism industry.* Unpublished Masters in Business Leadership dissertation, University of South Africa, Pretoria.

Ellis, S., & Joubert, R. (1996). *Barriers facing small, micro and medium enterprises in the South African tourism industry.* Unpublished paper presented at the International Conference on Urban and Regional Tourism, Potchefstroom (9–12 January).

Fakir, S. (1999). Eco-tourism — A sustainable avenue for SMMEs in South Africa: A critical look. In: A. Stavrou (Ed.), *Eco-Tourism: A sustainable avenue for SMME's in South Africa* (pp. 9–20). Durban: DRA-Development Report No. 23.

Fennell, D. A. (1999). *Ecotourism: An introduction.* London: Routledge.

Freitag, T. G. (1994). Enclave tourism development: For whom the benefits roll? *Annals of Tourism Research, 21,* 538–554.

Gartner, W. C. (1999). Small scale enterprises in the tourism industry in Ghana's central region. In: D. G. Pearce, & R. W. Butler (Eds), *Contemporary issues in tourism development* (pp. 158–175). London: Routledge.

Goodwin, H. (1998). *Sustainable tourism and poverty alleviation*. Unpublished discussion paper presented at the DFID/DETR Workshop on Sustainable Tourism and Poverty (13 October).

Goodwin, H. (2000). Pro-poor tourism: Opportunities for sustainable local development. *Development and Cooperation*, 5(September–October), 12–14.

Grierson, J., & Mead, D. (1996). *Business linkages in Manicaland*. Unpublished background paper for the CZI Manicaland Business Linkages Project Development Workshop (16–18 January).

Grierson, J., & Mead, D. (1998). *Business linkages in Zimbabwe: The Manicaland business linkages project*. Unpublished paper presented at the Workshop on Business Development Services, Harare (28 September to 1 October).

Hampton, M. (2001). *Poor relations?: Tourist attractions, local communities and economic development in Indonesia*. Unpublished paper presented at the International Conference on Tourism Development and Management in Developing Countries, Guilin, China (11–14 November).

Hamzah, A. (1997). The evolution of small-scale tourism in Malaysia: Problems, opportunities and implications for sustainability. In: M. J. Stabler (Ed.), *Tourism and sustainability: Principles to practice* (pp. 199–217). Wallingford: CAB International.

Harrison, D. (1992). International tourism and the less developed countries: The background. In: D. Harrison (Ed.), *Tourism and the less developed countries* (pp. 1–18). Chichester: Wiley.

Harrison, D. (1994). Tourism, capitalism and development in less developed countries. In: L. Sklair (Ed.), *Capitalism and development* (pp. 232–257). London: Routledge.

Hughes, H., & Vaughan, A. (2000). The incorporation of historically disadvantaged communities into tourism initiatives in the new South Africa: Case studies from KwaZulu-Natal. In: M. Robinson, N. Evans, P. Long, R. Sharpley, & J. Swarbrooke (Eds), *Management, marketing and the political economy of travel and tourism* (pp. 241–254). Sunderland: Centre for Travel and Tourism and Business Education.

Jansen van Veuren, E. (2001). Transforming cultural villages in the Spatial Development Initiatives of South Africa. *South African Geographical Journal*, *83*, 137–148.

Jansen van Veuren, E. (2003). Capitalising on indigenous cultures: Cultural village tourism in South Africa. *Africa Insight*, *33*, 69–77.

Kamsma, T., & Bras, K. (2000). Gili Trawangan — from desert island to marginal paradise: Local participation, small-scale entrepreneurs and outside investors in an Indonesian tourist destination. In: G. Richards, & D. Hall (Eds), *Tourism and sustainable community development* (pp. 170–184). London: Routledge.

Kirsten, M., & Rogerson, C. M. (2002). Tourism, business linkages and small enterprise development in South Africa. *Development Southern Africa*, *19*, 29–59.

Lea, J. (1988). *Tourism and development in the third world*. London: Routledge.

Letsema Consulting (1999). *Black economic empowerment and tourism*. Unpublished report for The Cluster Consortium, Johannesburg.

Letsema Consulting and Infonomics SA (2002). *South African tourism industry: Empowerment and transformation annual review 2002*. Unpublished report for the Tourism Business Council of South Africa, Johannesburg.

Lewis, J. D. (2001). *Policies to promote growth and employment in South Africa*. Washington, DC: Discussion Paper No. 16, Informal Discussion Papers on Aspects of the Economy of South Africa, The World Bank.

Mafisa (2001). *Developing tourism and conservation skills for economic sustainability in small businesses and tourism enterprises through trans-frontier conservation areas, national parks and provincial conservation authorities*. Unpublished discussion document for Theta Workshop (9–10 August).

Mathfield, D. (2000). *Impacts of accommodation and craft-based tourism on local economic development: The case of the Midlands Meander*. Unpublished Masters dissertation, University of Natal, Durban.

McCormick, D., & Atieno, R. (1998). *Linkages between small and large firms in the Kenyan food processing and tourism industries*. Unpublished paper prepared for the Workshop of the European Association of Development Institutes, Institute of Social Studies, The Hague (18–19 September).

Mowforth, M., & Munt, I. (1998). *Tourism and sustainability: New tourism in the third world*. London: Routledge.

Ndlovu, N. (2002). *Ecotourism as a rural development strategy: A case study of the Matatiele ecotourism project, Eastern Cape*. Unpublished MA Research Report, University of the Witwatersrand, Johannesburg.

Ndlovu, N., & Rogerson, C. M. (2003). Rural local economic development through community-based tourism: The Mehloding hiking and horse trail, Eastern Cape, South Africa. *Africa Insight, 33*, 124–129.

Oppermann, M. (1993). Tourism space in developing countries. *Annals of Tourism Research, 20*, 535–556.

Page, S. (1999). *Tourism and development: The evidence from Mauritius, South Africa and Zimbabwe*. Unpublished report prepared for the Overseas Development Institute, London.

Page, S. J., Forer, P., & Lawton, G. R. (1999). Small business development and tourism: Terra incognita? *Tourism Management, 20*, 435–459.

Pillay, S. (2000). *Towards a strategy to transform tourism in South Africa*. Unpublished Report, Department of Environmental Affairs and Tourism, Pretoria.

Rajotte, F. (1987). Safari and beach-resort tourism: The costs to Kenya. In: S. Britton, & W. C. Clarke (Eds), *Ambiguous alternative: Tourism in small developing countries* (pp. 78–90). Suva: University of South Pacific.

Ranck, S. R. (1987). An attempt at autonomous development: The case of the Tufi guest houses, Papua New Guinea. In: S. Britton, & W. C. Clarke (Eds), *Ambiguous alternative: Tourism in small developing countries* (pp. 61–77). Suva: University of South Pacific.

Rodenburg, E. (1980). The effect of scale in economic development: Tourists in Bali. *Annals of Tourism Research, 7*, 177–196.

Roe, D., Goodwin, H., & Ashley, C. (2002). *The tourism industry and poverty reduction: A business primer*. London: Pro-Poor Tourism Briefing No. 2, Overseas Development Institute.

Roe, D., & Urquhart, P. (2001). *Pro-poor tourism: Harnessing the world's largest industry for the world's poor*. London: International Institute for Environment and Development.

Rogerson, C. M. (1998). Investment-led entrepreneurship development. *Development Southern Africa, 15*, 917–942.

Rogerson, C. M. (1999). Small enterprise development in post-apartheid South Africa: Gearing up for growth and poverty alleviation. In: K. King, & S. McGrath (Eds), *Enterprise in Africa: Between poverty and growth* (pp. 83–94). London: Intermediate Technology Publications.

Rogerson, C. M. (2001a). Investment-led entrepreneurship and small enterprise development in tourism: Lessons for SDIs from the international experience. *South African Geographical Journal, 83*, 105–114.

Rogerson, C. M. (2001b). Tourism and Spatial Development Initiatives — The case of the Maputo development corridor. *South African Geographical Journal, 83*, 124–136.

Rogerson, C. M. (2002a). Tourism — A new economic driver for South Africa. In: A. Lemon, & C. M. Rogerson (Eds), *Geography and economy in South Africa and its neighbours* (pp. 95–110). Ashgate, Aldershot.

Rogerson, C. M. (2002b). Tourism and local economic development: The case of the Highlands Meander. *Development Southern Africa, 19*, 143–168.

Rogerson, C. M. (2003). Changing casino tourism in South Africa. *Africa Insight, 33*, 142–149.

Rogerson, C. M., & Sithole, P. M. (2001). Rural handicraft production in Mpumalanga, South Africa: Organization, problems and support needs. *South African Geographical Journal, 83*, 149–158.

Saayman, M., & Saayman, A. (1998). *Tourism and the South African economy: Growing opportunities for entrepreneurs.* Unpublished paper, Institute for Tourism and Leisure Studies, Potchefstroom University for Christian Higher Education.

SAFIRE (Southern Alliance for Indigenous Resources) (2002). *Regional community-based tourism association consultation: Discussion paper.* Unpublished document SAFIRE, Harare.

Schneider, D. (1999). *The role of buyers in the development of the hotel furniture industry in Kenya.* Brighton: Working Paper No. 93, Institute of Development Studies, University of Sussex.

Shah, K., & Gupta, V. (2000). *Tourism, the poor and other stakeholders: The experience of Asia.* London: Overseas Development Institute.

Sharpley, R., & Telfer, D. J. (Eds) (2002). *Tourism and development: Concepts and issues.* Clevedon: Channel View Publications.

Shaw, G., & Williams, A. M. (1998). Entrepreneurship, small business culture and tourism development. In: D. Ioannides, & K. G. Debbage (Eds), *The economic geography of the tourist industry: A supply-side analysis* (pp. 235–255). London: Routledge.

Sinclair, M. T. (1998). Tourism and economic development: A survey. *Journal of Development Studies, 34,* 1–51.

Sinclair, M. T., & Stabler, M. (1998). *The economics of tourism.* London: Routledge.

South Africa, Republic of (1995). *National strategy for the development and promotion of small business in South Africa.* Cape Town: Department of Trade and Industry.

South Africa, Republic of (1996). *White paper on the development and promotion of tourism in South Africa.* Pretoria: Department of Environmental Affairs and Tourism.

South Africa, Republic of (1998). *Tourism in gear: Tourism development strategy 1998–2000.* Pretoria: Department of Environmental Affairs and Tourism.

South Africa, Republic of (1999). *Programme of action 1999/2000.* Pretoria: Department of Environmental Affairs and Tourism.

South Africa, Republic of (2000). *Unblocking delivery on tourism strategy by government departments.* Pretoria: Department of Environmental Affairs and Tourism.

Spenceley, A., Relly, P., Keyser, H., Warmeant, P., McKenzie, M., Mataboge, A., Norton, P., Mahlangu, S., & Seif, J. (2002). *South African responsible tourism manual.* Pretoria: Department of Environmental Affairs and Tourism.

Stavrou, A. (Ed.) (1999). *Eco-tourism: A sustainable avenue for SMME's in South Africa.* Durban: DRA-Development Report No. 23.

Telfer, D. J. (2002). The evolution of tourism and development theory. In: R. Sharpley, & D. J. Telfer (Eds), *Tourism and development: Concepts and issues* (pp. 112–148). Clevedon: Channel View Publications.

Telfer, D. J., & Wall, G. (1996). Linkages between tourism and food production. *Annals of Tourism Research, 23,* 635–653.

Telfer, D. J., & Wall, G. (2000). Strengthening backward economic linkages: Local food purchasing by three Indonesian hotels. *Tourism Geographies, 2,* 421–447.

The Cluster Consortium (1999). *The South African tourism cluster: Strategy in action.* Unpublished report prepared for the Tourism Clustering Initiative, The Cluster Consortium, Johannesburg.

Timothy, D., & Wall, G. (1997). Selling to tourists: Indonesian street vendors. *Annals of Tourism Research, 24,* 322–340.

Tourism Business Council of South Africa (2001). Charter of Empowerment and transformation in the tourism industry: A commitment to furthering black economic empowerment in the tourism industry. Press statement released 29 June, TBCSA, Johannesburg.

Wahnschafft, R. (1982). Formal and informal tourism sectors: A case study of Pattaya, Thailand. *Annals of Tourism Research, 9,* 429–451.

Wanhill, S. (2000). Small and medium tourism enterprises. *Annals of Tourism Research, 27,* 132–147.

Weaver, D. B. (1988). The evolution of a 'plantation' tourism landscape on the Caribbean Island of Antigua. *Tijdschrift voor Economische en Sociale Geografie, 79*, 319–331.

Weaver, D. B. (1991). Alternatives to mass tourism in Dominica. *Annals of Tourism Research, 18,* 414–432.

Weaver, D. B. (1998). *Ecotourism in the less developed world.* Wallingford: CAB International.

Williams, S. (1998). *Tourism geography.* London: Routledge.

World Travel and Tourism Council (1998). *South Africa's travel and tourism: Economic driver for the 21st century.* London: World Travel and Tourism Council.

World Travel and Tourism Council (2002). *South Africa: The impact of travel and tourism on jobs and the economy — 2002 plus special report on September 11th impacts.* London: World Travel and Tourism Council.

Chapter 3

Factors Affecting Small Firms in Tourism:
A Ghanaian Perspective

William C. Gartner

Much of the academic tourism literature is demand side focused. That is it deals with the tourist. What they like to do, how much they spend, what they think of places etc are common themes one can find in almost all professional tourism journals. What is not so common is a supply side micro focus on firms engaged in providing touristic goods and services. Yet it is these very firms that often provide the basis for an individual's trip satisfaction evaluation.

Small firm development is different than that for large firms. This difference was frequently overlooked in developing countries as Ongile & McCormick (1996) argue that it was not until the 1970s that the International Labor Office began to study small firm development on the African continent. Much of the blame for Africa's failed development efforts is explained by proponents of either the neo-classical school or the dependency theorists (Anunobi 1994). Members of the neo-classical school argue that development is stymied by poor or inadequate infrastructure, an uneducated and unskilled workforce, weak management skills, low or non-existent levels of savings and capital formation, and strained international relations. Proponents of the dependency school claim that developing countries are in fact economic colonies of developed nations and suffer from poor trade terms both importing and exporting. The dependency school argues further that small enterprises are most severely affected by import liberalization programs effectively crowding them out of the market. This is especially important in Africa where most of the businesses are classified as Small Scale Enterprises (SSEs) and most GNP is generated by SSEs (i.e. small firms). Are these two schools of thought mutually exclusive or do the conditions that affect small firm development overlap the conditions embraced by each school? This question is behind the discussion that follows.

One often hears that tourism businesses are predominantly small businesses but what defines a small business? The U.S. government has defined small businesses as having less than $2 million U.S. in annual gross revenue. Others define small firms as having less than 50 employees (Hansohm 1992). Certain qualitative characteristics have also been proposed to define small firms in developing countries. Some of the more common include just in time production for direct sale of product to consumer, lack of specialization in the labor force,

Small Firms in Tourism: International Perspectives
Copyright © 2004 Published by Elsevier Ltd.
ISBN: 0-08-044132-7

poor or non-existent bookkeeping, and heavy employment of family workers (Scheider & Barthold n.d. from Hansohm 1992). It is estimated that the number of small firms in many developing countries is far larger than the number of medium or larger firms and accounts for between 40 and 90% of non-government employment. Although most of the small firm research in developing countries has been for traditional enterprises (e.g. agriculture, textiles, and trading) there is no reason to suspect conditions for tourism dependent firms are vastly different from small firms in other sectors at the microeconomic level.

The preponderance of small firms in developing countries may not be that dissimilar to what is encountered in developed countries. For example the Federal Reserve Board, District 9 which includes the north central states of the U.S. has surveyed tourism related businesses in the District and claims, that depending on sector, from 50 to 90% can be classified as small businesses. Smith (2003) has examined tourism related firm structures in Canada and concluded that the dominant size of firms across sectors, with the exception of some forms of local transportation, can be classified as small businesses. Smith's findings and those of the U.S. Federal Reserve Board of the 9th District are intriguing in that they appear to show that level of country development (i.e. developed vs. developing) may not have any influence on the size of firms operating in tourism. Another of Smith's findings is even more enlightening. His analysis of the percentage of tourism dependent businesses by sector reveals that tourism dependent businesses are no more weighted in favor of small firms than other non-tourism sectors. In other words there is no evidence, at least in the case of Canada, to claim that tourism dependent businesses are more likely to be small firms than for the rest of the non-tourism related sectors in the economy. Small firms in tourism will be affected by not only development conditions under which they operate but also by the unique properties of the tourism distribution system and trends that affect how tourism systems function.

The purpose of this chapter is to put into perspective some of the conditions under which small firms operate and how they affect firm performance. This chapter begins by examining the tourism distribution channel, moves into a discussion of tourism trends and resulting implications for small firms and then offers a look at the beginning of small firm development, tied to tourism, in the country of Ghana. The Ghana case study is drawn heavily on some research conducted when a new wave of tourism development occurred in the Central Region of the country during the 1990s. After the discussion of small firm development in Ghana the chapter concludes by returning to an examination of the conditions offered for the lack of development in the developing world with reference to how those conditions may be affecting small firm development.

Tourism's Distribution Channel

Tourism's distribution channel is inverted from that found for most consumer goods. Manufacturing and/or extractive industries are concentrated at the points of production with their products dispersed at the points of final delivery. When examining tourism flows we see a dispersion of potential tourists in the market that are concentrated at the points of final demand. Another way of looking at this is the points of production and consumption, which occur simultaneously at and enroute to the destination, need tourists as factors of production.

How to attract tourists to a destination has been a well researched area of study. The role of National Tourism Organizations, Destination Management Organizations, and local tourism organizations in this process has been documented and forms the basis for many tourism marketing studies. Since tourism products can not be stored and there are no pre-testing opportunities it becomes extremely important for tourism organizations to develop and project the types of images expected to convince people to visit their destination. The different ways touristic images are formed has been discussed by Gartner (1993). It is the process of image formation that brings up one of the major issues with small tourism dependent firms. Image formation is often a time consuming and costly process. Small firms, by their very nature, do not possess the resources for a sustained image formation campaign. This responsibility then devolves to the umbrella organization in charge of tourism promotion. If a tax paying small firm is unhappy with the types of images presented there is very little that can be done about it. This then puts small firms at the mercy of an agency that may or may not act in the interests of an individual firm. The issue of giving up control over marketing activities, even though the marketing activities may be funded by a special tax collected from tourists by the small firms which then turn over the proceeds for use by a public or quasi-public body, is one characteristic that plagues many small firms. Lack or limited control over how special tourist tax money collected by small firms is used is just one example that relates to the larger issue of dependency that is also an issue in other parts of the distribution channel.

When the tourism distribution channel is examined we find two exceptions to the argument of small firms dominance in tourism. The first deals with air transportation. Air transportation is a costly activity for both the consumer and the company providing the service. In Smith's (2003) study he noted the dominance of small firms in transportation in destination areas where access to remote places was desired. These small firms were predominantly "bush" pilots taking small groups of customers to remote camps or water access points. Small firms also dominate the taxi sector. He did not identify any small firm dominance in the long haul transportation sector. It is this part of the distribution channel that concerns many small firms located at a destination. In an ideal situation airlines do not concern themselves with how a destination organizes for tourism. If a destination is successful at developing and marketing its tourism potential the airlines serving that destination benefit from higher load factors. If the destination fails to acquire significant market share an airline company, unless prevented by some regulation, will stop serving the route. In this way airlines respond to market demand that they usually do not help to create.

The second exception to small firms as the dominant business model in tourism is a recent phenomenon and has to do with consolidation within the ranks of tour operators. Cavlek (2000, 2003) examines the consolidation that has taken place within the ranks of European tour operators since the formation of the EU and liberalization of laws governing foreign ownership of firms. The World Tourism Organization (1999) states that as much as 25% of international travel is organized by tour operators with approximately 50% of that travel organized within the European sphere. This much control by as few as four companies (Cavlek 2003) creates a power imbalance. In the early stages of tour operator consolidation within Europe it was primarily restricted to horizontal integration. In recent years vertical integration has been practiced with some firms controlling their own fleet of charter airlines and in some cases hotel properties within selected destinations. What this means for small

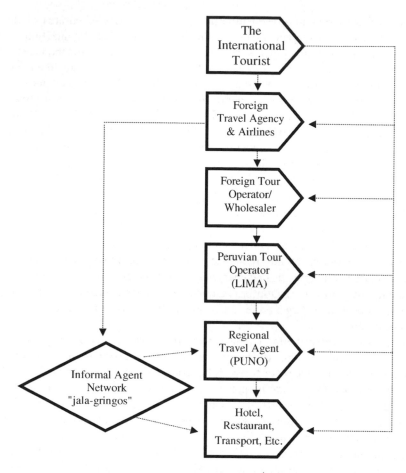

Figure 1: Small firm distribution channel for Puno, Peru.

firms located in the destination is that the distribution channel is being controlled by fewer and fewer firms leading to significant dependency relationships.

An examination of the distribution channel operating for the city of Puno, Peru will reinforce this point. Puno is a small town on the shores of Lake Titicaca. It operates as the Peruvian gateway to the various attractions, both environmental and socio-cultural, found throughout the Lake Titicaca area. Figure 1 shows the distribution channel for small firms, predominantly lodging, operational in the city. The reader will notice that there are four levels to this distribution channel. The first is at the destination and is comprised of small hotels, restaurants and transportation companies and tour operators. These firms sell their products through local agencies which then combine offerings and sell them wholesale to large tour operators located in the capital Lima. Lima brokers, of which there are only two large ones, sell their packages through tour operators and agents located in the primary international markets. These firms then sell the packaged products directly to customers who most likely are unaware of the existence of all the middle agents. Figure 1 also shows a local reaction to the control exerted by the companies firmly ensconced in the distribution channel. The "jala gringos" with its literal translation meaning "pull the foreigners" operates as an unconsolidated group of independent agents who offer direct to destination provider services to tourists fresh off international flights. For the most part they provide legitimate services but they get few takers as tourists have either pre-purchased their tour or are somewhat hesitant to be buying services from someone off the street.

The dependency relationship exerted primarily by the Lima based operators who deal directly with international agents and operators force prices to increase. In order to stay competitive Lima based operators will push discounting down the distribution channel where it ultimately affects local providers. Local providers, which are virtually all small firms, feel helpless to affect change. They must accept the price offered or forgo business. Often price offered may not be enough to reserve funds for necessary maintenance with the result a deteriorating physical property. During a research visit to the area (Puno) in May 2000 a focus group of approximately 15 independent owners of small tourism firms was convened to discuss the issue of distribution channels and dependency. There was unanimous agreement that dependency on Lima based tour operators cut significantly into profit margins. When the discussion turned to e-commerce and the hope of the internet to lessen dependency and allow small firms to sell directly, or through a shared company, the firms' products and services each owner argued that any move to create such a system would be viewed as a hostile act by the Lima based operators who have threatened, when the idea had been broached before, to stop selling the services of any small firm that had the audacity to act in such a way. Owing that there are only two major firms in Lima selling directly to the international market Puno based small firms took the threat as serious with high likelihood of being implemented. These concerns, raised in a confidential way during the focus group meeting, were repeated again in a confidential manner during independent visits to other small tourism dependent firms in the Region.

Whether or not threats issued by Lima based operators are legitimate and would be acted upon should a coalition of Puno operators began to sell to international tourists in any way that bypassed the Lima operators is not known. It is also not known how the Lima based operators have reacted to any firm that has established a relationship directly with an international operator. What is known from the work performed by Cavlek and the result of my own research in Peru is that dependency threats expressed by small firms are real and the potential for control of the distribution channel is present. If small firms were equally distributed along the distribution channel than the threat imposed by a dependency relationship would not exist to the extent they now do in many parts of the world. When large firms dominate in one or more parts of the distribution channel then small firms face a precarious future regardless of the level of tourism demand.

Factors Affecting the Small Firm Environment

There are a number of trends that affect small firm operations in tourism. Trends are not predictions but expected future scenarios based on past occurrences. Trends can also be analyzed based on global significance (i.e. mega trends) or those that just affect a particular economic sector such as tourism. This section begins by examining the mega trend of population growth with its ancillary trends and their implications and then moves into viewing trends specific to tourism.

Population Growth

Population growth is the mega trend that affects all aspects of how we live and play. World population stood at approximately 1.6 billion in 1900 and one hundred years later exceeded 6 billion people. The number of cities with over 10 million inhabitants in 1900 was zero whereas today over 14 cities have at least that many inhabitants (Brown & Flavin 1999). Age distribution of world population is uneven between countries. For the most part developed nations have achieved low birthrates equal to replacement levels or less but developing nations are still averaging birthrates above replacement levels. In developed nations the percentage of older inhabitants (>55) is steadily increasing with respect to rates of younger age cohorts (<25). Quite the opposite is found in developing nations where a large percentage of the inhabitants are less than 25 years old. This disparity in birth rates and population distribution has led to major economic rifts between citizens of the developed world and their counterparts in developing nations. Economic growth is desperately needed to deal with the new generation of young restless people but where will it come from? Tourism is one answer but only a partial one as it will be shown later that tourism is not yet fully rooted in developing nations.

An ancillary trend related to population growth is the discovery and spread of new diseases. As people concentrate in cities they become opportunistic hosts and carriers for old and new diseases. Diseases for which a person has not been able to build up antibodies can be extremely devastating. Exploration and colonization of new lands and their people often led to devastating disease rampages taking out a significant portion of native populations. Disease vectors worked both ways with the conquerors facing disease epidemics in the new land they occupied for which local people had built up antibodies and immunity over generations. Today two diseases, AIDS and SARS, threaten world economic systems.

Aids has been around in a significant way since the 1980s. Even though the disease can be somewhat controlled by a costly and complex mix of drugs most people in the developing world do not have access to the drugs or the money to buy them. Because of this especially hard hit nations in Africa and Asia are in danger of losing their security control which will ultimately lead to failed nation states. Failed nation states lead to breeding grounds for terrorist organizations which has direct relevance to tourism.

SARS is the latest serious potentially pandemic disease to appear in the world. Originating in southern China and spreading to numerous places around the globe the most serious outbreaks, as of this writing, have been in southeast Asia. Reports of travel being down 30% or more to southeast Asia are common news items. Even though the cause of the disease has been identified there is yet no known cure or treatment. Compared to the flu which annually kills in the tens of thousands SARS is a minor killer to date. However, it is the uncertainty over the way SARS spreads and the health community's inability to treat it that has led to alerts about travel to infected parts of the globe with some companies and public organizations in the west banning travel until the epidemic can be brought under control. Here we have a situation that may or may not have long term effects but in the short term the effects are substantial. What is the fate of small firms in tourism as a result of SARS? Given that small firms share some common traits such as limited resources and inability to control the distribution channel the expected result should be a reduction in small firm growth in areas affected by the disease. Depending on how long SARS remains a disease with no known treatment it is possible that entire international tourism dependent regions may enter into a long state of suspended animation with resulting significant economic losses.

AIDS with the possible legacy of failed nation states and SARS with its epicenter being southeast Asia will focus more of the worlds' international travel to developed nations that appear to have control over the diseases and/or effective treatment regimes. This calls into question whether tourism is really a global phenomenon. Aramberri (2003) argues that although tourists can be found in all parts of the world tourism is not a global economic activity. He points out that 84% of all international travel is between Europe, East Asia, and the United States. Even so, international travel is only a fraction of all touristic travel with domestic tourism being the backbone of a country's tourism economy. Given the health issues now focused on Southeast Asia which, according to the World Tourism Organization (1999), was the fastest growing region in the world for international travel it is expected that domestic and international travel will decline, at least in the short term. This should further solidify U.S./European dominance as markets and destinations for the majority of the world's tourists.

The impact of increasing population and its ancillary effects may be the opposite of what one might expect. Instead of increasing population leading to more and more tourists it has led to more and more strife and opportunistic transmission of disease organisms than anyone predicted. With respect to small firms it is becoming more apparent that any destination relying almost entirely on international tourists for its tourism base creates a high risk environment for success. High profile terrorist attacks in New York and Bali, Indonesia or SARS scares in Hong Kong and Singapore have similar effects. Tourism, both domestic and international, declines precipitously in the short run. This does not mean that tourism simply declines. There are some indications it was re-directed at least in relation to domestic tourism. Numerous destinations throughout the United States reported higher than expected tourist numbers in 2002. New York City, and other large U.S. cities suffered declines in number of tourists but those declines seem to have been offset by increases in other, rural, destinations in the U.S. The same can not be said for other destinations in the world (e.g. Singapore) where international tourism is much more heavily relied upon than for the entire United States.

Small firms find themselves at the mercy of exogenous forces that they can not control. The impact on small firm viability increases as the ratio of international tourism to domestic tourism increases. Population increases do not just bring the potential for expanding markets. Instead they bring the potential for disease and terrorist outbreaks to effect small firms at a much higher rate than in the industrialized economies that have a cushion of domestic tourism to fall back on should international tourist flows be disrupted. Therefore we should expect tourism dependent small firms in developing nations to practice a form of risk avoidance by not investing exclusively in activities that are only for the benefit of tourists.

This subject will be addressed again when the Ghanaian case study is presented at the end of this chapter however before moving into that discussion a few other trends, specific to tourism will be discussed.

Consumption Center Development

Consumption center development can be traced back to the idea of firm concentration for consumption purposes. Early forms of consumption center development not directly tied to tourism were shopping malls. What led to the success of shopping malls was the ease in which people could move around in a region by transport other than human powered. Small and large cities of 50 or more years ago concentrated all their basic services and shopping opportunities in a central downtown area. When suburban development, a product of housing expansion after World War II, hit the United States the net effect was to move resident centers from the heart of the downtown area to suburbs located some distance from the center. These new bedroom communities countered the downtown cluster of businesses by building shopping malls located close to their new suburban population centers. In addition as small towns and villages began to suffer significant population decline coinciding with reduced demand for personnel to work in primary industries tourism was "discovered" as a way to keep small towns alive. Some of these towns embarked on a major redevelopment exercise with expected increased levels of tourism being the primary reason for the change. Some examples from tourist towns in the United States will help emphasize this point. Deadwood, South Dakota has become a historical city with gaming as its basic tourist attraction. Deadwood's history is tied to the days mining was a major economic activity in the region and Deadwood was where the wealth concentrated. With mining no longer a major economic activity in the area tourism, through gaming, is viewed as the means to maintain the historical nature, including architecture, of the community. Other cities have adopted the consumption center philosophy for their development approach. Branson, Missouri has become a center for country and related music performances. Orlando, Florida has become the home of Disney World and a host of other theme parks existing off the draw of the primary attraction. Las Vegas, Nevada has redefined itself as a gaming center than also caters to family needs. Each of the above mentioned cities/villages has become a major touristic consumption center with little else but tourism to rely on for economic development. Even older industrial cities are redefining their landscape to have it take on more of a consumption center "look" (Wanhill 2003).

One major reason for developing consumption centers is simply to reduce access costs. Large scale consumption centers benefit from major infrastructure development by capturing economies of scale especially with respect to transportation costs. Low price charters and commercial service operations become possible once enough demand for accessing a particular area is achieved. This has the effect of lowering the access price to the area thus creating additional visitation. The key to success for consumption centers is volume leading to profit through mass sales. Market forces then come into play by making access to consumption centers less expensive for larger numbers of visitors.

The main advantage of consumption center development has to do with reducing the risk from concentration in the distribution channel. As discussed above small firms may be at the mercy of larger firms that control all or a significant part of the distribution channel. However if consumption center development is successful it will be virtually impossible for one company to control tourists flows to the consumption center. As demand for the products/services at the center grows competition will be created among the firms operating in the distribution channel. Situations, such as described above for Puno, Peru, happen because demand is not strong enough to encourge numerous companies to compete in bringing tourists to the destination. Once demand is of sufficient level a destination reverses the order of influence in the distribution channel. Instead of destination firms at the mercy of companies that control the distribution channel destinations become the dominant force and reduce the likelihood that one or a few outside companies can control prices and services within a destination. In a similar way destinations that rely on a "drive to" domestic market have little problems with concentration in the distribution channel as individual tourists are not at the mercy of a controlling authority when it comes to transport.

Consumption center development is not the answer for many destinations as there are other issues that must be addressed. First is the cost for consumption center development. In some cases (e.g. Deadwood, South Dakota) there may have been no other economic alternatives to saving the town. In other cases, such as Las Vegas, the impetus may have come from external forces that led to a proliferation of their core business, gaming, in other areas thus necessitating a development strategy to "break out of the pack." Whatever the impetus for embarking on consumption center development once started it never stops. Competition from other centers and competitors, the need to change the product mix and look, are forces that consumption center development strategy brings with it. Costs will continue to accrue as consumption centers change in response to market or competitive forces. Another concern is the transformational character of consumption center development. Consumption centers must be viewed as what they are: artificially contrived destinations that seek to concentrate tourists in a manner that induces spending. As the cost of consumption center development increases small firms may find themselves under as much pressure as those firms in destinations controlled by concentration in the distribution channel. Consumption center development may reach such a level, as it has for hotels in Las Vegas, that small firms are priced out of the market and/or unable to compete on price against larger firms that are responsible for much of the consumption center development.

Consumption center development, occurring as it has mostly within the developed nations, further concentrates tourists in the regions of the world accounting for over 80% of all tourism both domestic and international. Small firms located in these destinations stand to benefit from the concentration of tourists in geographically tight areas but as mentioned above they may lose their ability to compete as costs of competition increase and large firms move to consolidate their position by offering many of the services now offered by small firms.

Public Involvement

Almost all the community development workbooks (Messer 2001) call for higher levels of public involvement in local tourism development decisions. However not all societies value public involvement in the same way it is intended by the authors of the workbooks.

Centrally planned economies, of which there are few left in the world, do not embrace active local public involvement. Even in those societies that do place emphasis on different points of views, and the publics right to be involved, have a difficult time making the process fair and transparent.

McCool & Patterson (2000) argue that planning issues of the past are considered "tame" when compared to the "wicked problems and messes" with which today's planners are confronted. Most of the concern revolves around the goals and objectives to be attained through products offered rather than dealing with more concrete or physical types of planning issues. Since goals and objectives are subjectively determined they are bound to be questioned by a percentage of the affected population that desires other outcomes. Often legal avenues become the only recourse for solving some of the contentious issues. Nonetheless McCool & Patterson state that planning is embracing ever more the concept of managing for desired social or biophysical conditions.

Propst *et al.* (2000) reinforce some of the arguments offered by McCool & Patterson but they also add another dimension when dealing with environmental issues related to planning. They contend that humans are often unaware of human-natural resource interactions and impacts. Because of this public involvement may be more emotionally charged than factually directed. What all this means is that present and future managers involved in tourism development projects will likely face an increasing amount of interest group dissension with their decisions.

Small firms find themselves more affected by greater public involvement than their larger counterparts. This is due primarily to the limited resources small firms have for purposes other than selling. If small firms find themselves somehow involved in contentious issues surrounding tourism development their opportunity for success diminishes the longer the issues remain unresolved and take resources away from revenue generating activities.

Technology

Buhalis (2000) states that "Information Technology (IT) . . . at the same time propels it by providing effective tools both to consumers for identifying and purchasing suitable products and to suppliers for developing, managing, and distributing their offerings on a global scale." Essentially what this statement says is that all sizes of suppliers can use IT to their advantage. In other words it levels out the playing field between the big and small. However even if the technology supports this type of application the larger companies still possess economies of scale for product development and have the resources to reach the market.

Information technology is used for more than selling. Perdue (2000) discusses how certain providers of goods and services are using IT to increase their levels of service and guest satisfaction. The IT wave which began some 10–15 years ago has reached a point where in the five year period between 1995 and 2000 touristic service providers have been able to advance their offerings and delivery mechanisms more than they did in the three decades previously. "Developments in the IT represent a revolution for the tourism industry, comparable only to the introduction of the jet engine" (Buhalis 2000: 47).

It has become increasingly apparent that the internet is used more for product purchasing or product comparison than it is for creating product awareness. In a recent study of visitors to different Minnesota (U.S.) communities only the internet, when compared to other types of information dissemination, was consistently viewed as being more important in planning a trip than for creating awareness of the destination area (Gartner *et al.* 2002). If this finding is not exclusive to the Minnesota visitor then it suggests the small scale operator will have to find ways to partner with destination service providers that are able to reach the market in such a way and through various means that they benefit from the destination awareness marketing undertaken by these larger firms. Similarly associations that create destination awareness in the market would also be ideal candidates with which the small operator could become more involved. Whatever the course of action chosen it could lead to even more dependency issues, possibly similar to those that currently exist as the information flow, another part of the tourism distribution channel, becomes more concentrated with fewer primary sellers.

Ghana Case Study

The trends and implications discussed above will now be reviewed with respect to a small firm study in the Central Region of Ghana. The Republic of Ghana is located on the West Coast of Africa approximately 750 miles north of the Equator. A tropical country with temperatures ranging from 21 to 32 °C it is relatively moist in the south along the coastal zone with annual rainfall averaging 2,030 mm. Tropical forests at one time encompassed all of the southern and middle section of the country. Few extensive tracts remain today. Ghana has substantial gold and, at one time, timber reserves and is also a major exporter of cocoa. In spite of its resource wealth, development has been hampered by a burgeoning population (estimated at 15 million) and a series of coups from independence through 1981. It has been the coups, both attempted and successful that have, more than anything else, retarded tourism development (Teye 1988). Twelve years ago Ghana embarked on another attempt at instilling democracy which appears to be working and is somewhat responsible for an improving economic situation.

Tourism development is not new to Ghana as during the mid-1970's there was substantial development of touristic products facilitated by the construction of some very large hotels throughout the county. What is new about the recent level of tourism development is the focus on private sector ownership of the industry. Where in the 1970's all tourism development was conducted by government, supported by high earnings from primary products, that all changed as world prices for primary products declined in the late 1970s and have yet to return to 1970s levels in real value terms. Recent tourism growth is being fueled by private initiatives that in many cases, especially in rural areas, has led to small firm growth.

Small firms were studied in Ghana's Central Region. The Central Region with its historic capital of Cape Coast and the city of Elmina are the sites where the first European contact with West Africa occurred. The epicenter of this contact is Elmina Castle (Fort George Castle under British rule) which was originally a small fort erected by the Portuguese in 1482 to facilitate contact and trade with West African indigenous peoples. The fort later grew into a major trading center and fortification to protect European interests on the continent. Both Elmina and the nearby Cape Coast castle are on the World Heritage list of significant historical buildings. One of the most valuable, in economic and socio-cultural terms, commodities to pass through these castles was people — slaves. It is estimated that millions of slaves were processed through these castles and today the journey of the slaves from their homes to the castles is the basis for the World Tourism Organization's Slave Route project.

Significant other resources exist in the Central Region including small tropical forest reserves that hold great bio-diversity importance since they once were part of the great, isolated West Africa tropical rain forest belt. The Region's cultural resources are another major tourism attraction as parts of the culture are readily shared with visitors.

Study results important to the discussion presented in this chapter were first published in 1999 (Gartner 1999). I have extracted a few of the findings on small firm development that relate to the points made in this chapter. Table 1 provides a good picture of the development of the hotel sector operating in the Central Region in 1997. Notice that in 1995 a record number (6) of new hotels opened. To the casual observer this might seem to coincide with the development at Kakum Park, in particular the opening of the canopy walkway (one of only six in the world), and the inauguration of a new museum in Cape Coast Castle both which occurred in 1995. However, further analysis reveals a different story. In 1994 the government of Ghana passed a new investment code, effective in 1995, containing special provisions affecting the hotel sector. The two most important were a tax reduction from 35 to 25% of net profits from hotel operations and duty free importation of hotel equipment, furnishings or vehicles tied to operating the hotel (Ghana Investment Promotion Center Act 1994). A further incentive for hotel development came from the provision of low interest loans backed by the Ghana tourist board. These provisions in the tax code appear (from Table 1) to have encouraged hotel development but it is also important to note that anyone purchasing one of the old government hotels or even starting a small bed and breakfast using their own home would be entitled to these tax code benefits as they had the type of property identified in the legislation. In practice many Ghanians have more than one business venture operating at a time. Taking advantage of the tax code privileges reserved for the hotel sector meant many imported products could be purchased for the hotel but also diverted to other businesses owned by the same person.

Table 1: Hotel development by year in Ghana's Central Region.

Year Business Started	Number of Hotels
Before 1970	1
1970–1979	3
1980–1989	1
1990	1
1991	1
1992	1
1993	0
1994	1
1995	6

Table 2: What do you do with year-end profits?

Use of Year-End Profit	Number of Hotel/Restaurants
Don't have any yet	3
Plough it back into the business	11
Take out a little each month	3

What is done with year end operating profits? Most of the businesses claim there are no year end operating profits for reallocation to uses outside of their hotel. Most prefer to reinvest or as stated in Table 2 "plough it back into the business" when a profit is realized. This should not be an unrealistic finding for relatively new businesses that are in the development stage but observational data indicates that only five of those indicating they reinvest the profits in the business actually show, at least to the interested observer, some developmental change.

Part of the answer to what happens with profits may be revealed in Table 3 which shows that 10 of the 14 hotels responding hire friends or relatives of the owner. This is in keeping with the Ghanaian culture of assisting an extended family member and may be one of the reasons for the response that profits are reinvested as that phrase may also mean the write off of costs incurred from conducting business.

The final table (Table 4) shows the importance of external influences in business decisions. When asked to respond to whether they feel business owners seek input from a priest or priestess before making a business decision the overwhelmingly majority responded in the positive. Only one indicated this would not happen. It should be mentioned here that a priest or priestess in this context is not an ordained minister but rather someone who is in contact with the spirit world (i.e. shaman). This does not mean people who seek information from the spirit world deny the existence of a God. Most Ghanaians believe strongly in a God but also in spirits who do a great deal more to control everyday life than an all powerful God. Sarpong (1974) explains the role of spirits in daily life and the influence they have on behavior. Priests are held in high regard within the community. It is not a position that one can lay claim to even though it may be gained through hereditary succession or conferred by the deity the priest represents. All priests apprentice for the position and must be able to win the trust of the people they serve. There will be at least one priest for each recognized deity. Individuals may have a favorite spirit which they will constantly seek advice from through his intermediary, the priest. Even though in the study no one who was interviewed admitted

Table 3: Are hometown friends, family or acquaintances of the owner(s) employed here?

Friends, Family, Acquaintances Employed?	Number of Hotel/Restaurants
Yes	10
No	4

Table 4: Is it true that some business owners see priests or priestesses when making decisions?

Consult Priest/Priestess in Business Decisions?	Number of Hotel/Restaurants
Yes	12
Maybe	2
No	1

to seeking advice from a priest the vast majority were quite sure others did. This indicates that the practice remains an important part of daily life albeit one that is not readily shared with those outside the culture. If this is the case then it is quite possible that economic rationale would be a secondary consideration when seeking assistance for a business decision. The two, economic and cultural, are not mutually exclusive. It is entirely possible that one's favorite deity is also one that provides the best business advice. Nevertheless, the importance of cultural influences in the business life of the Ghanaian entrepreneur appears quite strong.

Conclusions

Where the discussion in this chapter, along with the case study results, appears to lead is that small firms operate in a different milieu, especially in the developing world, than their larger counterparts. Development economists that subscribe to the dependency school claim that developing countries are still subject to terms of trade dictated by developed countries. In this chapter an attempt has been made to show that dependency operates as well within the tourism distribution channel. Despite claims that the internet would allow small and medium size firms to compete on an equal footing against their larger competitors for the most part that prediction has not come true. There still exists constriction in the distribution channel and firms that control the constriction can force dependency relationships on small firms.

There is also evidence, presented in this chapter, that the neo-classical school's arguments for why countries have failed to develop can be directly related to small firms in tourism as well. The age old practice of taking care of one's own is still evident today in the Ghanaian context presented above. Hiring relatives and friends may not be the smartest business decision as often you end up with an uneducated and unskilled workforce but it does satisfy cultural obligations. Similarly low or non-existent levels of savings and capital formation retard development. The trends analysis presented above shows the potential for consolidating forces to impose dependency relationships on small firms thus negating the small firm's ability to reinvest in itself. Even when, as in the case of Ghana, the firms claim reinvestment takes place there may be no outward sign of this happening.

Weak management skills is another sign of the neo-classical argument for slow or no development in developing countries. There was evidence presented in this chapter that new hotel investment in Ghana resulted from favorable legislation. There was no evidence that those who invested in hotels had the skills to manage the hotel. Employment of friends and relatives coupled with the use of priests to help in business decisions (although no one would admit to using priests themselves although they were sure others did) are indications that management skills are weak. Even when legislation is proposed to spur sector development it was not at all clear that those owning and operating hotels did so because they saw it as a good investment and revenue generator or more as a way to import expensive items at a discount rate. As noted many of the items listed as needed for the hotel sector had uses for other industrial pursuits and even for personal consumption.

Trends discussed above underscore the risks entrepreneurs accept when investing in tourism dependent small firms. The market is for the most part restricted to Europe and North America with Asia trying very hard to hold unto tourism gains which are constantly buffeted by economic concerns as well as new disease vectors. Small firms located in developing countries that do not have a strong domestic tourist market as insurance are subject to volatile swings in revenue brought on by situations they have no control over (e.g. terrorism, disease). The Ghanaian entrepreneurs who started a tourism related business because the tax code was favorable are practicing risk avoidance by taking advantage of government policy even if tourism is not their main business interest.

One advantage for small firm development in developing countries not mentioned in this chapter is favorable terms of trade when it comes to prevailing wage rates (Keller 2000). Since the costs of a holiday are in large part determined by access cost and destination prices lower local prices may make a destination, and the small firms operating there, more appealing. However as was discussed this favorable condition may be offset by the control exerted by large firms operating in the distribution channel. By the time destination prices reach the consumer they may be no lower than those encountered in parts of the developed world. In a similar way consumption center development will exert competitive forces in the distribution channel thereby driving prices down to the point where developed country destinations can compete on prices against developing countries even with the disparity in wage rates.

Finally public involvement affects small firms by increasing litigation costs and by increasing the amount of time small firms must wait before they can physically develop. This is where small firms in developing countries that do not have a tradition of public involvement may actually be able to get something done much quicker than their counterparts in a developed nation but that is not a given. What appears to be clear is that the public involvement process is becoming more time consuming, more costly, and adds additional risk to investment decisions faced by small firms.

In conclusion it appears small firms in tourism, especially in developing nations, have a great deal working against them. Yet as agents of economic development small firms, which are the dominant form of tourism business at the destination level, are the backbone of a destination's tourism economy. In spite of the risks inherent in starting a small business there does not seem to be any shortage of them. As was shown in this chapter small firms face risks from global conditions (e.g. SARS, HIV, terrorism) over which they have no control. They also deal with dependency relationships that might arise from too much reliance on the global market. Finally they face risks from their inability to raise capital, lack of managerial skill and cultural obligations leading to hiring of family and friends. Not all small firms face the same obstacles. Obviously firms in nations where the public involvement process is well rooted must deal with that trend but they may not have to contend with other trends affecting small firms in other parts of the world. What is evident in the discussion presented in this chapter is that small firm development is needed for active tourism destination development but there are many obstacles in the way of their success. Understanding the context of small firm development, whether they exist in the developed or developing world, whether they are affected by the trends presented in this chapter, whether they rely more on an international vs. domestic market etc are necessary preconditions before any attempt can be made to deal with issues faced by small firms in tourism. In this chapter no solutions to the problems identified have been offered as it was not the intent of this discussion to pose solutions. Rather an examination of some of the major issues small firms might have to deal with were discussed in order to help frame any future discussion about solutions.

References

Anunobi, F. (1994). *International dimensions of African political economy: Trends, challenges, and realities*. University Press of America.

Aramberri, J. (2003, in press). How global is tourism. In: J. Aramberri, & R. Butler (Eds), *Tourism development: Issues for a vulnerable industry; international academy for the study of tourism*. Channel View Publications.

Brown, L., & Flavin, C. (1999). A new economy for a new century. In: *State of the World 1999*. New York: W. W. Norton and Company.

Buhalis, D. (2000). Trends in information technology and tourism. In: W. Gartner, & D. Lime (Eds), *Trends in outdoor recreation and tourism*. London: CABI.

Cavlek, N. (2000). The role of tour operators in the travel distribution system. In: W. Gartner, & D. Lime (Eds), *Trends in outdoor recreation and tourism*. London: CABI.

Cavlek, N. (2003, in press). The impact of tour operators on tourism development: A sequence of events. In: J. Aramberri, & R. Butler (Eds), *Tourism development: Issues for a vulnerable industry; international academy for the study of tourism*. Channel View Publications.

Gartner, W. (1999). Small scale enterprises in the tourism industry in Ghana's central region. In: D. Pearce, & R. Butler (Eds), *Contemporary issues in tourism development*. International Academy for the Study of Tourism. London: Routledge.

Gartner, W. (1993). Image formation process. *Journal of Travel and Tourism Marketing*, 2(3), 191–212.

Gartner, W., Love, L., & Erkkila, D. (2002). *Profile of visitors to five Minnesota communities*. St. Paul: Tourism Center, University of Minnesota.

Ghana Investment Promotion Center Act (1994). Act 478, Ghana Investment Promotion Center. Accra: Ghana Publishing Corporation.

Hansohm, D. (1992). *Small industry development in Africa — lessons from Sudan*. Munster: Lit Verlag.

Keller, P. (2000). Globalization and tourism. In: W. Gartner, & D. Lime (Eds), *Trends in outdoor recreation and tourism*. London: CABI.

McCool, S., & Patterson, M. (2000). Trends in recreation, tourism and protected area planning. In: W. Gartner, & D. Lime (Eds), *Trends in outdoor recreation and tourism*. London: CABI.

Messer, C. (2001). *Community tourism development*. St. Paul: Tourism Center, University of Minnesota.

Ongile, G., & McCormick, D. (1996). Barriers to small firm growth: Evidence from Nairobi's garment industry. In: McCormick, & Pederson (Eds), *Small enterprises: Flexibility and networking in an African context* (pp. 40–62). Nairobi: Longhorn, Kenya.

Perdue, R. (2000). Service quality in resort settings: Trends in the application of information technology. In: W. Gartner, & D. Lime (Eds), *Trends in outdoor recreation and tourism*. London: CABI.

Propst, D., Wellman, D., Campa, H., III, & McDonough, M. (2000). Citizen participation trends and their educational implications for natural resource professionals. In: W. Gartner, & D. Lime (Eds), *Trends in outdoor recreation and tourism*. London: CABI.

Sarpong, P. (1974). *Ghana in retrospect: Some aspects of Ghanaian culture*. Accra: Ghana Publishing Corporation.

Smith, S. (2003, in press). The geographical structure of Canadian tourism. In: J. Aramberri, & R. Butler (Eds), *Tourism development: Issues for a vulnerable industry; international academy for the study of tourism*. Channel View Publications.

Teye, V. (1988). Coups D'etat and African tourism: A study of Ghana. *Annals of Tourism Research*, *15*, 329–356.

Wanhill, S. (2003, in press). The ownership of attractions. In: J. Aramberri, & R. Butler (Eds), *Tourism development: Issues for a vulnerable industry; international academy for the study of tourism*. Channel View Publications.

World Tourism Organization (WTO) (1999). *Tourism highlights 1999*. Madrid: WTO.

Chapter 4

Government Assistance for Tourism SMEs: From Theory to Practice

Stephen Wanhill

Introduction

The aim of this chapter is to examine the theory and practice of government intervention in the tourism industry to correct for market failure. Having reviewed the significance of small firms, the first part deals with issues relating to investment strategy and then goes on to look at the principal instruments for implementation, namely investment incentives. But its is argued later that the myriad of small and micro-businesses, which dominate the sector, are faced with so many other difficulties that investment incentives alone are likely, in many instances, to be insufficient to guarantee success. What is required is a multi-tasking approach and the practicalities of this are discussed under four headings: structuring small business finance; upgrading standards; improving communications channels; and raising the level of market intelligence.

The rationale for intervention lies in the complex nature of the tourist product, which makes it unlikely that private markets will satisfy a country's tourism policy objectives to produce a balance of facilities that meet the needs of the visitor, benefit the host community and are compatible with the wishes of that same community. Thus, the market mechanism and governance should not be seen as mutually exclusive activities, but rather complementary. As witnessed by the developments in Russia post-1990, inadequate agencies to make use of market transactions, the unregulated acquisition of knowledge and resources (leading to widespread corruption), and the unethical concealment of information may be counterproductive to development, resulting in unsuitable directions for the market and disillusionment on the part of many in the society.

Importance of Small Firms

The growing interest in community tourism development is paralleled in the developed world, though less so in LDCs because of limited capital markets, by a switch of emphasis away from large automatic grants to attract inward investment projects, towards small firms

Small Firms in Tourism: International Perspectives
Copyright © 2004 Published by Elsevier Ltd.
ISBN: 0-08-044132-7

and indigenous development. This is a change in direction from the "Fordist" production era of economies of scale that had been so influential in the development thinking of governments prior to the "oil crisis ridden" 1970s (Curran & Blackburn 1991). The proponents of these ideas see such constructs as offering sustainable models for the future development of outlying economic areas, since the emphasis is on the need to build regional autonomy and to foster the collaboration of industry, employees and the public sector at that level. The promotion of SMEs is on the basis that small firms provide the community structure for entrepreneurship and job creation and should ideally be a business that is flexible in terms customising products to customers, adapting production techniques to the specifics of place and in networking.

Within the European Union (EU), the objectives of the Common Regional Policy (CRP) are to create a greater convergence between the economies of the Member States and to ensure a better spread of the economic activities throughout the Union. Thus the position of SMEs is critical to progress towards regional convergence. In a European-wide context, SMEs are defined as a companies with a workforce fewer than 250 employees, a definition that embraces quite readily the majority of the tourism businesses in Europe, for micro-businesses (fewer than 10 employees) form the largest division within the overall category of tourism SMEs (Middleton 2000; Thomas 2000).

Currently, the most common forms of multinational assistance for SMEs in the Union are the Structural Funds, specifically the European Regional Development Fund (ERDF). Multinational assistance for SME development in Eastern Europe and the Commonwealth of Independent States (CIS) within the Russian sphere of influence is the province of the European Bank for Reconstruction and Development (EBRD). The ERDF is focused mainly on productive investment, infrastructure, and SME development (principally grant aid and "soft" finance) in less favoured regions, and holds the bulk of EU money for regional aid. Disadvantaged regions in Europe usually have a strong representation of micro tourism firms that perform an important role both economically and socially in stabilising fragile areas (Middleton 2000). In this respect, tourism has received increasing amounts of regional aid under successive EU programmes (Wanhill 1997): a notable example of the use of these funds has been Ireland, whereby a combination of liberalisation on the demand side and investment in the product (particularly special activities, cultural heritage and genealogy), supported by grants and a reduced rate of VAT, has produced a renaissance in Irish tourism since the mid 1980s (Deegan & Dineen 2000).

Investment Strategy

The precise nature of a country's stance on tourism investment is determined by the kind of development the government is looking for and what role it envisages for the private entrepreneur. As a rule, the extent of political involvement is directly related to the importance attached to tourism as an economic activity and so, to realise the objectives of a tourism development plan, governments have to put forward an investment policy that is conducive to developers and investors. For example, the stated overall objective of the U.K. Government's support for tourism is to maximise the economic benefit of tourism to the nation, in terms of higher output and employment creation, an objective that can be found in most national tourism strategies. Section 4 assistance (S4), under the 1969 Development of Tourism Act (House of Commons 1969), was intended to help realise this objective by counteracting market failure in an industry characterised by SMEs and was a practical response to the "funding gap" for small firms, which has a long history in the U.K. (Taylor *et al.* 1998). The Welsh Office Review put the matter this way:

> Overall the development and growth of tourism in Wales will depend upon the availability of a combination of features — including an attractive environment and interesting leisure facilities. To create such combinations will typically require a number of related investments. But the return to any one investment *on its own* may be insufficient to persuade the small-scale investors who dominate Welsh tourism to go ahead, even though the whole combination of investments would earn a satisfactory rate of return. In the presence of such market failure there remains a need for some strategic pump priming (Welsh Office 1995: 5).

The extreme case is where governments themselves set up a Tourist Development Corporation (TDC) and invest directly, perhaps up to 100% ownership in revenue-earning activities such as hotels, which are traditionally regarded as the preserve of the private sector. Instances around the world include Egypt, India, New Zealand, Malaysia, Mexico and many African countries. In theory, once the resort has been built, the TDC's function ceases and the assets are transferred to the private sector (at a price) and the local authority. This is the general drift in market-orientated economies, where the rising trend towards greater economic freedom, which gathered momentum during the 1980s, led states increasingly to divest themselves of trading operations that could be undertaken by the commercial sector. On the other hand, the counter to increasing market power has been the growing concern for the environment and the concept of sustainable tourism. Given that tourist movements will increase both nationally and internationally, there will be a need for more regulation and improved management of tourism resources to prevent environmental degradation. For example, some time ago, the European Commission (1995) identified three objectives for governing EU involvement in the field of tourism:

- Supporting improvements in the quality of tourism by taking greater account of the trends in tourism demand;
- Encouraging the diversification of tourist activities and products through improving the competitiveness and profitability of the industry;
- Incorporating the concept of sustainable and balanced growth into tourism by giving due regard to the cultural and environmental dimensions of tourism.

These objectives have a wide level of support and it may be thought that the learning process of market interaction might lead to some regulating structure that can overcome identified weaknesses in the industry, thus ensuring that businesses remain economically viable, while environmental and other free goods are conserved and maintained in line with Local Agenda 21, so that the basis of the tourist industry is sustained. In practice, seldom is this case: evidence suggests that only government intervention will facilitate this to happen, because of the high degree of fragmentation in the industry and asymmetric information flows (DOE 1990).

Structure of Investment Incentives

Early work by Bodlender (1982) and Jenkins (1982), and again by Boldender & Ward (1987), considered the variety of incentives that were available in tourism and made it possible to draw a broad classification along the following lines (Wanhill 1999):

- Financial incentives;
- Reductions in capital costs;
- Reductions in operating costs;
- Investment security.

Illustrative examples of the kinds of incentives given within such a classification are shown in Table 1. The objective of financial incentives is to improve returns to capital so as to ensure that market potential, which is attractive to developers and investors, may be turned into financially sound projects. Where there is obvious commercial profit to be gained, the government may only be required to demonstrate a commitment to tourism by, say, marketing and promoting the region, particularly abroad, and giving advice and information to prospective developers. Such circumstances occurred in Bermuda during

Table 1: Structure of investment incentives.

Capital Cost Reductions	Operating Cost Reductions	Investment Security
Capital grants	Direct and indirect tax exemptions or reductions	Guarantees against nationalisation and adverse legislation changes
Soft loans	A labour or training subsidy	Repatriation of invested capital, profits, dividends and interest
Equity participation	Subsidised tariffs on key inputs such as energy	
Provision of infrastructure	Special depreciation allowances	Ensuring the availability of trained staff
Provision of land on concessional terms	Double taxation or unilateral relief	Loan guarantees
Tariff exemption on construction material		Provision of work permits for "key" personnel Availability of technical advice

Table 2: Investment incentives in the European union tourism industry.

Country	Special to Hotels and Tourism	Financial Incentives		Investment Security
		Capital	**Operating**	
Austria	Yes, more favourable than manufacturing	Grants and soft loans	Reduced VAT	State loan guarantees
Belgium	Yes	Grants and soft loans	Indirect and direct tax reductions	
Denmark	No, general schemes only			
Finland	No, general schemes only, save for VAT		Reduced VAT	
France	Yes, manufacturing similarly provided for if to do with regional development	Grants and soft loans	Indirect tax exemptions/ reductions, special depreciation allowances	
Germany	No, general schemes only			
Greece	Yes, wide range of incentives for tourism	Grants, soft loans and interest rate subsidies	Indirect and direct tax exemptions/ reductions, special depreciation allowances	
Ireland	Yes	Grants	Special depreciation allowances	
Italy	Yes	Grants and soft loans	Indirect and direct tax exemptions/ reductions, special depreciation allowances	
Luxembourg	Yes	Grants	Indirect and direct tax exemptions/ reductions	
Netherlands	Yes	Grants and soft loans	Reduced VAT	

Table 2: (*Continued*)

Country	Special to Hotels and Tourism	Financial Incentives		Investment Security
		Capital	Operating	
Portugal	Yes, tourism particularly favoured	Soft loans and interest rate subsidies	Indirect and direct tax exemptions/ reductions, special depreciation allowances	
Spain	Yes	Soft loans principal form of aid but grants also available	Indirect tax exemption	
Sweden	Yes, but only for regional development	Grants and soft loans	Reduced VAT	
UK	Yes, but only in parts of the UK	Grants principal form of aid; occasionally soft loans		

Source: NTAs and industry departments of Member States.

the early 1970s and so, in order to prevent over exploitation of the tourism resources, the Bermuda Government imposed a moratorium on large hotel building (Archer & Wanhill 1980).

Table 2 presents an overview of investment incentives within the EU: it appears that all Member States provide incentives for investment, but not all make any special provision for hotels and tourism and, as a rule, Southern European countries, with their greater dependence on tourism, exhibit more generosity in the terms and the rates at which they support tourist developments. Investment security is not usually questioned within the Union, where the most common approach is state loan guarantees, though not usually specific to tourism. For example, the U.K. government has been operating a general Small Firms Loan Guarantee Scheme since 1981, whereby banks have been offered up to 85% surety on loans, thus supplementing the collateral on offer from small businesses (Taylor *et al.* 1998).

Financial Incentives

The impact of financial incentives on the amount of investment is illustrated in Figure 1. The schedule SS_1 represents the supply of investible funds in the first instance, while D_1D is the schedule of post tax returns to capital employed. D_1D slopes downwards from left to right as

Return on Capital

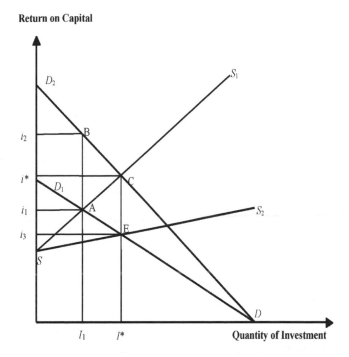

Figure 1: Macroeconomics of financial incentives.

more and more investment opportunities are taken up — the declining marginal efficiency of investment. In the initial situation, equilibrium is at A with the amount of investment being I_1 and the internal rate of return i_1. Conditions of market failure imply that the community benefits from tourism investment are not entirely captured in the demand function D_1D. Optimal economic efficiency is where the demand function that includes these externalities D_2D, intersects the supply curve at I^*, yielding a return I^*. To achieve this, the government implements a range of financial incentives, commonly in the form of tax adjustments and subsidies that reduce operating expenses, which have the effect of raising the private rate of return per unit of capital towards the higher economic rate of return (or social rate, if issues related to the distribution of income are taken into account), by moving the marginal efficiency of investment schedule to D_2D. At i^*, the amount of government subsidy to induce entrepreneurs to invest I^* is the area i^* CE i_3, and the effective rate of subsidy, say s, is $(i^* - i_3)/i_3$, which implies that $i^* = (1+s)i_3$ and the total subsidy is sI^*. The private opportunity cost of the investment funds is the area under the supply curve, I_1 AC I^*, while the public willingness-to-pay for correcting the externality is the area I_1 BC I^*: subtracting the two areas gives a net gain represented by the area ABC.

If the amount of investible funds available for tourism is limited at I_1, then the impact of incentives serves merely to raise the return to investors by raising the equilibrium point to B. The loss to the government treasury is the area i_1 AB i_2, which equals the gain to private investors and there is no net economic gain to the community. There is no doubt that many countries have been forced into situations that are similar to those above by the competitive pressures to obtain foreign investment. Countries can become trapped in a bidding process to secure clients and, as a result, the variety of financial incentives multiplies, together with an escalation of the effective rate of subsidy, without evaluating their necessity or their true cost to the economy.

The alternative to stimulating demand is to increase the supply of investible funds. In Figure 1, this is shown by a shift in the supply function to $S\, S_2$, which reduces the cost of capital to the private sector, thus permitting the marginal project to earn an internal rate of return of i_3, and generating the optimal level of investment I^*. Typically, governments attempt to do this by establishing Development or Investment Banks, arranging special credit facilities through sector specific agencies such as the National Tourism Administration (NTA), or, as noted above, constituting TDCs. The economic rationale for this is that governments are usually able to borrow at lower rates than the private sector, since they have ultimate recourse to taxation to cover their debts. In the case of LDCs, finance may be obtained from international banks and multinational aid agencies on favourable terms.

Investment Security

All the issues on investment security shown in Table 1 are important to tourism, which requires considerable public sector support to flourish. This may be demonstrated by the promotional activities of the NTA, reducing administrative delays, simplifying the planning process, easing frontier formalities, initiating liberal transport policies and so on. The converse, such as foreign exchange controls and restrictions on market access through protective air policies and visas, will retard tourism development and investment. To counter bureaucratic inefficiency, complicated administrative processes and the lack of transparency in the legislation affecting businesses, together with frequent modifications to the legislation, governments, as for example in Eastern Europe and the CIS, have established "one-stop-shop" agencies to ease the path of investors, as well as including "grandfathering" clauses in the legislation. The latter apply to legislation that exempts new enterprises from unfavourable fiscal changes for up to 10 years.

Options for Tourism SMEs

Tourism SMEs are dominated by family businesses and owner-managers, whose motivations have been found to encompass a spectrum that runs from commercial goals and policies to lifestyle intentions (Foley & Green 1989; Hornaday 1990). In their study of Cornwall, Shaw & Williams (1990) noted critically that family enterprises have limited market stability, low levels of capital investment, weak management skills and are resistant to advice or change. This makes them financially vulnerable in the sense that the value of the firm is largely based on intangible assets (the opposite of production industries), leaving them little collateral to put up as surety for debt finance. Similar aspects are also highlighted in the work of Morrison *et al.* (1998), where they conclude that such businesses are managed essentially by their owners and have negligible market power to influence purchases and sales. The owners are often married couples, which Getz & Carlsen (2000) describe as "copreneurs." Their incomplete management expertise is no help in dealing with a difficult business climate in respect of securing finance and penetrating the market. They have a widespread inability to think more than one year ahead and so act as "price-takers" in the manner of the perfectly competitive economic model, because they are unaware of market trends. It appears that transactions and information costs are taken as major barriers to obtaining knowledge of their demand curves. This forces them to behave in a cost-orientated manner in what is a market-orientated industry (Kotas & Wanhill 1981). Hence, it is not surprising that local bank managers operate a "rule of thumb" to the effect that about one third of SMEs are successful, one third are surviving in a struggle that could go either way, and the remaining third should not be in business in the first place! The goal, therefore, of public intervention should be to help SMEs manage their own future, rather than spend their time "fire-fighting" in every situation.

Microeconomic Aspects

The theoretical foundations that should underpin the public sector intervention process may be drawn out from the standard business model. Let Π, net profit before tax, so that

$$\begin{aligned} \Pi &= R - C \\ &= R - C^* - C^k \end{aligned} \tag{1}$$

where R is revenue and the total cost schedule C is divided into the operational costs C^* and the amortisation of the capital investment C^k This is shown on Figure 2: R is the revenue line and CC the total cost schedule attributable to running the business in a given year. The line C^*C^* represents the costs of operation excluding the provision for capital recovery, the difference $CC - C^*C^*$ being C^k.

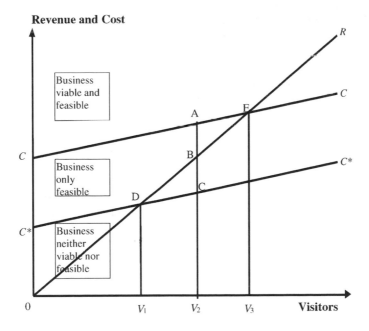

Figure 2: Microeconomics of investment incentives.

Decomposing R in Equation (1) into price P and the number of visitors V, and C^* into a variable component MV, where M is the unit variable or marginal cost, and a fixed sum C_f^*, then

$$\Pi = PV - MV - C_f^* - C^k \qquad (2)$$

Assuming that price is given by the market and is not under the firm's control, then taking differentials of Equation (2) gives

$$d\Pi = PdV - MdV - VdM - dC_f^* - dC^k \qquad (3)$$

Equation (3) allows the outcomes of various policy options to be separated into three distinct categories as well as combinations:

Option 1: Reduction in capital costs

$$d\Pi = -dC^k \qquad (4)$$

Option 2: Raising turnover

$$d\Pi = (P - M)dV \qquad (5)$$

Option 3: Reduction in operating costs

$$d\Pi = -VdM - dC_f^* \qquad (6)$$

where VdM is the reduction in variable costs and dC_f^* represents savings in fixed operating expenses.

In deciding the appropriate intervention policy, an important distinction to make is between the "feasibility" and "viability" of tourism businesses. From Figure 2, it may be seen that at a level of V_2 visitors the business is feasible, since it produces a surplus BC over C^*C^*, but it is not viable because there is a gap AB in the funds available to service the capital, as the business falls between CC and C^*C^*. To the left of D the business is neither viable nor feasible as it falls below C^*C^*, whereas the converse is true at point E, because the revenue line now lies above CC. If intervention policy is discretionary rather than mandatory, then the area of economic interest for tourism policy should normally reside between the two cost lines where the business is feasible but not viable. The rationale for this is that viability depends upon the cost of capital, which has a floor rate that is a macroeconomic variable set by the monetary authorities. To assist a business operating at a level to the left of D would likely involve the public sector in providing continuous support and might just be "throwing good money after bad." Beyond point E, the business is viable and has no need of public assistance: this has been termed (Wanhill 2000) the "additionality rule," which is practised in the U.K. to the effect that public assistance will only be given if the business or project would not go ahead without it, thus allowing the government to earn "best value" for the money that it disperses to private bodies.

On the assumption of the desirability of the firm in terms of the overall tourism development strategy, the tourism authorities must have as a target the viability of the business after assistance has been given. In practice, the requirements may be wider than this: for example, if one looks at S4 as implemented by the Wales Tourist Board (Wanhill 2000), all aspects of any proposed investment are considered, though the accountability for public funds lays stress ultimately on economic criteria, which may be summarised as:

- The project should be feasible;
- Viability is assured after financial assistance;
- Compliance with the additionality rule;
- Displacement effects on surrounding businesses should be minimized;
- Multiplier effects in terms of employment and grant cost per job should be met.

To ensure viability the tourism authorities have a number of options presented by Figure 2: they could implement capital incentives, commonly "substitute" equity in the form of grant aid or soft loans, so as to move CC down in a vertical direction to B, until the enterprise becomes viable at V_2 visitors. From a financial perspective, this is the most satisfactory option as capital incentives act directly on the main source of risk, which is the high operating leverage (Wanhill 1986). Alternatively, the authorities may reformulate the business plan and provide technical support to facilitate market expansion to raise turnover, so as to drive the business outwards towards the break-even point E on the revenue line R at V_3 visitors. Finally, they could reduce operating costs directly by subsidising inputs or assist in implementing efficiency/productivity measures, so as to drive down C^*C^* and bring the firm to a break-even at B. However, when dealing with tourism SMEs, there may be a range of concerns and the authorities may want to "hedge" their position by trying to implement a variety of instruments — in other words, a general action programme for SMEs.

Programme for SMEs

In order to implement regional strategies at the micro-economic level and address the many issues that were raised earlier, so as to improve the competitiveness of the tourism economy, there is a case for countries to have an ongoing action programme for tourism SMEs. Examples from Wales (Wanhill 2000), Hungary (Zapalska & Zapalska 1999) and Norway (Aasbrenn 1995), suggest that a multi-tasking approach to create the right business environment for SMEs will increase the occurrences of new ventures, expansion and survival. In the light of the importance being attached to indigenous development at the community level and given that many small tourism businesses are trading marginally and have great difficulty in planning ahead and investing, then there are a number of activities that are likely to suggest themselves as priorities for an integrated programme to combine the three general options resulting from Figure 2.

Structuring Small Business Finance

Business finance and the ensuing funding package are in essence the result of a strategy to spread the risk inherent in any scheme in such a way as to reconcile the divergent views of borrowers and lenders. In this respect, investment incentives, besides being used to attract new business ventures, may also have the important catalytic effect of defining an acceptable risk strategy, particularly when they provide investment security and therefore act as substitute collateral to protect the interests of lenders. The most common themes to emerge from investigations into small business finance (Stanworth & Gray 1991) are:

- The establishment of small business loan funds, supported, as necessary, by investment incentives, to bridge the gap in the availability of medium to long term finance that exists between the retail and investment banking sector;
- The creation of a small business advice or extension service.

The issue as to whether the public sector should be involved with funding SMEs depends on the effectiveness of existing financial intermediaries. A common argument is that where there is a sophisticated capital market, the task of the state is merely to set the right economic climate via the appropriate macroeconomic controls. Yet most countries have some form of small business schemes and, as noted earlier, special consideration may be given to tourism on the basis of the complex nature of the product and the fragmented nature of the industry. An examination of Table 2 will show that for most Member States within the EU the mechanisms for tourism are already there. What is needed is an element of fine tuning to ensure that prospective investors only have to deal with one organisation and that the rates of grant and the terms on which loans are made are compatible with the needs of SMEs, where the most common complaint is about access to low interest long term loans and the complexity of grants. An important aspect, of which Austria is an example, is the provision of soft loans not only for new capacity (which is not always needed), but also improving and modernising existing facilities.

Small business funds may be channelled through the existing banking system with the appropriate state guarantees and agreements as to terms and conditions, thus reducing government administration. Funds may even come from international institutions, thus the EBRD has arrangements for providing loans and making equity investments in approved domestic financial intermediaries for onward lending to SMEs. Alternatively, funds may be made available through a Development or Investment Bank. There are usually restrictions on how much of the equity in a single business that such banks can hold (varies from minimal to 30%), with arrangements for selling after 8–10 years, once the business has reached financial stability. For micro businesses, grant aid is often most appropriate, as they usually have substantial debt already and are in no position to lever in more. In some cases, there are separate funding schemes for particular ethnic groups, for example, the Maori in New Zealand and the Sami in Sweden. Particular sectors may also be targeted with individually tailored loan schemes: craftworkers are important for the provision of souvenirs, so special provision has been made for them in New Zealand through the Arts Council.

It would be difficult to meet the strategic objectives laid out by the EU without the creation of a small business advice or extension service. The fragmented structure of the tourist industry imposes transaction costs that are too high for the normal workings of the market mechanism to bring about the necessary changes, except at the margin. Trade associations are unlikely to have the legitimate authority and support to create such a service on their own. It follows that such a service has to come from a government created body, usually the NTA, or, at a more local level, a partnership formed between the local authority or municipality, the tourist bureau and the various trade associations. Such actions would be an appropriate step for those regions bidding for European Structural Funds to develop their tourism. Where the tourist authority facilitates grants or loans in support of SMEs, an audit of the business is usually common practice and support should be conditional on the essential benchmarks and verification systems either being currently in place or in place at the end of any sponsored investment.

A small business agency may also take on a co-ordinating role for funding sources: SMEs can obtain sponsorship money from outside organisations, particularly when they have charitable objectives. This money can come from commercial organisations, which are looking for public relations benefits, and also other charitable institutions. Of recent years, a major player in the U.K. has been the Heritage Lottery Fund. However, it is also possible to source equity funds through institutional contacts, lawyers, insurance brokers, or business "angels." The latter are normally high net worth individuals with substantial business experience participating in informal venture capital networks. In the U.K., for example, there is the National Business Angels Network (NBAN), which estimates that there are some 20,000 angels, investing up to £500,000 in developing a particular business, with an average of £25,000 (most investing less than £50,000) on a single deal.

Upgrading Standards

There is always the danger that investment support for SMEs is confined largely to physical capital, whereas investment in human capital may be equally, if not more, important. The latter is, for example, a particular aspect of Swedish regional policy, in which a central element is the diffusion and spread of knowledge in order to stimulate innovative development at the local level. Nilsson (2000) and Nilsson *et al.* (2004) report on a project in Arjeplog, northern Sweden, where the implementation of Options 2 and 3 above, as well as providing for investment security, was through investing in the human competencies of the owners of the businesses. This was done by focusing upon motivation and business education for tourism in eight tourism SMEs over a four-year period. The objectives were to expand the participants' ability to utilise and adjust to the changing business climate, thus raising economic efficiency. It was not simply giving consultancy advice, because it was attempting, through long term involvement, to bridge the divide between commercial and lifestyle goals by demonstrating a substantial degree of complementarity rather than mutual exclusiveness between the two goals, namely, that a better business organisation can give rise to a better lifestyle. From a NTA's perspective, it is not essential that small firms should grow and abandon lifestyle goals. Many "boutique" operations generate considerable customer satisfaction and repeat business through personalised services, in that the owners are part of the tourist experience and act as "brokers" in effecting introductions to the local area. The emphasis is on viability to ensure that the destination product stays in place and is not continually being interrupted through the "turbulence" of firms entering and leaving.

In general, activities that may be considered to raise standards and improve competitiveness are "benchmarking," sharing good practice and investing in the skills of both the management and labour force. Because of generally low skill levels and long hours of work, many owners and managers of small businesses have limited knowledge of industry standards of good practice. They may be unaware of the levels of business being achieved by similar establishments, how much repeat custom that is being generated, profitability ratios, and so on. The aim of benchmarking is to help SMEs achieve basic standards of good working practice and be credited for this achievement. Exemplars can be communicated to others through trade association meetings and journals, and similar activities undertaken by the local tourist bureau. Subject areas that are candidates for benchmarking are:

- Management and financial accounting methods for improving profitability;
- Employment and development of staff, including working conditions and training;
- Quality control systems;
- Environmental management;
- Health and safety procedures;
- Equal opportunities;
- Involving staff directly in the business;
- On-site tourist information.

Benchmarking will need to be accompanied by the assessment of training needs and the development of training programmes, for example, national customer care schemes (Sweeney & Wanhill 1996). The British Hospitality Association runs an "Excellence through People" programme to create a virtuous circle of employment conditions that encourage people to stay in the industry and Tourism Training Scotland has a complete suite of human resource training programmes (Baum 1999). There is also a U.K. government sponsored national quality standard scheme, "Investors in People" (1997), an appraisal of which can be found in Scott (1999). The scheme sets a level of good practice for improving an organisation's performance through its people. Its aims are to ensure that everyone who works in the organisation understands the business objectives, is properly qualified and skilled, is committed to continual improvement and knows that the business is committed to them. This is part of the process of improving standards, thereby increasing "value for money," and enabling operators to raise prices for a better quality product that is effectively marketed. Quality assurance is developed through classification and grading schemes, which are normally run at the national level via the NTA, and the entry of new operators into the market to displace those who do not have the means or the skills to come up to the required level. While raising the skills base can create barriers to entry, this may be regarded as beneficial if it serves to improve the products of existing firms and reduce the exit rate.

Improving Communications Channels

Technology is continually making it easier to customise, package, book, and price the product for the visitor. Global CRS networks have made it easier to book a foreign trip (with unequivocal price transparency) than a domestic holiday and have enabled the large players to switch to highly sophisticated database marketing to communicate their product offers to potential customers. Global CRSs are targeted at travel intermediaries who give priority to the security of the booking, instant confirmation and the certainty of receiving commission (Beaver 1996; Buhalis 1998); thus the majority of suppliers, unless they are part of a tour operator's itinerary at the destination, are excluded (admittedly in some cases on their own volition by their refusal to pay commission) from selling either at home or abroad through the modern communication and reservation systems of the travel trade. Instead they resort to traditional methods of promoting themselves through marketing consortia, travel guides, tourist board guides and brochures, newspaper supplements and magazines, leaflet distribution, local media and "word-of-mouth" in order to place their product in the market place and take bookings. This situation is not so serious in terms of domestic tourism where the general pattern is still one of customers using local knowledge to make their own travel arrangements, but it does mean that SMEs are missing out on their share of international visitors (Buhalis 1999).

On the other hand, the World-Wide Web is growing fast and has the potential for direct holiday information, direct bookings, and consumer feedback, although SMEs are generally poor in e-marketing and e-commerce technologies. In addition, CRS networks are gradually becoming open to the general public through Internet portals, thus giving potential visitors the opportunity to adjust their trip to their specific needs. Internet access to airline reservation systems has also opened new possibilities for discounted last-minute air travel with established carriers and has also seen the rise of low cost airlines such as Ryanair and Easy Jet, who are not on the global networks.

For a number of years there has been government interest in creating computer-based national reservation systems. NTAs in Europe have already been operating "Holiday Hotlines" and out-of-hours telephone information. In many areas, local Tourist Information Centres (TICs) offer a booking service to personal callers, though still very much a manual system requiring TIC staff to telephone accommodation establishments to check availability. In Britain, the TIC network was used to develop the "Book a Bed Ahead" scheme for the independent traveller touring different parts of the country. However, as more and more bookings are being made electronically, what is ideal and in the spirit of Option 2 above, is a fully networked computerised reservation system, which will generate for SMEs the additional benefits of:

- A database to assist with direct mail campaigns;
- Assisting in monitoring occupancy;
- Providing information on source markets;
- Evaluating improvements to packaging and pricing to meet changes in demand;
- Enhancing sales promotion through recommendations from satisfied visitors.

The key to penetrating the source markets from the regions lies in using the CRS to link suitable accommodation to a range of "things to see and do," so what is being sold is a complete holiday, not just accommodation. Although desirable, this does not necessarily mean complete packaging of other products: it would be an improvement just to use complementary suppliers in marketing and to couple this with the provision of good information on site. Beaver (1996) goes further and recommends a complete destination management system that acts as a neutral facilitator to the tourist industry.

Implementation of such a system via the NTA or regional tourist association is no easy task: in the past, proposals at the local level have foundered on the unwillingness of SMEs to give commission, to make booking allocations available, competitive jealousies concerning the equity of how bookings will be distributed by TIC staff and arguments over classification and grading, an essential ingredient for the inclusion in such a scheme, as in all tourist bureau publications. Such experiences suggest that a computerised destination management system cannot be implemented or sustained without a great deal of public sector involvement, particularly if the Commission's ideal of Europe as a single destination is to be realised (Commission 1995). Examples of such systems can be found in Austria, Denmark and Switzerland, but it appears that the most likely route is for NTAs to act as facilitators to bookings through provision of information on their Web Sites and links to agencies providing reservation services.

Raising the Level of Market Intelligence

Wood (2001) observes that marketing information systems used within SMEs are largely confined to internal data that are supplemented by customer surveys and informal investigations about local competitors. External data tend to be drawn from personal contacts and episodic monitoring of a miscellany of sources such as trade associations and magazines. Information technology is not greatly used to aid information gathering, analysis and management. Yet raising the level of market intelligence is essential if SMEs are to plan their business and target their marketing expenditure more effectively.

In order to move SMEs from a cost-orientated stance to one that is proactive in the market place, there is a need to create an interactive database, which can be accessed from PC networks, to research and analyse market trends. Specifically, small businesses need tailored printouts to:

- Understand their customers' needs and profile;
- Monitor the effectiveness of their marketing effort;
- Understand customer satisfaction levels;
- Monitor sources and times of bookings to establish patterns;
- Compare their demand position to the wider picture.

Wood advocated the use of the Internet as a low cost way of gathering market intelligence, though this did not find favour with her respondents.

Conclusions

In many parts of the world governments have intervened in tourism because the complexity of the product makes it unlikely that private markets will meet national tourism policy objectives. Investment incentives are policy instruments that can be used to correct for market failure and ensure a development partnership between the public and private sectors. The appropriateness of the various financial incentives depends on understanding the nature of the business risk and the likely returns of the tourist industry, as well as the ability of the country to afford them. As a rule, to control costs, government treasuries are against giving blanket reductions in general taxation, since it is difficult to prevent them applying to "old" capital as well as new investment. The emphasis on incentives is their ephemeral nature for the purposes of providing the foundation for new investments to establish themselves, but equally what is to be avoided are confiscatory tax policies at a later stage to try and recover what has been given through incentives. Of critical importance to the progress of tourism is the position of SMEs, which dominate the operational aspects of the industry and can act, in many ways, as barriers to sustainable improvements of the product. Apart from a range of investment incentives, what is outlined here is an action programme to create the right business environment for SMEs in order to improve their quality, diversity, competitiveness and profitability.

Acknowledgments

The author gratefully acknowledges the funding support from the Danish Social Science Foundation via the Danish Centre for Tourism Research.

References

Aasbrenn, K. (1995). *Livskraftige Uttynningssamfunn* [*Vibrant Out-migration Communities*]. Oslo: NordREFO.

Archer, B., & Wanhill, S. (1980). *Tourism in Bermuda: An economic evaluation*. Hamilton: Bermuda Department of Tourism.

Baum, T. (1999). Human resource management in tourism's small business sector: Policy dimensions. In: D. Lee-Ross (Ed.), *HRM in tourism and hospitality: International perspectives on small to medium sized enterprises*. London: Cassell.

Beaver, A. (1996). Lack of CRS accessibility may be strangling small hoteliers, the lifeblood of European tourism. *Tourism Economics*, *1*, 341–355.

Bodlender, J. A. (1982). The financing of tourism projects. *Tourism Management*, *3*, 277–284.

Boldender, J. A., & Ward, T. J. (1987). *An examination of tourism incentives*. London: Howarth & Howarth.

Buhalis, D. (1998). Strategic use of information technology in the tourist industry. *Tourism Management*, *19*, 409–421.

Buhalis, D. (1999). Tourism on the Greek Islands: Issues of peripherality, competitiveness and development. *International Journal of Tourism Research*, *1*, 341–358.

Commission of the European Communities (1995). *The role of the union in the field of tourism*. Brussels: COM (95), 97 final.

Curran, J., & Blackburn, R. (1991). *Paths of enterprise: The future of small businesses*. London: Routledge.

Deegan, J., & Dineen, D. (2000). Developments in Irish tourism 1980–1996. *International Journal of Tourism Research*, *2*, 163–170.

DOE (1990). *Tourism and the inner city*. London: HMSO.

Foley, P., & Green, H. (1989). *Small business success*. London: Paul Chapman Publishing.

Getz, D., & Carlsen, J. (2000). Characteristics and goals of family and owner-operated businesses in the rural tourism and hospitality sectors. *Tourism Management*, *21*, 547–560.

Hornaday, R. (1990). Dropping the E-words from small business research. *Journal of Small Business Management, 28*, 22–33.

House of Commons (1969). *Development of tourism act 1969.* London: HMSO.

Investors in People (1997). *Better people, better business.* London: Investors in People U.K.

Jenkins, C. (1982). The use of investment incentives for tourism in developing countries. *Tourism Management, 3*, 91–97.

Kotas, R., & Wanhill, S. (1981). PSA: Its nature, significance and applications. *International Journal of Tourism Management, 2*, 176–188.

Middleton, V. (2000). The importance of micro-businesses in European tourism. *Proceedings of the 34th TRC Meeting.* Bologna.

Morrison, A., Rimmington, M., & Williamson, C. (1998). *Entrepreneurship in the hospitality, tourism and leisure industries.* Oxford: Butterworth-Heinemann.

Nilsson, P. (2000). Tourism's role in new rural policy for peripheral areas: The case of Arjeplog. In: F. Brown, & D. Hall (Eds), *Aspects of tourism: Tourism in peripheral areas.* Clevedon: Channel View Publications.

Nilsson, P., Petersen, T., & Wanhill, S. (2004). Public support for tourism SMEs in peripheral areas: The Arjeplog project, northern Sweden. *The Service Industries Journal* (in press).

Scott, A. (1999). Investing in people? *The Hospitality Review, 1*, 26–30.

Shaw, G., & Williams, A. (1990). Tourism, economic development and the role of entrepreneurial activity. In: C. Cooper, & A. Lockwood (Eds), *Progress in tourism, recreation and hospitality management.* London: Belhaven Press.

Stanworth, J., & Gray, C. (1991). *Bolton 20 years on: The small firm in the 1990s.* London: Paul Chapman Publishing.

Sweeney, A., & Wanhill, S. (1996). Hosting the guest: Changing local attitudes and behaviour. In: L. Briguglio, R. Butler, D. Harrison, & W. Filho (Eds), *Sustainable tourism in islands and small states: Issues and policies.* London: Pinter.

Taylor, S., Simpson, J., & Howie, H. (1998). Financing small businesses. In: R. Thomas (Ed.), *The management of small tourism and hospitality firms.* London: Cassell.

Thomas, R. (2000). Small firms in the tourism industry: Some conceptual issues. *International Journal of Tourism Research, 2*, 345–353.

Wanhill, S. (1986). Which investment incentives for tourism? *Tourism Management, 7*, 2–7.

Wanhill, S. (1997). Peripheral area tourism: A European perspective. *Progress in Tourism and Hospitality Research, 3*, 47–70.

Wanhill, S. (1999). The economic aspects of location marketing. In: T. Baum, & R. Mudambi (Eds), *Economic and management methods for tourism and hospitality research.* Chichester: Wiley.

Wanhill, S. (2000). Small and medium tourism enterprises. *Annals of Tourism Research, 27*, 148–163.

Welsh Office (1995). *Review of Section 4 tourism grants.* Cardiff.

Wood, E. (2001). Internet use for market intelligence. *International Journal of Tourism Research, 3*, 283–300.

Zapalska, A., & Zapalska, L. (1999). Small business venture in post-communist Hungary. *Journal of East-West Business, 5*, 5–21.

Chapter 5

Short-Run Output and Employment Effects Arising from Assistance to Tourism SMEs: Evidence from Israel

Aliza Fleischer and Daniel Felsenstein

Introduction

To a great extent, tourism small firms share much in common with the general small business population. Barriers to entry are low, activities generally center on niche markets, the entrepreneur is the center of the small firm universe and personal equity capital is likely to form the initial resources of the business. Furthermore, tourism SME's like other small firms invariably have a distinct local orientation. They are likely to be locally owned, consume local inputs and generate larger local multipliers than larger enterprises. More than anything else however, interest in tourism SME's has been centered on their perceived employment benefits (Hudson & Townsend 1992; Wanhill 2000). Public support for small tourism enterprises is often couched in terms of creating job opportunities to deal with cyclical unemployment, diversifying economic opportunities and generating supplementary income. Small tourism enterprises ranging from family lodgings, through low-investment recreation operators (jeep rides, cycling trails) to traditional food and transportation activities (country restaurants, guided tours, etc.) are often viewed as having under-utilized capacity. When demand picks up they can easily assimilate under-used resources, accommodating extra labor without the need for extra investment. In this way, assistance for small tourism business should yield positive employment effects.

But do small tourism firms really warrant a plethora of dedicated assistance programs aside from the regular arsenal available to small firms? Is their response to public support schemes any more pronounced than that of the general small firm population? This chapter endeavors to answer these questions by comparing the short-run effects of an assistance program on small tourism firms and a sample of other similar (non-tourism) small firms.

The attention given in the literature to the employment effects of small firms (for a review and critique see Davis *et al.* 1996), often means a neglect of other indicators of SME performance such as output growth and productivity. In the context of assistance programs, the effects on different performance measures, such as employment and output are of course linked. Capital assistance to small firms can result in differing short-run impacts on firm output and employment. This chapter investigates whether these effects are more pronounced in the context of small tourism firms. Our a-priori hypothesis is that small tourism firms respond even more vigorously than other small firms to assistance programs in the area of employment over the short run because of the immediate absorption capacity of small scale tourism activity. In terms of output however, we do not expect to find any differences in short-run effects. Assuming a u-shaped short run cost function common to all small firms, there is no reason to believe that a small tourism firm's output rate will respond any differently to a sudden injection of capital to that of any other small firm.

These hypotheses are tested empirically below using a unique data set of small firms that were recipients of public assistance via a nation-wide small firms loan guarantee program, over the period 1993–1995. Distinguishing between small tourism firms and other small firms, the data set includes performance indicators collected from the firms on the basis of site visits both before and after receipt of assistance thereby adding a measure of actual short-run performance change. The chapter proceeds by setting up a simple model of output and employment response to capital assistance and estimating its results.

Assistance Programs for Tourism SMEs

The promotion of tourism small business is inevitably linked to the creation of local employment and output. However, the case for public support of tourism SME's is not unequivocal. On the one hand the typical tourism SME such as a bed and breakfast operation is perceived as having low barriers to entry and employing existing and under-utilized capital. This relates to both fixed and human capital. Assisting such an effort would seem to be promoting the highest and best use for local resources. On the other hand, the small-scale character of these operations can often render them marginal in terms of effecting any real local or regional economic change (Fleischer & Felsenstein 2000).

Furthermore, while much of the public rhetoric for assisting tourism SME's is bound up with employment creation, small-scale tourism is also charged with creating low-wage and seasonal employment in weak and unstable markets (Fredrick 1993; Shaw & Williams 1990). The same is true for claims relating to new tourism SME output. Some claim that new tourism small firms simply serve to displace or uproot existing output in the tourism market (Hoy 1996). In fact, nearly all the arguments for assisting small tourism activities are met with counter arguments opposing such activity. Small scale tourism as a local revenue source is challenged by claims that it is revenue-draining and a burden on the local service base. The claim that much small-scale tourism is environmentally sustainable is matched with the charge that it depletes valuable and finite resources.

A familiar array of instruments is available for assisting small tourism enterprises. On the supply side, capital assistance (grants and loans), tax concessions, business and management advice and tourism incubators are available (Fleischer 1999; Wanhill 2000). On the demand side, marketing efforts, local vacation campaigns, preferences for local content and input suppliers and the development of "export" (i.e. non-local markets) through visitor exchange programs are all utilized (Gibson 1993). While all of these mediate the failure of markets in the tourism sector in one way or another (failure in capital markets, asymmetric information and so on), none of them directly address the issue of risk associated with the small firm. Intuitively, this factor is considered a barrier to assisting small firms, which are perceived as likely to fail over time. However, Wren (1998) has shown that in fact smaller and newer firms are more responsive to assistance and that the risk involved in supporting them is therefore minimized.

One financial assistance instrument that directly addresses the small firm risk issue is the loan guarantee. Using this instrument, the onus of loan recovery is shifted to the loan guarantor (generally a public agency) and in this way the risk associated with small firm lending is mediated. The stereotypical small tourism enterprise operating in unstable markets, invariably under-capitalized and with weak management skills is particularly exposed to risk with all the concomitant difficulties in capital markets. Rather than attach a subsidy directly to the borrower (the small firm), the loan guarantee program changes the behavior of lenders encouraging them to lend to firms they would not otherwise consider. In this respect, the program represents the operation of a "second best" decision rule under conditions of market failure.

Analyses of the effectiveness of loan guarantee programs point to their relative cost-effectiveness and their ability to deliver assistance on the basis of area targeting (Cowling & Clay 1994; Harrison & Mason 1986). However, as in all assistance schemes, the litmus test lies in the true "additionality" of the subsidy and the extent to which the small firm would not have found any alternative in the absence of the assistance. The higher risk the market, the more likely this condition will be fulfilled. High levels of uncertainty associated with small tourist enterprises imply that assistance is less likely to be "deadweight."

Modeling the Output and Employment Effects of a Capital Assistance Program

While a firm receiving a capital subsidy is expected to register an increase in output, the impact of assistance on employment is ambiguous. The standard approach to looking at the effect of a capital subsidy is to assume a substitution effect. Upon receipt of assistance labor becomes relatively more expensive than capital and firms will tend use relatively less workers per unit of capital. An output effect can arise if the capital subsidy reduces average costs allowing the firm to produce additional output at a fixed cost level. While the substitution effect clearly reduces demand for labor, the effect of additional capital is less clear. If the output effect is greater than the substitution effect a capital assistance program can result in increased demand for labor. If the opposite is the case and the substitution effect is greater than the output effect, the result is less determinate: employment may both increase and decrease with capital assistance program (Swales 1981).

Our approach is to model output and employment effects as separate but structurally linked phenomena. By modeling the optimum output level of the firm with respect to capital and labor, we estimate the adjustment in output resulting from the capital assistance program. This is done while distinguishing between tourism firms and all "other" firms. We then proceed to model new employment as a function of previous employment and additional capital (i.e. the assistance program), differentiating again between tourism SME's and the other recipients of assistance. These models can be empirically tested and enable us to investigate the differences in the adjustment processes between tourism firms and other small firms.

Output Effects

In order to estimate the impact of the assistance on output we assume the following production function:

$$Q_{ij} = f(K_{ij}, E_{ij}) \tag{1}$$

where: Q_{ij} is the level of output for firm i in sector j, $j = 1, \ldots m$ (in our case $m = 2$, i.e. tourism and other firms), K_{ij} is the level of capital for firm i in sector j, E_{ij} is the level of employment for firm i in sector j.

Change in the output level, dQ_{ij} can be written as follows:

$$dQ_{ij} = f_j^k dK_{ij} + f_j^e dE_{ij} \tag{2}$$

where f_j^k and f_j^e are the partial derivatives of Q with respect to K and E respectfully. f_j^k and f_j^e are constant for each sector in competitive markets. Under the assumption of a competitive market, firms from all sectors face same price for capital (r) and labor (w) while firms from sector j face the same product price (p_j). In equilibrium, the value of the marginal product of input equals the input price. Thus, the following equations hold:

$$f_j^k = \frac{r}{p_j} \tag{3}$$

$$f_j^e = \frac{w}{p_j} \tag{4}$$

Based on Equations (1)–(4), Equation (5) is estimated. For our purpose, we assume two sectors, tourism and other. Accordingly, the dummy variable (D) equals 1 if the firm belongs to the tourism sector and 0 otherwise. The coefficients in Equation (5) are the partial derivatives of the output with respect to capital and labor. The dummy variable allows variability of the coefficient between the two sectors. In our case, a significant positive (negative) coefficient of the dummy variables means that the marginal product of labor or capital in the tourism sector is higher (lower) than the other sectors. In order to get values per worker, both sides of the equation are divided by E.

$$\frac{dQ}{E} = f^k \left(\frac{dK}{E}\right) + f^k D \left(\frac{dK}{E}\right) + f^e \left(\frac{dE}{E}\right) + f^e D \left(\frac{dE}{E}\right) \tag{5}$$

Employment Effects

Equation (5) allows us to assess the contribution of the assistance program to output. Since one of the major justifications for assistance programs such as the current is the need to create jobs, it is also necessary to focus on the employment impacts of SME support programs.

Wren & Waterson (1991) develop a framework to compare the employment impact of different industrial assistance programs. This is based on a combination of two frequently-used approaches. The first, in line with the current paper, is based on modeling the optimization problem of the firm. The second specifies the employment level as a loosely defined function including variables that theory dictates are likely to affect the level of employment.

Starting from the second approach we can write the partial adjustment model for firm employment in any sector j in the following form:

$$E_t - E_{t-1} = \lambda(E_t^* - E_{t-1}) + u_t \tag{6}$$

where: E_t is the level of employment in time t, E_t^* is the planned level of employment, λ is an adjustment coefficient, $0 \le \lambda \le 1$, u_t is random error.

The difference between E_t^* and E_{t-1} is comprised of L^* and some proportion of E_{t-1}:

$$E_t^* - E_{t-1} = L_t^* - \delta E_{t-1} \tag{7}$$

where: L^* is the planned level of employment to be induced by the assistance program, δ is the proportion of redundant employment expected to be absorbed due to the assistance program.

The relationship between L^* and the receipt of financial assistance is derived from the structural model depicted in Equation (1). Dividing Equation (3) by Equation (4) produces the following relationship between additional labor and level of assistance.

$$\frac{f_j^k}{f_j^e} = \frac{r}{w} \tag{8}$$

Using our notation where L^* is the additional labor and K^* additional capital and assuming a homothetic production function leads to the following:

$$\frac{K^*}{L^*} = \alpha \tag{9}$$

where α is a constant ratio between the capital and labor since in a homothetic production function the firm expands along a ray. α is a parameter that depends on r, w and the firm's production technology.

Additional capital (K^*) can come from the assistance program (AP) and/or private funds. Since we want to investigate the impact of the assistance program we assume that additional capital comes solely from the program and thus K^* equals AP.

$$K^* = AP \tag{10}$$

By substituting (10) into (9), (9) into (7) and (7) into (6) and rearranging, we get the following equation:

$$E_t = \left(\frac{\lambda}{\alpha}\right) AP + (1 - \lambda\delta)E_{t-1} + u_t \tag{11}$$

Following Wren & Waterson (1991), the equation for estimation equation takes the following form:

$$E_t = a + b\,AP + cE_{t-1} + dD + u_t \tag{12}$$

where a, b, c and d are the estimated coefficients and D is a dummy variable with a value of 1 if the firm is in the tourism sector and 0 otherwise.

The Assistance Program and Data

The small firms assistance program examined here is the national small firms Loan Guarantee Program (LGP). This was initiated in 1991 in response to the mass immigration of Jews from the former USSR, the specter of large-scale unemployment and a general public sector infatuation with the role of SME's as job generators. The program was administered jointly by the national Small Business Authority and a local commercial bank. Loan terms offered up to $165,000 over a 5-year period with 100% loan guarantee provided by the government (80%) and the commercial bank (20%), respectively. Cost-of-living linked interest rates rose over the period 1993–1995 from 3.75 to 5.35%. All authorized loans needed to be backed by personal funds to the extent of 25% of the loan with assets of the small business acting as loan collateral.

Table 1 presents basic indicators of the operation of the loan guarantee scheme over the period 1993–1995. This is the period covered in our empirical analysis and represents the most active years of the program. As can be seen, the average size of the loan was less than half of the loan ceiling. While more than 5,500 loan applications were submitted, some 44% were authorized. The level of actual loan utilization (loan materializations as a share of loan authorizations) was even lower and stood over the study period at 39%. The sectoral distribution of loan authorizations closely reflected the sectoral distribution of small firms in the economy: services (42–46% of authorizations) industry (33–39%) and tourism SME's in third place (8–10%).

The empirical data used below represents a unique longitudinal sample of 285 firms that received assistance over the period 1993–1995. The data were collected by a management consulting firm mandated by the government to monitor the program. All firms that received government guarantees were visited at least once by the consulting company, subsequent to having received assistance. This visit took place roughly two years after receiving the loan guarantee and represents our short-run time frame. The data set therefore contains output and employment observations for each firm both before and after receiving assistance.

Table 1: National small firms loan guarantee fund — basic indicators 1993–1995.

	1993	**1994**	**1995**
Requests submitted	1529	2265	1767
No. of guarantees authorized	588	1190	665
Total value of guarantees authorized	140	265	170
Total value of guarantees materialized ($m)	26.5	31.4	19.1
Average value of guarantee ($ Th)	83.5	74.3	75
Anticipated employment increase	2596	6109	2950
Loan period (months)	60	60	60

While the loans were administered over the period 1993–1995, the monitoring process for this period extended up to 1998.

Table 2 presents a description of these variables and their summary statistics for the entire sample and for the sub-groups of tourism SME's and others. The variables relate to output and employment before and after receipt of assistance, level of assistance and period of time

Table 2: variable description and summary statistics by sectors.

Variable	Description	Total Sample	Tourism	Other
emp_t-1	Number of employees before receiving assistance	5.78 (8.2)	6.16 (9.5)	5.74 (8.1)
emp_t*	Number of employees after receiving assistance	10.77 (15.6)	19.84 (19.3)	9.91 (15.0)
emp_d*	Increase (decrease) in number of employees after receiving assistance	5.69 (7.1)	12.57 (15.0)	5.08 (5.6)
Assist	Level of assistance (000' $)	82.7 (61.6)	89.4 (61.2)	82.0 (61.6)
emp_d_w	Rate of increase (decrease) in employees after receiving assistance	0.56 (1.6)	1.06 (1.4)	0.53 (1.6)
assist_w	Level of assistance per worker	49.32 (63.5)	21.58 (17.0)	50.91 (46.7)
output_t-1	Annual output before receiving assistance (000'$)	252.8 (424.6)	160.6 (296.3)	262.1 (516.6)
output_t	Annual output after receiving assistance (000'$)	733.3 (1042.6)	695.3 (856.0)	736.6 (1195.6)
output_d_w	Increase (decrease) in annual output after receiving assistance, per employ (000' $)	74.1 (131.4)	36.1 (31.8)	76.5 (135.0)
No_months	Number of months between receiving assistance and monitoring visit	26.9 (12.6)	25.1 (14.3)	27.1 (12.5)

Note: Standard deviations are in parentheses.
*Means are significantly different at 5%.

that elapsed between receipt of assistance and the post-assistance monitoring visit. A difference of means test was also performed to see if statistical differences exist across mean values for the tourism small firms versus the rest. As can be seen, ex ante, there are no significant differences across the two sets of firms in terms of employment output and size of assistance. The only significant difference relates to the ex-poste employment size of the firm.

Results

In the first instance, we estimate Equation (5) (above), empirically testing the adjustment of output per worker as a function of the marginal product of capital and labor. The estimated coefficients appear in Table 3. They show that while the marginal product of labor is lower in the tourism firms than in the rest (the coefficient of the dummy is negative and significant), the marginal product of capital is the same. Under the assumption of competitive labor market, i.e. all sectors face the same price of labor and decreasing marginal product, lower marginal product in the tourism sector means that it employs more workers than the other sectors. However, the marginal product of capital is the same. Thus, if we expect the capital assistance program to increase output, tourism small firms do not seem to have any advantage over other firms. Public assistance may increase output, but there is no a priori case for assuming this will be more pronounced in the tourism sector than in any other sector.

The role of the "number of months" variable is to normalize the time frame for the different firms. The time period between receiving the assistance and the follow up visit varies across firms and since we assume there is an adjustment or maturation process we expect that the longer the time period the greater the increase in output. As to be expected this is positive and significant. It can also be interpreted as the time period for absorbing

Table 3: Model estimates for change in output per worker.

Variable	Coefficient
emp_d_w	126.8[*]
emp_d_w_dummy[a]	−143.7[*]
assist_w	2.06[*]
assist_w_dummy[b]	0.9
no_months	5.3[*]
Constant	−896[*]
No. of observations	165
R^2	0.6

[a] emp_d_w multiplied by the sector dummy variable; this receives a value of 1if the firm is in the tourism sector and 0 otherwise.
[b] assist_w multiplied by the sector dummy variable; this receives a value of 1if the firm is in the tourism sector and 0 otherwise.
[*] Significant at 5%.

Table 4: Model estimates for change in employment level.

Variable	Coefficient
emp_t-1	1.01^{*}
Assist	0.01^{*}
Dummy[a]	9.6^{*}
no_months	0.13^{*}
Constant	-2.2
No. of observations	285
R^2	0.42

[a] Sector dummy: 1 if firm is in the tourism sector and 0 otherwise.
[*] Significant at 5%.

public assistance. The coefficient seems to suggest that it is not simply the magnitude of assistance that is important for increasing SME output but also the way this resource is utilized.

The results of the effect of the capital assistance program on employment change (Equation (12)) are presented in Table 4. This estimates, ex poste, employment as a function of the pre-assistance employment level, additional capital (assumed to come solely from the assistance program) a sector dummy and the amount of time elapsed since receipt of assistance. As can be seen, all coefficients are positive and significant. This means the larger the firm (in employment terms) at the time of filing the request, the greater the level of assistance and the longer the time interval between request and follow up visit, the greater the employment effect. The positive and significant coefficient for the tourism dummy implies that *ceteris paribus*, capital assistance to tourism firms has a greater employment impact than to other firms. This result is in accordance with the smaller magnitude of marginal product of labor reported in Table 3. In both cases, but from different angles, we can see that in the short-run adjustment process, tourism firms will increase their labor input faster than other firms and thus register higher impacts on employment.

Similar to the output adjustment process, the change in employment level is found to be significantly related to the time-frame over which the capital assistance is absorbed by the firm. As above, while the main object of this variable is to standardize the time frame while estimating the capital and labor impacts, it does convey information on the adjustment process. Just as an increase in output does not adjust immediately to the stimulus of additional capital, a similar result is likely in employment which will increase over time.

Conclusions

This chapter has endeavored to address the question of whether tourism SME's respond any more vigorously to public assistance than other small firms over the short run. Our hypotheses relating to the employment and output effects of tourism enterprises would seem to be upheld. Capital assistance seems to simulate a greater reaction in the tourism firms in employment than it does in output. Assuming no other sources of additional capital, a public sector subsidy will increase tourism small firm employment more than employment in other firms but will not simulate any significant differences in output. This could be due to two reasons. First, tourism is a labor-intensive industry and customers expect to be served by people rather than machines. Second, the seasonal nature of tourism forces small firms to choose a technology which enables them to costlessly adjust to fluctuations in customer demand. Adjustments to labor, especially non-skilled labor, seem to be best suited for this purpose and thus tourism SME's opt for labor-intensive technology.

These findings also have bearing on the wider issue of justification for special assistance programs for tourism SME's outside the framework of general small business support. Based on the loan guarantee program examined here, our results indicate that public support enables those small firms to increase capital, that otherwise would not have been able to do so. This additional capital induces a higher increase in the level of employment in the tourism sector than in the other sectors. The impact on level of output however is the same across sectors. Thus, in a situation where employment is a major public policy concern, preference for a dedicated tourism small firm assistance program may be warranted. This assumes that firms are small enough and that there is demand for their expansion.

Acknowledgment

The authors would like to thank the Michlol Consulting Company for access to the data.

References

Cowling, M., & Clay, N. (1994). Factors influencing take-up rates on the loan guarantee scheme. *Small Business Economics, 7*, 141–152.

Davis, S. J., Haltiwanger, J., & Schuh, S. (1996). Small business and job creation: Dissecting the myth and reassessing the facts. *Small Business Economics, 8*, 297–315.

Fleischer, A. (1999). Incentive programs for rural tourism in Israel: A tool for promoting rural development. In: P. Rietveld, & D. Shefer (Eds), *Regional development in an age of structural economic change* (pp. 97–110). Ashgate, Aldershot.

Fleischer, A., & Felsenstein, D. (2000). Support for small-scale rural tourism: Does it make a difference? *Annals of Tourism Research, 27*(4), 1007–1024.

Fredrick, M. (1993). Rural tourism and economic development. *Economic Development Quarterly, 7*, 215–224.

Gibson, L. (1993). The potential for tourism in non-metropolitan areas. In: D. L. Barkley (Ed.), *Economic adaptation: Alternatives for non-metropolitan areas* (pp. 145–164). Boulder, CO: Westview.

Harrison, R. T., & Mason, C. M. (1986). The regional impact of the small firms loan guarantee scheme in the United Kingdom. *Regional Studies, 20*(6), 535–550.

Hoy, F. (1996). Entrepreneurship: A strategy for rural development. In: T. D. Rowley, D. W. Sears, G. L. Nelson, N. J. Reid, & M. J. Yetley (Eds), *Rural development research: A foundation for policy* (pp. 29–46). Westport, CT: Greenwood Press.

Hudson, R., & Townsend, A. (1992). Tourism employment and policy choices for local government. In: P. Johnson, & B. Thomas (Eds), *Perspectives on tourism policy* (pp. 49–68). London: Mansell.

Swales, J. K. (1981). The employment effects of a regional capital subsidy. *Regional Studies, 15*(4), 263–273.

Wanhill, S. (2000). Small and medium tourism enterprises. *Annals of Tourism Research, 27*(1), 132–147.

Wren, C. (1998). Subsidies for job creation: Is small best? *Small Business Economics, 10*, 273–281.

Wren, C., & Waterson, M. (1991). The employment effects of financial assistance to industry. *Oxford Economic Papers, 43*, 116–138.

Chapter 6

Risky Lifestyles? Entrepreneurial Characteristics of the New Zealand Bed and Breakfast Sector

C. Michael Hall and Kristy Rusher

Despite substantial definitional issues (Thomas 2000), small businesses in regional New Zealand, as elsewhere around the world, are widely regarded as important employment and economic development generators. According to the New Zealand Ministry of Economic Development (2001) 84.9% of New Zealand businesses are small enterprises, and 11.6% are medium sized enterprises. SMEs account for 35% of New Zealand's economic output and account for a greater amount of employment than in other international economies. For the purposes of comparability, this chapter uses the definition of SME developed by the New Zealand Ministry of Economic Development. The Ministry of Economic Development (2001) defines a medium enterprise as any business that employs 6–19 full time employees (FTE), and a small enterprise as one that employs 5 or less FTEs. Nevertheless, despite their supposed significance, there has been no comprehensive study to date on the overall business profile and management character-istics, and entrepreneur profile of small business in New Zealand. However, anecdotal evidence suggests that such businesses are characterised by a small number of employees — usually less than 5, the owner being responsible for a high degree of operational and management duties and few companies that implement "best practice" business management principles on a day-to-day basis (Ministry of Economic Development 2001).

The New Zealand tourism industry is also dominated by SMEs although estimates vary on the exact number. According to the New Zealand Tourism Industry Association (2002) "Tourism has 10 publicly listed companies and about 16,500 small to medium enterprises." The New Zealand Tourism Strategy completed in 2000 estimated that the tourism industry has "between 13,500 and 18,000 SMEs, approximately 80% of which employ less than 5 people" (Tourism Strategy Group 2000). Table 1 indicates the overall composition of the New Zealand tourism industry on a sectoral basis. The New Zealand Tourism Strategy 2010 recognised that SMEs lie at the heart of tourism even though they "have limited ability to

Small Firms in Tourism: International Perspectives
Copyright © 2004 Published by Elsevier Ltd.
ISBN: 0-08-044132-7

Table 1: Composition of the New Zealand tourism industry by sector (excluding airlines).

Sector	%
Accommodation providers	34
Attractions/activities	16
Adventure tourism	13
Retail/hospitality	11
Transport (excluding air)	7
Eco/nature tourism	5
Conference, incentives, events	4
Organised tour group	4
Culture/heritage	3
Other	3

Source: Tourism Strategy Group (2000).

invest in its development" (2000), with the Strategy Group observing that, among other factors, that "upskilling and capability building of sector participants, particularly small and medium sized businesses" was "critical to the success of the New Zealand Tourism Strategy 2010."

Yet despite such recognition, the knowledge base of the actual business behaviours of tourism SMEs in New Zealand is extremely limited (Page *et al.* 1999), particularly when the strategies of some tourism SMEs may well be aimed as much towards maintaining the desired lifestyles of the owners as they are towards profit maximisation or growth oriented strategies (Ateljevic & Doorne 2000; Getz & Carlsen 2000; Hall & Kearsley 2001; Miciak *et al.* 2001). For example, little is known of the risk tolerance and uncertainty management behaviours of tourism SMEs which are associated with business decision-making and activities, including business entry and exit strategies, even though it is a major theme within the wider small business and entrepreneurship literature (e.g. Brockhaus 1980; Busenitz 1999; Palich & Bagby 1995).

"Risk" consists of two distinct but related concepts (Busenitz 1999). Firstly, risk refers to the propensity and probability of an event occurring and secondly, of accepting the consequences of having acted in a particular manner. In the entrepreneurial environment, "taking a risk" describes a process of assessing probabilities and acting or making decisions to ensure that as far as possible, the consequences of those actions are favourable for the business and the entrepreneur. Inherent, but silent within this is the small business entrepreneur's commitment to the business and of being ultimately responsible for the outcomes of those decisions. Therefore, how this silent commitment and responsibility to the business in terms of managing the risks in operational decision making and business development are balanced against the sometimes competing commitments of fulfilling personal, family and lifestyle objectives is an important issue that this chapter addresses with respect to the bed and breakfast component of the accommodation sector.

The Bed and Breakfast sector

A bed and breakfast (B&B) is a small business where the owners rent out a small number of rooms in a private home to travellers for a short-term basis (Angowski Rogak 1995). Long the subject of jokes regarding British tourism in the 1960s, the B&B sector has gained an important international profile in recent years through the growth of more personal forms of travel with the B&B providing accommodation in friendly, intimate surroundings, where the visitor is welcomed into the home of the host (Mangin & Collins 2001). For example, in examining the motivations which surround choice of lodging in New Zealand, Johnston-Walker (1998) observed that B&B guests place far more emphasis on social interaction than do hotel guests, while aesthetics, setting and friendly staff are also regarded as extremely important. Internationally, research on B&Bs has also grown (e.g. Vallen & Rande 1997; Warnick & Klar 1991; Zane 1997) with lifestyle motivations being noted as a significant factor in business development (e.g. Miciak *et al.* 2001).

In New Zealand lifestyle concerns have been demonstrated to be significant in the development of rural homestay accommodation (Hall & Kearsley 2001; Høgh 1998; Oppermann 1998; Warren 1998). However, such developments have at times not come without perceived negative or unexpected consequences. Although not solely concerned with rural homestay businesses, Warren's (1998) survey of rural businesses echo a number of concerns found in the New Zealand and international literature regarding the development of rural B&Bs and the relationship between business and lifestyle issues (Tables 2 and 3).

Table 2: Changes in personal life from tourism business.

	Main (*n* = 430)		Secondary (*n* = 324)	
	Number	**%**	**Number**	**%**
Increased personal income	102	24	86	27
Greater social contact with visitors	302	70	68	21
Meeting people from other cultures	210	49	100	31
Something to do/hobby	94	22	51	16
Loss of personal space	87	20	91	28
Loss of personal time	152	35	98	30
Loss of social contact with family & friends	91	21	67	21
Increased stress	100	23	70	22
Enabling home improvements	43	10	52	16
Increased travel opportunities	40	9	52	16
Decreased travel opportunities	58	14	58	18
Increased employment opportunities	50	12	42	13
Decreased employment opportunities	7	2	11	3
Enjoyment/satisfaction	4	1	3	1
Other	15	4	5	2

Note: Multiple responses.
Source: Warren (1998: 13).

Table 3: Changes in family life from tourism business.

	Main (*n* = 430)		Secondary (*n* = 324)	
	Number	%	Number	%
Increased personal income	92	26	59	24
Greater social contact with visitors	182	52	72	29
Meeting people from other cultures	145	41	62	25
Something to do/hobby	46	13	40	16
Loss of personal space	76	22	61	24
Loss of personal time	120	35	59	24
Loss of social contact with family & friends	67	19	55	22
Increased stress	75	21	41	16
Enabling home improvements	26	7	33	13
Increased travel opportunities	25	7	35	14
Decreased travel opportunities	32	9	25	10
Increased employment opportunities for family	44	13	54	2
Decreased employment opportunities for family	3	1	7	3
Other	7	2	3	1

Source: Warren (1998: 14).

The exact number of B&Bs operating in New Zealand is extremely hard to ascertain. Many B&B businesses are unregistered while some are also "casual" or "hobby" businesses operating only at times of peak demand or at convenient times for the owners (Cheyne-Buchanan 1992). The perceived low entry costs of B&B start-ups, particularly with respect to ownership of existing property with unoccupied bedrooms (Hall & Kearsley 2001) reflects wider research on the attraction of low entry costs for encouraging business start-up in other sectors (Amit *et al.* 1995). In research conducted by Oppermann (1998) the perceived low entry barrier to running a homestay (including farmstay) and B&B operations, often due to the availability of existing accommodation facilities, was regarded as a major incentive for many farm properties to venture into the accommodation sector as a means of maintaining farm operations and maintain or enhance income levels, although the social opportunities offered through contact with visitors was also a very significant factor. On the other hand, there was also an equally low exit barrier and the hosts could essentially decide on a daily basis to terminate their involvement in the provision of accommodation.

The growth in the number of bed and breakfast accommodation businesses has coincided with the overall development of international tourism in New Zealand, as demonstrated by an increase in the volume of B&B advertisements, as well as regional economic restructuring (Hall & Kearsley 2001). An analysis of phone books, advertising in Visitor Information Centres, and other tourism media suggests that in early 2002 there were at least 640 self-described B&B businesses in New Zealand, although this figure is likely a substantial underestimate. However, it is difficult to accurately estimate how B&B operations have contributed to either SME economic activity or even the tourism industry. The primary reason is that B&B businesses usually do not formally register themselves with the Companies Office unlike other business types. Indeed, because of their characteristics many B&Bs could well be described as part of the informal economy or as micro-businesses. Therefore, it is not possible to accurately monitor the birth, death and economic activity or contribution of these enterprises. A second difficulty in measuring the activity in this sector is that New Zealand's national international visitor monitoring survey records the use of hotel and motel accommodation, but does not record the use of bed and breakfast operations. Similarly, the recently recommenced domestic visitor survey also does not record B&B guest nights. It is therefore difficult to measure the changes in demand that are occurring for this form of accommodation, and the impacts that the emergence of this accommodation style has had on the existing industry structure.

Apart from the obvious difficulty in surveying B&B small businesses mentioned above, a further explanation for not including B&Bs in formal accommodation monitoring is that it is that it is unclear whether in fact B&Bs formally constitute a new and independent accommodation sector. This confusion arises because of the diversity of product that B&B businesses offer guests, as some provide a unique and clearly distinct product and others appear to supplement or mimic existing accommodation sectors such as boutique hotels/motels. Traditionally, the accommodation sector has been differentiated by the level or degree of service offered, however, this is not helpful when categorising bed and breakfast businesses due to the wide variety of services provided by hosts. Some service offerings in New Zealand's B&Bs exceed that offered by New Zealand's finest hotels and some service offerings are similar to that offered by backpacker accommodation. However, despite these difficulties, it is possible to identify the importance of behavioural traits as a unifying feature of this small-scale, homestay type of accommodation in that it is hosted and characterised by a high degree of social interaction between host and guest.

As with comparable Canadian research (Miciak *et al.* 2001), this chapter therefore seeks to provide a basic profile of New Zealand bed and breakfast businesses in order to identify the owners' management attitudes and operational decision making. The regional context for this is the upper North Island, a rapidly developing area of small business enterprise promoted for its lifestyle benefits (Hall & Kearsley 2001; Page 2000).

The Regional Context

New Zealand's upper North Island is a region of great contrasts. The major city is Auckland, which contains New Zealand's largest urban population of more than one million residents as well as New Zealand's major international airport. Auckland city is therefore the primary tourist gateway for travel to this region as well as the primary city for international arrivals to New Zealand. However, although this region contains New Zealand's largest city, it is also characterised by a large number of disperse rural communities. These contrasts can be illustrated by examining the earning capacity and occupation of the upper North Island's residents. Auckland is an affluent area in terms of the average income of its residents.

New Zealand Census 1996 figures show that Auckland City had an above average number of residents earning more than NZ$30,000 per year. In contrast, residents in the northern most part of the North Island have an above average number of people earning less than NZ$20,000 per year (Statistics New Zealand 1996).

Tourism is an emerging industry in the rural areas of the upper North Island. Approximately 533 people are employed in the accommodation, café and restaurant industry in Northland. The majority of the rural and coastal residents in the Northland region are employed in the agriculture and fishing industries. In contrast, Auckland's tourism industry is well developed with 2,695 people being employed in the accommodation, café and restaurant sector with the majority of residents employed in professional occupations (Statistics New Zealand 2000).

The International Visitor Monitor shows that the most common form of accommodation used by international visitors to the North Island is a motel. Backpacker hostels and hotels are the second and third most commonly used accommodation styles respectively. As statistics on the use of B&B businesses for tourist accommodation are not collected, it is not possible to report how the major visitor groups used this style of accommodation. However, the use of motels, backpacker hostels and hotels grew by an average of 15% in 2001, consistent with an increase in tourist activity of 16% (International Visitors Survey 2002). This suggests that B&B enterprises, along with other niche forms of accommodation are not yet posing a significant threat in terms of diverting new visitor volume to other forms of accommodation.

Methodology

A survey of the Bed and Breakfast operators in the North Island of New Zealand was undertaken between February and June 2002. The indepth questionnaire consisted of 147 questions in a mixture of discrete and scaled quantitative questions plus open-ended qualitative questions. Eligible businesses were selected for participation in the survey by mailing a copy of the questionnaire to owner/manager's address listings in a purpose built database. The database was compiled from several accommodation guide sources, and included properties listed on the Internet and print publications (AA Accommodation Guide 2002; Jasons 2002; Travelwise 2002; New Zealand Yellow Pages 2002). For inclusion in the database, the business must have been advertised or listed in the electronic and/or print media as a B&B enterprise. This resulted in identifying 175 B&B businesses that were operating in this region.

Questionnaires and a reply paid envelope were mailed to the identified B&B businesses. A second questionnaire was mailed to those businesses that did not respond to the first mailing. During the three month survey period, 87 questionnaires were returned, equating to a response rate of 49%, 67 were usable responses, equating to a final response rate of 38%. The response rate was higher than expected as the survey period overlapped with the end of the peak tourist season. All businesses who did not return a questionnaire in the survey period were telephoned after the survey period to identify non-response bias.

Three significant non-response biases were found. Sixteen percent of non-respondents declined to participate because they did not wish to supply the information requested from the questionnaire, in particular information relevant to the profitability of their business.

Eleven percent of B&B businesses were in the process of being sold or had recently been taken over. Their owners did not wish to participate because they had insufficient knowledge regarding the details of the survey questions, or no interest in receiving the report that summarised the survey findings from survey participants. Eleven percent of non-respondents declined to participate because they perceived that answering the questionnaire was too time consuming and would interfere with the normal functioning of their business or the enjoyment of their lifestyle. Such respondents also indicated that they were required to complete a Statistics New Zealand survey form each month requesting details about guests who stayed, and completing an additional survey was too onerous. The remaining non-respondents (62%) indicated such a broad variety of other reasons for not participating in the survey, and these did not fall into specific categories but some examples included, that the survey had been completed but not yet mailed, recent illness, or that the owners perceived that "the survey was not relevant to them as they operated their business as a hobby" and were therefore "not a true business" or "too small" to be considered.

A second difficulty with achieving a representative sample of B&B operators in this region was that some of these businesses rely solely on word of mouth to generate business, and therefore do not advertise. Businesses who did not advertise, or who did not advertise they provided a B&B style of accommodation could not be included in the survey sample. Despite the possible bias of the survey results reflecting the answers from respondents of smaller, less busy B&B businesses, the results are still regarded as indicative of attitudes, patterns and trends within the business environment of New Zealand's upper North Island region.

Business and Entrepreneur Profile of Businesses Within New Zealand's Upper North Island Region

The research found that B&B businesses in this region clearly fall into the New Zealand Ministry of Economic Development category of small enterprises. The majority of properties only employ the business owners who work full time, or between 36 and 50 hours per week during both peak and low seasons. Only one property intends to hire an additional staff member within the next year.

Eighty-six percent of respondents were more than 50 years old and identified their business as a family company. The majority of respondents indicated their spouse was involved to some degree in the running of the business. However, the respondents' concept of a "family" business is quite narrow, as although 90% of respondents are married with 2.5 adult children in their mid-30s, in 73% of cases these children had no involvement with running the business. There was no significant relationship between the age of the adult children and the degree of involvement in the business, although it is difficult to draw a definitive, reliable conclusion given the sample size.

Businesses typically make two bedrooms (32% of responses) or three bedrooms (30% of responses) available for hosting guests. On average, these rooms contain in total, 3.32 single beds and 3.01 double beds. The average rate charged for single beds per night is NZ\$81.53 and for doubles NZ\$127.34.

When examining respondents' financial commitment to the business, an interesting dichotomy emerged. 23.3% of respondents reported having invested between 90 and 100%

Table 4: Average monthly occupancy from January to December 2001.

Month	Occupancy Rate (%)	Month	Occupancy Rate (%)
January	47.72	July	13.87
February	51.43	August	16.86
March	40.18	September	18.19
April	27.65	October	24.25
May	15.58	November	33.35
June	15.15	December	42.25

of their personal savings in the business. A similar proportion (18%) reported investing less than 10% of their personal savings in the business. This reflects the age of the respondents who have combined savings from a 20-year working life and are likely to own their own home and have financial resources in excess of the start-up costs of the B&B business. This conclusion is consistent with 42% respondents reporting other forms of investment, and 54% stating that the business does not access any form of external finance.

Sixty-two percent of respondents have owned a business previously, but only 25% had experience in the tourism industry prior to the opening of their B&B. Respondents with prior industry experience had spent on average, 11 years in the hospitality sector. Fifty-one percent of properties record occupancy rates, but only half of these operators provided monthly occupancy rate figures. A clear pattern of seasonality emerges in the occupancy rates provided as shown in Table 4, where the high season is identified as the summer months of November to February (similar to Oppermann 1998). Such a pattern of seasonality as well as personal comments from respondents clearly suggested the development of seasonal entrance and exit strategies for the B&B business component of many respondents wider business strategies.

Respondents were selling at least one bed on approximately 203 nights each year, and 73% of businesses were generating average annual gross revenue of less than $50,000. This level of revenue is significantly low when compared to the average market value of the property which 20% of respondents stated was valued at more than $500,000. When examining the income that these businesses provide their owners, again there is a strong dichotomy. Eighteen percent of respondents derive less than 10% of their income from the business, while 15% derive more than 90% of their income.

The management expertise of the owners is supplemented by advice sought from other professionals such as accountants and lawyers, rather than employing a person with the necessary skills or seeking training in those areas. As no additional staff are employed, most properties do not have a training programme for staff in place and do not intend to do any future training. Within the previous year 68% of respondents had consulted an accountant. The most common forms of advice requested were for financial advice and marketing. However, few respondents were aware of government assistance schemes and often did not belong to the industry organisations and associations created for the tourism industry and accommodation sector. Nevertheless, respondents had lived an average of 15 years in the region the business is located in, suggesting they are well integrated within the region's business and social community within potential access to the regional business networks.

Examining Attitudes About Entrepreneurs' Balance Between Risk and Lifestyle

Respondents were asked to rate the importance of a series of goals (after Carlsen & Getz 1998) when getting started in the business on a scale of 1–7, where 1 = Not at all important and 7 = Very important) (Table 5). The responses to this question illustrate the twin tensions of operating a business while trying to enjoy a quality lifestyle. "To permit me to become financially independent" was the goal which received the highest ranking. However, the presence of three different mode values at both ends of the scale, and a high standard deviation value illustrate that not all bed and breakfast operators agree that this is a high priority. In contrast, few indicated that "to make lots of money" was an important goal when beginning the business, further illustrating the disparity of opinion regarding the role of profit making in this type of business. Lifestyle is a highly significant factor when deciding to enter a B&B business, as "to enjoy a good lifestyle" was the second highest ranked goal. The least important goal was for the business owners to gain prestige by owning their own business.

Respondents were also asked to indicate how much they agreed or disagreed with a series of statements about business attitudes by circling a number on a scale of 1–7 where 1 = Totally agree and 7 = Totally disagree. The raw results are presented in Table 6.

Table 5: Question: "How important were the following goals to you when entering this business? (1 = Not at all important; 7 = Very important)

Statement	Mode Rating	Average Rating	Standard Deviation
To permit me to become financially independent	2, 6, 7	4.08	2.21
To meet interesting people	7	6.06	1.36
To enjoy a good lifestyle	7	5.83	1.54
To live in the right environment	7	5.60	1.93
To be my own boss	7	5.37	1.92
To provide a retirement income	7	4.68	2.15
To support my/our leisure interests	7	4.45	2.05
To provide me/us with a challenge	6	4.95	1.68
To keep this property in the family	1	3.36	2.44
To keep my family together	1	3.08	2.46
To make lots of money	1	3.03	1.91
To gain prestige by operating a business	1	2.22	1.77

Note: Multiple modes are separated by commas.

Table 6: Attitudes to aspects of business management (1 = Totally agree; 7 = Totally disagree).

Statement	Mode Rating	Average Rating	Standard Deviation
I want to present a good public/corporate image	1	1.49	1.215
I would rather keep the business modest and under control than have it grow too big	1	2.12	1.69
I come into daily contact with customers	1	2.36	1.91
Accepting the responsibility of this business has been worth the gains in lifestyle	1	2.09	1.31
The advantages of this occupation outweigh the disadvantages	1	2.31	1.35
It is crucial to keep the business profitable	1	2.45	1.74
Enjoying the job is more important than making lots of money	1	2.46	1.83
It is hard to separate work and family life in a tourism business	1	2.56	1.65
The business is highly seasonal	1	2.62	1.96
I want to keep the business growing	1	2.76	1.76
My personal/family interests take priority over running the business	1	3.23	1.91
Eventually the business will be sold for the best possible price	1	3.41	2.43
There are more risks in owning this business than in my previous occupation	1	3.87	2.3
Government assistance is essential for industry growth	1	4.05	2.2
In this business, customers can not be separated from personal life	2	2.87	1.62
Business meets my performance targets	3	3.05	1.53
Business should run purely on business principles	6	4.43	1.93

The most interesting aspect of the results is the divergence of attitudes regarding the strength of the pure business philosophy guiding the management of the business. The statement, "the business should run purely on business principles" received the strongest disagreement. The largest diversity of answers was in response to the statement "eventually the business will be sold for the best possible price." The strongest agreement was with the statement, "I want to present a good public/corporate image," indicating that B&B operators place a high importance on running their business to a professional service standard, but that this standard is a management concept that is separate and perhaps unrelated to business profitability. The responses to these parameters combined with a weak positive response to the statement "my personal/family interests take priority over running the business" suggests that B&B operators balance the strict application of business management philosophy with the pragmatics of operating a business they expect to fulfil lifestyle goals.

However, evidence of a strong business management philosophy emerges with respondents favouring responses that indicate taking responsibility for managing profit and business growth. Respondents agreed strongly that accepting the responsibility of operating the business has been worth the gains in lifestyle. Surprisingly, respondents demonstrated only weak agreement with the statement that there were more risks in owning the B&B business than in their previous occupation. This is contrary to the anecdotal perception that owning a business involves greater risk than being in full time or part time employment. This contrary result can perhaps be explained by the fact that unlike other businesses, in the case of a B&B enterprise, the business owner lives and resides within the business premises and that fulfilling the owners' lifestyle goals takes precedence over making a large profit. Perhaps just as importantly the perceived low entry costs, in terms of both direct costs as well as opportunity costs, are likely also a significant factor in entrance and exit strategies.

The responses to these questions demonstrate overall, that owner/managers of this type of small business do engage in balancing a business philosophy of profit management and business growth with their personal interests of enjoying their lifestyle. The difficult issue for most entrepreneurs in this study appears to be deciding how much profit is reasonable, given the constraints of meeting their lifestyle objectives, rather than how much profit it is possible to earn — a philosophy more traditionally associated with a non-lifestyle oriented business. Moreover, the results of this research contest some perspectives on lifestyle business owners (Ateljevic & Doorne 2000), by suggesting that profit and a professionally run business are strongly desired goals of entrepreneurs in this business segment, and are as important in small business strategies as achieving lifestyle objectives.

This chapter has discussed the attitudes of the B&B owner/manager towards the day-to-day risks associated with owning a bed and breakfast enterprise. However, as previously mentioned, most respondents indicated their spouse was involved to some degree in the running of the business. This means that the risk is shared between the business partners. The survey asked respondents to indicate what degree of involvement their partner/spouse had in performing tasks associated with running the bed and breakfast on a scale of 1–7, where 1 = Not responsible and 7 = Totally responsible (Table 7). A broad interpretation of the results from this question would suggest that the tasks listed are shared relatively equally between the survey respondent and their spouse/partner. However, when these tasks are correlated with gender, a slight division of labour emerges. Male spouses tended to be rated as having a greater responsibility for the transportation of guests than female spouses. Similarly, female spouses were rated as having a greater responsibility for bookings, cooking, and cleaning. Tasks such as business planning were shared almost equally between genders and neither gender had a high rating for being responsible for financial management. This finding is consistent with the high number of respondents who seek professional advice from an accountant. Significantly, while some gender division is therefore apparent in the running of the business, the results of this study as well as personal interviews and discussions with respondents seem to suggest a far greater sharing of business responsibilities then in some other studies of small tourism businesses (Lynch 1998), with consequent implications for our understanding of the role of gender in small business performance (Baines & Wheelock 1998; Chell & Baines 1998; Cliff 1998; Rosa *et al.* 1996).

Table 7: Activity sharing between spouses in a New Zealand bed and breakfast businesses.

Task	Average Degree of Responsibility	Standard Deviation
Cleaning	4.12	2.04
Cooking	3.91	2.43
Taking bookings	4.14	1.82
Marketing/promoting	3.59	1.97
Financial management	3.71	2.05
Staff management	3.06	2.38
Transporting guests	3.60	2.13
Business planning	3.87	1.97

Conclusions

This chapter has demonstrated that the profile of B&B operations in New Zealand's upper North Island region consists of small businesses as defined by the New Zealand Ministry of Economic Development. Predominantly these businesses are family owned, generate a small amount of revenue relative to the market value of the business and only employ the business owners. The typical B&B business in the region was very small, with management and operational duties split between the married owners, and little involvement from adult children. This study also found that respondents indicated strongly that the risks and responsibility of operating a B&B business were worth the perceived gains in lifestyle. An examination of the attitudes of owners to the issues of applying strict business principles to a business that is known for its lifestyle benefits has shown that there is evidence of a strong business philosophy being balanced against the personal goals of the business owners to enjoy a good lifestyle. These characteristics are consistent with those exhibited by small family owned tourism enterprises (Carlsen & Getz 1998; Getz & Carlsen 2000). However, in the context of New Zealand's broader small business environment, these B&B businesses present some unique insights into understanding the business goals and entrepreneurial behaviours of tourism SMEs particularly with respect to the situation that fulfilling the lifestyle goals of the owners is almost equally important than meeting more traditional business goals and objectives. Indeed, for vast majority of the respondents *lifestyle is a strategic business objective*. Therefore, these findings illustrate the need to incorporate lifestyle goals within the development of models of the entrepreneurship process within tourism and, arguably, within much small business knowledge overall (e.g. Gibb & Davies 1990, 1992; Glancey 1998; Greenbank 2001; Perren 1999). Interestingly, at least two other consequences emerge from understanding the importance of lifestyle as a strategic business objective of small tourism businesses. First, our understanding of small business performance and entrepreneurial success would therefore need to incorporate lifestyle' quality-of-life measures as an important component (Hornaday & Aboud 1971; Keats & Bracker 1988). Second, lifestyle and amenity factors therefore also become a significant factor in the decision-making regarding the location of new small tourism business ventures (Williams & Hall 2002).

The bed and breakfast sector of New Zealand's accommodation industry is still emerging, but has experienced rapid growth within the past five years. This niche product has now become a significant player in the accommodation sector although it is marked by poor formal linkages with tourism industry associations, RTOs and other sectors of the tourism industry. Quite possibly one of the most significant reasons for poor linkages are the different goals of small businesses within emergent tourism networks (see Hall, Chapter 11 of this volume). For example, the lifestyle goals of many tourism entrepreneurs may well be at odds with some of the profit maximisation goals of other entrepreneurs within a tourist destination. These conflicts have been observed first-hand by the authors within the study area. Comments from members of economic development agencies or tourism organizations that such lifestyle entrepreneurs are "hippies" or "a danger to the industry" are not uncommon. Many tourism organizations often perceive such lifestyle businesses as being "unprofessional." However, the evidence from this study suggests that this is not the case although there are potentially significant areas for goal conflict in terms of business objectives. From a network development perspective such issues clearly need to be addressed if regions are to effectively maximise the economic and social benefits of tourism development (Hall 2000).

At this stage of accommodation industry development in New Zealand, it is unclear whether the Bed and Breakfast sector will threaten the hotel and motel accommodation sectors by eroding their traditional target markets, or whether this niche product will complement the existing industry structure by responding and attracting an entirely new travel market. Nevertheless, regardless of the sectoral issues that this research raises, if the New Zealand tourism strategy is to be successfully implemented it is apparent that government and the tourism industry association will need to have a far better understanding of the entrepreneurial and business characteristics and motivations of the small businesses which form the bulk of the tourism industry. It is readily apparent from the results of this study that the economic development goals of the national tourism strategy may not be the same as some of the SMES that lie at its intended core.

References

AA Accommodation Guide (2002). http://www.nz-accommodation.co.nz/ [Accessed on January 12].

Amit, R., Muller, E., & Cockburn, I. (1995). Opportunity costs and entrepreneurial activity. *Journal of Business Venturing*, *10*, 95–106.

Angowski Rogak, L. (1995). *The upstart guide to owning and managing a bed and breakfast*. Chicago: Upstart Publishing Co.

Ateljevic, I., & Doorne, S. (2000). Staying within the fence: Lifestyle entrepreneurship in tourism. *Journal of Sustainable Tourism*, *8*(5), 378–392.

Baines, S., & Wheelock, J. (1998). Working for each other: Gender, the household and micro-business survival and growth. *International Small Business Journal*, *17*(1), 16–35.

Brockhaus, R. H. (1980). Risk taking propensity of entrepreneurs. *Academy of Management Journal*, *23*, 509–520.

Busenitz, L. (1999). Entrepreneurial risk and strategic decision making: It's a matter of perspective. *The Journal of Applied Behavioral Science*, *35*, 325–340.

Carlsen, J., & Getz, D. (1998). Relatively speaking: Business goals and operating issues for rural, family owned/operated tourism and hospitality businesses. Trinet Publication, http://www.sbaer.uca.edu/Research/2000/ICSB/pt1/020REL.PDF [Accessed on January 15].

Chell, E., & Baines, S. (1998). Does gender affect business "performance"? A study of micro-businesses in business services in the U.K. *Entrepreneurship and Regional Development, 10,* 117–135.

Cheyne-Buchanan, J. (1992). Issues of marketing and promotion in farm tourism: A case study of the Manawatu region of New Zealand. *Australian Journal of Leisure and Recreation, 2*(3), 15–19.

Cliff, J. E. (1998). Does one size fit all? Exploring the relationship between attitudes towards growth, gender, and business size. *Journal of Business Venturing, 13,* 523–542.

Getz, D., & Carlsen, J. (2000). Characteristics and goals of family and owner-operated businesses in the rural tourism and hospitality sectors. *Tourism Management, 21,* 547–560.

Gibb, A., & Davies, L. (1990). In pursuit of frameworks for the development of growth models of the small firm. *International Small Business Journal, 9*(1), 15–31.

Gibb, A., & Davies, L. (1992). Methodological problems in the development of a growth model of business enterprise. *The Journal of Entrepreneurship, 1*(1), 3–36.

Glancey, K. (1998). Determinants of growth and profitability in small entrepreneurial firms. *International Journal of Entrepreneurial Behaviour and Research, 4*(1), 18–27.

Greenbank, P. (2001). Objective setting in the micro-business. *International Journal of Entrepreneurial Behaviour and Research, 7*(3), 108–127.

Hall, C. M. (2000). *Tourism planning.* Harlow: Prentice-Hall.

Hall, C. M., & Kearsley, G. (2001). *Tourism in New Zealand: An introduction.* Melbourne: Oxford University Press.

Høgh, L. (1998). Farming the tourist: The social benefits of farm tourism in Southland, New Zealand. In: R. Mitchell, B. Ritchie, M. Thyne, & A. Carr (Eds), *Pacific Rim tourism: Past, present and future* (pp. 43–48). Dunedin: Centre for Tourism, University of Otago.

Hornaday, J. A., & Aboud, J. (1971). Characteristics of successful entrepreneurs. *Personnel Psychology, 24,* 141–153.

Jasons Travel Guide (2002). http://www.jasons.co.nz/country.cfm?country=nz&CFID=67567&CFTOKEN=77860685 [Accessed on January 18].

Johnston-Walker, R. (1998). The accommodation motivations and preferences of international free and independent travellers to New Zealand. In: R. Mitchell, B. Ritchie, M. Thyne, & A. Carr (Eds), *Pacific Rim tourism: Past, present, future* (pp. 49–55). Dunedin: Centre for Tourism, University of Otago.

Keats, B. W., & Bracker, J. S. (1988). Toward a theory of small firm performance: A conceptual model. *American Journal of Small Business* (Spring), 41–58.

Lynch, P. (1998). Female micro-entrepreneurs in the host family sector: Key motivations and socio-economic variables. *Hospitality Management, 17,* 319–342.

Mangin, E., & Collins, A. (2001). *An investigation into service quality variation within a tourist brand: The case of the Shamrock.* Discussion Paper No. 35. Cork: Department of Food Business and Development, National University of Ireland.

Miciak, A. R., Kirkland, K., & Ritchie, J. R. B. (2001). Benchmarking an emerging lodging alternative in Canada: A profile of the B&B sector. *Tourism Economics, 7*(1), 39–58.

New Zealand Ministry of Economic Development (2001). *SMEs in New Zealand: Structure and dynamics.* Wellington: New Zealand Ministry of Economic Development.

New Zealand Yellow Pages, Telecom Directories Ltd (2002). http://www.yellowpages.co.nz [Accessed on January 15].

Oppermann, M. (1998). Farm tourism in New Zealand. In: R. Butler, C. M. Hall, & J. Jenkins (Eds), *Tourism and recreation in rural areas* (pp. 225–235). Chichester: Wiley.

Page, S. J., Forer, P., & Lawton, G. (1999). Small business development and tourism: Terra incognita? *Tourism Management, 20*(4), 435–460.

Palich, L. E., & Bagby, D. R. (1995). Using cognitive theory to explain entrepreneurial risk-taking: Challenging conventional wisdom. *Journal of Business Venturing, 10*, 425–438.

Perren, L. (1999). Factors in the growth of micro-enterprises (Part 1): Developing a framework. *Journal of Small Business and Enterprise Development, 6*(4), 366–385.

Rosa, P., Carter, S., & Hamilton, D. (1996). Gender as a determinant of small business performance: Insights from a British study. *Small Business Economics, 8*, 463–478.

Statistics New Zealand (1996). *Census of New Zealand population and dwellings.* http://www.stats.govt.nz/ [Accessed on April 2, 2002].

Statistics New Zealand (2000). *Business activity statistics.* Wellington: Statistics New Zealand.

Thomas, R. (2000). Small firms in the tourism industry: Some conceptual issues. *International Journal of Tourism Research, 2*, 345–353.

Tourism Industry Association of New Zealand (2002). *Key facts and figures.* Wellington: Tourism Industry Association of New Zealand. http://www.tianz.org.nz/ind/ind01.htm [Accessed on April 3, 2002].

Tourism New Zealand (2002). *International visitors survey.* Wellington: Tourism New Zealand. http://www.tourisminfo.govt.nz/cir_randd/index.cfm [Accessed on April 8].

Tourism Strategy Group (2000). *New Zealand tourism strategy 2001.* Wellington: Office of the Minister of Tourism/Tourism Strategy Group.

Travelwise (2002). *Charming bed and breakfast in New Zealand.* New Zealand: Travelwise.

Vallen, G., & Wallace Rande, W. (1997). Bed and breakfasts in Arizona: Demographics and operating statistics. *Cornell Hotel and Restaurant Administration Quarterly* (August), 62–66.

Warnick, R. B., & Klar, L. R., Jr. (1991). The bed and breakfast and small inn industry of the commonwealth of Massachusetts: An exploratory study. *Journal of Travel Research, 29*(3), 17–25.

Warren, J. (1998). *Rural tourism in New Zealand.* Wellington: Centre for Research, Evaluation and Social Assessment.

Williams, A. M., & Hall, C. M. (2002). Tourism, migration, circulation and mobility: The contingencies of time and place. In: C. M. Hall, & A. M. Williams (Eds), *Tourism and migration: New relationships between production and consumption* (p. 152). Dordrecht: Kluwer.

Zane, B. (1997). The B&B guest: A comprehensive view. *Cornell Hotel and Restaurant Administration Quarterly, 38*(4), 69–75.

Chapter 7

From Lifestyle Consumption to Lifestyle Production: Changing Patterns of Tourism Entrepreneurship

Gareth Shaw and Allan M. Williams

Introduction

The increasing attention given to the role of small firms in the tourism sector has led to a recognition of the significance of entrepreneurship in such businesses. The uncovering of factors conditioning patterns of entrepreneurship within tourism contrasts in part with more general studies of small firms that have emphasised organisational structures (Goffee & Scase 1983) and features of entrepreneurial personalities. In terms of the latter, particular research has been directed at so-called proactive entrepreneur personalities (Kickul & Gundry 2002), alongside notions of risk taking (Das & Tend 1997). Studies of small firm entrepreneurs in tourism have, by contrast, identified a range of entrepreneurial cultures (Shaw 2003), only a few of which appear to embrace formal ideas of entrepreneurship and innovation. Such cultures range from a preoccupation with economic motives through to a range of entrepreneurs for whom non-economic factors are of primary importance. As Dewhurst & Horobin (1998) explain, such non-economic motives create difficulty in applying economic models of small enterprises within the tourism industry. In this situation, the concept and definition of the entrepreneur is far more complex and, according to Swedburg (2000), necessitates the adoption of different perspectives. This includes sociological and psychological views which highlight the knowledge, background characteristics and personality traits of the entrepreneur.

This suggests that the small-scale entrepreneur in tourism is somewhat different from those in other economic sectors. Certainly, the tourism industry is characterised by a relative ease of access in terms of skill requirements and, to a lesser degree, levels of capital; features matched only in the retail sector. There is also another major characteristic of the small-firm entrepreneur in tourism which appears to set them apart from other sectors of the small-firm economy. This concerns the close relationship between elements of consumption and production. In broad terms, commentators on tourism development have drawn attention to the need to understand the interplay between tourism consumption and production (Britton 1991; Shaw & Williams 2002). Within this context Ateljevic (2000) viewed tourism as an interrelated framework of circuits of consumption and production. Such circuits revolve around the interplay of "interests, infrastructure and social relations of production, and consumption forces" (Ateljevic 2000: 377). More specifically, situated within these perspectives are those studies that have sought to expose the direct link between consumption and production that operates through the process of small-business formation. Early work by Williams *et al.* (1989) drew attention to the blurring of the boundaries between consumption and production, as many of the entrepreneurs operating tourism businesses within Cornwall were former tourists. In many cases, such people had made repeated visits to the tourism destination, creating strong aspirations for wanting to live and work within the area. In these instances, entrepreneurial motives were dominated by quality of life and local environmental variables. Snepenger *et al.* (1995) have termed this process "travel stimulated entrepreneurial migration," although in their case study of Yellowstone in North America, they were examining the role of tourism in attracting entrepreneurs to all types of economic sectors.

Increasing numbers of studies have identified a complex combination of motives and aspirations characterising the small business entrepreneur in tourism. Within the Cornish case study, almost one-third of the tourism entrepreneurs were motivated by non-economic factors, whilst less than 17% of those operating hotels and guesthouses were local to the county. The importance of lifestyle motives within tourism entrepreneurship is seen as a significant feature of small firms in this sector, with Ateljevic & Doorne (2000) arguing for greater attention to be given to this theme. This chapter takes up this challenge in three ways. First, we review the debates surrounding the small business entrepreneur and lifestyle motives. Second, we explore the changing patterns of tourism entrepreneurship in the face of new forms of consumption and production. Finally, the chapter develops some of the ideas on lifestyle entrepreneurship in the context of Cornwall's surf-tourism industry.

Changing Lifestyles: Motivational Behaviour in Tourism Entrepreneurship

The entry into entrepreneurship is in itself a life-changing experience for most people and is often related to a desire to exercise some control over their working lives. Within many studies of small businesses in all economic sectors, such motives are often expressed by the notion of "being your own boss" (Storey 1994). Morrison *et al.* (1999: 13) argue that the "majority of small firms in the U.K. can be termed life-style businesses," on the basis that they are mainly motivated by survival and enough income to maintain their way of life. Within tourism such motives are especially prevalent, but are also part of a complex web of desires and motives that are socially constructed. The increasing attention given to tourism entrepreneurship in the context of the small firm has highlighted the importance of non-economic motives. Dewhurst & Horobin (1998) have, for example, stressed such behaviour and how this creates problems in applying economic models of entrepreneurship to many of the small enterprises within the tourism industry. Their work in Yorkshire found that owners of small enterprises within tourism were twice as likely to state non-economic motives, compared with economic factors, as reasons for establishing the business.

Similarly, Morrison *et al.* (1999) have explored, across a range of settings, the notion of tourism entrepreneurship, including the importance of lifestyle motives.

The extent of non-economic motives have also been highlighted in larger-scale surveys by Thomas *et al.* (1997). They examined some 1,300 small tourism firms across the U.K. and found that almost 80% of owners gave prominence to non-economic motives. At a more regionally specific level, successive surveys of small firms in Devon and Cornwall have found a consistent trend in the importance give to particular non-economic factors (Shaw *et al.* 1987; Tourism Associates 1997; Tourism Research Group 1996). The last of these surveys conducted in 1997 as part of an EU Leader programme focused on some 555 tourism and retail businesses in Cornwall. As Table 1 shows, a series of non-economic or lifestyle variables were rated very important, including being "able to live in the area" and the idea of being in control of their working lives, as expressed by "being my own boss" along with "doing interesting work." This study, along with others, also draws attention to the relative complexity of the interactions between non-economic and economic factors. For example, "making a good profit or good return" was rated as "important" by 48% of the sample, whilst a further 38% stated this was a "very important" motive. It would seem that, in many cases, lifestyle motives are, to some extent, embedded within an economic agenda. This follows Shailer's (1994) view that the two types of motives are intrinsically linked.

Dewhurst & Horobin (1998) have attempted to set these motives into a strategic management model and, in doing so, emphasised the personality traits of the entrepreneur. More importantly, they have sought to use motives and goals as a means of providing a taxonomy of small business entrepreneurs by combining a subjective goal orientation model with that of a management orientation one. This suggests a possible combination of positions in terms of lifestyle-oriented goals and commercial ones, and with lifestyle as opposed to commercially-oriented strategies.

Such an approach raises the important issue of the degree to which motives impact on entrepreneurial activity or, as Dewhurst & Horobin (1998: 34) put it, "are lifestylers likely to content themselves with smaller businesses?" Research by Shaw & Williams (1998) has drawn attention to two differing models of small-business entrepreneurship within tourism.

Table 1: Motivations for operating tourism business: The case of Cornwall.

Reasons	Degree of Importance (%)		
	Not Important	Important	Very Important
Making a good profit	14	48	38
Being able to live in area	9	27	64
Doing interesting work	3	28	69
Flexibility of work patterns	19	30	51
Expanding the business	33	38	29
Being own boss	5	19	76

Source: Tourism Associates (1997).

One is characterised by owners who had moved into tourism destinations, very often for non-economic reasons. Many of these had wanted to live in the area and established their business with the aid of personal savings, whilst some had come to semi-retire. They were also attracted by a way of life that involved "being their own boss" by operating a small hotel, guesthouse or small shop. The non-economic motives in themselves were not a full determinant of strategy, but when they combined with a lack of business experience and an ageing owner, then entrepreneurial activity was extremely limited. To all intents such people operated their businesses as non-entrepreneurs. If they had any aspirations for development, these tended to be ill-defined and lacked any coherent business strategies. This group shares some similarities, with Carland *et al.*'s (1984) group of so-called "small business owners." In contrast to non-entrepreneurs, it was also possible to recognise a group of "constrained entrepreneurs." These were characterised by younger people with a greater level of economic motives, and drawn from more professional, though mainly non-business backgrounds. In this group, lifestyle motives were still significant, but did combine much more with economic ones and a potential for business development, if training and support were provided.

Whilst such typologies are important, it should also be recognised that they have short-comings, especially in their failure to understand the linkages between different motives, along with the fact that they tend to ignore other variables associated with tourism en-trepreneurship. Of particular importance is the relationship between lifestyle motives and migration. This has been highlighted in a number of studies of tourism entrepreneurship (Paniagna 2002; Williams *et al.* 1989), although as Snepenger *et al.* (1995) explain, such processes occur in other economic sectors. In the case of Cornwall, less than 17% of the tourism entrepreneurs were native to that county (Shaw & Williams 1998). More recently, Paniagna's (2002) work on the urban-rural migration of tourism entrepreneurs in Spain has provided a richer detail of the motives and processes. Once again, it seems that a series of motives are linked together, usually related to "a modification of professional activity to fulfil life goals" (Paniagna 2002: 361). In this study, three main types of entrepreneurial migrants could be identified in terms of their motives for moving:

- those moving for economic-professional reasons, whose motives are mainly economic;
- moves for professional-environmental reasons; motives are mainly lifestyle ones;
- moves based on environmental-rural reasons; motives are negative feelings of the city.

In Spain, the process is also complicated by the case of return migrants who are moving back to their village. In the majority of cases the move coincided with the establishment of a new business, mainly providing rural holiday accommodation. However, despite the different circumstances, the results from this research do correspond with other studies in which one of the key reasons for migration in tourism entrepreneurship is "to become self-employed or be their own boss" (Paniagna 2002: 365). There are differences over the factors conditioning the choice of destinations between migrant tourism entrepreneurs in Spain and those in the U.K. In the former, selection of the destination in which to establish the business is strongly influenced by family background and inherited property. Within the U.K., studies of migrant entrepreneurs to major coastal tourism destinations such as Cornwall have shown choice is mainly determined by previous patterns of tourist visits.

Limited studies of rural tourism destinations in the U.K. show more the influence of property prices alongside perceptions of high quality environments as major determinants. It would seem that the migration patterns of entrepreneurs are contingent on culture factors and types of tourism destinations. However, in this context, we know very little of the characteristics of tourism entrepreneurs in urban settings and whether these are more likely to be local people or migrants.

The movement of most tourism entrepreneurs into a holiday destination does, of course, create a different set of problems for the operation of the small enterprise. In many studies, the migration unit has been shown to be that of the family. Indeed, family-run businesses have been identified across a range of tourism studies. This link operates mainly by providing cheap and flexible labour, but is also conditioned by family-related goals. In this context, Getz & Carlson (2000) working in Australia have identified two motivational types of entrepreneur (see also Carlsen *et al.* 2001). One they have termed "family first," which accounted for two-thirds of the enterprises, many of which they labelled "copreneurs" or married couples operating a business. The second group of so-called "business first" were motivated more by business related factors despite the fact that half of them had no formal business goals. The role of the household in the small business enterprise is obviously important, but within the tourism sector is little understood in its entirety.

We would argue that the family often becomes more important for migrant entrepreneurs, especially in the formative years of the business. The migrant entrepreneur is moving into an environment of which they may have little knowledge, few contacts and, in many instances, perceptions formed through being a tourist in that destination. In contrast, the literature on the development of small firms has increasingly stressed the importance of entrepreneurial networks (Tinsley & Lynch 2001). Johannisson (2000) has drawn particular attention to such networks which, to a large extent, are created from the personal contacts of entrepreneurs. These social networks are the entrepreneurs' contact and relations with others and the degree to which these facilitate the utilisation of other resources (Gibson & Cassar 2002). Such networks are also significant in terms of information, support, credibility and governance (Birley 1985; Birley *et al.* 1990).

According to Hill, McGowan & Drummond (1999) the overall strength of a social network is determined by geographical, psychological and cultural distances between the actors, along with the nature of the entrepreneur's past experiences. In terms of the migrant tourism entrepreneur, all these determinants are against the easy establishment of a working network, since they initially tend to have poorly developed social networks. Furthermore, as immigrants, they may have considerable psychological and cultural distances with the host population. Successive studies have also highlighted the limiting nature of past work experiences of many tourism entrepreneurs, which have often been outside of the business world. In all of these circumstances, the migrant entrepreneur very often falls back on the family unit and places increased reliance on family members, which may act as substitutes for social networks.

In a wider context, debates focussed on the urban-rural shift in small firm formation across a range of economic sectors have also contested the links between small firms and local economic networks. Curran & Blackburn (1994) for example, argue that there is very little integration between many small firms with their local economies. Certainly, such a perspective would seem to describe the situation for the early stages of development for migrant tourism entrepreneurs, although lack of detailed research limits knowledge of the extent of such trends. In contrast, Phelps *et al.* (2001) suggest that within parts of the U.K., especially in the South of England "there is considerable evidence that businesses in small settlements are able to borrow size from Greater London" (p. 164). This notion of "borrowed size," originally described by Alonso (1973), alters the perspective on local networks and shifts it "toward an emphasis upon the interactions between businesses in groups of localities" (Phelps *et al.* 2001: 614). Research by Hitchens *et al.* (1994) on manufacturing firms in mid-Wales partly revealed patterns of sourcing centred upon Birmingham and London, adding some evidence to the notion of "borrowed size." Unfortunately, studies of the networks of small tourism firms is limited and the relevance of the concept of 'borrowed size' remains untested.

Changes in Tourism Consumption and Production: The Rise of New Lifestyle Entrepreneurs

Shifts in tourism consumption and production from a Fordist regime to a post-Fordist one have been given increasing attention in the literature (Richards 1996; Sharpley 1994; Urry 1995). Certainly, a range of authors have described not only so-called new forms of tourism consumption associated with heritage, themed landscapes, ecotourism and adventure tourism, but also recognised new types of tourists. Particular attention has been directed at the rise of ecotourists in all their various forms, including so called ego-tourists. In this context, Mowforth & Munt (2003) highlight the discourse of a new wave of tourists characterised by the young adventurous ego-tourists with limited economic capital and a desire to meet other like-minded people often around certain types of adventure tourism.

It is within this context of more individualistic forms of tourism, characterised by post-Fordist elements of increased market segmentation, that Ateljevic & Doorne (2000) highlighted a closer correspondence between lifestyle and tourism entrepreneurship. Their research, based on a seven-year case study in New Zealand, argued that it was possible to identify an emerging cohort of tourism lifestyle entrepreneurs . . . who also do not subscribe to the inevitable path of "progress" as an end in itself' (Ateljevic & Doorne 2000: 381). Such entrepreneurs seemingly rejected a range of economic and business growth opportunities, especially those concerned with large-scale mass tourism, because of their socio-political ideologies.

This perspective, which identifies tourism entrepreneurship around a set of lifestyle value positions that encompass; cultural-community values of egalitarianism, organisational ideologies around the individual, market positions based upon the local and post-modern tourist, alongside an industry perspective which highlights business reciprocity and quality of life. Ateljevic & Doorne (2000: 388) claim that many small tourism firms in New Zealand are selecting combinations of these value positions "in order to preserve both their quality of life in their socioenvironmental contexts and their niche market positions."

The evidence for such a perspective is as yet limited and centred around the growth of adventure and backpacker tourism in New Zealand. Ateljevic & Doorne (2000) recorded the growth of backpacking from the late 1980s onwards. Of particular note was the fact that many early owners of these small businesses were attempting to establish an alternative set of values which stressed "social, cultural and environmental relationships" (p. 386). These owners were entrepreneurial in that they were developing new tourism products, albeit within a distinctive "lifestyle" framework. Over time, these innovations were reproduced and imitated by another group of businesses whose values and motives were very different. Indeed, in further research, Ateljevic & Doorne (2001) have outlined an evolutionary model of change for the backpacker market in New Zealand. This is characterised by increased commercial, economic activity over time along with a strong degree of integration between the various elements of the backpacker and adventure tourism industries. Such trends result in greater levels of market segmentation and far more differentiation in business motives.

The evidence from New Zealand suggests a new form of lifestyle entrepreneurship that has its origins in new forms of tourism consumption. Many of the initial small business owners were key to the innovation of new tourism products. In this sense, these entrepreneurs differ from those described in previous studies. For example, those small-scale entrepreneurs identified in British resorts merely reproduced elements of the traditional tourism product and had little thought for innovation. Furthermore, the notion of lifestyle also differed for, in the New Zealand study, it encompassed a range of value positions. In contrast, research on other tourism entrepeneurs have identified a much narrower focus of lifestyle associated with escapism and a pleasant environment, with few attempts to transfer such values into concrete business ethics and strategies.

Apart from these significant differences, there are also common features. For example, for both groups of lifestyle entrepreneurs, there is a process of migration. However, even within this common mechanism, there are subtle differences. In New Zealand, the migrant entrepreneurs were "seeking closer relationships within a natural environment, together with opportunities to be involved in . . . inclusive community relationships' (Ateljevic & Doorne 2000: 386). Such place identity is expressed in different terms by entrepreneurs in British resorts, where the primary reason for migrating was the environment. A further point of common ground is the restrictive nature of capital accumulation, along with the reliance of family labour, although this remains to be more closely researched.

We now turn to the third part of this chapter, which is the search for new lifestyle entrepreneurs in British resorts through the growth of surf tourism. We start by briefly exploring the growth and characteristics of surf tourism as a new form of tourism consumption and production before focussing on the nature of lifestyle entrepreneurship in this sector.

Surf Tourism: Characteristics of Consumption and Production

It is estimated that there are well over 10 million surfers worldwide and that by the turn of the century the industry turnover was $10 billion per annum (Buckley 2002). An estimated rate of growth of 12–16% per annum, together with its embracing of surf-branded clothing and specialised equipment, has made it a major sector of tourism that is being increasingly commoditised on a global scale. As Buckley (2002) explains, it also shares many features of adventure tourism, including its establishment as a recreational activity and its subsequent development as a component of the tourism industry. There is also evidence of the establishment of surf tourism businesses by people involved in surfing, in other words, the shift from consumption to production. In addition, there has been a more recent growth of commercial operators and the development of a large industry supplying equipment and clothing. These developments have been driven on by changes in demand and the manipulation of consumption patterns by a specialised media, especially through the www. This has proved to be a dominant marketing tool as well as a means of communicating ideas between the global surfing community. The commercial and non-commercial dimensions of the www epitomise the differences between surf tourism and surf culture proper. The former is becoming increasingly dominated by tour operators and the growth of packages — albeit offered in flexible ways, characterised by more neo-Fordist trends. These commercial companies tend to offer either low-budget or high budget tours based in surf camps and surf lodges. Buckley (2002: 407) defines commercial surf tourism "as purchasable holiday packages where clients travel more than 40 km from home, stay overnight, and intend to devote their active leisure time principally to surfing." This contrasts with more individual-istic forms of travel for surf tourism where trips are arranged away from major commercial establishments, use their own transport as far as possible. Buckley terms this as "recreational surf travel."

Surf tourism has also linked culturally and economically with adventure tourism via the backpacker market. Many companies offer surf trips by charter bus and use backpacker hostels, with a strong focus on the youth travel market. The industry is therefore highly segmented, but there is growing evidence of the rise of a more dominant market segment, catering for what Buckley has defined as the commercial surf tourist.

The limited academic literature on surf tourism suggests that the commodification of the activity has occurred in a series of stages and that the market has become complex and highly segmented. Furthermore, other commentators such as Preston-Whyte (2002) have viewed surfing through a cultural lens with a focus on "social practices and social processes" (p. 308). There is certainly evidence that many surfers are bound together by social practices and an interest in alternative lifestyles (Green & Chalip 1998). In this context, work by Booth (1995) in Australia demonstrated that surfers were resistant to regulation and that they were influenced by a variety of social problems. Others have stressed the desires of freedom and escapism as typical values held by surfers (Augustin 1998). Entwined within these values are also interests in the environment, which is not surprising given the close association between surfing and certain features of the natural landscape. Such environ-mental interests tend, however, to be fairly specific as, for example, in Southwest England and the campaign of "Surfers Against Sewage," combating the problems of beach and water pollution (Ward 1996). More recently, these environmental concerns have turned to surfers opposing the commodification of certain surf beaches and the privatisation of recreational spaces.

As we have argued, around this core culture has developed a larger, more commodified, market for surfers — mainly young people under the age of 30. This market is increasingly being served by larger tour companies, offering trips to popular surf destinations across the globe. There has also been a growth in surf lodges, surf schools and surf shops to service the growing demands of surf tourists. All these new forms of production provide opportunities for the small-scale entrepreneur who wishes to link a certain lifestyle with entrepreneurship. The remainder of this chapter focuses on the nature of lifestyle entrepreneurship in surf tourism within the context of Cornwall in England and, more especially, the resort of Newquay, which is the centre of the U.K.'s surf tourism industry.

Changing Patterns of Tourism Entrepreneurship: The Case of Surf Tourism in Cornwall

Newquay is in the top seven seaside resorts in England which together account for at least 75% of the volume and value of coastal tourism (Shaw & Williams 1997). Recent estimates claim Newquay accounts for 30% of all visitors to Cornwall, which would total approximately 1.4 m visits per annum. Compared to many other large resorts such as Blackpool or Brighton, Newquay has a significantly high proportion of long-stay holidaymakers. In this respect, the resort still markets itself as a destination for family based holidays. Monthly visitor numbers (at the peak of the season) peaked in 1989 with 26,400 visitors compared with a low of 19,300 in 1994, although since then numbers have increased rapidly to over 25,000 in the late 1990s (www.cornwall.gov.uk). These recent changes reflect not only national trends but significant local factors. Of the latter, two main ones can be identified. The first is the growth of Newquay as the U.K.'s main surfing centre, which has also stimulated a growth in youth tourism within the resort. Details on this are sketchy, as little research has been undertaken. However, local tourist officials claim that surf tourism brings in an estimated visitor spend of some £26 m per annum or 10% of all visitor spend within the resort (Williams 2002).

Newquay's tourism sector, like the rest of Cornwall, is also dominated by a small firm economy (Shaw *et al.* 1987). Current statistics show that 74.8% of all Cornish businesses have fewer than 5 employees and within tourism this proportion rises to over 87% (www.cornwall.gov.uk/Facts/Socio-ec/SE009.htm). It is within the context of surf tourism businesses that our research is focused. In particular we explore two main themes. The first concerns the characteristics of entrepreneurship in surf tourism, the role lifestyle motives play in business start-ups. Our second and more important theme is to explore the development of new lifestyle entrepreneurs within the surf tourism industry and their value systems, in the light of research in New Zealand.

The research is based on three small-scale surveys. The first of which was based around an internet search of surf tourism business in Cornwall and particularly Newquay. In terms of the latter, the internet search was supplemented by a detailed field survey of surf businesses within the resort. The second survey was a face-to-face questionnaire survey of all the identifiable surf businesses in Newquay. This was aimed at business owners although, in a number of cases, it was only possible to interview business managers. The questionnaire was, including the characteristics of the owner, lifestyle motives and business strategies, designed to collect some basic information around a number of key themes and to provide detail on the structure of Newquay's surf tourism industry. Some 28 businesses were contacted, but only 20 questionnaires were fully completed. Finally, six in-depth interviews were undertaken to gain detailed information on the aspects of lifestyle and entrepreneurship. These interviews were taped and, of course, these respondents had already completed an early questionnaire which the interview could build upon. All the survey work was undertaken during March and April 2003. It is the in-depth interviews which we mainly draw on for this chapter.

Cornwall's surfing industry is long established and well developed (Ford 2004). Three main elements have been identified in this survey, namely: retail outlets, accommodation units and surf schools. The distribution of these is shown in Figure 1. In many cases, there are strong linkages between the different elements, especially surf lodges and surf schools. There is also a dominant use of the www for marketing, with some 90% of businesses

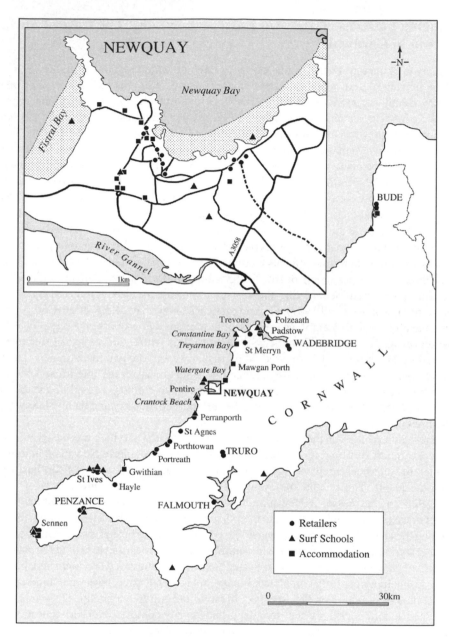

Figure 1: Distribution of main surf businesses in Newquay and Cornwall.

within our survey having a www site. Indeed, these sites appear to act as the main media for promoting the linkages between different businesses, with Newquay acting as the key focal point even in a national context.

Evidence from the Newquay survey suggests that the industry has developed in a series of stages. The first dating back to the 1970s saw the initial growth of surf shops providing equipment and clothing for the growing number of recreational surfers. A small number of these early establishments survive and accounted for a quarter of all the retailers in our survey, although the majority of retailers had established their businesses during the last 10 years.

The second phase of development dates from around the mid-1990s and has seen the growth of a more complete surf tourism industry, in particular the establishment of back-packer hostels and surf lodges, alongside a growing number of surf schools (Figure 1). This second phase has also witnessed the increasing segmentation of the industry as more facilities have been directed at the commercial surfing sector. Such changes have brought new business opportunities, initially for the small-scale operator and, more recently, for slightly larger enterprises. These opportunities are likely to change again with the development and commodification of surfing facilities at Fistral Beach. In this instance, there are strong parallels with evolution of the backpacking industry as outlined by Ateljevic & Doorne.

As we have argued, the growth of commercial surf tourism is having a marked impact on Newquay. The increasing number of young tourists being drawn into the resort has led to a thriving club scene, which is also strongly promoted on many of the www sites of surf lodges. Such developments are operating to attract more young people into the area, not only as tourists, but in search of work within the tourism sector. In this context, our survey has recorded a number of managers and operatives of surf businesses who have migrated into the area to pursue their recreational interests in surfing. This is especially the case in the surf shops, half of which were run by managers rather than owner-managers. Of the former group, 4 out of 5 respondents rated "being able to surf" as either "very important" or "important" motives. This is typified by the joint manager of one surf shop who had moved to Newquay to surf. He had selected shop work because it allowed him to "combine surfing with work as there was another assistant manager and they could work out a rota when they could go surfing." Owner-managers also recorded similar motives and a majority were dedicated surfers who had moved to Newquay to pursue their lifestyle.

The owners of surf tourism businesses were characterised as small-scale entrepreneurs, although two did operate more than one shop outlet. As with previous surveys in the small business sector, our sample was dominated by owners who had funded their business start-up with informal capital sources — personal or family savings. This was the case in the retail sector, although amongst the owners of surf-lodges it was more typical to have a combination of informal and formal funding, including bank loans. There was also another important difference between the owners of surf tourism enterprises and those from other tourism businesses previously surveyed. This concerns levels of expertise which, in the former, revolved around a strong knowledge of surfing from participating in the activity. Typical of this background was one owner of a surf lodge, aged 32, who started his business in 1996 with personal savings and a bank loan (Respondent A). He had moved from London where he was employed as an estate agent but had considerable experience as a surfer, and believed he understood what tourists would require in terms of facilities. He saw Newquay as the country's surfing mecca and undertook some market research before finding a suitable location for his business. These characteristics are similar to other owners as illustrated by another respondent. In this case, the 31 year old male had moved from Somerset to establish a surf lodge in 2001 (Respondent B). He also had combined formal and informal sources of capital, including a bank loan, to establish his business. His previous employment had been diverse and included managing restaurants and bars along with working in France as a supervisor for a holiday company. He was a long-standing surfer and believed this gave him a "strong insight into running a business based on surf tourism."

There were, however, interesting variations amongst the owners of surf accommodation, including one female respondent who owned a small surf lodge. She was older, 50 years old, had moved from London but had no connections or current interest in surfing (Respondent C). Her start-up capital was personal and came from the sale of a house in London. Surf tourism had "seemed like a good thing to be involved in as there were lots of surfers," was the respondents reasons for focussing on this sector. This case was the exception, certainly within our survey results.

The contrasts between previous studies on tourism entrepreneurs and this smaller group of owners involved in surf tourism also extend to business operations and motives. In terms of operations, the majority of businesses employed non-family labour. In contrast, the last respondent (50 year old female owner) employed only family labour. Of course, this may be purely a function of age in that many of the respondents were in their early 30s and had no children. It is also the case that the owners with surfing backgrounds did not need to rely on family networks — as many of the traditional small-scale entrepreneurs have to. The surfers appeared to have strong social networks within the surfing community, mainly of young people, from which their employees were drawn. It may also be that these networks provided important business contacts, although this remains to be investigated.

Our second main theme is to explore the nature of lifestyle entrepreneurship amongst these owners. This is in the context of differences from other owner's motives and possible similarities with the findings of work in New Zealand. In other words, are these new forms of tourism consumption producing different sets of lifestyle motives for tourism entrepreneurs. Our research had explored this theme by examining in detail the motives for establishing a business. In the majority of cases, respondents highlighted the importance of being able to surf and to allow time in their working lives to do this. For example, respondent A, detailed earlier, stated he had moved to Newquay to be able to surf and work within the surf tourism industry and to "a nicer quality of living." These strong links between lifestyle and entrepreneurship are also evident in some of the www advertising. For example, "Fistral Backpackers," a surf lodge, profiles the owners:

> Roger (joint owner) is an experienced surfer (a former member of the English Surfing Team) who has surfed all local beaches . . . as well as many locations around the world' (www.FistralBackpackers.co.uk/).

Most respondents claimed their lifestyles were now better, less stressful and, more significantly, more fulfilled because they could combine surfing with working. Respondent A, for example, claimed he would spend at least 5 hours per week surfing. In the in-depth interviews, respondents were asked to rate the main motives for operating the business and, in all six cases, two key sets of motives were identified. One set relates to lifestyle and obviously surfing, but also includes strong motives of living in a pleasant area and being in control (i.e. being their own boss). The second set related to the importance of profit motives which were rated as important by all six, as was being part of a "dynamic industry." There was, in all cases, a strong perspective on business development in that many owners had already opened other businesses or were thinking of doing so. For example, one respondent (respondent D, male of 42) owned two other surf shops in Cornwall, developed from the original business in Newquay.

It would seem that whilst lifestyles based around surfing are significant motives, these are related to entrepreneurial factors of business expansion. This does mark out these entrepreneurs from those researched in earlier surveys, some of whom could be described as non-entrepreneurs in that they were merely surviving. This certainly was not the case within the surfing businesses in this survey, where there was clear evidence of plans for expansion and development. These were not owners who had semi-retired to Cornwall showing little interest in business growth.

In terms of comparisons with the ideas developed by Ateljevic & Doorne (2000), who describe lifestyle values conditioning business operations, our evidence is less convincing. We did, however, identify a common bond between most owners who were surfers and their customers. These appear to operate at a number of levels. Firstly, surfers were perceived as being less troublesome than other tourists, second, owners understood the needs of surfers and, finally, they often shared similar views on the future growth of surfing in Newquay. However, we found very limited evidence that such owners had more ethically-orientated values in the way the businesses were operated.

Conclusions

This chapter has attempted to raise the issue of tourism consumption and production practices as a framework for understanding small-scale entrepreneurs in the tourism sector. We have argued that there appear to be visible differences in the lifestyle motives and behaviour of these entrepreneurs that relate to Fordist and post-Fordist trends in tourism consumption. These were first highlighted in New Zealand around the backpacker and adventure tourism markets. Our survey in Cornwall argues that similar trends are operating in the surf-tourism industry. In the case of Newquay, it is possible to detect a new, more dynamic group of entrepreneurs operating in the surf tourism industry for whom lifestyle factors are significant. These entrepreneurs, moreover, have distinctive differences in motives and, importantly, business operation methods, compared with their counterparts in other parts of the tourism industry. Obviously, our evidence is limited to a small-scale study and, in this context, requires further research in other parts of the industry. Our final conclusion is to strongly suggest that small-scale tourism businesses not only reflect lifestyle motives generally but also, in certain circumstances, more specific lifestyles related to new forms of tourism consumption.

References

Alonso, W. (1973). Urban zero population growth. *Daedalus, 102*, 191–206.
Ateljevic, I. (2000). Circuits of tourism: Stepping beyond the 'production/consumption' dichotomy. *Tourism Geographies, 2*(4), 369–388.

Ateljevic, I., & Doorne, S. (2000). Staying within the fence: Lifestyle entrepreneurship in tourism. *Journal of Sustainable Tourism, 8*(5), 378–392.

Ateljevic, I., & Doorne, S. (2001). Nowhere left to run: A study of value boundaries and segmentation within the backpacker market of New Zealand. In: J. A. Mazanec, G. I. Crouch, J. R. Brent-Richie, & A. G. Woodside (Eds), *Consumer psychology of tourism, hospitality and leisure* (Vol. 2, pp. 169–187). Wallingford: CABI Publishing.

Augustin, J.-P. (1998). Emergence of surfing resorts on the Aquitaine littoral. *The Geographical Review, 88*(4), 587–595.

Birley, S. (1985). The role of networks in the entrepreneurial process. *Journal of Business Venturing, 1*, 107–117.

Booth, D. (1995). Ambiguities in pleasure and discipline: The development of competitive surfing. *Journal of Sport History, 22*(3), 189–206.

Britton, S. (1991). Tourism, capital and place: Towards a critical geography. *Environment and Planning D: Society and Space, 9*, 451–478.

Buckley, R. (2002). Surf tourism and sustainable development in Indo-Pacific islands. *Journal of Sustainable Tourism, 10*(2), 405–424.

Carland, J. W., Hoy, F., Boulton, W. R., & Carland, J. A. C. (1984). Who is an entrepreneur? Is a question worth asking. *American Journal of Small Business* (Spring), 33–39.

Carlsen, J., Getz, D., & Ali-Knight, J. (2001). The environmental attitudes and practices of family businesses in rural tourism and hospitality sectors. *Journal of Sustainable Tourism, 9*, 281–297.

Curran, P., & Blackburn, R. (1994). *Small firms and local economic networks: The death of the local economy?* London: Paul Chapman.

Das, T. K., & Tend, B. S. (1997). Time and entrepreneurial risk behavior. *Entrepreneurship Theory and Practice, 22*, 69–88.

Dewhurst, P., & Horobin, H. (1998). Small business owners. In: R. Thomas (Ed.), *The management of small tourism and hospitality firms* (pp. 19–39). London: Cassell.

Ford, N. (2004). Surfing in Cornwall and the Romantic Sea. In: S. Fisher, M. Duffy, & P. Payton (Eds), *The maritime history of Cornwall* (forthcoming). Foxher: Exeter University Press.

Getz, D., & Carlson, J. (2000). Characteristics and goals of family and owner-operated businesses in rural tourism and hospitality sectors. *Tourism Management, 21*, 547–560.

Gibson, B., & Cassar, G. (2002). Planning behaviour variables in small firms. *Journal of Small Business Management, 4*, 171–186.

Goffee, R., & Scase, R. (1983). Class entrepreneurship and the service sector: Toward a conceptual classification. *Service Industries Journal, 3*, 146–160.

Hill, J., McGowan, P., & Drummond, P. (1999). The development and application of a qualitative approach to researching the marketing networks of small firm entrepreneurs. *Qualitative Market Research: An International Journal, 2*, 71–81.

Hitchens, D. M., O'Farrell, P. N., & Conway, C. (1994). Business use by manufacturing firms in mid-Wales. *Environment and Planning A, 26*, 95–106.

Johannisson, B. (2000). Networking and entrepreneurial growth. In: D. L. Sexton, & H. Landström (Eds), *The Blackwell handbook of entrepreneurship*. Oxford: Blackwell.

Kickul, J., & Gundry, L. K. (2002). Prospecting for strategic advantage: The proactive entrepreneurial personality and small firm innovation. *Journal of Small Business Management, 40*, 85–97.

Morrison, A., Rimmington, M., & Williams, C. (1999). *Entrepreneurship in hospitality, tourism and leisure industries*. Oxford: Butterworth Heinemann.

Mowforth, M., & Munt, I. (2003). *Tourism and sustainability: Development and new tourism in the third world* (2nd ed.). London: Routledge.

Paniagna, A. (2002). Urban-rural migration, tourism entrepreneurs and rural restructuring in Spain. *Tourism Geographies, 4*, 349–371.

Phelps, N. A., Fallon, R. J., & Williams, C. L. (2001). Small firms, borrowed size and the urban-rural shift. *Regional Studies, 35,* 613–624.

Preston-Whyte, R. (2002). Constructions of surfing space at Durban, South Africa. *Tourism Geographies, 4*(3), 307–328.

Richards, G. (1996). Production and consumption of European cultural tourism. *Annals of Tourism Research, 23,* 261–283.

Sharpley, R. (1994). *Tourism, tourists and society.* Huntingdon: ELM Publications.

Shaw, G. (2003). Entrepreneurial cultures and small business enterprises in tourism. In: M. Hall, A. Lew, & A. Williams (Eds), *Blackwells companion to tourism geography.* Oxford: Blackwell.

Shaw, G., & Williams, A. M. (1997). The private sector: Tourism entrepreneurship — a constraint or resource? In: G. Shaw, & A. Williams (Eds), *The rise and fall of British coastal resorts* (pp. 117–136). London: Mansell.

Shaw, G., & Williams, A. M. (1998). Entrepreneurship, small business culture and tourism development. In: D. Ioannides, & K. D. Debbage (Eds), *The economic geography of the tourism industry* (pp. 235–255). London: Routledge.

Shaw, G., & Williams, A. M. (2002). *Critical issues in tourism: A geographical perspective* (2nd ed.). Oxford: Blackwell.

Shaw, G., Williams, A. M., & Greenwood, J. (1987). *Tourism and the economy of Cornwall.* Exeter: Department of Geography, University of Exeter.

Snepenger, D. J., Johnson, J. D., & Rasker, R. (1995). Travel — stimulated entrepreneurial migration. *Journal of Travel Research, 34,* 40–44.

Storey, D. J. (1994). *Understanding the small business sector.* London: Routledge.

Swedburg, R. (Ed.) (2000). *Entrepreneurship: A social science view.* Oxford: Blackwell.

Thomas, R., Friel, M., Jameson, S., & Parsons, D. (1997). *The national survey of small tourism and hospitality firms: Annual report 1996–1997.* Leeds: Centre for the Study of Small Tourism and Hospitality Firms, Leeds Metropolitan University.

Tinsley, R., & Lynch, P. (2001). Small tourism business networks and destination development. *International Journal of Hospitality Management, 20,* 367–378.

Tourism Associates (1997). *China clay area business survey: Tourism/retail sector.* Exeter: Tourism Associates, University of Exeter.

Tourism Research Group (1996). *TEMPT survey report.* Exeter: Department of Geography, University of Exeter.

Urry, J. (1995). *Consuming places.* London: Routledge.

Williams, J. (2002). *A study of the influence of surfing and surf culture on the identity of its participants, inside the case study of surf tourism in Newquay.* Unpublished dissertation, Department of Geography, University of Exeter. www.cornwall.gov.uk/Facts/tour08.htm (Accessed March 2003).

Williams, A. M., Shaw, G., & Greenwood, J. (1989). From tourist to tourism entrepreneur, from consumption to production: Evidence from Cornwall, England. *Environment and Planning A, 21,* 1639–1653.

Chapter 8

Success and Growth in Rural Tourism Micro-Businesses in Finland: Financial or Life-Style Objectives?

Raija Komppula

Introduction

Rural tourism is tourism that takes place outside densely populated communities and tourist centres. It is often considered small-sized and connected to the farming industry and outdoor activities that offer the guests individual service (Borg 1997). Rural tourism is local tourism, tourism "of the area," sought after and controlled by local authorities (Grolleau 1996: 7). According to Bramwell (1993), the small scale of firms and their functional relationship with nature, heritage or traditional societies make them rural.

Rural tourism in Finland includes cottage holidays, farm holidays, bed and breakfast lodging, farm visits and group catering, organised activity services and holiday villages (Finnish Tourist Board 1994: 1–2). The estimated number of this kind of rural tourism businesses in Finland is about 4000 (Ahlgren 2000; Martikainen 2002). In accommodation statistics, only businesses with more than ten rooms or cottages are included, which means that only about 5% of rural tourism accommodation units are included in the statistics.

According to the National Rural Tourism Working Group three quarters of the rural tourism businesses have originally been farms. However, today tourism is a major source of income for only 25% of the rural tourism entrepreneurs (Martikainen 2002). The average turnover of a full-time rural tourism business in Finland is about 120.000€ (Puurunen 2001). Profitability of full-time tourism enterprises is also weak (Kupiainen et al. 2000), which in most cases is a consequence of the seasonality of the businesses (Martikainen 2002).

While rural tourism has much to do with farms, agriculturalists view rural tourism as a category of farm diversification, whereas tourism researchers and regional tourism promoters consider it to be a sector of tourism in its own right (Busby & Rendle 2000: 635). Diversification is one way for a small rural firm to reduce a firm's risk of being too dependent upon one product, to gain growth and confirm the income of the owner-manager. Tourism is the third most popular means of farm diversification in Finland (Rantamäki-Lahtinen 2002) and 39% of the rural tourism entrepreneurs are still farmers, too (Martikainen 2002: 10–11).

The rural tourism industry in Finland is characterised by part-time tourism entrepreneurship, limited financial resources, limited entrepreneurial skills and a low level of commitment to long term development of the businesses (Komppula 2000b).

The promotion of tourism SMEs by the European union and its member states is seen as particularly significant in relation to the development of the remote regions of the union (Wanhill 2000). Tourism is seen as a tool for developing the rural areas and the national, as well as local, authorities set development goals for the regions, including goals for the growth of the industry. The national level authorities responsible for rural tourism development in Finland have set a goal for doubling the supply and the demand of rural tourism services in the first six years of the 21st century (http://www.mmm.fi/maasmatk/enggroup.htm 31.3.2001).

The rural tourism industries have low entry barriers. Many new businesses are created as a result of identifying an opportunity, following experiences of neighbours, or new businesses build on the back of a hobby or interest. For individuals with no business or industry background, many of the skills have to be learnt whilst "on the job" (Morrison *et al.* 1999: 128). A remarkable part of rural tourism businesses are started by immigrants, who seek "rural peace." For them, accessibility to a preferred way of life is more important than how large a business one has. Others vastly prefer to be with their family and spouse and live in a non-urban area they consider very attractive (Timmons 1999: 36).

If the rural tourism industry is to meet with the goals of the national, regional and local level development programs in Finland there are two ways to achieve the objectives: to expand the existing rural tourism businesses and/or to establish new businesses. But because the individual entrepreneurs are independent of each other in decisions and actions, the goals of the region may come into conflict: the entrepreneurs may have lifestyle-oriented goals with no expectations of growth, or the companies are willing but unable to grow. It can be argued that this is often the case in Finland.

Among many others Dewhurst & Horobin (1998) note that in the tourism industry there is a great number of entrepreneurs "who are not motivated by a desire to maximise economic gain, who operate business often with very low levels of employment and in which managerial decisions are often based on highly personalised criteria" (25). Based on this notion, they have suggested a model of owner-manager tendencies, a model of a continuum for small-business owner manager that lies between commercial and lifestyle goals and strategies. In this paper, I concentrate on the rural tourism entrepreneurs' definitions of success and growth. I argue that an entrepreneur's definition of success and growth is comprised of his/her attitudes towards the need for growth in business, needs and expectations for continuation of the firm and various quality aspects, i.e. quality of life, quality of service and quality of the product.

Small Firm Success

Chell & Baines (1998) argue that what counts as "success" may be judged differently from that of "performance." According to them, performance is most often compounded into hard criteria such as increased turnover, wider profit margins and so on, which are often taken to be the "male" attitudes towards the issue (Chell & Baines 1998: 118). Sandberg *et al.*

(2002) define the performance of small businesses as their ability to contribute to job and wealth creation through business start-up, survival and growth (Sandberg *et al.* 2002: 3).

Success is often equated with the achievement of clearly defined and measurable performance targets (Chell & Baines 1998: 118), which on the other hand may be of a subjective nature as well as financial. According to Keats & Bracker (1988), small firm performance is substantially influenced by the individual characteristics and behaviour of the owner, and task environment characteristics. In this study, the terms "success" and "performance" are used interchangeably, in the same manner as they are referred to in the literature.

Rosa *et al.* (1996) have outlined four different measures of performance: (1) Primary performance measures (number of employees, growth in employees, turnover, and value of capital assets); (2) proxy performance measures (geographical range of markets, VAT registration); (3) subjective measures (including the ability of the business to meet business and domestic needs); and (4) entrepreneurial performance measures (the desire for growth, the ownership of multiple businesses). Hard financial measures of success are easy to understand, apply, administer and to compare. An alternative to pure financial measures are affective or subjective measures, such as lifestyle and personal freedom, and a balance between work and domestic responsibility.

Financial performance and growth are closely associated: growth seems to be an appropriate strategy for small firms to enhance their financial performance (Wiklund 1998). The desire for growth has often been regarded to be the criterion by which the enterprises are classified into entrepreneurial or life-style oriented firms. The life-style entrepreneur targets survival and a maintenance of life-style that he or she may have been accustomed to in a previous life. For him/her, issues of family roots and location take precedent. The second type will be concerned with growth and expansion, with the entrepreneur eventually owning several companies (Freel 1999: 201). The definition of an entrepreneurial firm implies the promise of expansion and the building of long-term value and durable cash flow streams as well. Often it takes a long time for a new company to become established and grow (Timmons 1999: 34).

According to Gibb & Davies (1990, 1992), academic approaches to understanding SMEs growth can be categorized into four groups: an entrepreneur's personality and goals, the owner-manager's influence on the development of her/his business, various business skills related to growth and finally, sectored approaches that mostly concentrate on various industries and their practical problems, particularly those of external factors and constraints. Davidsson (1991) argues that all the specific low-level explanatory variables used earlier to explain small firm growth can be regarded as aspects of one of three major determinants, which are ability, need and opportunity. A firm's growth motivation is determined by subjective factors (perceived ability, need and opportunity), which influence growth motivation and direct behaviour, as well as objective factors (ability, need and opportunity) that only partly determine subjective perceptions. Nevertheless, they can have important direct effects on actual growth.

In Davidsson's (1991) model, three first-order factors are used as indicators of growth motivation: cognitive attitude towards growth, affective attitude and growth aspirations. The indicators for cognitive attitude towards growth are the expectations of what consequences growth would have with respect to eight specific dimensions: workload, work-tasks, employee well-being, private finances, control, independence, crisis survival ability and product/service quality. Affective attitude is an overall attitude measurement that reflects reactions towards a hypothetical increase of the firm's size by 25 and 100% respectively. Growth aspirations are measured with two indicators: (1) difference between present size and an ideal size five years ahead in terms of the number of employees and (2) the same for turnover.

Davidsson's (1991) empirical analyses supports the assumptions that perceptions of ability, need and opportunity influence growth motivation. Objective ability, need and opportunity can only, in part, explain differences in the perception of these factors. Truly direct effects of these three objective factors on growth may exist alongside the motivation mediated effects. Davidsson argues that, in particular, his results support the idea that the individual matters: the need factors included in the study suggest that the core of the matter is the subjectively perceived situation and its relation to personal goals.

Perren (1999) suggests that the owner-manager's desire to succeed is the most prominent factor influencing the owner's growth motivation. Perren refers to McCelland (1961) who originally proposed the "need for achievement" as an important component of entrepreneurship. In Perren's framework, the desire to succeed and the owner's growth motivation are separated: his data also supported the conception that some entrepreneurs had a high desire to achieve but it was not always directed towards the growth of the firm. According to Davidsson (1991), perceived need consists of economic satisfaction and the need for achievement. The more satisfied the entrepreneur is with the economic situation the less need there is for growth. Perren (1999), nevertheless, seems to take a need for growth as granted if the firm is to develop.

Enterprise growth has also been handled through various life cycle approaches in which enterprises follow predetermined phases from birth to death via periods of fast growth (Kolvereid 1992). Common to these described approaches is that they take growth for granted: firms are expected to be willing to grow and capable of growth (Johannisson 1990). Storey (1994) postulates that small firm growth is driven by three integral component sets, which are identifiable in different stages of the firm's life cycle: characteristics of the entrepreneur (identifiable pre-start), characteristics of the firm (identifiable at start) and characteristics of the corporate strategy (identifiable post start). Irwin (2000) suggests an alternative model basing the stages of the enterprise development on attitudinal stages through which an entrepreneur might progress. According to him, many, however, stop at the point where the barrier to moving to the next stage is too great to surmount. Many researchers have come to the conclusion that maintaining the present enterprise size is satisfying even for the majority of enterprises (Davidsson 1991).

Mäki & Pukkinen's (2000) study on barriers to growth and employment in Finnish small enterprises was based on Davidsson's model. According to their results, experts responsible for public sector support for developing the SMEs emphasised that the entrepreneur's need for growth depends on the motives for entrepreneurship. Cliff (1998) came to the same conclusion in her study. But the entrepreneurs' interviews only partly confirmed the effect of start-up motivation on growth: if the primary motivation for entrepreneurship was to avoid stress and pressure at work, then s/he does not want to grow. But even when in the beginning motivation was only towards self-employment or making one's living, objectives may change. And, originally a growth-oriented entrepreneur may realise that her/his plans for growth were not realistic.

According to Davidsson (1991), important factors that affect the objective need for growth are the age and size of the firm and the owner-manager's age. Perceived needs consist of economic satisfaction and need for achievement: the more satisfied the owner-manager is with the economic situation the less need there is for growth. Glancey's (1998) results amongst small manufacturing firms in a region in Scotland gave strong evidence that older firms grow less rapidly than younger firms, a result which is in contrast with most previous studies. According to Glancey, the differences in entrepreneurial motivations could provide one with a possible explanation for these results.

According to Cliff (1998), female entrepreneurs seem to prefer a smaller size company than men; a size, which is comfortably manageable, which enables her to maintain control of the organization, devote a reasonable amount of time and energy to the firm and/or balance work and personal life. For female entrepreneurs in particular, personal considerations appear to override economic considerations in business expansion decisions.

Chell & Baines' results (1998) among 104 micro-businesses show no significant difference between the performance of the business of sole male and sole female owners but clear evidence of the underperformance of spouse-owned businesses. According to Baines & Wheelock (1998), family involvement in micro-businesses is most commonly spouses. Often the spouse may have separate work but still offers unpaid support in some way which indicates that they often regard the business as a family-business (Baines & Wheelock 1998: 23–24). Although Rosa *et al.*'s (1996) results demonstrated some considerable gender differences in quantitative economic and financial performance measures, they concluded that the complexity of the overall pattern of results suggests that a more sophisticated interpretation was required than to simply attribute differences to gender alone.

Westhead & Cowling (1997) did not find significant contrasts between family and non-family companies with regard to a variety of hard performance indicators. According to their results, family companies are not solely profit maximizers. To a greater extent, their prime objectives are to maintain/enhance the lifestyle of the owners or to provide employment for family members in the management team. Baines *et al.* (1997, 1998) discovered that neither family resources and responsibilities nor the gender of the owner/s determine where businesses are positioned on the spectrum of "intention to grow" but these factors do impinge upon, with varying degrees of intensity according to the personal circumstances, the past experiences, and the values and beliefs of the owners. According to their results, becoming an employer for the first time is a hard and even painful process for many business owners.

The theory of lifestyle issues being equally, if not more, important as financial criteria with respect to the measurement of small business success was tested by Walker (2000) within one industry sector in Australia. Her results show that larger small businesses use financial measures of success to a greater extent than micro-businesses. Those who measure their success financially also place a high value on lifestyle and personal freedom. Pasanen's (1999) findings in Eastern Finland emphasize that there are several paths to success and that the growth rate is not the only and best measure of success. Pasanen suggests that for local and regional development it is possible to foster the preconditions of success of SMEs and to direct development actions to critical targets, by paying attention to the foundations of success.

Measurement of success often requires evaluation between objectives and achievements. According to Greenbank (2001), micro-business owner-managers invariably have objectives, but they do not always make them explicit. These objectives tend to relate to personal rather than business criteria. Greenbank argues that the vast majority of micro-business owner-managers indicate little inclination to maximise profit or pursue growth. In practice, micro-businesses generally pursue a number of economic and non-economic objectives such as income levels, job satisfaction, working hours, control and flexibility. Behaviour is most appropriately characterised in terms of satisfying behaviour.

According to Lynch (1998), it is arguable that firms in the hospitality sector have something unique or at least distinct about them, particularly with regard to hospitality micro-enterprises, where the private home is often used as the business unit. Carlsen & Getz (2000) also argue that there are good reasons to believe that in rural tourism motives and goals in running the businesses will be somewhat different from other sectors and from non-family businesses in general. The most important start-up goal in Carlsen & Getz's West-Australian sample was desired life-style in the countryside. In terms of operating goals, two factors clearly differentiate between family/lifestyle and business: although there is an emphasis on maintaining high moral standards and quality service, maintaining profitability is also an important operating goal. Growth of the business was not considered as important as enjoying the job and keeping the business manageable in size. A desire to maintain close personal contact with the customers was typical for rural tourism entrepreneurs. Seasonality was a big operational problem, business plans were not common. A conflict between business goals and goals for the family was evident. Another important issue was a lack of succession planning in rural tourism family business (Carlsen & Getz 2000; Getz & Carlsen 2000). Similar results have been reported by Ateljevic & Doome (2000) and Hall & Rusher (2002) in New Zealand as well as by King et al. (1998) in Australia. In a Cornish study (cited in Shaw & Williams 1990: 77–78), a desire for a better way of life might be a motivation for those 55% of entrepreneurs who were in-migrants to Cornwall.

Lassila's results from one region in Eastern-Finland show that the rural tourism entrepreneurs define success with non-economic measures. Ninety-two percent of the entrepreneurs see the future of the company as very or quite positive and about 70% aimed at developing or expanding its business in the near future (Lassila 2000b). But the measures of development were more quality than quantity oriented. Success as an entrepreneur meant to them more or less the continuity of the firm, and the possibility to offer the next generation an opportunity to earn their living as an entrepreneur (Lassila 2000a).

Rural Tourism Businesses in Finland

The aim of the study was to examine the growth motivation and definition of success in the rural tourism industry in Eastern Finland. The results of the study were to assist policy-makers in understanding the factors that stimulate or prevent growth with a view to informing the development of more effective business support strategies.

The empirical data were collected in two phases. The first part of the data were collected during autumn 2001 as a part of a more extensive study on the characteristics of rural tourism entrepreneurship in four regions in Eastern Finland:[1] North-Savo, South-Savo, North-Karelia and Kainuu. This paper presents the results of this study particularly for the aspects relating to growth and success, which refer to the growth- or life-style orientation of the entrepreneur. The data offer interesting information on the motives behind starting a rural tourism business, the capital structure of the business and the continuation planning (succession).

The population of the study consisted of 178 businesses, which produced tourism services either on a full-time or part-time basis outside the main cities or tourism centres. These businesses were first selected from the tourism marketing mailing lists of the regional tourism organisations within the area with the help of local rural tourism experts. The interviewed businesses were then selected from this population on a quasi-random sampling basis (every forth address). Personal interviews comprised of open as well as structured questions.

The second part of the study was carried out in the form of personal thematic interviews during spring 2002 in one of the regions, namely North-Karelia. In the light of results from previous studies (e.g. Komppula 1997, 2000b; Mäki & Pukkinen 2000), it was suggested that the ideas of entrepreneurs on growth and success could be dependent upon how long the enterprise has been in operation and how extensive its operations are. Based on this, fourteen enterprises, which were considered to be typical representatives of their own category, were selected amongst the population of 160 companies, taking into account that none of the companies interviewed in the first part of the study would be in this sample. The criteria for the categories were the full-time or part-time status of the business, the age of the enterprise, the extensiveness of operations and the speed of growth. For the interviews, those enterprises which were as varied as possible were sought after in order to highlight the differences between their concepts.

The entrepreneur was asked to describe the history of the business from inception to present day, his/her growth objectives at different development stages, factors enhancing and hindering growth and the entrepreneur's ideas on what success as an entrepreneur means. Finally, the entrepreneur was asked to describe how she/he envisages her/his enterprise's future in five year's time. The interviews were recorded and transcribed.

Results

Structured Interviews

The distribution of data by region and gender was as follows (Table 1).

Forty-eight percent of the respondents were at least 51 years old, and even 16% were over 61. The level of education amongst the interviewed entrepreneurs was fairly low, in that one third had no vocational training whatsoever and only 24% had done their matriculation examination. However, 81% of the entrepreneurs had participated in further training that dealt with tourism business during their entrepreneurship, female entrepreneurs were more active than men in further training. Rural tourism entrepreneurs seem to have very "entrepreneurial" roots: 70% of the respondents state that his/her parents were also entrepreneurs or farmers.

Thirty-four percent of the respondents state that they earn their living by having several sources of income. Only 49% of the respondents earn over 50% of their income from the tourism businesses. Over 70% of all businesses but only 35% of those businesses run by

Table 1: Male and female respondents by region.

Region	No. Respondents	%	Male (%)	Female (%)
South-Savo	67	38	67	33
North-Karelia	45	25	40	60
North-Savo	40	23	53	47
Kainuu	26	15	62	38
	178	100	56	44

over 61 years old entrepreneurs serve their customers all year round. Only 18% of the businesses use employed workers, whereas 82% operate with family members only. Thirty percent employ only one member of the family. 55% of the respondents state that the tourism business is profitable, 8% regard it loss-making.

The respondents were asked to evaluate the development of their businesses during the last 12 months. The results show that more than half of the respondents have succeeded to increase their profits, turnover and number of clients although money used in marketing, and number of personnel has in most cases been the same or even less than earlier (Table 2).

Less than half of the entrepreneurs have used external sources of finance to develop their tourism businesses. The most common sources of finance are cash-flow, revenues from other businesses, savings and different kinds of public support. Occupation rates in rural tourism were very low: in accommodation mean was 35%, in catering 33% and in activity services 29%.

The objective of the project was to examine the entrepreneurs' desire to grow their business's operations and the entrepreneur's attitude against business success. In the structured interview, the desire to grow was measured against the growth of the turnover, so that all the sub-branches of rural tourism (accommodation, catering and activity services) could be measured with one unambiguous meter.

Thirty percent of businesses stated that their aim was to maintain business activities as at present, with 6% of the respondents wanting to decrease activities. 10% of the respondents aimed to expand the businesses rapidly, with 55% aiming to grow slowly in the long run.

Table 2: Development of tourism business within the past 12 months.

	Same (%)	Higher (%)	Lower (%)	I Don't Know (%)
Number of clients	25	66	7	2
Average stay of clients	51	37	5	6
Turnover	21	69	6	4
Number of personnel	79	16	4	2
Profit	29	62	3	4
Money used for marketing	47	31	18	2

Since the frequencies in categories "aim to grow rapidly" and "aim to decrease" are so low, the two first mentioned categories are here combined and called as established businesses (36%) and the two others as growth-oriented businesses (65%).There is a clear difference in the willingness to grow the turnover between male and female in the data: 70% of male and 56% of female entrepreneurs were growth-oriented. The growth-oriented entrepreneurs operated in a clearly wider domain than the established businesses: 42% of the established companies offered accommodation only and 17% offer accommodation, catering and activity services, whereas the corresponding percentages for the growth-oriented were 32 and 27%. Businesses that employed workers were more often growth-oriented than those that did not.

Those who want to grow their businesses quickly were significantly younger than the others and those who were going to decrease the business were in 63% of cases more than 61 years old. The quickly growing entrepreneurs also operate most often all year round and have in most cases a wider domain of businesses than the established ones.

The respondents were asked to evaluate their motives for becoming a tourism entrepreneur (Appendix 1). The most important motives were the interesting and challenging character of the industry, independence and freedom of entrepreneur and coming across a good opportunity. For the growth-oriented the interesting character of tourism businesses was even more important than for the established. A good opportunity and earning extra income, however, were more often the motive of the established businesses, although the difference was not statistically significant. Independence and the freedom of the entrepreneur were more important for males than females. For male respondents the existing premises were a more important motive for starting the tourism businesses than for females. The importance of maintaining the business activity to leave it to the children was also more important for the males.

Fifty-three percent of the growth-oriented respondents and even 70% of the established prefer to avoid economic risk and investment than to go into debt in order to expand business activities.

More than half of the entrepreneurs were reluctant to mortgage personal property as collateral for business debts. Half of the respondents state that development of the businesses with borrowed capital does not belong to their principals. The established businesses apparently aim to develop their businesses mainly through cash-flow financing; they believed more often that without borrowed capital growth was too slow (Appendix 2).

Forty-one to sixty years old entrepreneurs desire, more often than other age categories, time with their family. Seventy-nine percent felt that entrepreneurship was challenging and interesting from the point of view of the whole family. Women were more often than men fairly happy with their career prospects and their possibilities to develop as entrepreneurs. Seventy-five percent of the respondents considered the physical setting of the business (buildings, childhood home, scenery, surroundings) a significant reason for acting as an entrepreneur. This was significantly more important for the growth-oriented than for the established businesses. More than half of the respondents believed that the quality of life as a tourist entrepreneur was better than if the person were a wage earner, and of the growth-oriented this is the case even more often than amongst the established companies. Seventy-three percent of the respondents considered happiness and the quality of life more important than great economic profits.

The entrepreneurs were also asked to describe their own tourism entrepreneurship with one word or expression. The dispersion of the answers was large, but a few typical categories could be found: Challenging work, Desire to serve, Interesting work, Source of livelihood, and Way of life. 54% of the respondents worked in a business whose premises had been passed to their current owner within the same family, 26% had bought the business from an outsider. Half of the respondents considered that their children might continue the businesses after they retired. Half of these businesses are considering succession within the next ten years.

In-depth Interviews

Four of the fourteen interviewees had ended up as entrepreneurs through coincidence and only two completely new enterprises had started their operations on a full-time basis from the start. With respect to the others, the operations were still either part-time (6) or at least had started as such. Over half of the interviewed companies had previously worked within agriculture. The growth in all but one had been very slow and there were normally no long-term business plans. The capacity was increased if there seemed to be a demand for it. The problem with the rapidly grown company turned out to be an over-estimated capacity and a low occupation rate during the recession.

Growth was considered specifically to be growth through investment and increase in the capacity, which also entails hiring an outside work force. Other financial measures of success, like an increase of turnover or profits were understood as "normal objectives of business" but not as measures of growth, as such. All but two of the interviewees may be characterised as life-style entrepreneurs, since growth was not an objective in their operations. Entrepreneurs who had an agricultural background or owned fixed property considered the return on investment as important, and additional building was, in these cases, related specifically to this objective. An increase in capacity and number of clients was deemed necessary only within the limits of securing a livelihood, because extensive growth requires more full-time employees. Only one enterprise regarded hiring outside labour as desirable and one as possible, the others wanted to specifically ensure that the company only employed family members. Employment was seen as troublesome, strangers were not wanted for work in the home and the expenses related to employment were considered high in general.

Only two entrepreneurs mentioned growth as a measure of success. Eleven respondents considered customer satisfaction and the creation of long-term customer relationships as the most important indicator of success. Getting rich is not even an objective; a reasonable livelihood was considered sufficient and if this were the outcome of not having to worry about extensive debts and sufficient demand, then the entrepreneurs would consider themselves to be successful. Nevertheless, two of the respondents mentioned profits as a primary measure of success and one as one of the measures. Eight of the interviewed entrepreneurs also mentioned quality of life factors as indicators of success.

Of factors affecting success, co-operation with other entrepreneurs in the same field rose above all others. Networking was seen as particularly important amongst activity operators. The quality of the product and the capabilities of the entrepreneur were also important factors affecting success. Those entrepreneurs who had previously worked within agriculture also considered a healthy capital structure as a particular key factor to their success; growth was financed with cash-flow or revenue from selling forest, not with loans.

Half of the respondents felt that the most important barrier to firm growth was low demand for the services, which caused insufficient profits. Four entrepreneurs felt that growth was restricted by some external factors, high taxation, and other state actions. In relation to two other enterprises, it became evident that the transfer of the business to the descendant was financially problematic and might even lead to closing down the business. Family estates were not sold to outsiders, so if there were no one to take on the business or the transfer were too complicated, the operations may be stopped rather than sold.

In five year's time, one of the new and two of the older enterprises hoped to have operations on a wider scale than at present, five in the development stage hope to have reached their growth objectives in relation to the number of customers and to have established their position, two believed that their operations would continue as they are at the moment, and one intended to downsize. The rest will either have been transferred to their children or to a new entrepreneur, provided that they have not closed down the business due to problems related to continuity.

Discussion

The data show that the motives for starting rural tourism businesses in Eastern Finland are in most cases related to existing premises, which make the accommodation or activity services as an opportunity to earn extra income and/or employ one or even more family members. Many rural tourism businesses start as part-time enterprises. Entrepreneurs also have, at least in the beginning of the businesses, several sources of income. The diversification of the businesses is probably one of the reasons why the growth in tourism businesses is often very slow: the entrepreneur has to choose between several options when deciding whether to concentrate in one field of business or to maintain several ones. If the entrepreneur has to manage several at the same time, the personal resources to develop all of them are limited.

The results also support the findings of Baines *et al.* (1997, 1998), Carlsen & Getz (2000) and Lynch (1998): another barrier to rural tourism firm growth is the entrepreneurs' reluctance to employ a full-time workforce from outside the family. Becoming an employee is seen a troublesome and risky process and having strangers working in one's home is felt displeasing. Entrepreneurs want to maintain their close personal contact with the customers. Customer satisfaction and the creation of long-term customer relationships is — for many — an important indicator of success. Satisfied customers are important marketers of rural tourism, and regular customers will guarantee the growth of turnover in the long-run.

A typical rural tourism entrepreneur rather avoids economic risks than wants to make rapid growth investments in his/her businesses. In many cases the family has already reached a certain standard of living, which the entrepreneurs do not want to risk. Most of the entrepreneurs seemed to have an image of an ideal size of businesses that was the objective for the development of the activities. In general, success was primarily measured by affective and subjective measures: reasonable level of income was more important than getting rich, time for family and hobbies was respected, interesting and challenging work and the opportunity to work at home or in the countryside were very important for the entrepreneurs.

According to the in-depth interviews, growth of turnover was not seen as a measure of firm growth because increasing the turnover is, in most cases, possible and even probable without an increase in employment or investments in equipment, which the entrepreneurs seem to count as measures of firm growth. Growth in turnover was desirable according to most entrepreneurs but without any growth in labour or investment in expansion of the capacity. Given the low occupation rates of the industry, this is easy to understand. Investment in the quality of existing capacity (for example, refurbishment of the accommodation) may increase the occupancy rate as well as turnover, but not the capacity itself, which means that the firm will not expand, but the profitability will develop.

In consequence, the results show that rural tourism entrepreneurs do have need for achievement, but in most cases it is directed towards rather qualitative than quantitative objectives. However, regardless of which measures of success are used, it can be argued that owners of small rural tourism establishments are in business primarily to earn their living, which calls for at least sufficient profit.

The results of this study do show only limited evidence about the differences between the growth-oriented and established entrepreneurs. It can be argued that rapid growth expectations might be more likely among young, full-time operators that have bought or inherited the premises of the tourism businesses. Nevertheless, the affective and subjective measures of success, and the tendency to avoid economic risk are as common among those, who wish rapid or slow growth, or among those, who wish to maintain the business as it is. The cognitive attitude towards growth (the expectations of what consequences growth would have with respect to workload, work-tasks, employee well-being, private finances, control, independence, crisis survival ability and product/service quality) seems to have a crucial role in rural tourism entrepreneur's growth-orientation. The results also give some support to Mäki & Pukkinen's (2000) and Cliff's (1998) results and suggest that the growth objectives may change over time.

Reasons for a minor desire for growth in these data are often related to the entrepreneurs' age or state of health: an entrepreneur near retirement does not have the motivation to invest more in the tourism business, especially if there is no possibility for succession or other means of continuity. This, together with the above mentioned finding about rapid growth entrepreneurs, suggests that in order to discover the real growth potential of the rural tourism industry in Finland, in-depth research should concentrate on younger proprietors, who, at the moment, are a clear minority in the rural tourism businesses in Finland.

Conclusion

The results presented in this chapter are broadly in accordance with many other studies conducted in the tourism field (see Ateljevic *et al.* 2000; Busby & Rendle 2000; Carlsen & Getz 2000; Clarke *et al.* 2001; Dewhurst & Horobin 1998; Getz & Carlsen 2000; Grolleau 1996; Hall & Rusher 2002; King *et al.* 1998; Lassila 2000a, b; Lynch 1998; Morrison *et al.* 1999; Shaw & Williams 1990; Thomas 2000; Walker 2000). The results also support the argument of Shaw & Williams (1990), who suggest that future research on tourism and economic development will need to more closely examine the relationships between the nature of entrepreneurship, the structural characteristics of the tourism industry and its impact on economic change. The affective and financial performance of local entrepreneurs also holds the key to developing stronger benefits from tourism. According to Thomas (2000), it is clear that although the relative importance of small tourism firms in terms of employment is not increasing, they remain a significant component of the tourism industry. The effectiveness of various dimensions of tourism policy would be enhanced if more attention were given to understanding small tourism businesses.

A new approach is needed in the small tourism business support policy and its implication. Many of the support systems in rural tourism development currently necessitate a high degree of commitment and involvement on the part of small firms. In most cases, the financial support is allocated on condition that the company may commit to growth objectives. Nevertheless, many of the lifestyle-oriented owner-managers may be reluctant to make such a commitment and they may, therefore, be unwilling to participate in development programs (Dewhurst & Horobin 1998; Komppula 2000a, b). Watts *et al.* (1998) emphasize that growth should more usefully be placed within an environmental context and should not be confused with progress. Growth can be characterised as symbiotic with environments, i.e. growth is not an "imposition" but rather an adaptation (Watts *et al.* 1998: 109–110). In the tourism development programs, the acceptance for "growth in quality but not in volume" might be the way to balance the divergence between common development policy and private interests.

Note

1. The data were collected together with Principal Lecturer Hilkka Lassila from North Savo Polytechnic. She analysed the data concerning succession planning in these businesses.

References

Ahlgren, H. (2000). Tilastotietoja maaseutumatkailusta [Rural Tourism Statistics]. *Maaseutumatkailu [Rural Tourism Journal]* (Autumn). http:www.mmm.fi/maasmatk/lehti/b0007b.htm (31.3.2001).

Ateljevic, I., & Doome, S. (2000). Staying within the fence: Life style entrepreneurship in tourism. *Journal of Sustainable Tourism, 8*(5), 378–392.

Baines, S., & Wheelock, J. (1998). Working for each other: Gender, the household and micro-business survival and growth. *International Small Business Journal, 17*(1), 16–35.

Baines, S., Wheelock, J., & Abrams, A. (1997). Micro-business and the household: Micro-businesses owner-managers social context: Household, family and growth or non-growth. In: D. Deakins, P. Jennings, & C. Mason (Eds), *Small firms. Entrepreneurship in the nineties* (pp. 47–60). London: Paul Shapman Publishing Ltd.

Borg, P. (1997). Maaseutumatkailun suuri tuleminen. *Maaseudun uusi aika* 1/97.

Bramwell, B. (1993). *Tourism strategies and rural development.* Paris: OECD.

Busby, G., & Rendle, S. (2000). The transition from tourism on farms to farm tourism. *Tourism Management, 21*(2000), 635–642.

Carlsen, J., & Getz, D. (2000). *Relatively speaking: Business goals and operating issues for rural, family owned/operated tourism and hospitality businesses* (pp. 1–20). Paper presented at ICSB Brisbane, Queensland (June).

Chell, E., & Baines, S. (1998). Does Gender affect business "performance"? A study of micro-businesses in business services in the U.K. *Entrepreneurship and Regional Development, 10,* 117–135.

Clarke, J., Denman, R., Hickman, G., & Slovak, J. (2001). Rural tourism in Roznava Okres: A Slovak case study. *Tourism Management, 22*(April), 193–202.

Cliff, J. E. (1998). Does one size fit all? Exploring the relationship between attitudes towards growth, gender, and business size. *Journal of Business Venturing* (13), 523–542.

Davidsson, P. (1991). Continued entrepreneurship: Ability, need and opportunity as determinants of small firm growth. *Journal of Business Venturing, 6,* 405–429.

Dewhurst, P., & Horobin, H. (1998). Small business owners. In: R. Thomas (Ed.), *The management of small tourism and hospitality firm* (pp. 19–38). London: Cassel.

Finnish Tourist Board (1994). *Loma maalla on mukavaa. Maaseutulomailuprojekti 1989–1993 loppuraportti* MEK E:28 [Country holidays are nice. Finnish Country Holidays. Rural tourism Project 1989–1993]. Final Report.

Freel, M. (1999). Entrepreneurial and growth firms. In: D. Deakins (Ed.), *Entrepreneurship and small firms* (2nd ed.). Glasgow: McGraw-Hill.

Getz, D., & Carlsen, J. (2000). Characteristics and goals of family and owner-operated businesses in the rural tourism and hospitality sectors. *Tourism Management, 21*(2000), 547–560.

Gibb, A., & Davies, L. (1990). In pursuit of frameworks for the development of growth models of the small firm. *International Small Business Journal, 9*(1), 15–31.

Gibb, A. A., & Davies, L. (1992). Methodological problems in the development of a growth model of business enterprise. *The Journal of Entrepreneurship, 1*(1), 3–36.

Glancey, K. (1998). Determinants of growth and profitability in small entrepreneurial firms. *International Journal of Entrepreneurial Behaviour and Research, 4*(1), 18–27.

Greenbank, P. (2001). Objective setting in the micro-business. *International Journal of Entrepreneurial Behaviour and Research, 7*(3), 108–127.

Grolleau, H. (1996). Putting feelings first. In: *Marketing quality rural tourism: The experience of LEADER I.* Bruxelles: LEADER European Observatory.

Hall, M. C., & Rusher, K. (2002). A risky business? Entrepreneurial and lifestyle dimensions of the homestay and bed and breakfast accommodation sector in New Zealand. In: E. Arola, J. Kärkkäinen, & M.-L. Siitari (Eds), *Tourism and well-being* (pp. 197–210). The 2nd Tourism Industry and Education Symposium, May 16–18, 2002, Jyväskylä, Finland.

Irwin, D. (2000). Seven ages of entrepreneurship. *Journal of Small Business and Enterprise Development, 7*(3), 255–260.

Johannisson, B. (1990). Economies of overview — Guiding the external growth of small firms. *International Small Business Journal, 9*(1), 32–44.

Keats, B. W., & Bracker, J. S. (1988). Toward a theory of small firm performance: A conceptual model. *American Journal of Small Business* (Spring), 41–58.

King, B. E. M., Bransgrove, C., & Whitelaw, P. (1998). Profiling the strategic marketing activities of small tourism businesses. *Journal of Travel and Tourism Marketing, 7*(4), 45–59.

Kolvereid, L. (1992). Growth aspirations among Norwegian entrepreneurs. *Journal of Business Venturing* (7), 209–222.

Komppula, R. (1997). *Pohjois-Karjalan matkailustrategian synty ja yritysten valmius sitoutua strategiaan.* Lieksan oppimiskeskuksen julkaisusarja A:3.

Komppula, R. (2000a). *Matkailuyrityksen sitoutuminen verkostoon — tapaustutkimus Pohjois-Karjalan maakunnallinen matkailuverkosto.* Acta Universitatas Lapponiensis 30. Väitöskirja.

Lapin yliopisto. [The commitment of a tourism entrepreneur to a network — case North Karelia regional tourism network]. Doctoral dissertation.

Komppula, R. (2000b). Planning and managing the nature tourism for sustainability at rural destinations in Finland — some entrepreneurial aspects. In: L. Loven (Ed.), *Responsible nature tourism. Proceedings of the conference at Koli National Park, Finland (3–4 February 2000)* (pp. 77–93). Finnish Forest Research Institute, Research Papers 792 2000.

Kupiainen, T., Helenius, J., Kaihola, O., & Hyvönen, S. (2000). *Maaseudun pienyrityksen menestyminen* [*Performance of Small Rural Enterprise*]. Agricultural Economics Research Institute, Finland. Research Reports 239. Helsinki.

Lassila, H. (2000a). *Factors affecting the success in rural tourism enterprises. A case study*. Paper presented in the Finnish National Symposium in Tourism Research (May). Rovaniemi. Unpublished.

Lassila, H. (2000b). Problems in developing tourism entrepreneurship in a rural region: A case study. In: Robinson *et al.* (Eds), *Developments in urban and rural tourism* (pp. 179–190). Gateshead: Atheneum Press.

Lynch, P. (1998). Female micro-entrepreneurs in the host family sector: Key motivations and socio-economic variables. *Hospitality Management, 17*, 319–342.

Mäki, K., & Pukkinen, T. (2000). *Barriers to growth and employment in Finnish small enterprises* (pp. 1–18). Paper presented at ICSB Brisbane, Queensland. June 2000.

Martikainen, R. (2002). *Maaseutumatkailu*. Toimialaraportti. KTM. Infomedia.

McCelland, D. C. (1961). *The achieving society*. New Jersey: Van Nostrand, Princeton.

Morrison, A., Rimmington, M., & Williams, C. (1999). *Entrepreneurship in the hospitality, tourism and leisure industries*. Bath: Butterworth-Heinemann.

Pasanen, M. (1999). *Monet polut menestykseen*. Pk-yritykset Pohjois-Savossa. [Many ways to success: A study of SMEs in Northern Savo]. University of Kuopio, E. 15. Kuopio.

Perren, L. (1999). Factors in the growth of micro-enterprises (Part 1): Developing a framework. *Journal of Small Business and Enterprise Development, 6*(4), 366–385.

Puurunen, J. A. (2001). *Majoitus- ja ateriapalveluja tarjoavien päätoimisten maaseutumatkailuyritysten kannattavuus* [Profitability of the full time rural tourism enterprises offering accommodation and catering services]. Agricultural Economics Research Institute, Finland. Working Papers 2/2001. Helsinki.

Rantamäki-Lahtinen, L. (2002). On-Farm diversification from the management perspective. In: *CD-proceedings of 12th Nordic conference on small business research. Creating welfare and prosperity through entrepreneurship* (pp. 1–14). Kuopio Finland (May 26–28).

Rosa, P., Carter, S., & Hamilton, D. (1996). Gender as a determinant of small business performance: Insights from a British study. *Small Business Economics, 8*, 463–478.

Sandberg, K., Vinberg, S., & Pan, Y. (2002). An exploratory study of women in micro enterprise; owner perceptions of economic policy in a rural municipality: Gender-related differences. In: *CD-proceedings of 12th Nordic Conference on Small Business Research. Creating Welfare and Prosperity through Entrepreneurship* (pp. 1–14). Kuopio Finland (May 26–28).

Shaw, G., & Williams, A. M. (1990). Tourism, economic development and the role of entrepreneurial activity. In: C. P. Cooper (Ed.), *Progress in tourism, recreation and hospitality management* (pp. 67–81). London: Belhaven Press.

Storey, D. (1994). *Understanding the small business sector*. London: Routledge.

Thomas, R. (2000). Small firms in the tourism industry: Some conceptual issues. *International Journal of Tourism Research, 2*, 345–353.

Timmons, J. A. (1999). *New venture creation*. Entrepreneurship for the 21st century. Singapore: McGraw-Hill International Editions.

Walker, E. (2000). *An empirical study of measures of success in micro businesses* (pp. 1–14). Paper presented at ICSB Brisbane, Queensland (June).

Wanhill, S. (2000). Small and medium tourism enterprises. *Annals of Tourism Research, 27*(1), 132–147.

Watts, G., Cope, J., & Hulme, M. (1998). Ansoff's Matrix, pain and gain. Growth Strategies and adaptive learning among small food producers. *International Journal of Entrepreneurial Behaviour and Research, 4*(2), 101–111.

Westhead, P., & Cowling, M. (1997). Performance contrasts between family and non-family unquoted companies in the U.K. *International Journal of Entrepreneurial Behaviour and Research, 3*(1), 30–52.

Wiklund, J. (1998). *Small firm growth and performance. Entrepreneurship and beyond.* Jönköping: International Business School.http://www.mmm.fi/maasmatk/enggroup.htm 31.3.2001

Appendix 1

21. Why have you become a tourism entrepreneur. Level of significance, circle the most appropriate statement. 1 = very important, 2 = important, 3 = somewhat important, 4 = not so important, 5 = not at all important.

	Valid	1 + 2 (%)	3 (%)	4 + 5 (%)	Mean	Med	Mode	Pearson Chi-Square[a]	Pearson Chi-Square, Growth-Orient
Independence and freedom of entrepreneur; I am my own boss	176	66	19	15	2,3	2	2	Gender 0,01	
Tourism industry is interesting and challenging, I enjoy this work	177	75	11	14	2,15	2	2		0,015
I came across a good opportunity, which suited me well	177	60	21	19	2,35	2	1		
I have appropriate training in this field and/or I have know-how in this field	176	46	24	30	2,88	3	2	Age 0,001 educ. 0,043	
My income level is better as an entrepreneur	176	27	30	43	3,30	3	3	Voc. train. 0,021	
I have inherited or bought premises for a tourism business which had no other use	174	36	11	53	3,44	4	5	Gender 0,004 educ. 0,022	
I wanted to earn extra income and/or employ myself at the same time	177	61	18	21	2,45	2	2	Educ.0,000	

Appendix 1 (*Continued*)

	Valid	1 + 2 (%)	3 (%)	4 + 5 (%)	Mean	Med	Mode	Pearson Chi-Square[a]	Pearson Chi-Square, Growth-Orient
I wanted to return to my place of origin	170	19	7	74	4,21	5	5		
I have retired and want to have an interesting and challenging pastime	169	18	4	74	4,22	5	5		
I want to maintain my tourism business activity to leave it to my children for an income	174	37	25	38	3,13	3	5	Gender 0,044	
I want to work at home	177	52	20	28	2,66	2	1		

[a] Age, gender, education, vocational training.

Appendix 2

29. Choose the best alternative in scale 1–5 so that 1 corresponds to the least and 5 to the most. There is no one correct alternative, please answer in a way which best describes your business activities.

	Valid	1 + 2 (%)	3 (%)	4 + 5 (%)	Mean	Med	Mode	Pearson Chi-Square[a]	Pearson Chi-Square, Growth-Orient
Development of tourism business activities with borrowed capital does not belong to our principal of operations	177	28	22	50	3,51	4,00	5		0,014
I do not want to mortgage the fixed assets of our family as collateral for the loans to develop tourism business activities	177	23	20	57	3,65	4,0	5		
Developing business activities without borrowed capital with only cash-flow would slow down too much the development of business activities	177	23	24	53	3,53	4,0	5	Age 0,050	
Tourism entrepreneurship is interesting and challenging for the whole family	178	6	15	79	4,28	5,0	5	Educ. 0,031 voc. training 0,011	

Appendix 2 *(Continued)*

	Valid	1 + 2 (%)	3 (%)	4 + 5 (%)	Mean	Med	Mode	Pearson Chi-Square[a]	Pearson Chi-Square, Growth-Orient
I believe that avoiding economic risk is more important than rapid development of business activities and increasing the profits through investments	177	18	23	58	3,68	4,0	5	Educ. 0,007	0,017
Tourism entrepreneurship consumes so much time that there is none left for the family and/or one's own hobbies	178	51	21	29	2,64	2,0	1	Age 0,012	
As a tourism entrepreneur I am not able to adequately develop myself and advance the development of my own career path	178	67	19	14	2,13	2,0	1	Gender 0,008	
The greatest risk within tourism entrepreneurship is experiencing failure in business activities and "losing face" before relatives and acquaintances	176	74	15	11	1,90	1,0	1		0,038

Statement	N				Mean	Median	Mode	Significance	
I want to be a tourism entrepreneur, because the setting for this entrepreneurship is important to me (the surroundings, buildings, childhood home etc)	176	10	14	76	4,10	4,50	5	Gender 0,01	0,033
I want to be a tourism entrepreneur because there are no other opportunities to earn an income here.	177	46	24	29	2,68	3,0	1	Educ. 0,049	
As a tourism entrepreneur I feel that the quality of life is better than if I was a wage-earner	177	16	27	57	3,59	4,0	5		
Happiness and quality of life are more important factors in my business activities than great economic profit	177	7	20	73	4,11	4,0	5	Educ. 0,042	
The continuation of this business and succession are not part of our long-term business plan and I have never considered this alternative	176	51	17	32	2,76	2,0	1	Age 0,02 educ. 0,02	

a Age, gender, education, vocational training.

Appendix 3

Summary of interviews

Company No.	1	2	3	4	5	6	7	8	9	10	11	12	13	14
Operations started part-time x-years ago	20	8	4		7	30	1	12	20	9	10	35	8	11
Operations started/changed x years ago from part-time into full-time	18		2	1		1	1		10	7				3
Initial motives														
Planned full-time	x								x	x				
Planned part-time								x			x	x		x
Coincidence or chance			x		x								x	
Growth objectives														
Extra income, no need for full-time status		x									x		x	
Employment of one family member/self-employment				x	x		x	x						
Employment of family	x					x			x	x				
Employment of family and paid permanent staff			x											
Increasing profit from property/capital ≥ investments			x		x			x	x			x		
Increasing capacity utilization		x		x	x	x	x	x	x	x	x	x		x
Transfer to full-time in next few years												x		
What is success														
Customer satisfaction, permanent customer relations	x	x		x	x	x	x	x	x	x	x	x		x
Moderate income	x		x	x	x	x	x	x	x	x			x	

Factor										
Work that is deemed interesting and significant	X			X	X	X			X	X
Physical and mental well-being, time for hobbies, peace of mind		X	X	X	X	X	X	X		
Sufficient return on capital investments	X									
Profit						X	X	X	X	X
Growth	X					X	X	X	X	
What factors promote success										
The product itself	X	X		X	X	X	X		X	X
Financial and development support from authorities					X	X			X	X
Previous experience and training in other fields	X	X	X	X	X			X	X	
Training	X	X	X	X	X		X	X	X	
Entrepreneur's own well-being	X	X				X				
Cooperation and networking in one's own area and field	X	X	X	X	X	X	X	X	X	X
Projects, advisory organisations		X	X						X	
Healthy capital structure of enterprise		X	X	X	X		X	X	X	X
What factors restrain growth										
No desire to employ or make extra investments	X	X	X	X	X		X			
High employment expenses			X			X				
No one to continue the business or related uncertainty	X					X				
Low demand, insufficient cash-flow		X	X	X	X	X		X	X	
Remote location		X	X							
Negative attitude of municipality or environment towards entrepreneurship						X				X
Taxation or other state payments, regulations or actions		X	X	X		X		X	X	X

Appendix 3   (*Continued*)

Company No.	1	2	3	4	5	6	7	8	9	10	11	12	13	14
Resources for expanding used up (land, buildings etc.)														
Unsound competition											x			
Five-year vision														
Operations as at present				x	x	x								
Objectives achieved, no envisaged growth							x	x					x	
Operations expand			x											
Operations ceased or sold	x													
Operations transferred to descendants		x												
Operations have been reduced														
Plenty of factors creating uncertainty related to succession									x					

Chapter 9

The Interaction of Community and Small Tourism Businesses in Rural New Zealand

Donna Keen

Introduction

In the increasingly competitive environment that is rural tourism, the ability of small business operators to provide a unique and enjoyable experience is a key to the development of a sustainable tourism industry within the region. A factor in this development is the presence of entrepreneurs, whether they are business operators or community leaders. These entrepreneurs have the ability to recognise opportunities within the area and in the case of successful rural areas they provide an impetus for other business operators to develop or expand tourism products.

The realisation of success for rural tourism businesses is often highly dependent upon the interaction between the operator and the wider community. Small business research often focuses on the business background and management skills of operators. However, the ability of the entrepreneurial operator to understand the dynamics of community is an important factor on the path to successful rural tourism.

Drawing in the first instance on a survey conducted on rural tourism businesses in Southern New Zealand during 2000, this chapter begins by discussing the background of tourism business operators in rural areas and the nature of rural tourism in New Zealand. Developing further upon themes of community, highlighted in this research, the chapter continues to discuss the implications of community in the formation and operation of small business within a rural community in Central Otago, New Zealand. Notably the presence of entrepreneurial personalities in both private small business and community-initiated enterprises are highlighted. Within this community, the utilisation of existing community structures and facilities has been one of the primary reasons for a massive growth in the tourism products offered in this area. Moreover, it is argued in this chapter that the utilisation, by small tourism businesses, of community infrastructure and social capital is a key feature to the development of sustainable tourism not only in this region but in other rural areas which seek to change from a primarily production based society.

Small Firms in Tourism: International Perspectives
Copyright © 2004 Published by Elsevier Ltd.
ISBN: 0-08-044132-7

Tourism in Rural Areas of New Zealand

The New Zealand tourism product is largely based on wilderness and rural landscapes. Wilderness is embodied through tourist icons such as Milford Sound and Aoraki/Mount Cook. While wilderness has been the main icon of New Zealand tourism, rural tourism is a steadily growing component of both domestic and international tourism (Hall & Kearsley 2002). Rural New Zealand is represented through packaged performances such as the Agrodome in the tourist hub of Rotorua through to experiences of "authentic" rural lifestyles by the opportunity to stay with families on large sheep stations.

The initiation of rural tourism businesses has been partially motivated by changes in the agricultural and rural environment. These global changes, which have revolutionised the face of rural areas, have affected the New Zealand rural environment in a unique way (Cloke 1989). Key factors influencing this change have been the removal of protectionist strategies during the mid-1980s, the loss of key export markets, advances in technology and the migration of people between urban and rural environments (Keen 2000). Despite the negative portrayal of these changes they have created opportunities; the realisation of these opportunities being dependent upon the entrepreneurial ability of individuals or communities (Wilson 1994).

The resilience of New Zealand farmers and rural areas to the loss of both income and employment has been to diversify, gain other employment and increase farm size (Wilson 1994; McCrostie *et al.* 1998). Farm sizes have increased in order to maintain viable economic units and make more use of areas not traditionally used for farming (Hargreaves 1987). One form of diversification has been tourism (McCrostie *et al.* 1998). Tourism has provided an alternative source of income both to farmers and to rural service centres. In part tourism has been generated by diversification into wine and forestry, which provide features to enhance rural areas. Not only has tourism been generated as a response to changes in the agricultural environment, it has also resulted from the migration of people to rural areas. A number of people are moving from urban to rural areas; these people are further adding to the diversity of the tourism experience.

The impact of these changes has been substantial in influencing the way in which rural areas and regional development are viewed and this in turn, as Hall & Kearsley (2002: 168) note has resulted "not only to an economic restructuring of rural areas, but substantial cultural restructuring as well." Therefore, the emergence of entrepreneurial tendencies, the changing shape of the rural landscape and the increases in migrants to the area are contributing to much more dynamic environmental and cultural landscapes from which rural tourism businesses are operated.

Small Business and Rural Tourism

Rural tourism is heavily reliant on tourists' perception of rurality. Hall & Kearsley (2002) note the role that individual businesses have in operating in such a way so as to promote and manage these rural areas. Page *et al.* (1999) note that the tourism industry in New Zealand is characterised by small firms. These small firms have the ability to provide tourists with a typically New Zealand experience and to adapt to the changing perceptions of tourists (Deloittes 1994).

As noted above, tourism is about the provision of experience (Pine & Gilmore 1999). The current national promotional campaign focuses on the branding of New Zealand as "100% Pure," with this idea of purity centred around the natural environment and increasingly on what can be described as the purity of New Zealand culture. Arguably, tourism in rural areas allows the tourist greater opportunities for an "authentic" experience of a New Zealand way of life. A core component of the rural tourism product in New Zealand, are Bed and Breakfasts and Farmstays (Hogh 1998; Oppermann 1996; Warren 1998). People often operate home hosting accommodation with strong links to agriculture and the community (Keen 2000). This type of tourism is more than just a form of accommodation; due to its very nature it allows tourists to interact with "real" members of the local community and to experience rural life from a very personal perspective (Tucker 2002). Indeed, this opportunity to gain backstage experiences into the life of rural areas is an often cited motivation and expectation of guests to home hosted accommodation (Tucker & Keen 2002).

These more traditional core tourism products are being augmented by the development of other tourism products such as hotels (pubs), restaurants, lodges, specialist shops (e.g. antiques), museums and guided tours. These all offer tourists similar opportunities for experience; they are often run by locals and represent part of the communities' heritage. In turn each of these is also supported by a number of service suppliers such as petrol stations and grocery shops, whose focus is not predominately on the tourist. The role of these businesses is significant given the importance of developing a diverse tourism product (Hogh 1998). Hogh notes the difficulties that respondents felt in operating home hosting accommodation in an area where no other activities or services were provided for tourists. However, a diverse range of service and activities creates an increasingly complex environment from which rural tourism is operated. This complexity ensures that the interaction between the tourists, business operator and the community is undeniable.

Table 1 outlines the key findings of research conducted by the author into the nature of rural tourism businesses in New Zealand. As well as looking at the motivations of business operators this research also highlighted the link between tourism and other business, the role that community has in motivating business formation, the age of tourism businesses and the sources of advice and support used by operators.

The results of this research were largely consistent with the findings of other research into rural tourism in New Zealand (Hogh 1998; Warren 1998). One of the most interesting findings of rural tourism research in New Zealand is the relative lack of importance that economic considerations have had with respect to the rationale behind business formation. By their very nature many tourism businesses were attached to existing businesses and provided little income, in fact operators are significantly motivated by the social benefits perceived in operating the business (Hogh 1998; Keen 2000; Warren 1998). In comparison to the situation in many other countries, farmers are now receiving high prices for agricultural products. The need for financial gains from tourism is no longer as paramount, if indeed it ever was; yet many people linked to the agricultural sector continue to develop and run tourism businesses. The continuing involvement in tourism of people attached to traditional industries arguably highlights the importance of the social benefits gained from the tourism business; a point which has been substantiated by this research and the work of both Hogh (1998) and Warren (1998) into rural tourism businesses.

Table 1: Key findings of research into rural tourism businesses in New Zealand.

Profile of rural tourism businesses
- Characterised by a number of components but with an emphasis upon accommodation particularly farm-stays
- A large number of businesses are in the early stages of operation

Background profile of rural tourism operators
- Most operators have a business background; a large majority being linked to agriculture
- Two-thirds are still involved in other businesses
- Few operators have any tourism experience
- Characterised by formal education, but not by any type of education specifically

Entrepreneurial aspects of rural tourism businesses
- Majority of operators accessed advice on the formation of their business
- Most use some form of marketing and most make an attempt to keep track of trends in the tourism environment
- Show awareness of the performance of the business and can attribute the reasons for this performance

Economic rationale of tourism businesses
- Low revenue from tourism businesses
- Tourism income not the overwhelming factor behind business formation
- Importance of income is of no importance for 35% of the sample
- Social aspects, especially meeting people, are important as a motivation and benefit of operating the business

Other issues
- Most operators indicate they feel the business is relatively successful
- For nearly a third of the sample, enhancing the local district was a key motivation behind the operation of the business

---

Source: Keen (2000).

Another crucial finding of the study related to "enhancing the local district" as being a significant motivation for the operation of the business. In the rural areas included as part of the research, these formal tourism businesses were supported by a number of individuals or groups who were involved in the creation of information centres, facilities and other services for the same reasons. As the case study will highlight the role of these "Social entrepreneurs" (Dees 1998) plays a vital role in supporting these businesses and in some respects they act both as an instigator and incubator for entrepreneurship.

Entrepreneurship and Rural Tourism

The above point then leads on to what indeed is entrepreneurship. In terms of a classical definition, entrepreneurs are characterised by a propensity toward risk taking, creativity and innovation and business skills (Echtner 1995; Stewart *et al.* 1999). Entrepreneurship is seen as increasingly synonymous with rural tourism (Petrin 1994). However, the reality is that in many cases entrepreneurship is absent in small rural tourism businesses. Though academic thought has at times described entrepreneurship in terms of all small business operations, it is best that this description is not adopted given the role that those individuals who are characterised by entrepreneurial tendencies have in instigating regional development. For example table one discusses the characteristics of business operation in rural areas. Upon closer reflection some of the businesses in this study were not successful either from an economic or a social dimension. Whereas other operators were to a degree responsive for the increasing development of tourism in their area both in terms of attracting tourists and encouraging the development of other tourism businesses and are more reflective of entrepreneurial personalities.

Wilson *et al.* (2001) state that tourism entrepreneurs are one of the key factors to tourism success. However, they also note that because tourism is place oriented, success is not just about the individual entrepreneur but also about the community and environment surrounding the business (Murphy 1985 in Wilson *et al.* 2001). Entrepreneurship within rural communities is not principally about pure economic business success but should also be defined by "the skills that will be needed to improve the quality of life for individuals, families and communities and to sustain a healthy economy and environment" (Petrin 1994: 4). Entrepreneurship is increasingly seen as the key to successful regional development. Petrin notes the development of entrepreneurship within rural areas is a complex one given the role that entrepreneurs have in the economic and social development of rural communities. Petrin also argues that in comparison to urban entrepreneurs, the link between the entrepreneur and the social aims of development are much closer, and the role of community much greater. Therefore, one could argue that the ability of individuals to positively interact with the community is a significant determinant of success and a characteristic of entrepreneurship. The dynamic between community and entrepreneurship is something which needs to be better understood.

The interrelationship between community and entrepreneurship is evident in two ways. The first dimension of this dynamic is the way that entrepreneurs utilise the community as part of their tourism product and the way they manage community to ensure the smooth running of the business. As a feature of the tourism product this chapter has already addressed the importance of community in rural areas as part of the tourist experience and noted the way in which elements of success can be judged through the skill of the business operator in utilising this effectively, hence this skill can be seen as a characteristic of rural entrepreneurship.

The second influence of community has been briefly referred to above as social entrepreneurship. Social entrepreneurship is not a new term and it is not something which is entirely synonymous with rural tourism either. Social entrepreneurship can be simply stated as entrepreneurs with a social mission (Dees 1998). The characteristics of social entrepreneurs include engaging in innovation, adaptation and learning, and adopting change to create and sustain social value (Dees 1998). The Ashoka (2003) organisation note the importance of social entrepreneurs is that they can influence change in large-scale social problems. In comparison to individual entrepreneurs the identification of opportunities is done with the primary focus toward the way in which success of an enterprise can positively impact upon either the community as a whole or on a social group. In relation to rural communities in particular the role of community groups is not a new phenomenon, these groups have utilised fundraising and government funding to provide support back into particular groups. However, the phenomenon of community acting as entrepreneurs is still relatively new. In terms of tourism, community entrepreneurship is being directed toward the utilisation of government or community funds for the creation of services or tourism products which while not directly giving back to the community help to stimulate both business development and community pride.

The following case study discusses the presence of entrepreneurship in a rural community. Arguably the success of tourism in this area is due to the presence of entrepreneurs. In relation to the above discussion the case study discusses the way in which entrepreneurs have utilised the community and the influence that community or social entrepreneurs have had toward creating a successful tourism destination.

Case Study: The Interaction of Community and Small Tourism Businesses in the Maniototo, Otago, New Zealand

The Maniototo is located in the province of Otago in Southern New Zealand. The area is typified by a large barren plain surrounded by three main mountain ranges; creating a landscape which is unique for Southern New Zealand and a key point to the promotion of the area for tourism. Historically industry was based upon goldmining and agriculture. The gold rush lasted throughout the 1880s–1890s and though not long in duration was important in developing the cultural heritage of the Maniototo. Agriculture still remains the principal industry of the region. The industry has changed since the 19th Century to reflect much smaller farms and a diversification from sheep farming to horticulture, dairying and tourism.

The 2001 census showed the Maniototo region to have a permanent population of 948 (Statistics New Zealand 2003). The main service centre for the area is Ranfurly which has a population of 735. There are a number of other villages which make up the Maniototo community. These villages are the centres for a number of distinct sub-regions. As with New Zealand rural areas in general the Maniototo has been subject to rural depopulation and agricultural change. The population of the Maniototo has declined from 1,134 in 1991 to 948 in 2001 (Statistics New Zealand 2003). Moreover, the community has had to deal with a number of other problems. The closure of a forestry processing plant during the 1990s resulted in the loss of thirty families from the district. Agricultural problems have been compounded by severe drought. These problems have resulted in rural depopulation and economic hardship. As a result of the changes to the Maniototo many of the features of these communities were closed such as schools, village shops, pubs and agricultural supply shops. Despite these closures distinct communities have still survived. Community is maintained through the continuation of sports teams and other community organisations. The endurance of these organisations can be seen as a result of the strong historical links of many of the residents and the history of tradition, which appears to provide a greater reason for ensuring the continuation of these societies. In terms of tourism, the maintenance of community ensures that an identity is sustained which can then be utilised both as a feature of the tourism experience and as support for small business formation.

Tourism Development within the Region

The development of tourism within the Maniototo is strongly connected to the history of the region. Though a number of the tourism products or activities are based around the natural environment the integration of heritage in those activities is undeniable. For example, many guiding activities interpret the history of the environment as part of the tourist experience despite the fact that with such things as fishing, the primary activity is based upon the natural environment. Within the Maniototo the influence of the past is very strong. This has implications in terms of how important the community is to the tourism product and to the operation of tourism businesses. Moreover, this is the case with many rural areas where heritage is significant in defining both the natural and the cultural landscapes. Hence, the implications of this case study can be applied to other rural areas. Tourism development in the Maniototo can be seen in two stages (see Table 2). The first stage has been characterised by few tourism specific businesses, with most tourism focused around second homes. The second stage, which is the principal focus of this case study, is centred on the creation of a number of dynamic small tourism businesses and community-initiated enterprises.

Tourism in the Maniototo has largely been centred on domestic tourism. In 2000, 80% of the visitors were domestic, most coming into the Maniototo through the Christmas period (Warren & Taylor 2001). Historically, second homes have been the primary feature of tourism within the region. Second home owners have utilised the large number of redundant housing which has come about largely as a result of the end of the gold boom (Keen 2002). Second homes can be found in many of the rural communities throughout the Maniototo. They are beneficial in providing an economic boost to the area — through expenditure and in terms of the role of second homes as a part of the accommodation supply —and in the role they have in maintaining the heritage buildings, and as a part of the community. Naseby, for example, has 51 houses that are occupied by permanent residents and 210 which conceivably

Table 2: Stages of tourism development in the Maniototo.

	Key Occurrences
	Stage 1
1950s	First second home settlements
Late 1980–1990s	Development of tourism specific businesses
	Severe rural downturn
1999	Formation of revitalisation movement
	Stage 2
2000	Opening of rail trail
	Rural art deco theme
	Mountain bike capital of Naseby (new business formation)
2003	Proposal for development of lodge/conference centre
	Number of new business development
	Increase in real estate demand

represent second home use (Statistics New Zealand 2003). Second homes owners are a component of the community in this village and have similar historical ties that many permanent residents have as well. Second homes are still an important component of the tourism industry in the region, if one which is not recognised by relevant authorities. At the end of the 1990s, small tourism businesses in the Maniototo were based primarily around the provision of accommodation facilities; this has basically been the use of accommodation in pubs and the development two farmstays. There had been no cohesive identification of the resources of the area and the utilisation of those resources into comprehensive products for tourism.

The success of tourism in recent years is probably best indicated by this comment from a tourist "I was here in 1992 and I saw nothing; now I see it all." The development of tourism in the Maniototo has not focused on the creation of new facilities but has been centred on the identification of what already exists and creating ways of modifying them or highlighting their significance. Activities utilise the unique landscape and cultural heritage of the Maniototo; significance is given to these features through successful interpretation. The key developments have included the development of a cluster of tourism businesses in the village of Naseby, the Central Otago Rail Trail and the identification and use of Art Deco buildings.

Naseby was once the centre of a large goldmining boom. The end of the goldmining boom left a large number of redundant buildings. Since the 1950s these have been utilised as second homes. Currently the permanent population of Naseby is around 90, in the peak summer period when second home owners are resident the population of the village is close to 1000. When the researcher first came into contact with the village two years ago the only significant form of tourism was the second homes. The village was increasingly becoming know as a mountain biking Mecca but the lack of supporting infrastructure and attractions meant cyclists only came for recreation and then left. There were two pubs, a village shop, and two small but very well resourced museums. The service provided by the pubs was inconsistent and anyone coming into the very quaint village, outside of the few peak weeks of the year, could not find services to keep them in the area. At that time many people in the village were expressing ideas for the development of the village, noting the influence that the Art Deco trail was having in relation to tourism, however no one was willing to develop any of these idea.

Returning to the village 14 months later it was noticeable that someone had developed these ideas. In the space of one month the four main tourism businesses had new owners. This included new owners of the camping ground, the two pubs and the opening of a B&B. Two of these are operated by very entrepreneurial personalities. These people are characterised as entrepreneurial for two main reasons; firstly they have identified opportunities for innovative products and secondly the level of risk associated with operating a full time tourism business in the village was quite high. In the first instance, one couple have opened up a B&B in a renovated historical house. As well as offering general B&B they provide Devonshire teas, themed dinners and plan to run craft retreats. This couple invested their life savings into the renovation and promotion of their business. The second business is the local pub, in tandem with this mountain biking guiding and hire has been opened. One of the owners stated "Í had a hankering to have a dabble at tourism. Two pubs for sale that were run down and had tired people in them you didn't have to be the very top of your game to see. I think we went to the right place for us." The operators of the pub have also been fundamental in creating events to bring locals and tourists to the area. Between these two businesses they have created what can only be described as a boom in tourism for the village. From observations it is argued that their efforts in developing tourism, based on a strong understanding of the community have also benefited the other businesses. The increase in visitors and length of stay of visitors to the village has provided more customers for the existing businesses, community craft shops and for the museums in the area. As a result of the rising number of tourists, property prices in the village have increased; where two years ago properties had been on real estate agents books for years, the market of available land and housing is now limited. Currently, development is planned of a lodge and conference centre, a restaurant and an international curling rink.

The Central Otago Rail Trail has also been responsive for bringing both tourists and business into the area. As a result of the closure of the rail line in 1990, the Central Otago Rail Trail was created to stimulate tourism development in the area. (Kulczycki 2001). The trail was a result of both the Department of Conservation and the Otago Central Rail Trust. The Department of Conservation is responsible for the daily management of the trail and the Rail Trust for the promotion and collection of funds for the trails operation (Kulczycki 2001). The trail has resulted in the both the diversification of existing businesses and the creation of new businesses to support trail users. Businesses have noted that the trail has provided benefits to both themselves and the community as a whole (Kulczycki 2001). The trail has also been beneficial in providing another dimension of recreational use for the Maniototo region.

The third development of note has been he identification of Ranfurly as a rural Art Deco town. The justification for embarking on the Art Deco theme came as a response to the need for community rejuvenation. At the primary instigation of one individual the local council created the "Vision Maniototo" plan as a way of creating both economic and social rejuvenation. The first phase of this plan was the theming of Ranfurly as Art Deco. Though not an obvious example of a tourist attraction, particularly when compared with opulent examples of the Art form, rural Art Deco involved the identification of a large number of Deco buildings. The aim of the project was that if given meaning and packaged well, Art Deco could become a successful means of stimulating pride in both the town and the wider region and act as a stimulator for business development.

Community Involvement

One of the important components to the success of the three developments listed above has been the influence and involvement of community. The last part of this chapter will look at the role of community in these developments, in terms of community entrepreneurship and the role of community as a feature of the tourism product.

Community Entrepreneurship

What makes this an interesting case study is the role that community entrepreneurship has had in successful tourism development. Relating specifically to the Art Deco movement, the influence of the work of one person has been so significant within this community that one could state tourism development has hinged on this individuals drive and initiative. As one tourism operator commented "Anybody that is getting a dollar out of tourism must appreciate that it is her doggedness that had put them on the map. The little town that was dying, she made a hell of a difference. I think even the people who mock her begrudgedly know that she has made a difference." This individual has also been involved in the development of the Central Otago Rail Trail, particularly in developing events to promote the use of the trail. This woman is the classic example of a community or social entrepreneur; she gives the community as her main motivation, stating specifically that it is "about doing something to get us out of the doldrums." She states "I have always been involved in community work and always loved where I lived and particularly interested in promoting the area to share the beautiful place we live in with other people basically." Through her efforts she has developed the community organisation which acted as the official body for fund raising and development, has been in charge of the renovation of Art Deco buildings and their operation as tourism products and utilisation as businesses and as part of specific events. She largely attributes the success of the venture to herself "And I'm not skiting or anything like that because if I had have walked away it would of fallen over and its been three and a half years that you have to nurture something and hold it and get other people to believe it and now its working wonderfully." Personally she has benefited from the success of rural Art Deco by opening her own antique shop. However, she noted the reason for this as; "It took a while for people to get the confidence, even when we had finished the milk bar no one would have done anything and that's why we got into this (antique shop) this was never part of my vision and this is why that happened." The degree to which personal gain is achieved is significant in discussions of what classifies a community or social entrepreneur. Arguably the crucial point of consideration in relation to this example, is that the main motivations have been to advance the community and that the benefits from this venture have indeed benefited a greater circle of people both economically and socially in terms of the value that the project has had in terms of community revitalisation.

Both individuals and groups working for community good have been significant in the creation of facilities and tourism services. Addressed above in greater detail is the work of an individual toward community revitalisation, however a number of community groups have also been significant. Community organisations have been behind the protection and interpretation of heritage buildings and artefacts, they have been crucial for the operation of museums. These contribute toward a more diverse tourism product for the area. Many community members volunteer hours for the operation of museums and visitor centres, maintain facilities and provide support to the running of these businesses. Even with the presence of entrepreneurs the community is still a crucial component to the success of enterprise regardless of where the projects main impetus comes from.

Importance of Community to the Tourism Experience

Identifying the advantages the community has, as a tourism product, has been one of the keys to the achievements of the tourism businesses within the Maniototo. As mentioned above, the values that the community and the facilities of that community, are crucial to the provision of the tourist's experience. Those tourism business operators who have recognised this have been resourceful in engendering ways of becoming involved in the community. This is a relatively difficult task given the parochial nature of the community. Many times throughout the research members of the community expressed half in jest, yet with an element of sincerity, that if someone was not born in the Maniototo or even within specific areas of the Maniototo, they were not local. In the case of some of these comments the implied meaning was that those people not born in that community did not have the necessary knowledge or right to make comments about the village and surrounding environment; this includes the knowledge they share with tourists. The parochial nature of this community and the importance of tourism operators finding their place within in it is a significant point given the "non-local" status of many of the operators of small tourism businesses. Understanding the nature of this community and managing the business in a way that reflects this is a method of achieving some sort of acceptance into this community. One such method is the awareness that certain types of personalities or personal backgrounds play a significant role in acceptance. As one operator noted, "by putting * in as a Manager who had been a commercial fisherman and a South Island representational shearer he was actually not alienated. They will still talk about the hippies that owned it in the early 1990s." Other operators have also become heavily involved in community organisations. Thereby they have instead of utilising the social capital of the community contributed to it as well. Community ownership also serves to avoid any potential antagonism. As one business stated, allowing a prominent local family who has historically been connected to their property to use it for a family gathering increased the support that the community gave them. Given this parochial dynamic of rural communities, another crucial basis from which to judge entrepreneurship within communities is the degree to which business operators successfully deal and utilise communities.

Conclusions

The development of rural tourism is dependent upon the abilities of individuals and communities to recognise the opportunities inherent in an area. This chapter has described the situation of tourism in a rural area of New Zealand, focusing on the interrelationship between small tourism business and the wider community. While the entrepreneurial abilities of business operators and community members represent only part of this dynamic, the role they have in shaping the development is undeniable. It is the presence of entrepreneurs and their ability to recognise the attributes of areas and manage them in such a way as to draw tourists that is the key to success. As the case study has shown one of the keys to the success of these entrepreneurs has been their ability to identify the use of the community as a feature of the tourists experience and also the role community has in the successful running of their operation. The chapter has also highlighted the role of community or social entrepreneurs as facilitators of development. Small business and entrepreneurial research need to focus more on understanding issues relating to the interaction of community and business. Despite the fact that business background and management skills are a crucial component of understanding tourism business, developing knowledge of the integration of community and business is essential. This includes developing knowledge of the ways of managing the relationship of business with community and the skills needed to achieve symbiosis between themselves and the wider environment in which the business operates. Due to the very social nature of many tourism businesses in rural areas of New Zealand this community dynamic is arguably as important as the traditional economic features underpinning business operation. And finally the understanding of community is yet another dimension to understanding the successful entrepreneur.

References

Ashoka (2003). *What is a social entrepreneur?* Ashoka Organisation www.ashoka.org/fellows/ social_entrepreneur.cfm, accessed 3 February.

Cloke, P. (1989). State deregulation and New Zealand's agricultural sector. *Sociologia Ruralis*, *XXIX*, 1

Dees, J. G. (1998). *The meaning of social entrepreneurship*. Centre for Social Innovation Stanford Business School www.gsb.stanford.edu/csi/SED.html, accessed 3 February.

Deloittes (1994). *Small business survey: New Zealand tourism industry*. Deloitte Touche Tomatsu, Tourism and Leisure Consulting Group, Christchurch: 28.

Echtner, C. M. (1995). Entrepreneurial training in developing countrie. *Annals of Tourism Research*, *22*(1), 119–134.

Hall, C. M., & Kearsley, G. (2002). *Tourism in New Zealand: An introduction*. South Melbourne: Oxford University Press.

Hargreaves, R. (1987). People farming — is this our 4th tier. *New Zealand Farmer* (January), 8.

Hogh, L. (1998). *From farm to farm-stay: Is developing a farm-stay personally satisfying to the operator? A study of farm based tourism in the Southland Region of New Zealand*. Unpublished Dissertation for the Diploma of Tourism, University of Otago.

Keen, D. (2000). *Rural tourism entrepreneurship*. Unpublished Dissertation for the Diploma of Tourism, University of Otago.

Keen, D. (2002). Second homes in New Zealand. In: G. Croy (Ed.), *New Zealand tourism and hospitality research conference* (3–5 December).

Kulczycki, C. (2001). *Perceptions of the Otago central rail trail*. Unpublished thesis submitted for the degree of Master of Tourism, University of Otago.

McCrostie Little, H., & Taylor, C. N. (1998). *Off-farm employment and entrepreneurship: The New Zealand farm family in the 1990s*. Paper presented for the conference of the Rural Sociological Society. Portland, USA (5–9 August).

Oppermann, M. (1996). *Spotlighting farm tourism in New Zealand towards a more sustainable tourism*. Proceedings of Tourism Down Under 2 (3–6 December).

Page, S., Forer, P., & Lawton, G. (1999). Small business development and tourism: Terra incognita. *Tourism Management*, *20*, 435–459.

Petrin, T. (1994) Entrepreneurship as an economic force in rural development. *Seventh FAO/REU International Rural Development Summer School*. Herrsching, Germany (8–14 September).

Pine, J., & Gilmore, J. H. (1999). *The experience economy: Work is theatre and every business a stage*. Boston: Harvard Business School Press.

Statistics New Zealand (2003). *Census 2001*. New Zealand Government http://www.stats.govt.nz/census.htm, accessed 12 February.

Stewart, W. H., Watson, W. E., Carland, J. C., & Carland, J. W. (1999). A proclivity for entrepreneurship: A comparison of entrepreneurs, small business owners and corporate managers. *Journal of Business Venturing*, *14*(2), 189–214.

Tucker, H. (2002). *Front-stage, Backstage: Experiencing the "real" New Zealand. Tourism and hospitality of the edge*. Twelfth International Research Conference of the Council for Australian University Tourism and Hospitality Education. Council for Australian University Tourism and Hospitality education. Freemantle Esplanade Hotel, Western Australia (6–9 February).

Tucker, H., & Keen, D. (2002). The role of small tourism home-hosted accommodation in regional tourism and development. *Small firms in the tourism and hospitality sectors*. Leeds Metropolitan University (13 September).

Warren, J. (1998). *Rural tourism in New Zealand: The experience of individual businesses*. Centre for research evaluation and social assessment.

Warren, J., & Taylor, N. (2001). *Heritage tourism in New Zealand*. Centre for research evaluation and social assessment.

Wilson, O. (1994). They changed the rules: Farm family responses to Agricultural Deregulation in Southland, New Zealand. *New Zealand Geographer, 50*(1), 3–13.

Wilson, S., Fesenmaier, D. R., Fesenmaier, J., & Van Es, J. C. (2001). Factors for success in rural tourism development. *Journal of Travel Research, 40*, 132–138.

Chapter 10

Whale Watching — The Roles of Small Firms in the Evolution of a New Australian Niche Market

Noel Scott and Eric Laws

Introduction

This chapter discusses and compares the development of a new niche market in two coastal resort destinations on the East Coast of Australia. The research draws on two cases, part of a larger study focusing on the development of new types of tourism products in established resort destinations. These cases utilize data "triangulation" (Jick 1983) to develop an event history of the development of commercial aspects of viewing of humpback whales in Australia. Data are drawn from in-depth interviews with wildlife experts, industry and community leaders, archival analysis and personal observation. This has allowed a number of key events in the development of this specialized niche market to be identified. The chapter discusses the development of latent demand arising from increasing interest in environmental issues and the serendipitous recognition by an experienced entrepreneur of whale watching as a new business opportunity. However, the local community was reluctant to see a full development of this business sector in one resort destination while in the other case examined here, many local small businesses were able to benefit from the development of whale watching.

From Whaling to Whale Watching

The development of whale watching in Australia is based on the remarkable changes in general community attitudes to the environment and to the recovery of whale populations after near extinction. Australia, along with many other western countries, has a history of catching and processing whales from small ships that began as early as the late 1700s and is memorably described in Moby Dick (Melville 1926). Whale products such as oil and baleen were in fact amongst Australia's first exports (Tucker 1989). Beginning in 1954, land based whale processing plants were established along the east coast of Australia as a regional

Small Firms in Tourism: International Perspectives
Copyright © 2004 by Elsevier Ltd.
All rights of reproduction in any form reserved
ISBN: 0-08-044132-7

economic development activity. This type of whaling involved spotting whales travelling along their migration path, intercepting them with small fast boats and towing the carcass back to port. Whaling continued to 1962 when the industry became uneconomic due to falling whale numbers. Whaling stations were located at Eden in New South Wales, Byron Bay in New South Wales and Tangalooma (on Moreton Island) in Queensland. The main target species for whalers was the humpback whale (*Megaptera novaeangliae*) that makes an annual migration from its feeding grounds near Antarctica each June or July and returns in September or October. Several populations of humpback whales have been identified and are classified according to their migratory routes. Humpback whales travelling along the East Coast of Australia are classified as Population V. Whales travel on their migration in small groups referred to as pods.

Methodology

There is a strong tradition for the use of case studies in examining dynamic tourism phenomena. Recent examples of tourism case studies in these areas include the effects of a natural disaster on the Town of Katherine and of the dynamics of change on the Gold Coast, Australia (Faulkner 2000; Russell & Faulkner 1999). Two basic types of case research, single case design and multiple case designs are noted in the literature (Yin 1994). Multiple-case designs have distinct advantages and disadvantages in comparison with single case designs. The evidence from multiple cases is considered more compelling, and the overall study is often considered more robust. Multiple case study research typically examines a phenomenon with the focus on causation so as to explain the "how and why" of historically and/or culturally significant phenomena (Ragin & Becker 1992). However, the conduct of a multiple case study can require extensive resources and time beyond the means of a single student or independent research investigator (Yin 1994). Pearce (1993) suggests that comparative case studies are commonly used in situations with small numbers of cases and large numbers of variables.

The three main techniques used in this research are convergent interviewing, archival analysis and triangulation. Three other research techniques were also used to supplement these primary techniques; face-to-face and telephone interviews as well as affinity group in-depth interviews (Decrop 1999; Hartmann 1988; Oppermann 2000; Ralston & Stewart 1990; Richins 1999).

Convergent interviewing was chosen as the method for use in interviewing. Dick (1987) views convergent interviewing as multistage or cyclic data-collection and interpretation. At each stage or cycle the questions and the interpretation of the responses need only be specific enough to allow the next stage to be designed. The interpretation of the data converges gradually towards its final form. The convergence occurs both within each interview, and from one interview to another. Both content (subject matter) and process (details of the interviewing process itself) can converge over the course of interviews. Convergent interviewing leaves the content unstructured, but structures the process very tightly. It starts in a very open-ended way, which confers flexibility. The structured process provides a means for dealing with the large amounts of data that is produced.

To use convergent interviews efficiently, an interviewer looks for two patterns in the emerging data. Patterns of convergence or agreement, and discrepancy or disagreement are examined. These provide the criteria for deciding whether to analyse particular data further, or discard them. Each interview terminates when the respondent has no more to say, and the interviewer is satisfied that the data meet three other criteria. Firstly, an overall pattern can be seen in the data, or at least the key information has been identified. Secondly, as far as possible all convergence from prior interviews has been confirmed (or disconfirmed). Thirdly, all discrepancies are explained if possible. The series of interviews terminates when fairly clear agreement emerges between all or most people interviewed, and where their differences are explained. The views expressed by those interviewed are seen by the interviewers to converge to one or a small number of distinct views on the topic being investigated.

The second major research technique used in this thesis was archival analysis. Lincoln & Guba (1985) distinguish between documents and records on the basis of whether the text was prepared to attest to some formal transaction. Thus records include statistical data collections and newspaper articles while documents are of a personal nature: diaries, memos, etc.

Triangulation implies that a single point is considered from three different and independent sources. Authors like Jick (1983) consider triangulation as mixing qualitative and quantitative methods, advocating that both should be viewed as complementary instead of rival camps. Triangulation has also received attention in qualitative research as a way to ground the acceptance of qualitative approaches (Denzin 1978). Triangulation as a research technique enhances the trustworthiness of qualitative data (Decrop 2000), although other approaches are also available such as testing rival explanations, looking for negative or atypical cases, or keeping methods and data in context. Triangulation limits personal and methodological biases and enhances a study's generalizability. Four basic

Figure 1: Map of whaling and whale watching areas.

types of triangulation have been discussed (Denzin 1978). These are data sources, methods, investigators, and theory triangulation. In this study the triangulation approach adopted is based on method and data triangulation.

In addition to collecting data, the researcher sought confirmation from the respondents or other sources that the material collected was valid. This involved providing transcripts and feedback to respondents on the findings of the research (Figure 1).

Early Development of a New Niche

After whaling ceased on the east coast of Australia in 1962, it was estimated that only 200–500 humpback whales remained in east coast waters out of an estimated population of 15–20,000 prior to commercial whaling (Centre for Coastal Management 1995). This decline in whale populations was a worldwide phenomenon; the humpback whale became a protected species worldwide in 1966. It remains on the protected species list (Kaufman & Forestell 1993), although limited catches are allowed for scientific research, conducted almost exclusively by Japanese fleets. Currently, humpback whale numbers on the East Coast of Australia are growing at 10% per year.

"Whale watching" has been defined as tours by boat, air or from land, formal or informal, with at least some commercial aspect, to see, swim with, and/or listen to any of the some 83 species of whales, dolphins and porpoises (Hoyt 2001). Between 1964 and 1987 when whale watching started in Hervey Bay, there was an increase in environmentalism in Australia and other developed countries. This increasing concern for the environment is attributed (Udall 2000), to a reaction against the rampant developmental ethos of the 1960s and was heralded by the publication of "Silent Spring" (Carson 1963).

Whale watching began as a non-consumptive economic activity in the 1950s in locations such as California and New England in the United States. A second wave of whale watching destinations began in the 1980s including operations in New Zealand, Canary Islands, Japan and Norway (Hoyt 2001). Cousteau & Paccalet (1988: 23) write that in 1988, whale watching was a significant economic activity in Cape Cod Newfoundland, San Diego, California (300,000 people on land and sea) and Peninsula Valdes Argentina (36,000 per year). In fact they suggested at that time that the *"popularity of whales is such that 'nature safaris' to breeding lagoons are beginning to be problematic."* A third wave of whale watching destinations became popular in the 1990s including Iceland, Philippines, Indonesia, Hong Kong, Tonga and Taiwan (Hoyt 2001).

Whale watching has been seen as a wildlife tourism activity and is *"often located under the broad banner of eco-tourism"* (Muloin 1998: 201). It is distinct from a simple outing on a boat as whales are a central focus for the trip (Orams 2000).

Humpback whales are amongst the largest living mammals, yet the business of viewing them is almost exclusively operated by small companies. Individual boat owners and operators typically conduct commercial whale watching operations. Most commercial operations are water based activities although both air and land based operations are also found. Land based whale watching tends to be non-commercial in nature. At some locations the migrating pods of whales pass very close to high cliffs, or they may congregate there for short periods, making an easy spectacle for people enjoying unrestricted access to cliff

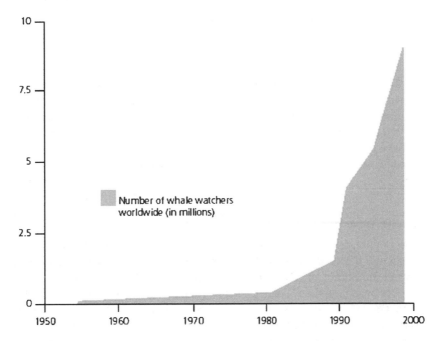

Figure 2: The growth of whale watching worldwide 1955–1998. *Source:* Hoyt (2001: 12).

top parklands. Water based tours tend to be for half a day or a day in length although a number of other formats are available (for example dawn and dusk tours). The duration of tours is largely determined by the proximity of whale viewing areas to the local harbour, although other factors include the degree of expertise of the boat captain and the levels of interest and commitment of the passengers. The boats tend to be quite small, and can be uncomfortable in certain combinations of wind and water conditions.

The overall growth of whale watching between 1955 and 1998 has been rapid as shown in Figure 2 (Hoyt 2001). This information has been based on survey data collected from whale watch operators, tourism departments and researchers by Erich Hoyt. These data must be viewed as indicative only since they are based on a sample survey method. However, the overall pattern suggests that whale watching became significantly more popular in the 1980s and continued to grow in popularity, at least until 1998, when the last survey was conducted. Hoyt estimates that in 1998 whale watching around the world provided direct expenditure of USD$300 million with over 9 million visitors undertaking commercial whale watching. Hoyt also estimates that whale watch numbers grew by around 14% annually between 1994 and 1998.

Whale Watching Case Studies

Byron Bay is the most easterly point in Australia, and is a key location along the Australian humpback whale migration routes. It combines a high vantage point close to a narrow continental shelf, thus providing ideal conditions for whale viewing. The earliest recorded commercial whale watching activity in Byron Bay occurred while the whale processing plant was still operating.

> . . . the company that ran the whaling station here, saw people were coming to watch the whales being brought in. So they actually encouraged that as a tourism industry environment. There was a small shop built opposite the whaling station and it sold drinks and that sort of stuff. And it certainly became popular especially on the weekends. And literally hundreds of people would go around the whaling station to see the whales (Byron Bay Resident).

A photograph of people watching a whale being cut up probably taken in the 1960s was displayed on the walls of the Byron Bay Hotel during a visit by the researcher in 2001.

In June/July 1979, Project Jonah, a Brisbane-based voluntary organization involved in whale conservation, arranged a field trip to look for whales at Cape Byron. Project Jonah was subsequently renamed the Australian Whale Conservation Foundation, and continued counting whale numbers from Byron Bay headland from 1979 to 1998. In that year the task was taken over by the Southern Cross University Whale Research Centre (SCUWRC). The Cape Byron Trust (CBT) took over of the management of Cape Byron from the Maritime Safety Authority in 1989. In the early 1990s the CBT undertook to promote whale watching from the Cape Byron headland and first ran a very successful Whale Watch weekend event in 1993. This received extensive coverage in local and national media. However, local community concerns about environmental degradation caused by the effects of large numbers of visitors on Cape Byron led to this successful event being discontinued. Land based whale watching, however has continued and is now supported by interpretation from the SCUWRC during the peak of the northern whale migration in June/July. These activities remain free of charge. In 2002, interpretation consisted of whale information leaflets, whale researchers able to provide commentary, hydrophones so that whale "song" could be heard, and computer plots of whale movements to facilitate better viewing of passing whales.

Currently, one operator conducts water-based commercial tours from Byron Bay on which according to his publicity material it may be possible to view whales close up. These tours cost in the vicinity of $A80. The development of water-based whale viewing in Byron Bay is restricted because of the concerns of the CBT about possible negative impacts on the whale population. In particular, access to the water is through land controlled by the CBT. Thus they are able to exercise control over water-based whale watching. Some incidental water based whale watching occurs during scuba diving and kayak tours that take place off Cape Byron. Thus, whale watching as a commercial activity is at a very early stage of its development in Byron Bay.

Five hundred kilometres further north in Hervey Bay, whale watching began serendipitously in September 1987. In that year a husband and wife business team bought a second hand boat and began a fishing tour operation in Hervey Bay. While on a fishing charter, the boat encountered rough weather and motored into the calmer waters of Platypus Bay, Fraser Island in order to avoid discomfort for his passengers. There, the boat encountered whales, creating a strong impression on the passengers:

> ... basically the reaction of the passengers who were all fishing people who forgot about fishing when they saw the whales and that gave me the idea that maybe, people would be interested in whale watching (Whale watch Operator).

On returning from the first trip, the local television studio and paper were contacted and immediately provided media coverage.

> So I rang channel 7 (the local TV station in Hervey Bay) and they asked me to come down and do an interview, in the interview they were just mind blown because here were all these people getting off boats (Whale watch Operator).

This resulted in an immediate reaction from the public and further media interest:

> our phones just went berserk ... it was absolutely incredible. So then all the (other) media started coming in (Whale watch Operator).

They began whale-watching tours three days later on his fishing boat to immediate success. As a result competitors began to also offer tours from the local harbour.

> We leased another boat and between those two boats we carried three and a half thousand people. By the end of that first season there were six boats operating. We were running two of them (Whale watch Operator).

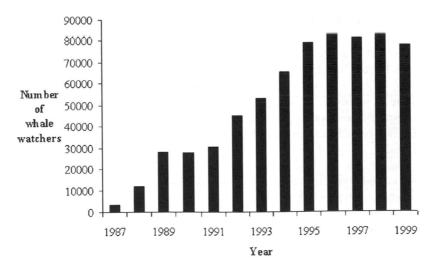

Figure 3: Whale watch passengers in Hervey Bay 1987–1999. *Source:* Queensland Parks and Wildlife (2002).

In the second year (1988) they again operated two boats, one a larger 188 passenger capacity vessel, and carried 11,000 of the 13,000 total whale watchers during the season. In 1989 there were 21 operators offering whale watch tours. In that year, the Queensland National Parks and Wildlife Service issued licences to all 21 operators. Figure 2 shows the number of whale watch passengers visitors from 1988 to 2001, based on official statistics as well as whale watch operator records. The number of passengers has grown significantly since 1987. It can be said that a niche market in whale watching has been successfully established in Hervey Bay (Figure 3).

The adoption process and diffusion process was rapid for whale watching in Hervey Bay

> From the very beginning of whale watching here, incredible media interest gave Hervey Bay promotion that no amount of money could buy, and led to thousands of people heading this way for the next whale season (Burger 1996: 94).

Analysis of the Development of Whale Watching

A number of features distinguish the evolution of a niche market in Hervey Bay in whale watch tourism from the relatively immature status of the sector in Byron Bay. Our analysis of the experience documented here of these two resorts is that it is the small enterprises that establish and lead local development of commercial whale watching.

The dynamics of the growth of the new market niche reflect the actions of individuals and also the effect of the social structures in the destination. In the case of Hervey Bay, the prior effects of the growth of environmentalism in Australia provided a large potential market for whale watching. In addition, the introduction of commercial whale watching was supported by the actions of other organizations such as news television and established companies interested in being associated with "ecotourism."

The influence of key people is evident at critical points of the development of whale watching in Hervey Bay. Firstly, the actions of the first husband and wife team are seminal. They had a history of entrepreneurship. They had retired in 1986 after developing and then selling a successful concrete batching company. This company was responsible for introducing a number of innovations into the concrete industry such as patterned concrete. Their entrepreneurial action began whale watching in Hervey Bay. The incident is described as:

> He came home after a really long trip and said "I saw whales and I think we might run a whale watching trip," and I went "Yeah right, how do you know if the whales are still going to be there?" And he said "Tomorrow I want you to go to the paper and put an ad in," so I went to the local paper (Whale watch Operator).

Apart from doing the first whale watch tour, they also introduced a number of innovations to the industry including whale spotting.

... we would fill up the plane with toilet rolls and fly out and find the whales and if we found them we would fly back to the boat, we'd give the boat about two hours start and if we flew around the boat three times clockwise then it meant we'd found the whales and then we'd fly off in the direction of the whales and drop a toilet roll for every two miles we thought the boat had to go, if we dropped three toilet rolls it meant they had to go six miles. That was right from day one that's how we signaled the boat ... (Whale watch Operator).

... as well as setting out many of the whale watch standards and, working with other local small businesses to develop a set of service suppliers required for the further development of his business and the whale watch sector.

Yeah. Within two or three we'd changed the whole thing around to ... introduced the major boats. We went out and bought busses, we introduced that, we introduced putting meals on boats to serve passengers where they used to bring a sandwich before (Whale watch Operator).

This raises the following question posed by the researcher

... I'd like to talk to you about the later years. Was what everyone was offering fairly similar to the product that you were offering?

Well, everyone pretty much followed us, we set the benchmark, such as to guarantee our trips, which is a big advertising advantage because there's nowhere else in Australia that will guarantee whale sightings and our guarantee is that we give them a free ticket to come back. The only time you wouldn't see a whale is at the beginning or end of the season or if we turn around because of rough weather (Whale watch Operator).

However, the effect of other individuals or organizations apart from the initial entrepreneur is also evident. These include the effect of the actions of Sea World, a marine wildlife research and visitor centre together with the impact of another boat owner and local identity Mimi McPherson. The initial success of whale watching in Hervey Bay is partly attributed to the actions of Sea World and their interest in being associated with wildlife preservation.

Sea World could see the potential in it, and they wanted to be on the right side, see they've got whale there that were captured and they wanted to show sort of wild things too ...

Because Sea World was saying that they were donating, I think, fifteen thousand to conservation and that was there big thing to say that. It was starting to happen where the Zoos and Circuses were having trouble because they had all the captured animals were trained so this was their way of getting o the environmental side of things (Whale watch operator).

In addition, the presence of Mimi McPherson (sister of the international supermodel Elle McPherson) in the industry added significant publicity.

> If was, funny enough, busier than what it is now, um, Mimi had what was then "Matilda 2" and she was a very high profile person for the area. There were very mixed feelings from people, they didn't like her or they did like her, you know, but whatever you thought of Mimi as a person, you could never . . . and I'll disagree with anyone, you could never take away the publicity that she received. She got more free press than the rest of the industry could pay for. That's very, very sorely missed and it's been evident from the marketing trends since her departure. So, good publicity, bad publicity, whichever way you want to look at it, it was all publicity and it was brought about by Mimi McPherson and whale watching Harvey Bay and it was all that, you know, that fantastic coverage (Whale watch operator).

Finally, the legislation determining the industry capacity was another important factor impacting on small operators.

> So, then in 1990 they decided that it would become a marine park, and because we saw seven pods of whales, we recommended that no more than three boats) go through each pod so they put out twenty one permits, which was way too many and we got an influx of boat here (Whale watch operator).

The development of whale watching in Byron Bay developed in quite a different manner. However, the underlying dynamics maybe described again by the interaction of individual actions and the structure of social organization in the destination.

In comparison to Hervey Bay, the key individuals in Byron Bay have resisted the development by local small businesses of commercial whale watching. The initial interest in whale watching in Byron Bay was derived from the interest of a whale conservation group, Project Jonah later the Australian Whale Conservation Foundation. A member of Project Jonah and whale expert described the early history of whale watching in Byron Bay . . .

> And after we've done that stuff (antiwhaling campaign) for about 18 months, someone said let's see ourselves a whale. There was no such thing as commercial whale watching anywhere at all so we decided to have a look for whales and the options were to go to Tangalooma because there was a whaling station there so there must be whales around, or go to Byron Bay because there was a whaling station there and both of those (whaling stations) closed in the mid-1960s. This was in 1979. So we decided on Byron because it had a pretty good observation. And we went down their in the hope of seeing whales (Whale expert).

As was noted earlier, whale watching in Byron Bay was also influenced by the actions of the Cape Byron Trust. This organization has acted to reduce the commercial nature of whale watching in Byron Bay on at least two occasions. In the early 1990, a whale watching weekend festival was organised on the Cape Byron Headland. The initial success of this whale watching promotion led to unwanted impacts on the amenity of Cape Byron and as a result the festival was discontinued.

> As far as how (whale watching) developed from a land-based point of view, the Cape Headland Reserve Trust used to actually promoted land-based whale watching but it got to the stage that we created a monster that we couldn't manage. It used to be that on a good Sunday we would get in excess of 12,000 people on the Cape and it got to the stage where parking was totally out of control, toilets were overflowing, people were getting grumpy because they were getting their cars booked for illegal parking they couldn't get up there the roads were blocked we were getting vegetation damage, they were safety issues about people climbing over some of the barricades, climbing down the rocky faces and things so it got to the stage that the Trust made a conscious decision to downplay whale watching, because they used to have what they called whale watch weekend (Park ranger).

A second cause of restricted supply of whale watching capacity is due to the concerns about commercial impacts by the Cape Byron Trust.

> because this reserve has the only beach access and we control that, it's fairly limited for growth because we are not allowing any more licences for vessels to go out. And one of our main aims is that this is such a good land-based whale watching area why encourage boats? (Park Ranger).

Discussion

Whale watching in Hervey Bay began at a propitious time. Public goodwill towards whale watching already existed, and the attention given by the media to the new opportunities to see whales close up rapidly increased the number of visitors. Thus the effect of prior communication and activity by environmentalists created a latent interest in whales that subsequently allowed the rapid development of whale watching by entrepreneurial small business owners.

We can see from the case studies that other operators rapidly imitated the entrepreneurial actions of one operator in Hervey Bay. The new operators offered similar products following the pattern of suppliers networks previously established. Later, the implementation of whale watch regulation effectively ensured that the standard product was "locked in." Development of whale watching in Hervey Bay is dependent on the actions of individuals as well as the interaction with existing structures and organizations and the creation of new structures and organization.

However, in the case of whale watching in Byron Bay, a different set of circumstances meant that entrepreneurs were not able to develop marine whale watching. The major resource required for whale watching in Byron Bay, (Cape Byron Headland) was controlled by a community organization and hence removed from commercial exploitation. Because the local community was aware of whales and was pro-environment the community also had a number of values and beliefs that were inconsistent with commercial whale watching. As a result, whale watching in Byron Bay did not develop into a specific commercial activity. However, it may be examined as the action of individual people within a community structure.

The actions of an entrepreneur have established a niche tourism market in Hervey Bay. However, imitation by competitors in Hervey Bay is inhibiting the potential for further growth. The nature of the product in Hervey Bay is undifferentiated making it difficult to attract new market segments. Furthermore, the competition is increasing as other resorts on Australia's East Coast have also developed whale watch tourism based on similar types of boats. Hervey Bay's special advantage is that the whales stay for periods of up to a week in the area rather than passing on their migration as is found in other destinations. There are a number of potential areas for development of new products in the region but there is little evidence of it. In fact competition in Hervey Bay appears to be hampering further growth.

> The tourism industry here has never worked in total co-operation, but with the advent of big investment it seems everyone is working individually to secure for themselves a larger share of the cake, rather than working together to try and increase the size of the cake. The growth of the whale watch industry is mainly due to the individual persistence in the market place, and not from coordinated or united approaches. There are those operators who simply do not believe a united approach would benefit them (Burger 1996: 94).

> About the only thing we do together is fund $7000 worth of television advertising and promotion, not tied to any one vessel and in the past even this has been the cause of dispute. Neither does any other sector of the Hervey Bay tourism industry offer support even to such meager joint promotion (Burger 1996: 95).

> In 1995 capacity increased by 60% as some local operators invested heavily in the industry with new vessels at the same time, as capacity usage was only 50% (May 1996: 154).

This competition operates both within the whale-watch sector in Hervey Bay and between this sector and others in the region (notably accommodation operators). A focus on new product development opportunities may enable this competition to be reduced.

Conclusions

This chapter has examined the roles of small businesses in the development of a new niche market and traces their interaction with small communities. Small businesses have been able to successfully develop a new niche market in one destination, but failed to in the other. In one region the benefits and development were primarily economic in orientation while in the other region, social values appear to have dictated limits to the development of whale watching.

The context within which small businesses can develop a new commercial niche is complex and this chapter has highlighted their interactions with the community, supplier networks and the marketplace as important factors in their success. The recognition of a new product niche does not necessarily mean that it will be successfully developed to its full potential. Instead, the values of the dominant stakeholders in the community may inhibit the growth of the new product. Additionally, the case study suggests that the supply requirements of an entrepreneur developing a new niche begin the formation of a network of supplier relations that increases the possibility of other competitors entering the market.

A number of practical and theoretical issues arise as a result of this case study that merit further research. The case suggests that a new product developed by entrepreneurial actions may become commodified as a result of the development of supplier networks. As the new product becomes established legislative responses may further define the nature of the product thus tending to define standards and reinforce commonality between suppliers. The case also suggests that the interaction of small businesses with their surrounding social and economic structure is critical in understanding their development over time.

Acknowledgment

This work has been supported in part by the Cooperative Research Centre for Sustainable Tourism, Gold Coast, Australia. It draws on the first authors' doctoral dissertation at University of Queensland.

References

Burger, A. (1996). Whale watching and regional tourism. In: K. Colgan, S. Prasser, & A. Jeffery (Eds), *Encounters with whales* (pp. 93–96). Canberra: Australian Nature Conservation Agency.

Carson, R. L. (1963). *Silent spring*. London: Hamilton.

Centre for Coastal Management (1995). *Humpback whales of eastern Australia*. Lismore, NSW: Centre for Coastal Management.

Cousteau, J., & Paccalet, Y. (1988). *Whales*. I. M. Paris (Trans.). New York: Abrams.

Decrop, A. (1999). Triangulation in tourism research. *Tourism Management, 20*(1), 157–161.

Decrop, A. (2000). *Tourism destination marketing*. Paper presented at the Tourism Destination Management, Dublin.

Denzin, N. K. (1978). *The research act: A theoretical introduction to sociological methods*. Boston: Allyn and Bacon.

Dick, B. (1987). *Convergent interviewing*. Brisbane: Interchange.

Faulkner, B. (2000). *The future ain't what it used to be: Coping with change, turbulence and disasters in tourism research and destination management*. Gold Coast: Griffith University.

Hartmann, R. (1988). Combining field methods in tourism research. *Annals of Tourism Research, 15*, 88–105.

Hoyt, E. (2001). *Whale Watching 2001: Worldwide tourism numbers, expenditures, and expanding socioeconomic benefits*. Yarmouth Port, MA, USA: International Fund for Animal Welfare.

Jick, T. D. (1983). Mixing qualitative and quantitative methods: Triangulation in action. In: J. Van Maanen (Ed.), *Qualitative methodology*. Beverley Hills, CA: Sage.

Kaufman, G., & Forestell, P. (1993). *Hawaii's humpback whales*. Maui, Hawaii: Pacific Whale Foundation.

Lincoln, Y. S., & Guba, E. G. (1985). *Naturalistic enquiry*. Beverley Hills, CA: Sage.

May, E. (1996). Developing legislation for whale watching. In: K. Colgan, S. Prasser, & A. Jeffery (Eds), *Encounters with whales* (pp. 153–157). Canberra: Australian Nature Conservation Agency.

Melville, H. (1926). *Moby Dick*. New York: Modern Library.

Muloin, S. (1998). Wildlife tourism: The psychological benefits of whale watching. *Pacific Tourism Review*, 2, 199–213.

Oppermann, M. (2000). Triangulation a methodological discussion. *International Journal of Tourism Research*, 2, 141–146.

Orams, M. B. (2000). Tourists getting close to whales, is it what whale-watching is all about? *Tourism Management*, 21, 561–569.

Pearce, D. (1993). Comparative studies in tourism research. In: R. Butler, & D. Pearce (Eds), *Tourism research: Critiques and challenges* (pp. 20–35). London: Routledge.

Ragin, C. C., & Becker, H. S. (1992). *What is a case? Exploring the foundations of social enquiry*. New York: Cambridge University Press.

Ralston, L., & Stewart, W. P. (1990). Methodological perspectives on festival research studies. *Annals of Tourism Research*, 17(2), 289–292.

Richins, H. (1999). Utilizing mixed method approaches in tourism research. *Pacific Tourism Review*, 3(1), 95–99.

Russell, R., & Faulkner, B. (1999). Movers and shakers: Chaos makers in tourism development. *Tourism Management*, 20(4), 411–423.

Tucker, M. (1989). *Whales and whaling in Australia*. Canberra: Australian National Parks and Wildlife Service.

Udall, S. L. (2000). How the wilderness was won (History of environmentalism). *American Heritage*, 51(1), 98–105.

Yin, R. K. (1994). *Case study research: Design and methods*. Thousand Oaks, CA: Sage.

Chapter 11

Small Firms and Wine and Food Tourism in New Zealand: Issues of Collaboration, Clusters and Lifestyles

C. Michael Hall

Introduction

Industrialisation, globalisation, tariff reduction, widespread growth in wealth and leisure, increased environmental awareness, growing land use conflict, ageing populations, inconsistent farm incomes and declining agricultural employment, and many other factors have served to change the face and structure of rural economies, and the lifestyles of rural people. In addition, people's expectations of rural areas are changing as greater emphasis is given to the conservation and maintenance of natural and cultural heritage and amenity landscapes with often little appreciation of the industrial forces which led to the creation of those landscapes and heritage. In short, economic, environmental and social developments and issues are putting increasingly varied and complex pressures on rural areas in many industrialised countries resulting in new forms of rural production and consumption associated with economic diversification and restructuring (Butler *et al.* 1998).

The present chapter discusses a specific type of small business response to the present rural context. It examines the means by which small food and wine tourism businesses can compete more effectively within the context of regional cluster and network theory. Case studies of the development of food and wine tourism networks are provided from New Zealand to illustrate some of the issues inherent in the establishment of competitive business and networks. The chapter concludes by highlighting the importance of social capital and communication flows in developing competitive regions as well as the role of intangible capital in binding small businesses together within wine and food tourism clusters and networks.

Food and Wine Tourism

Given the challenges facing many rural regions it should therefore not be surprising that tourism and new forms of food production are seen as potentially significant sources of economic development. For example, long seen as only a "bit part" or "minor" industry in terms of national development, tourism has now assumed centre stage as a major source of foreign income and overseas investment and as a key component in New Zealand's regional development strategies (Hall & Kearsley 2001). The reasons for the change of attitude towards tourism by politicians, business and the public alike are complex but several reasons can be put forward. First, New Zealand has suffered major recessions and concerns over foreign debt since the mid-1970s. International tourism in particular is seen as a mechanism to help boost export income. Second, economic deregulation and the impacts of globalisation have affected "traditional" employment in the manufacturing and agricultural sectors. Tourism is therefore seen as a "sunrise" industry that is labour intensive and which offers the potential to be a substantial source of employment. Finally, New Zealand has become a significant international destination which utilises a tourism brand strategy (100% Pure) which serves to leverage the brand strategies of a number of New Zealand agricultural products such as apples and pears, cheese and wine thereby creating overall national brand awareness (Tourism Strategy Group 2000).

However, not only are food production and tourism significant individual sectors in rural economies, the relationship between food and tourism also represents a significant opportunity for rural diversification. Specialised products offer the opportunity for the development of visitor product through rural tours, direct purchasing from the farm, specialised restaurant menus, and home stays on such properties (Bessiëre 1998). Indeed, in these circumstances, outsider interest in local produce may serve to stimulate local awareness and interest, and assist not only in diversification, and maintenance of plant and animal variety, but may also encourage community pride and reinforcement of local identity and culture (Centre for Environment and Society 1999; Hall *et al.* 1997).

The use of food and wine tourism to drive local economic development has already started in many rural regions and is often encouraged through state intervention in the development of business networks. For example, through the European Union's LEADER programme (Hall *et al.* 2000) or through the support of various Australian governments for the creation of food and wine tourism networks (Hall *et al.* 1997). Interestingly, in the Australian situation, the development of wine and food tourism initiatives has tended to occur "top-down" through the financial backing and policy involvement of the relevant state and federal governments (Macionis & Cambourne 2000). The Australian Bureau of Industry Economics (BIE) (1991a, b) identified four potential roles for government in the development of networks:

- disseminating information on the opportunities created by networks;
- encouraging cooperation within industries through industry associations;
- improving existing networks between the private sector and public sector agencies involved in research and development, education and training; and
- examining the effects of the existing legislative and regulatory framework on the formation, maintenance and breakup of networks relative to other forms of organisation, such as markets and firms.

In the case of wine and food tourism in Australia, government has directly utilised the first of the three roles in the creation of specific organisations and/or the provision of funding for research, education, cooperative strategies and mechanisms, and information provision.

The BIE (1991a, b) considered information gaps to be a major factor in the impairment of network formation. Indeed, there are substantial negative attitudes towards tourism by wineries and some food producers, whereas tourism organisations tend to be far more positive towards the wine and food industry. This situation is reflective of Leiper's (1989) concept of tourism's partial industrialisation that suggests that businesses need to perceive that they are part of the tourism industry before they will formally interact with tourism suppliers.

Although New Zealand shares numerous similarities with Australia in terms of attitudes of producers towards the tourism industry there has been virtually no national government involvement in trying to create wine and food tourism networks beyond having large producers participate in cooperative marketing and branding schemes (Hall *et al.* 1997). In Australia innovation and the creation of networks has occurred in great part at the regional level because of government involvement, in New Zealand where innovation has occurred it has primarily been because of champions and individual innovators who have been able to generate local interest and involvement. Although the election of a centrist Labour Government in 1999 did at least lead to a rediscovery of the potential role of the state intervention as a mechanism for regional development, through, for example, funding for America's Cup initiatives, this has not translated into developments in the rural tourism economy (Hall & Kearsley 2001).

From the perspective of small rural business development, tourism can be part of the core business activities for many boutique wineries, smallholdings or horticultural businesses, especially those who have chosen rural production as a lifestyle option. For example, newly established small-scale wineries tend to sell most of their wine at the cellar door, and gain an essential source of cash-flow in the early stage of business development, particularly as they experience greater per bottle returns from the cellar door than by selling through retail outlets. In addition, cellar door sales provide an opportunity to develop a mailing-list of customers which can then be used for direct-marketing. Some wineries also produce a newsletter and/or web site as a means of maintaining customer relationships. However, one difficulty of cellar-door sales for some small wineries however is that serving customers may take time away from other viticultural activities, particularly during harvest, while the small scale production of many boutique wineries means that they may have to close the cellar door to visitors for some periods of the year if they have run out of stock.

For more established rural producers, visitors provide a test-bed for new products. Tourism also facilitates producer-consumer interaction and involves education about and experience of products and the wider region. Furthermore, for both large and small scale businesses tourism can be very important in terms of brand development. However, tourism needs to be seen part of the overall development of small rural businesses rather than necessarily an end in itself. The manner in which wine tourism is used as a component of the business mix will therefore depend on the stage of business development, overall business goals, location, and target markets (Dodd & Biggotte 1995; Hall 2002; Hall *et al.* 2000).

Arguably, one of the keys to maximising the benefits of food, wine and tourism in rural regional development is through understanding the nature of the global intangible economy in which we now operate (Hall 2002). Therefore, not only will firms survive if they have access to priviliged capital but places and regions as well. What is increasingly recognised with respect to differentiation and perceptions of quality of rural produce is that the development of intangible capital can provide rural regions, and the businesses that lie within them, substantial competitive advantages.

Many rural regions and small businesses have intangible assets — knowledge, relationships, reputations and people. However, only some firms and regions succeed in converting these assets into intangible capital. Intangible assets create value when captured as intellectual property, networks, brand, and talent (Daley 2001). All these intangibles are significant for successful rural development through wine and food tourism. That is, if, over an extended period of time, a region can show that it learns and is able to move forward — from the framework of opportunities offered within declining industries — into new industries and new processes (Cooke 1995). For example, intellectual property and brand has served to reinforce the role of appellations within international food and wine production, e.g. Champagne, as well as the development of a system of legally protected geographic descriptors for certain products, e.g. Prosciutto di Parma, Roquefort, and Cornish clotted cream. However, for the purpose of the present chapter we are focussing attention on the role of networks as one component of the intangible capital of regions and small business.

Networks

Networks and cluster relationships are a significant part of the development of intangible capital and are a major focal point for much contemporary discussion of regional development. Networking refers to a wide range of cooperative behaviour between otherwise competing organisations and between organisations linked through economic and social relationships and transactions. Often the term is synonymous with inter-firm cooperation. Industry clusters exist where there is geographic concentration or association of firms and organisations involved in a value chain producing goods and services and innovating. Suggesting that business clusters add value to a region implies an entirely new set of public policies, one that shifts the focus of attention from an individual place or individual firm to a region and clusters of businesses and the interaction between them (Rosenfeld 1997). A cluster may therefore be defined as a concentration of companies and industries in a geographic region that are interconnected by the markets they serve and the products they produce, as well as by the suppliers, trade associations and educational institutions with which they interact (Porter 1990). Many commentators argue that such chains of firms are the primary "drivers" of a region's economy, on whose success other businesses, such as construction firms, for example, depend on in terms of their own financial viability. Nevertheless, for the cluster concept to become a legitimate and useful subject of analysis and policy, it must be defined more clearly than it has been. However, objective criteria for clusters have proven exceedingly difficult to pin down, and there are arguably "as many definitions as there are types of organizations using the term" (Rosenfeld 1997: 8). Rosenfeld (1997: 9) argues that to all intents and purposes, networks are a result of mature and animated clusters, not the source of a local production system, whereas clusters are systems in which membership is simply based on interdependence and making a contribution to the functioning of the system. Table 1 draws some comparisons between idealised notion of the cluster and network concepts.

Table 1: Networks or clusters?

Networks	Clusters
Networks allow firms access to specialized services at lower cost	Clusters attract needed specialized services to a region
Networks have restricted membership	Clusters have open "membership"
Networks are often based on contractual agreements	Clusters are based on social values that foster trust and encourage reciprocity
Networks make it easier for firms to engage in complex business	Clusters generate demand for more firms with similar and related capabilities
Networks are based on cooperation	Clusters take both cooperation and competition
Networks have common business goals	Clusters have collective visions

Source: After Rosenfeld (1997).

An industry cluster includes companies that sell inside as well as outside the region, and also supports firms that supply raw materials, components and business services to them. These clusters form "value chains" that are the fundamental units of competition in the modern, globalised world economy. Clusters in a region form over time and stem from the region's economic foundations, its existing companies and local demand for products and services (Waits 2000). Firms and organisations involved in clusters are able to achieve synergies and leverage economic advantage from shared access to information and knowledge networks, supplier and distribution chains, markets and marketing intelligence, competencies, and resources in a specific locality. The cluster concept therefore focuses attention on the linkages and interdependencies among actors in value chains (Enright & Roberts 2001).

Wine has been recognised as one industry in which clustering is a significant competitive factor. Indeed, Porter (1990) himself used the California wine industry as an example of successful cluster development. Similarly, Blandy (2000: 21) cites the example of the South Australian wine industry as "the classic example of a successful industry cluster in South Australia . . . a group of competing, complementary and interdependent firms that have given strong economic drive to the State through the cluster's success in exporting its products and know how nationally and internationally." Marsh & Shaw (2000) have similarly commented that clustering and collaboration have been the primary reason for the success of the Australian wine industry.

Cluster formation is regarded as a significant component in the formation of positive external economies for firms, including those of the wine industry, with tourism being recognised as a significant component (Porter 1990), while Telfer (2000) has argued that cluster development has been a significant component of wine and food tourism network development in the Niagara region of Canada. Tastes of Niagara in Ontario which is a Quality Food Alliance of Niagara food producers, winemakers, chefs, restaurateurs and retailers (http://www.tourismniagara.com/tastesofniagara/index.html). Established in 1993 members have joined together to promote the uniqueness of the region's agricultural products to consumers through the development of and maintenance of high quality regional produce, cuisine, events and service. Although one of the lessons of cluster development programs around the world "is that there is no precise, 'right' (one size fits all) formula for developing industry clusters" (Blandy 2000: 80), a number of factors have been recognised as significant in the development of clusters and the associated external economy which serves to reinforce the clustering process. These include:

- the life cycle stage of innovative clusters;
- government financing and policies;
- the skills of the region's human resources;
- the technological capabilities of the region's R&D activities;
- the quality of the region's physical, transport, information and communication infrastructure;
- the availability and expertise of capital financing in the region;
- the cost and quality of the region's tax and regulatory environment; and
- the appeal of the region's lifestyle to people that can provide world class resources and processes.

What is remarkable in many of the accounts of cluster development, with Blandy's (2000) review being typical, is that few of the models or accounts of clusters adequately capture and describe the underlying dynamics of clusters. They do not explain how they actually "work" or answer questions of whether and how firms interact and produce synergy. Scale is only part of reason that clusters and their regions prosper. In the case of the wine industry it could be argued that wine clusters form because of the environmental determination of where one can produce wine. Equally important to the circuitry of the system is the "current," or the flow of information, knowledge, technological advances, innovations, skills, people, and capital into, out of, and within the cluster, from point to point (Rosenfeld 1997). Conventional data cannot distinguish between a simple industry concentration and a working cluster. As Doeringer & Terkla (1995: 228) observed: "Although interindustry transactions incorporated within production channels can sometimes be detected in input-output tables, neither the character of relationships among firms nor the benefits of clustering can be discerned in this way." However, in a cluster, the social ecology is as important as the agglomeration economies. As Rosenfeld (1997: 10) comments, "The 'current' of a working production system is even less easily detected, often embedded in professional, trade and civic associations, and in informal socialization patterns . . . The 'current' depends on norms of reciprocity and sufficient levels of trust to encourage professional interaction and collaborative behaviour."

In light of the role of trust as a strategic factor in regional development (Hall 2001), Rosenfeld (1997: 10) redefined clusters as "A geographically bounded concentration of interdependent businesses with active channels for business transactions, dialogue, and communications, and that collectively shares common opportunities and threats." Importantly, this definition asserts that "active channels" are as important as "concentration," and without active channels even a critical mass of related firms is not a local production or social system and therefore does not operate as a cluster. Without such active channels it is extremely unlikely that the various firms in a region, large or small, can actively cooperate in order to achieve regional aims (e.g. see Saxenian 1994). Therefore, in seeking to understand the processes of cluster development recognition of social capital and the relative efficiency of channels of social exchange becomes a vital component of the research process. Indeed, the co-location of firms may at times lead to a lack of social exchange as often as it does to a positive sharing of knowledge and ideas unless the firms are seen to have some shared interests on which they communicate.

Such a situation may well be critical with respect to maximising the contribution of clusters to regional economy. In the case of Porter's (1990) citing of the wine industry of California as an example of a cluster and Blandy's (2000) reference to the South Australian wine industry cluster it seems that the authors failed to recognise that in both cases the wine industry had been in place for well over a hundred years (often with the establishment of substantial family networks over that period) and with tourism being a late, and often incidental, arrival in both cases as a component of the cluster. Furthermore, given that the areas had been wine regions for such a long-period and that wine is an environmentally dependent resource it is therefore not surprising that certain elements of a cluster formation had developed in this time. Perhaps a more significant question is therefore what understanding does existing work on clusters provide us for identifying the factors in developing new clusters particularly in rural areas which have undergone fundamental economic restructuring. Unfortunately, unless research indicates how firms interact and clusters actually work over time the answer is likely to be very little. The following case study discusses the development of wine and food tourism clusters in New Zealand. It details three regions and their relative success and posits reasons as to why this success has been achieved in relation to the importance of social capital.

Wine and Food Tourism in New Zealand

The wine industry has been one of New Zealand's rural success stories in recent years. Although other traditional rural industries have struggled to maintain growth in the light of industry restructuring, shifts in export demand and currency fluctuations, wine has had a cinderalla existence from being a minor agricultural industry to dominating the landscape in a number of rural areas. This growth can be charted not only in terms of number of wineries and the area under vine but also the substantial export returns that have developed.

Three leading New Zealand wine regions, Central Otago, Hawkes Bay, and Marlborough — which exhibit cluster characteristics have been studied since 1996 in terms of the development of wine and food tourism. Although Hawkes Bay is the longest established wine region it has recently witnessed a substantial growth in the number of wineries in the area, with Marlborough becoming established in the late 1980s and Central Otago in the 1990s as recognised wine producing areas (Table 2) (Cooper 2002). Nevertheless, although having similar numbers of wineries substantial differences exist in their capacity to establish interfirm cooperation particularly with respect to wine and food tourism.

Several barriers to creating effective links between wine and food producers and the tourism industry may be recognised (Hall *et al.* 1997, 2000, 2003a, b):

Table 2: Wineries by region.

	1992	1993	1994	1995	1996	1997	1998	1999	2000	2001
Hawkes Bay	21	21	23	24	31	33	35	41	44	50
Marlborough	13	20	28	35	43	47	52	60	62	63
Otago	6	7	8	8	11	14	23	26	39	44
Total	166	175	190	204	238	262	293	334	358	376

Note: All figures are for the year end June except 2001 which shows year to date. *Source:* After http://www.nzwine.com/statistics/

- the often perceived secondary or tertiary nature of tourism as an activity in the wine and food industries, accompanied by a common perception that there is an imbalance of benefits from food, wine and tourism relationships with the greater advantage accruing to tourism firms;
- a dominant product focus of wine makers and wine marketers;
- a general lack of experience and understanding within the food and wine industries of tourism, and a subsequent lack of entrepreneurial skills and abilities with respect to marketing and product development; and
- the absence of effective intersectoral linkages, which leads to a lack of inter and intra or-ganisational cohesion within the food and wine industries, and between the wine industry and the tourism industry.

In examining the development of wine, food and tourism clusters in the three study areas little differences were noted in the factors regarded as significant in the development of clusters and the reinforcement of the clustering process noted in the previous section. Instead, these being reasonably constant, Hall (2001, 2002) identified several other factors which may affect cluster and network success in relation to food and wine tourism in New Zealand:

- spatial separation — the existence of substantial spatial separation of vineyards and wineries within a wine region due to physical resource factors whereby physical distance may contribute to increased communicative distance between firms and stakeholders;
- administrative separation — the existence of multiple public administrative agencies and units within a region which potentially leads to institutional rivalry and lack of consistent message and support for cluster processes;
- the existence of a "champion" to promote the development of a network;
- the hosting of meetings to develop relationships and, related to this, the extent of local social capital.

Of which the role of champions as well as the involvement of the local state was regarded as especially important in the creation of wine and food tourism networks and associated new product development in the New Zealand situation (also see Henton & Walesh 1997). Such an observation is significant, as Audretsch & Feldman (1997) have argued that the generation of new economic knowledge tends to result in a greater propensity for innovative activity to cluster during the early stages of the industry life cycle, and to be more highly dispersed during the mature and declining stages of the life cycle.

In the case of Hawkes Bay such developments have occurred primarily because several local champions emerged convinced of the need to promote Hawkes Bay collectively as they saw that their own individual businesses would be more successful if there was a strong brand and producer network. According to one such champion, Graeme Avery of Selini Estate winery, "I think [Hawke's Bay Tourism] has mixed masters. It tried to please all its masters and I think that's where the mixed messages came in. Also it had no real industry clout" (Quaintance 2001: 40). In tourism terms they recognised that their individual business may not be sufficient to generate the required volumes of visitors but that if there was a critical and connected mass of visitor attractors then their own business would benefit because the overall marker for their business would have increased. Following their formation at a public seminar in July 2000 the Hawkes Bay Wine and Food group have developed a food and wine trail, brochures; improved signage, and have engaged in more effective joint promotion strategies, including the development of a wine and food oriented Hawke's Bay regional brand. Indeed, such has been the success of the group that local government is having to respond to their initiative. In November 2001 Hawkes Bay hosted the second New Zealand wine and food tourism conference as part of the development of a national food and wine tourism strategy. However, unlike the Australian examples discussed above, such initiatives have come out of the private sector and from the goodwill of certain individuals rather than having occurred because of government involvement. Critical to the development of the Food and Wine Group was the involvement of "experts" or "knowledge brokers" at the initial meeting who could provide what was perceived as "independent" advice to attendees and which helped create a climate of trust between potential small business members of the cluster and, just as importantly, allowed the work of champions to be perceived as wider than self-interest in the creation of the group.

In the case of the Hawkes Bay wine and food tourism network appropriate collaborative arrangements (Forde 2000, Hall 2001) have been put in place through.

Organisational arrangements between cluster members that give the cluster an identity and profile the industry sector, e.g. Hawkes Bay Food and Wine Tourism Group under the brand of Hawke's Bay Wine Country. They create the framework for development of the cluster and implementation of initiatives. Importantly, ownership of the brand has now been adopted by those external to the wine and food tourism sector which has helped reinforce the strength of the brand for regional development.

Standard operating procedures agreed by members for transferring information, communicating with each other and organizing around market opportunities, e.g. through regular group meetings.

Administrative support services that are developed to give effect to the above.

Marlborough held meetings to establish a farmers market in early 2001 with the first market being held in late 2001 although no distinct and consistently used food and wine tourism brand has been established. Interestingly, attempts to bring the food and wine sectors together within a regional context had been occurring since 1996 although the champions tended to come from the local tourist organisation. As individuals left the organisation (often because of frustration with local government and stakeholder politics) so interest was lost only for it to be "rediscovered" when another person committed to wine and food tourism joined the local tourism body. Although Marlborough has a strong food and wine tourism profile, and a very high profile internationally in the wine industry, there is no clear series of industry relationships and public-private sector partnerships as developed in Hawkes Bay.

Little multi-firm wine and tourism developments occurred in Otago over the same period although many individual firms were established and wine trails developed. Nevertheless, the wine trails consisted of sets of dyadic relations with a tour operator and individual wineries rather than a fully developed network although improved inter-winery cooperation has at least led to the development of cooperative marketing efforts. Indeed, common exporting issues appear to be more of a driver for small winery cooperation than interest in developing the synergies available through wine and food tourism. However, the arrival of a new local tourism organisation head for one of the towns in the region in late 2002 with an interest in wine and food tourism may provide a champion for cooperative action between the wine and food sectors.

From fieldwork conducted in the study areas since 1996 it is apparent that at an individual level many firms and public agencies are seeking the creation of networks and the benefits of clustering in both regions. Nevertheless, the pre-existence of wine and tourism organisations is not necessarily a forerunner to cluster development. Indeed, inter-organisational rivalry may work against new inter-sectoral networks being established because of threats they may pose to the organisations. Instead, two factors, the role of a champion to initiate cluster development and the associated holding of regular stakeholder meetings to facilitate cooperation and communication appear to be far more significant in facilitating stakeholder collaboration that other factors. In addition, the lack of continued leadership in terms of cluster development also becomes an issue. For example, in the case of Marlborough these has been a number of champions emerge seeking to encourage collaboration. However, they were not consistently in place long enough in their positions within local government to lead to the creation of long-term collaborative relationships in part because of the stakeholders they were directly answerable too. While stakeholder meetings provide part of the basis for the development of trust within a cluster it is readily apparent that someone has to organise. In some areas such a single act as this can prove difficult because of community politics.

An additional dimension to collaborative relations in all three areas is the role of lifestyle entrepreneurs. Wine and food tourism has tended to attract a number of entrepreneurs, many of whom are semi-retired, who are seeking the perceived lifestyle benefits of rural living. These small landholders have often focussed on wine and food (e.g. horticulture, cheese, truffle, nut, organics, herb production) as a means of earning an income. However, such lifestyle entrepreneurs are often not favourably looked at by the larger producers potentially leading to non-cooperative behaviour. Yet, such small scale producers are often at the forefront of product and service innovation in these rural regions and also substantially add to the diversity of the region and therefore its attractiveness. In the case of Hawkes Bay it is apparent that both large and small firms have recognised the mutual benefits of collaboration cluster activation. This is not the case in the other regions. In part this may be because of community attitudes, particularly regarding "new arrivals," although another significant factor does appear to be recognition of the products and skill sets available from lifestyle entrepreneurs. Yet, for such recognition to have occurred the role of champions, knowledge brokers and opportunities for information sharing at meetings appear critical. Indeed, whereas the information provided by a champion, particularly from someone "outside" of the rural community may be initially mistrusted by those "inside" the community, knowledge brokers provide information on which small businesses are able to potentially perceive the financial benefits of investing their scarce resources in network behaviours.

Conclusions

Cluster activation is a critical first step toward realizing the potential of a group of industries as an engine of economic growth. Clusters are activated when companies in related industries come together formally as an organised industry cluster (Connecticut Department of Economic and Community Development 1999). However, geographical co-location does not necessarily lead to cluster development and activation. Instead, communicative relationships need to be established between partners. Without an appropriate cluster champion and associated relationship creating strategy (formal or otherwise) co-location may as much lead to rivalry that works against cluster development as behaviours that do. The creation of trust becomes a critical component in this exercise and outside independent knowledge brokers appear extremely important in providing an understanding of the economic and social context of cluster development.

The further development of social capital through the creation of networks is extremely important in terms of its capacity to reduce the level of uncertainty for entrepreneurs in the creation of new businesses. Network-based relationships can provide entrepreneurs with critical information, knowledge and resources. Social and intellectual capital, including access to prior experience can therefore be used to maximise the scarce capital available to some small food and wine businesses. Particularly in the case of Hawkes Bay, discussed above, social capital has assisted in the development of trusting relationships which has allowed various network members to overcome issues of smallness and newness through their affiliation with prestigious and well-established businesses within the overall context not only of network membership but also brand association. Such a strategy represents a classic model of resource acquisition by new small business ventures (McGee *et al.* 1995; Starr & MacMillan 1990), the significance of which has been little recognised in studies of tourism networks and entrepreneurship (Hall *et al.* 1997).

The long term benefits of network relationships remains an interesting question for small wine and food tourism businesses. Venkataraman & Van de Ven (1998) argue that it only makes sense to leverage social capital in the early stages of a new venture. According to their research, as ventures progress businesses base their decisions on economic criteria, and social capital has less impact. Ironically, this means that the very network relationships that help to reduce risk and uncertainty in small business start-ups fade in importance when uncertainty becomes less. Such an interpretation may mean that the importance of social ties may therefore be a function of the level of uncertainty facing a small business entrepreneur. Yet the application of this to the food and wine tourism sphere may be problematic given the importance of regional brands as a means not only of destination promotion but also of place and product differentiation. Arguably once the geographical designation is established and accepted in the market (e.g. appellations such as Champagne, Burgundy, or Napa Valley) it

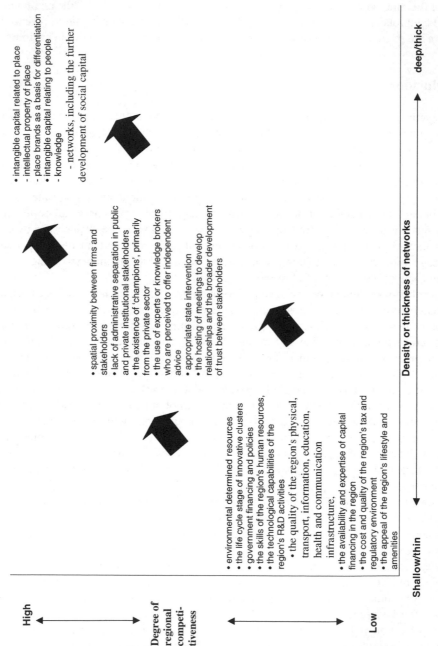

Figure 1: Ideal pathway for the increasing competitiveness of regional food, wine and tourism clusters and networks.

then becomes extremely difficult for ventures to withdraw from networks which support the place brand as it would potentially mean the loss of significant intangible capital and a direct economic resource. This observation may have substantial implications for the longevity and success of place and brand-oriented clusters and networks. Once place-brands have established their presence in the market they not only contribute to the success of the cluster and individual businesses but they also contribute to the development of further social capital because they become integral to the identity of place and the firms and individuals within it (Figure 1). This iterative and recursive process does not mean that such clusters have an infinite lifespan, nor does it mean that wine and food regions automatically shift in building block fashion from a basic cluster configuration to a network relationship and then form a dense network set of social, economic and intangible capital which comes to be deeply embedded in the region's social, cultural, economic, industrial and political formations. However, the particular congruence of intangible capital to be found within the food, wine and tourism industries does potentially lead to longer cluster life-cycles and the associated longer-term maintenance of social networks and capital.

This chapter has argued that within the food and wine tourism sectors small business success needs to be understood within the broader context of contemporary business research on clusters and networks. It has emphasised that such relationships need to be understood in social, cultural and communicative terms as much as they are from economic perspectives. Moreover, the role of place and intangible capital is regarded as highly significant for cluster and network characteristics particularly given the potential of strategic small business investment in network development. Therefore, future research on the role of clustering and networks in rural wine and food tourism which is usually seeking to bridge industrial firm and sectoral divides need to pay further attention to the social mechanisms which enhance and maintain collaborative relations in addition to locational strategies. Such mechanisms are obviously significant beyond the immediate domain of tourism. Nevertheless, this chapter has also raised fundamental issues with respect to the role of place, in the form of destinations, intellectual-property and branding, so central to the competitiveness of wine, food and tourism, to our understanding of the processes and life-spans of clusters and networks. Place matters!

References

Audretsch, D. B., & Feldman, M. P. (1997). *Innovative clusters and the industry life cycle.* C. E. P. R. Discussion Papers 1161. London: Centre for Economic Policy Research.

Bessiëre, J. (1998). Local development and heritage: Traditional food and cuisine as tourist attractions in rural areas. *Sociologia Ruralis, 38*(1), 21–34.

Blandy, R. (2000). *Industry clusters program: A review.* South Australian Business Vision 2010. Adelaide: Government of South Australia.

Bureau of Industry Economics (1991a). *Networks: A third form of organisation.* Discussion Paper 14. Canberra: Bureau of Industry Economics.

Bureau of Industry Economics (1991b). Networks: A third form of organisation. *Bulletin of Industry Economics, 10*, 5–9.

Centre for Environment and Society (1999). *Local food systems: Lessons for local economies conference proceedings.* Colchester: University of Essex.

Cooke, P. (1995). Keeping to the high road: Learning, reflexivity and associative governance in regional economic development. In: P. Cooke (Ed.), *The rise of the rustbelt*. London: University College Press.

Cooper, M. (2002). *Wine atlas of New Zealand*. Auckland: Hodder Moa Beckett Publishers.

Connecticut Department of Economic and Community Development (1999). *Industry cluster progress report — November/1999*. Hartford: Industry Cluster and International Division.

Daley, G. (2001). The intangible economy and Australia. *Australian Journal of Management, 26*, 3–20.

Dodd, T. H., & Biggotte, V. (1995). *Visitors to Texas wineries: Their demographic characteristics and purchasing behavior*. Lubbock: Texas Wine Marketing Research Institute.

Doeringer, B., & Terkla, D. G. (1995). Business strategy and cross-industry clusters. *Economic Development Quarterly, 9*, 225–237.

Enright, M., & Roberts, B. (2001). Regional clustering in Australia. *Australian Journal of Management, 26*, 65–86.

Forde, H. (2000). *Industry clusters and collaboration*. Occasional Paper SABV2010 Industry Cluster Project. Adelaide: Government of South Australia.

Hall, C. M. (2001). The development of rural wine and food tourism networks: Factors and issues. In: *New directions in managing rural tourism and leisure: Local impacts, global trends* (CDrom). Auchenvyre: Scottish Agricultural College.

Hall, C. M. (2002). Local initiatives for local regional development: The role of food, wine and tourism. In: *The 2nd tourism industry and education symposium, 'Tourism and well-being' (May 16–18, 2002)* (pp. 47–63). Jyväskylä, Finland: Jyväskylä Polytechnic.

Hall, C. M., Cambourne, B., Macionis, N., & Johnson, G. (1997). Wine tourism and network development in Australia and New Zealand: Review, establishment and prospects. *International Journal of Wine Marketing, 9*(2/3), 5–31.

Hall, C. M., Johnson, G., & Mitchell, R. (2000). Wine tourism and regional development. In: C. M. Hall, E. Sharples, B. Cambourne, & N. Macionis (Eds), *Wine tourism around the world: Development, management and markets* (pp. 196–226). Oxford: Butterworth-Heinemann.

Hall, C. M., & Kearsley, G. W. (2001). *Tourism in New Zealand: An introduction*. Melbourne: Oxford University Press.

Hall, C. M., Longo, A. M., Mitchell, R., & Johnson, G. (2000). Wine tourism in New Zealand. In: C. M. Hall, E. Sharples, B. Cambourne, & N. Macionis (Eds), *Wine tourism around the world: Development, management and markets* (pp. 150–174). Oxford: Butterworth-Heinemann.

Hall, C. M., Mitchell, R., & Sharples, L. (2003a). Consuming places: The role of food, wine and tourism in regional development. In: C. M. Hall, E. Sharples, R. Mitchell, B. Cambourne, & N. Macionis (Eds), *Food tourism around the world: Development, management and markets* (pp. 25–59). Oxford: Butterworth-Heinemann.

Hall, C. M., Sharples, L., & Smith, A. (2003b). The experience of consumption or the consumption of experiences: Challenges and issues in food tourism. In: C. M. Hall, E. Sharples, R. Mitchell, B. Cambourne, & N. Macionis (Eds), *Food tourism around the world: Development, management and markets* (pp. 314–336). Oxford: Butterworth-Heinemann.

Henton, D., & Walesh, K. (1997). *Grassroots leaders for a new economy: How civic entrepreneurs are building prosperous communities*. San Francisco: Jossey-Bass.

Leiper, N. (1989). *Tourism and tourism systems*. Occasional Paper No. 1. Palmerston North: Department of Management Systems, Massey University.

Macionis, N., & Cambourne, B. (2000). The development of a national wine tourism plan? Wine tourism organisations and development in Australia. In: C. M. Hall, E. Sharples, B. Cambourne, & N. Macionis (Eds), *Wine tourism around the world: Development, management and markets* (pp. 226–253). Oxford: Butterworth-Heinemann.

Marsh, I., & Shaw, I. (2000). *Australia's wine industry: Collaboration and learning as causes of competitive success*. Sydney: Australian Business Foundation.

McGee, J. E., Dowling, M. J., & Megginson, W. L. (1995). Cooperative strategy and new venture performance: The role of business strategy and management experience. *Strategic Management Journal, 16*, 565–580.

Porter, M. (1990). *The competitive advantage of nations*. London: Macmillan.

Quaintance, L. (2001). The bountiful bay: Let the good times roll. *North and South, 181*(April), 32–42.

Rosenfeld, S. A. (1997). Bringing business clusters into the mainstream of economic development. *European Planning Studies, 5*(1), 3–23.

Saxenian, A. (1994). *Regional advantage: Culture and competition in Silicon Valley and Route 128*. Boston: Harvard University Press.

Starr, J. A., & MacMillan, I. C. (1990). Resource cooptation and social contracting: Resource acquisition strategies for new ventures. *Strategic Management Journal, 11*, 79–92.

Telfer, D. J. (2000). The northeast wine route: Wine tourism in Ontario, Canada and New York State. In: C. M. Hall, E. Sharples, B. Cambourne, & N. Macionis (Eds), *Wine tourism around the world: Development, management and markets* (pp. 253–271). Oxford: Butterworth-Heinemann.

Tourism Strategy Group (2000). *New Zealand tourism strategy 2001*. Wellington: Office of the Minister of Tourism/Tourism Strategy Group.

Venkataraman, S., & Van de Ven, A. H. (1998). Hostile environmental jolts, transaction set, and new business. *Journal of Business Venturing, 13*, 231–255.

Waits, M. J. (2000). The added value of the industry cluster approach to economic analysis, strategy development, and service delivery. *Economic Development Quarterly, 14*, 35–50.

Chapter 12

Quality Homes, Quality People: The Challenge of Quality Grading and Assurance in Small Accommodation Enterprises

Paul A. Lynch and Hazel Tucker

Introduction

This chapter reflects critically on the relevance of current quality grading and assurance schemes to small accommodation enterprises in which a home dimension is a common feature. The discussion focuses specifically on the cases of New Zealand and Scotland, looking comparatively at the nature of small tourist accommodation businesses and at the quality grading and assurance schemes in place in those contexts.

A current trend in the tourist market in New Zealand is for increasing numbers of tourists to want to get off the beaten track, interact with local people and experience aspects of the destinations they visit apart from the usual tourist icons (Hall & Page 2002; Ombler 1997). In terms of accommodation, there is increasing demand for small tourism accommodation enterprises. In New Zealand, Bed and Breakfast (B&Bs), home-stays and farm-stays represent a rapidly growing sector of the tourism industry, providing tourists with a variety of accommodation choices over and above the more mainstream options such as hotels, motels, motor-camps and "backpackers" which were the standard up until the late 1980s (Ombler 1997). This growth and increase in importance of the home-hosted sector has led to the recent inclusion of this type of accommodation within New Zealand's national quality grading scheme.

Similarly, in the United Kingdom, in absolute numbers of tourism nights the following types of accommodation have all increased over the 1990–1999 period: friend's/relative's house, other private house/B&B, hotel/motel/guest house, self-catering in rented house/chalet (UKTS 2000). When examined in detail, during the period 1990–1999, other private house/B&B increased by a massive 86%, self-catering in rented friend's/relative's house by 33%, and only small increases in hotel/motel/guest house and self-catering in rented house/chalet. A reduction occurred in tourism nights in self-catering in rented flat/apartment of 13.3% and of 13.3% in self-catering in holiday camp/village. As in New Zealand, the demand therefore seems to be increasingly leaning towards private house, or "hosted," accommodation. In Scotland, a national quality assurance and grading scheme including all types of accommodation other than cultural homestays is well-established.

It might be questioned, however, whether supporting tourism infrastructures are sufficiently sensitive to the nature of such small accommodation establishments. Arguably, an important part of the success of small tourism businesses is about getting away from offering standardised accommodation products as might be found in larger accommodation establishments. Therefore, it becomes important to consider the extent to which, for example, quality grading and assurance schemes, are relevant to small tourism firms. Such schemes are, in the eyes of the authors, examples of essentially large firm models. As such, it is crucial to take a critical look at their relevance, particularly given the relative paucity of research concerning the smaller tourism firm. In this instance, a practical consequence of allowing a large firm model to predominate may be to harm the quality of the accommodation experience through the very mechanisms intended to raise the quality.

The purpose of this chapter, therefore, is to discuss the difficulty of applying large firm models, such as quality grading and assurance schemes, to small, home-based, tourism businesses, and to question the relevance of such applications. The chapter will begin by considering the characteristics of the home-hosted accommodation sector and then explore the concept of the home and its significance. Attention will then be paid to the hosts and guests of small accommodation firms prior to discussing and then evaluating the quality grading and assurance schemes. In conclusion, it will be argued that there is a particular need for enhanced subjective grading to inform quality grading and assurance schemes.

Characteristics of the Homestay or Home-Hosted Accommodation Sector

A difficulty experienced by the authors drawing upon Scottish and New Zealand studies is that of finding common terms with the same shared meaning to describe their units of study. Both authors' research has focused upon small accommodation establishments. In a New Zealand context the focus has been upon B&Bs, home-stay, and farm-stay establishments. In a Scottish context, this has ranged from host families, cultural stays, bed and breakfasts, farmhouse stays, self-catering accommodation, guest houses, and small hotels, collectively referred to as "homestay" or commercial home accommodation (Lynch 2003, forthcoming-a, b).

The term "home-stay" accommodation is inevitably a term with specific cultural associations. In Australia for instance the term is associated with farmhouse accommodation, B&B type accommodation within private homes (Craig-Smith *et al.* 1993; Ogilvie 1989). In the United Kingdom, it is traditionally associated with the English as a Foreign Language Sector. As a generic term it is used variously to refer to types of accommodation where visitors or guests pay directly or indirectly to stay in private homes. It embraces a range of accommodation types including farmstay accommodation, host families, some small hotels and B&Bs. Accommodation such as guest houses, boarding houses, lodging houses whose terms are sometimes used synonymously with hotels and B&Bs are also included as homestay establishments. Not only the objective description is important, but also the associations: private homes, interaction with host/family who live on the premises, sharing of space which thereby becomes "public." The associations may be described as linked by the concept of the home which may be perceived to distinguish homestay establishments from other forms of accommodation. For instance, those hotels where the host's (the manager, perhaps also staff) private home is not on the premises, and the boundaries distinguishing public space open to staff and visitors from private space open to staff only, are relatively distinct would not fall under the term homestay. Thus, one may refer to a sector of homestay accommodation to distinguish the accommodation from other types which do not share all the characteristics to the same degree.

Likewise, in New Zealand, a range of accommodation types falls under the "home-hosted" sector. Under the general label of Bed and Breakfast, both the New Zealand Bed and Breakfast Book (2002) and the Travelwise Guide to Bed and Breakfast in New Zealand (2000) include homestays, farm-stays, lodges, inns, and boutique accommodation. Yet, the distinctions between those establishments labelled a B&B and those as a home-stay, are often unclear. Craig-Smith *et al.* (1993) also make this point comparing home host accommodation in Australia and B&B accommodation in Europe. In the research carried out by Tucker, prices ranged from \$65 to \$170 or £20 to £60 for a double room. On average these establishments have 3 rooms offering mostly double accommodation. All establishments offer breakfast, usually in a shared dining area, although these range from full cooked breakfasts to cereal and toast. The range of facilities offered within home-hosted accommodation is also varied. For the purposes of quality assessments, the category "Guest and Hosted" accommodation as defined by Qualmark includes:

> bed and breakfasts, farm and home stays, guest houses, boutique lodges, inns, country hotels and similar establishments providing "home-like" or "character" accommodation. There's normally emphasis on the personal interaction between the guests and the host ... Breakfasts are a feature and are usually part of an all-inclusive tariff. In more remote areas, other meals may be provided on request (Qualmark New Zealand 2003: 14).

Interestingly, the category has no establishment size limit and permits establishments of more than fifteen rooms to fall under the same category, presumably those providing "character" rather than "home-like" accommodation.

The Issue of "Home"

Lynch & MacWhannell (2000: 104) suggest that even with a restrictive definition of the word "home," and including only guest houses, farmhouses, and B&Bs, 42% of the accommodation units in the United Kingdom may be classified as offering commercial hospitality within a home setting. As the authors acknowledge, this figure is itself highly problematic. For example, some guest houses may not have hosts living on the premises, and it excludes those hotels which are also a family home. It should be noted that the host and/or family do not need to live on the premises all the time. For instance, caravans or self-catering cottages may share the fact of being a private home but not that of a host/family living on the same premises, although one may nevertheless be very conscious of the presence of the host/family as a visitor through, for example, choice of reading material, furnishings, locked cupboards, or notices, for example, on operating the boiler. The important feature in such cases is the presence of the host *in absentia* i.e. evidence of the emotional engagement (Lynch 2000) or personal expression of the host.

The concept of home seems to have significant importance in the context of examining small commercial accommodation units. Thus, some consideration is given to the nature of a private home as being of key relevance to understanding small accommodation units.

Douglas (1991) identifies a number of conceptual characteristics of the home which are noteworthy and may help to draw out characteristics which may distinguish small commercial accommodation units from other accommodation which does not have a private home dimension. Douglas (1991) states the home may be viewed as a form of tyranny as well as holding affectionate images. Affectionate associations are related to the regularity of doings and this regularity is one of the distinguishing features of the home. Douglas describes the home as more than just a space. It is identified as having a structure in time. Further, for the people who live in that time and space, it also has aesthetic and moral dimensions. The home is further described by Douglas (1991) as a reflection of ideas. Likewise, Marcus (1995) perceives the home as a reflection of self i.e. the regular dwellers in the property. Other authors (Franklin 1991; Madigan & Munro 1991) highlight other associations, for example, the home may be a repository for memories, have associations of security, a castle (Darke 1996). Douglas (1991) also suggests a key differentiation is the idea of the home as a "virtual community" (p. 297) which requires "synchrony and order" (p. 300) to ensure that the home acts as "a collective good" (p. 297). Synchrony ensures balance, fair access to goods, it imposes obligations (types of social control) such as the right to information, for example, the timings of going out and in. It imposes obligations of order, for example, attending meals at agreed times. It also exerts order (tyranny) over speech, tastes, greed, over food one person dislikes. Thus, social control can have both positive and negative effects and the attribution of being positive or negative is a question of perspective. For instance, social control in a *commercial home* may be perceived as positive from a host perspective but negative from a guest perspective. Likewise, young people may perceive the home as a form of tyranny, but the parents, the householders, and imposers of social control, may perceive such control as necessary to ensure the efficient running of the home. One anecdote from a guest was of an occasion staying in a Scottish highland bed and breakfast. This guest had been admonished by the landlord not to get up in the morning before the landlord himself in order not to cause disturbance. This led to the guest lying awake in the early hours of the morning with a full bladder until it was "permitted" to go to the toilet.

According to Douglas (1991), the private home has "massive redundancies" (p. 298) and is contrasted to a commercial organisation as its justification is in its continuance. Perhaps here is a key difference underlying the meaning of "hospitableness," as offering massive redundancies against quantifiable commercial hospitality. Thus, the hotel acts as the contrast, the virtual market in contrast to the virtual community. Douglas (1991) perceives the idea of the hotel as a perfect opposite of the home, not only because it uses market principles for its transactions, but because it allows clients to buy privacy as a right of exclusion. This offends doubly the principle of the home whose rules and separations provide some limited privacy for each member (pp. 304–305).

PRIVATE HOME---------------------COMMERCIAL HOME-------------------------HOTEL

Figure 1: Home/Commercial Home/Hotel Continuum.

The home-hotel continuum has its merits as a means of conceptualisation. However, the process of providing commercial hospitality leads to changes in the way the home is used spatially, and in terms of the behaviours of the usual occupants. These changes may be perceived to change the intrinsic nature of the home. For example, associations of home, such as, castle, freedom, escape from the outside world are likely to be of less relevance. As such, it may be worth considering that what is being discussed are in fact *types of commercial homes*, a hybrid state between the private home and the hotel (see Figure 1).

On an individual unit basis, it would seem to make sense to market such establishments as homes. However, on an industry and academic basis it would make sense to recognise them under the generic term of being commercial homes. This chapter thus focuses upon the commercial home, in which, as Qualmark phrases the important feature of this category, there is emphasis placed on "the personal interaction between guests and hosts."

Hosts and Guests

On the basis of observations from staying in small accommodation units in Scotland, the politics of identity of both the host and of the guest are highly significant in constructing the homestay product. Central to this process is the subjective experience of the guest. The objective experience of the accommodation product is certainly an important part of the whole, but so too is the guest's subjective experience of staying in someone's (commercial) home. The extent to which engagement with the local people occurs, and insights into the lifestyle of people, would seem to vary according to where on the home/commercial home/hotel continuum the accommodation unit is located. Thus, the greater the opportunity for engagement, the closer the accommodation is to the private home end of the continuum. Certainly, as in the New Zealand example, the relationship with the home setting is an important part of the subjective experience of the guest.

It is important to note that New Zealand B&B and homestay accommodation tend to be as, or if not more, expensive than motels or hotels. Both hosts and guests therefore see this type of accommodation as the buying and selling of something more than "just a bed," but rather as an experience. In interviews, whilst the reasons guests gave for staying in B&Bs often included wanting the accommodation to be in beautiful settings, to be peaceful, "homely, and unique," the overriding reason they gave was "to have a relationship with local people," "to have the opportunity to talk with them," "to get to know the lifestyle of New Zealanders" and "to learn about their culture." Thus, it is the value that the experience holds for them, particularly the experience of a personal relationship with their hosts, that is key in this type of accommodation. Adding value to home-hosted accommodation is the way in which it allows tourists backstage into the lives of "average" New Zealanders, as represented by home-stay hosts. The level to which guests can enter into this "real life" is something which is dictated entirely by the hosts, and depends on the extent to which the hosts are prepared to interact with their guests. Apart from these more social experiences, home-hosted accommodation also offers tourists an opportunity to stay in comfortable accommodation, often in quite luxurious houses and beautiful locations, and to be pampered with excellent breakfasts and other special and more personal touches such as home-baking and home-made preserves.

Of course, the experience of the host-guest relationship goes both ways and is also important for the hosts in this type of more personalised accommodation. When asked about their motivations for operating a home-hosted accommodation business, New Zealand homestay hosts expressed their enjoyment in "having the company" and "meeting different people and sharing ideas." Many hosts also see themselves as being the "right" people to run B&B or home-stay accommodation, as they consider themselves to be "people people" and thus suitable to host guests. Most of the hosts suggested in interviews that their role as hosts placed them in the position of being representatives of the New Zealand people (and, more specifically, "ordinary" New Zealand people), and they felt particularly suited to the job if they felt they held some particular aspect of local knowledge, such as history or wildlife, or a "local" skill such as home-preserve making. These issues concerning the hosts' "hosting" identity are crucial when considering the quality of the experience in this type of accommodation.

The guest identity is also significant in the construction of the homestay product. A strong host role may encourage particular patterns of behaviour. For example, whilst experiencing a cultural stay in the context of a shooting lodge on a large estate in Scotland, one of the authors found himself cast in the role of an urban visitor finding out about rural life. This role-casting did not coincide with the visitor's self-perception but in the context it seemed easiest to go along with it.

Quality Assurance and Grading

Quality assurance is generally perceived by the hospitality and tourism industry, and the media as a whole, to be problematic in relation to the small accommodation sector (Bywater 1998). A major concern appears to be the variable quality of accommodation. A long-standing debate in the Scottish tourism industry is whether a "licence to practise," or compulsory registration, should exist based around the existing quality assurance and grading scheme. It is argued that such compulsory registration would aid in addressing problems of quality in accommodation. In order for such a scheme to be welcomed and command credibility, it is essential that the quality assurance and grading scheme is one that is beneficial both in theory and in practice. Consideration is therefore given to the schemes operating in New Zealand and Scotland.

In New Zealand, 2002 saw the inclusion of home-hosted accommodation under its own category "Guest and Hosted" within the *Qualmark* quality assurance system, operated jointly by Tourism New Zealand and the New Zealand Automobile Association. The purpose of quality assurance systems such as Qualmark is to ensure quality of tourism product, and hence overall visitor satisfaction. Qualmark claims that the benefits of becoming Qualmark licensed are credibility, increased visibility and thus opportunities for enhanced profitability (Qualmark New Zealand 2003).

Properties are visited each year by the organisation's accommodation assessors who conduct a detailed evaluation of the facilities and services. The assessment is divided up into approximately 20 quality criteria, each containing a series of minimum requirements that must be met to ensure eligibility for a star grade. The twenty or so criteria fall into 8 main quality areas. Four out of the eight relate to physical aspects of the establishment: the building and grounds, the bedrooms, the bathrooms and the lounge and dining areas. All of these categories are assessed for their size/space, their comfort and their appearance or quality. The other four main areas are cleanliness, service and hospitality, guest meals, and general business practice.

Each area includes quality scoring criteria to meet three different levels. The first level represents fairly basic customer expectations; the second level reflects higher quality expectations; and the third recognises aspects that "are likely to delight guests" (Qualmark New Zealand 2003). The score is then weighted to reflect the importance of the different quality areas to the overall guest experience and guest expectation, depending on the type of accommodation, its target market, and the type of visitor experience it aims to deliver. For example, the Guest and Hosted category places most emphasis on the "hosting" and "breakfast" criteria (Qualmark New Zealand 2003). Low emphasis is placed on such criteria as reservations service, general business practice, and kitchen hygiene.

Likewise, current methods of quality assurance employed in Scotland for members of the tourist board are conducted by Grading Officers. The scheme selects up to 51 areas of the property for examination covering: exterior, bedrooms, guest bathrooms/WC, public areas, dining room, food and beverage, and services (Scottish Tourist Board, n.d.). For each of the seven "features" between four and eight "details of property" are considered and total marks from a possible 10 per detail are awarded.

As an example of exactly what is being assessed, consider the "appearance of building" which is described in the following way

> In a modern building the absence of any weathering. Fresh, well-maintained paintwork, an overall clean "new" look
>
> In an older building no unsightly staining to stonework. All fabric in a sound and clean condition. Well-maintained paintwork, though some ageing (wearing of steps etc) may be apparent.
>
> Visible outbuildings to be of a similar high standard. Addition of such attractive features as flower tubs, window boxes or awnings where appropriate.
>
> External lighting. Good clear signs. Attractive architectural features (this may not apply to smaller establishments such as B&Bs) (Scottish Tourist Board, n.d., Guidance Notes for Serviced Accommodation: 3).

The above narrative is interpreted as focusing upon physical quality only and identifies all marks from 10 are being awarded in respect of the physical quality of the appearance of a building. Similar interpretations are made in respect of the other details of property in the feature and a subjective interpretation is reached of 40 out of 40 marks being awarded for physical quality in the exterior of the property feature. A similar process is followed in respect of the feature "bedrooms." Accordingly, the authors estimate that from

70 marks for the seven details of the feature, 50 are for physical quality, 10 are for weak qualitative consideration and 10 for aesthetic considerations. However, here, analysis of the description of the seven details suggests that there is some weak qualitative consideration of the details, for example, "comfortable . . . seating" (6) and some aesthetic consideration of the details involved, for example, "pleasant . . . appearance" (4). A similar process is followed in respect of the features guest bedrooms/WC, public areas, dining room, and food and beverage. The same process is also followed in respect of the feature called "services." Here, a new aspect of what marks are being awarded for is identified which is interpreted by the authors as being an emotional dimension of service, for example, "Warm, friendly smile. Helpful attitude." (20). For this particular feature and its 11 relevant details (porterage is also present as a 12th detail but interpreted as not being relevant to the homestay sector), it is estimated that of a possible 110 marks, 70 marks are awarded for qualitative considerations and 40 marks for an emotional dimension of service.

It should be noted that a conscious effort was made to generously interpret the descriptions of what was being assessed in order to identify features other than physical quality and to avoid the potential for criticism of interpreting the scheme for the purpose of the argument.

It would seem that in the New Zealand context and the Scottish context, the accommodation benchmarks for the grading scheme have their antecedents in the hotel and that this concept has largely determined the detail of the schemes on which measurement is based. In Scotland, the scheme has ostensibly been adapted for different types of accommodation, for example, self-catering, guest house, bed and breakfast. The true extent of the adaptation is debatable. Indeed, at the time of writing, it is understood that VisitScotland which has responsibility for quality assurance grading is giving consideration to subjective views of accommodation informing the current quality assurance and grading system.

Emphasising the Home Dimension

On a pragmatic level, it seems questionable whether a hotel benchmark is appropriate for all the units studied. The purpose of quality assurance systems such as Qualmark is to assure the quality of the tourism product, and hence overall visitor satisfaction. As mentioned above, Qualmark claims that the benefits of becoming Qualmark licensed are credibility, increased visibility and thus opportunities for enhanced profitability. However, given that the types of properties represented by these units represent a very significant proportion of total accommodation stock, on numerical grounds alone there would seem to be an argument for reviewing the accommodation grading scheme for these types of units and using the private home as the benchmark. The reality in New Zealand is that there is currently a tendency for the top end of the market to take part in the quality grading system and apply for a star rating (currently around 70% have received a four, four plus, or five star rating). Furthermore, it is questionable whether the experience of a grading officer, in the New Zealand case, based on one person visiting for only 2–3 hours, on a *prima facie* basis, can be a reasonable representation of the total experience had by overnight guests.

As said above, the Qualmark system in New Zealand has placed its highest emphasis for the Guest and Hosted accommodation category on the "hosting criteria." The requirements in this criteria include: "hosts friendly and confident in meeting people," "hosts very knowledgeable about their local area and relevant local attractions," and "hosts take an appropriate personal interest in guests" travels and are able to relate well with their guests including sharing stories of relevant travels'. These requirements must be met to achieve a one — three star rating respectively. Within the five star requirements in the "hosting" category, however, are "guest delight factors" such as "pampering options (spa, massage, facials etc)" and "multiple languages spoken." These criteria certainly appear to be based on a hotel model of assessment, relating more to "services" than home-based hospitality and a host-guest relationship.

The Qualmark system also places moderately high emphasis on the "Guest Welcome and Farewell" criteria. Within this criteria, to achieve a five star rating, the establishment must have "Efficient and complete registration procedures," and such "Guest delighters offered" as "customised merchandise available for sale." These criteria also appear to be based on a hotel model of assessment. It seems, then, that the system has appropriate criteria for this type of small home-based accommodation at the 1–3 star requirement level, but for them to obtain a five star grading, the criteria become more akin to a hotel benchmarking system. The additional point that the system by its very nature attracts more applications from the more "luxurious" end of the product-range raises the question further as to the appropriateness of the quality grading schemes for home-based accommodation. Many of the criteria necessary to achieve a five star rating throughout the categories are features that belong more to a hotel bench-marking system. Further examples are furniture and fittings available in bedrooms, such as extra phone by bed, TV, iron and ironing board. Such items would move the commercial home further along towards the hotel end of the continuum, and away from the sense of staying in a home. Moreover, it has been found that some features, such as TVs and tea and coffee-making facilities in guests rooms can have a significant affect on guests' perceptions of the host-guest relationship they can expect to have during their stay in that particular establishment (Tucker forthcoming). Having such facilities in rooms, for example, can tell guests that they should be fairly self-sufficient and stay in their rooms, thus removing the sense that the stay is all about interacting with their hosts in the hosts' living areas.

If it is accepted that the current accommodation grading scheme uses a benchmark of questionable relevance, is it not possible that this leads to, variously, inappropriate accommodation grading, recommendations on quality assurance improvements which may not be of relevance to the type of accommodation unit and so possibly "harmful" to those accommodation units that the scheme is intended to improve? For a small instance, the presence of an accommodation grading plaque on display in the hall of a B&B seemed more than incongruous in the context of a family home and detracted from the home as a product since it presented an artefact from "another world." There would seem to be a danger of seeking to standardise an, arguably, non-standard accommodation experience. The reality is that it is very difficult to quantify the dynamics of the host-guest relationship and this is key to this industry sector. One might question the extent to which consideration is given to a guest's emotional engagement with the property and overall accommodation experience which transcends imperfections. For example, an anecdote recounted by a couple with glee as being a positive experience was of staying in a family-run hotel where owing to rainwater flooding the dining-room, guests were called upon by the owner to help to mop up. This was perceived to be all part of the fun of the experience.

On a conceptual level, the grading schemes seem of partial relevance as they essentially represent providers' perspectives of quality derived from a hotel model "adapted" by omission of certain elements for small accommodation units. This hotel model is originally based on the aristocratic mansion and associated concepts of aristocratic hospitableness. The features of this model are those of service by servants who speak if they are spoken to, conforming to an "upstairs, downstairs" (where the family lives "above stairs" and the servants below) model of behaviour i.e. the opposite of the high level interaction identified in a New Zealand context. Whilst this model has evolved over time, arguably the essential features of its conceptual basis remain where the aristocratic home is held up as the quality benchmark for hospitality. This fits in to an essentially "trickle down" (class-based) view of the world where an ideal model exists and lower down the scale (sic) are "poorer" imitations of the same i.e. quality is raised from above. This approach seems fundamentally flawed. Historically, other forms of homes other than the aristocratic existed (Rybczynski 1988) but have received less attention. Indeed, perhaps the move of hotels to becoming more homely is a reflection that the approach was flawed. The absence of such home models does not detract from their intrinsic relevance and suitability.

Proposed Subjective Grading Needs

A consequence of challenging the primacy of the hotel benchmark and possibly to use a private home benchmark as the basis of a new means of grading small accommodation, would be to encourage new ways of conceptualising the accommodation experience. The current methods, leaving aside their possible low relevance, do not really challenge the accommodation providers to think upon the way that they do things such as manage space, the way that they present their accommodation, nor does it encourage reflection upon the way they present themselves. Using the home as a benchmark prompts new ways of thinking about the accommodation product. For instance, the nature of hospitableness vs. the concept of service.

The notion of hospitableness highlights more strongly the roles of "host" and "guest," and also the *relationship* between the host and guest. The experience of meeting people and having personalised interaction is the main reason both hosts and guests give for wishing to enter into this relationship in the B&B and home-stay setting. As Selwyn points out, "The basic function of hospitality is to establish a relationship or to promote an already established relationship" (2000: 19). Hospitality is a transformation process, wherein the key transformation taking place is that from a set of strangers into friends. Indeed, most of the hosts interviewed described this transformation process when discussing their guests. For example, one home-stay host said in conversation, "it gives me a great buzz that perfect strangers can come on in and I can see within an hour they feel quite relaxed." Many hosts stated that they saw their guests as "guests" when they first arrived but as "friends" when they departed. When asked, for example, what happens upon guests' arrival, one host couple answered:

> We always offer them a hot drink or a glass of water or whatever, and a
> muffin or a cookie or something and ask if they would like to sit down and

join us, and that to me is a very important time. To us it's a very important time. Because it's when you start to build up a relationship and find out what they want to do.

This can be compared and contrasted to Lynch's observations with regard to staying in a farmhouse bed and breakfast accommodation (the highest graded of those stayed in with 3 stars), and interactions with a rather Jeeves-like host. On arrival:

oh yes we shook hands in a fairly perfunctory fashion, and we introduced one another, and B (child), and he took us upstairs to our room, and just showed us it really, and I don't think he even said there's your room.

And later in the stay,

then gradually you know during the serving situation, as he would come in, deliver a plate or pick one up and ask is everything all right, like the first day he said is everything all right, it was like a statement rather than a question (Lynch 2003).

As this host-guest relationship is key to the experience in this type of tourist accommodation, it is necessary that a grading system for home-hosted accommodation should place significant emphasis upon it. Indeed, the Qualmark scheme does place importance on the "hosting category," but, as pointed out above, the criteria it states for the 1 through to 3 star categories seem to be identifying the qualities that guests in this type of accommodation really expect, whilst the 5 star criteria would tend to standardize the experience and be based on a hotel benchmark. In other words, there is a problem with the actual rating emphases, and the criteria that would currently score a 3 star in the hosting category (such as hosts present to offer guests a warm welcome and to thank and farewell guests; hosts very knowledgeable about local area and relevant local attractions; hosts take a personal interests in guests' travels and are able to relate well with their guests including sharing stories of relevant travels) should be qualifying of a 5 star rating in the homestay category.

One of the perceived advantages of current grading schemes is their "objectivity" achieved through the use of trained grading officers following specific assessment protocols. The following observations regarding the theoretical and actual use of space, as well as its control, in relation to a bed and breakfast in a family home, highlight limitations of the "objective" grading approach ignoring the subjective experience:

S. the dog was in the hall this morning, I didn't pay much attention yesterday, it was clearly a sort of security arrangement that they operate. I had a look in the brochure and the brochure quite clearly indicates that there is a TV lounge, that made me review, had I misunderstood the signal, about the usage of the lounge, it was certainly my impression has been that it is a guarded area, for meal time only and it was never introduced as being a TV Lounge you can use in such and such, and yet I found that in the brochure had

> TV lounge so that is maybe interesting in terms of the actualities of space compared to the theoretical position vis a vis the Tourist Board (Lynch 2003).

The Scottish accommodation grading system emphasises the cumulative experience on which the guidance notes are based. However, a thrust of the research methodology followed by Lynch (2003) was the importance of capturing the spontaneity of impressions in order to highlight the unique emotional response of the individual. Freshness of perceptions is an important aspect of Lynch's methodology and also a recognition that individuals will have unique perceptions and experiences. It should be noted that the methodology recognises the involvement of the guest in constructing the total hospitality accommodation experience. An implication of this is that, were a subjective quality assurance methodology to be adapted to become a practical grading tool, it is very unlikely that Grading Officers would be used. Instead, it would be preferable to make use of individuals, preferably "live" guests, who would not bring the Officers' perceptual and experiential "baggage." Thus, a holistic quality assurance scheme would include both the current "objective" approach to grading as well as a "subjective" customer-based grading approach. This type of customer-based grading would then supplement the existing "objective" quality assurance and grading system. It is suggested that the effects for the accommodation industry would be profoundly liberating and contribute over time towards a much improved guest product and experience.

Conclusions

In conclusion, this chapter has suggested that the quality assurance and grading schemes discussed are derived from hotel benchmarking systems, and so divert the guests' experience away from that of "home-based" accommodation. As a result, a number of implications arise. The current schemes do not place enough emphasis upon the host-guest relationship which has a particular importance in the context of homestay accommodation. Further, the schemes are too standardised in their approach and are unable to take account of the positive guest perspective that may arise in the event of mishaps. The criteria for 5 star accommodation are more suitable for hotels than for home-like accommodation. It is suggested that the benchmark for such quality assurance and grading schemes should be that of the home with much greater emphasis upon the importance of the host-guest relationship. Rather than simply being concerned with the objective facets of accommodation, allowance needs to be taken of subjective elements of the accommodation experience; what it feels like for the guest who is staying, and what the guest has to say about a place. In this way, it is suggested that a tendency towards standardization, perceived to be harmful to the reality of the accommodation product, might be avoided.

References

Bywater, M. (1998). The guests are sad and desolate. The owner is a sociopath. Welcome back to the Great British hotel. *The Observer* (4 October), 31.

Craig-Smith, S., Cody, N., & Middleton, S. (1993). *How to be successful at home hosting and farm tourism.* Gatton College: University of Queensland.

Darke, J. (1996). The Englishwoman's castle, or, don't you just love being in control? In: C. Booth, J. Darke, & S. Yeandle (Eds), *Changing places: Women's lives in the city.* London: Paul Chapman Publishing.

Douglas, M. (1991). The idea of a home: A kind of space. *Social Research, 59*(1), 287–307.

Franklin, A. S. (1991). Owner-occupation, privatism and ontological security: A critical reformulation. In: R. Madigan, & M. Munro (Eds), Gender, house and 'home': Social meanings and domestic architecture in Britain. *The Journal of Architectural and Planning Research, 8*(2), 116–132.

Hall, M., & Page, S. (2002). *The geography of tourism and recreation* (2nd ed.). London: Routledge.

Lynch, P. A. (2000). Homing in on home hospitality. *The Hospitality Review,* 48–54.

Lynch, P. A. (2003). *Conceptual relationships between hospitality, space and social control in the homestay sector.* Doctoral dissertation in preparation, Queen Margaret University College, Edinburgh.

Lynch, P. A. (forthcoming-a). Commercial homes. In: A. Pizam (Ed.), *International encyclopaedia of hospitality management.* Oxford: Elsevier.

Lynch, P. A. (forthcoming-b). Homestay sector. In: R. C. Wood, & B. Brotherton (Eds), *Encyclopaedia of hospitality management.* Oxford: Butterworth Heinemann.

Lynch, P. A., & MacWhannell, D. (2000). Home and commercialised hospitality. In: C. Lashley, & A. Morrison (Eds), *In search of hospitality: Theoretical perspectives and debates* (pp. 100–114). Oxford: Butterworth Heinemann.

Madigan, R., & Munro, M. (1991). Gender, house and 'home': Social meanings and domestic architecture in Britain. *The Journal of Architectural Planning Research, 8*(2), 116–132.

Marcus, C. (1995). *House as a mirror of self.* Berkley: Conari Press.

New Zealand Bed and Breakfast Book (2002). Wellington: Moonshine Press.

Ogilvie, B. (1989). *1990 homestay Australia: A guide to accommodation and travel, homes, farms, outback, Sydney's good accommodation and travel guide.* Bathurst: Pty Ltd.

Ombler, K. (1997). Motels vs. private lodging ... same game ... different rules. *Hospitality, 33*(6), 6–10.

Qualmark New Zealand (2003). www.qualmark.co.nz

Rybczynski, W. (1988). *Home.* London: William Heinemann Ltd.

Scottish Tourist Board (n.d.). Guidance notes for serviced accommodation.

Selwyn, T. (2000). An anthropology of hospitality. In: C. Lashley, & A. Morrison (Eds), *In search of hospitality: Theoretical perspectives and debates* (pp. 18–36). Oxford: Butterworth-Heinemann.

Travelwise Guide to Bed and Breakfast in New Zealand (2000). Dunedin: Travelwise Ltd.

Tucker, H. (forthcoming). 'Let me be': The host-guest relationship and its implications in rural tourism. In: D. Hall, L. Roberts, & M. Mitchell (Eds), *New directions in rural tourism.* Aldershot: Ashgate.

UKTS (2000). *The U.K. tourist: Key trends 1990–1999.* English Tourism Council, Northern Ireland Tourist Board, Scottish Tourist Board and Wales Tourist Board.

Chapter 13

Overcoming the Green Gap: Improving the Environmental Performance of Small Tourism Firms in Western Australia

Michael Schaper and Jack Carlsen

Introduction

Greening and sustainability are often issues associated with the global tourism industry. In many cases, tourism is often cited as one of the drivers for the conservation of natural areas and biological diversity. For example, ecotourism is often used to illustrate how the notion of sustainable development (that is, business practices which successfully accommodate the diverse goals of economic growth, biodiversity protection and community participation) can be put into action.

Tourism has environmental implications that go far beyond just ecotourism. As a major industry in its own right, tourism is a significant consumer of resources. A recent national profile of tourism businesses in Australia identified some 55,000 small- and micro-sized firms (that is, enterprises employing less 19 persons) in existence, located mainly in the food and beverage, accommodation, and travel and tour operations sectors. These represent almost 92% of all the tourism firms in the country. The profile also identified a large number of other micro- and small-scale enterprises (almost 270,000) which were not located specifically within the tourism sector, yet which drew significant proportions of their income from tourists (Bolin & Greenwood 2003). These 325,000 small firms represent almost one-third of the total 1.1 million small businesses currently found in Australia (Australian Bureau of Statistics 2002).

Clearly, the cumulative performance of these individual small firms can potentially have major implications on the environment. Although it is hard to gauge the overall environmental effect of small firms around the world, it has been previously claimed that they may indeed be responsible for up to 70% of global environmental pollution (Hillary 2000).

The vast bulk of tourism enterprises have traditionally been small-sized firms, and this remains the case today. This in itself creates problems, since it is much harder to measure and evaluate the performance of a small services-sector firm than a traditional "smokestack industry," such as is found in large-scale manufacturing or industrial production. Moreover, small firms usually lack many of the financial, human and knowledge resources that large enterprises can draw upon to improve their environmental performance.

In this chapter, the greening of small tourism firms is examined in detail. The paper begins with a discussion of the arguments in favour of greening, and the ways in which it can be achieved within small tourism firms. It then examines the actual performance of small firms to date, and the barriers that stand in the way of small tourism firms achieving improved "greener" performance. To help flesh out these concepts, a brief examination is provided of recent research into the environmental behaviour of small tourism firms in Western Australia. The chapter concludes with some suggestions to improve the level of "green" behaviour in small firms, and potential future research issues worthy of more examination.

As much of the research into the environmental performance of small firms is also found outside the tourism discipline, the paper draws on both general material (that is, research on SMEs in many other industries) as well as on tourism-specific data.

Why Go Green?

Why should business organisations deal with environmental matters? Is there any compelling reason why this issue should be given any special consideration or priority in the decision-making and operational aspects of business management? Often the drivers for environmental change are usually a complex mixture of risk and rewards, rather than a simple cause-and-effect relationship (Day & Arnold 1998). A number of arguments have been put forward as to why firms should adopt a "greener" perspective in their operations.

At the most basic level, it can be argued that human societies and the businesses which operate within them (such as tourism) are substantial consumers of natural resources. Both organic (such as fish and flowers) and non-organic stocks (such as landscape features) are limited in their capacity, and are a finite resource. Once consumed or destroyed, many of them cannot be recreated. Without sufficient resources, firms cannot service customers and so generate a profit (Burke & Hill 1990). During the twentieth century, the consumption and pollution of such natural resources proceeded at an unparalleled rate, during the course of which a significant amount of biodiversity was lost and many natural resources consumed beyond their recovery point (Hutchinson & Hutchinson 1997). Indeed, there are a number of historical examples — such as the desertification of North Africa, the deforestation of what is now modern-day Lebanon and the Levant region, and the loss of the Aral Sea — which suggest that the uncontrolled exploitation of physical resources by humans can ultimately damage or destroy whole social and economic systems. This behaviour has been described by Schmidheiny (1992) as "living off the capital, not the interest" of an industry's natural resource assets. Therefore, it is in the long-term self interest of business proprietors to extend and sustain renewable resources before such depletion damages their own survival (Hutchinson & Chaston 1994).

A second compelling factor is the role of external pressure. No firm exists in isolation. All organisations must operate in a world in which their actions, supplies, customer base, marketing and business strategies are also influenced by the activities, views and demands of external parties, such as consumers, governments, and competitors (Petts *et al.* 1998). Many of these external stakeholders, especially government and the general community, have come to demand higher levels of environmental performance by firms (Burke & Hill 1990).

At a more pragmatic level, firms may also be forced into undertaking environmental improvements by the imposition of government laws, licensing regimes, or policies. In many situations, this can be the prime impetus for a changed organisational focus on the importance of environmental responsibility. Studies by Murphy *et al.* (1995), Hutchinson & Chaston (1994), Merritt (1998), Tanner *et al.* (1996), and Petts *et al.* (1999), amongst others, appear to show that for many small firms the major reason for adopting environmental action is often legislation or regulation. Laws and policies often provide the initial "push" factor to commence environment improvements, and therefore legislation is likely to continue to be used as a public policy tool by governments and the community for the foreseeable future (Fineman 1997).

In Australia, codes of conduct, compliance guidelines and performance frameworks have also been introduced by a wide variety of industry associations and government bodies (Hutchinson & Gerrans 1997). This has further increased the direct and indirect pressure on individual firms to "go green."

Another perceived advantage of environmentally-responsible behaviour by businesses is that it can offer significant opportunities for new markets, competitive advantages, and stimulate greater innovation within a firm (Gallarotti 1995; Hodge 1995). As Charter & Polonsky (1999) point out, the last two decades have seen the emergence of a discernible new market segment, the environmentally-conscious purchaser or "green consumer." This has fuelled demand for environmentally-friendly products, a market niche which provides an opportunity for entrepreneurs to exploit. Many such consumers have shown a willingness to spend more on environmentally-friendly products, and firms are now innovating to produce goods with a "green" price premium, thus opening up new market segments (Porter & van der Linde 1995).

There is also a significant moral or value-based element to the arguments why firms should be involved in environmental matters (Hill *et al.* 1994). Sagoff (1988) argues that the prevention or rectification of environmental problems should be done by individuals and by firms because it is a good thing in itself — the correct or moral choice of action — not because of any potential direct or indirect benefits which may accrue to them as a result of such actions.

There is only a small body of literature which deals specifically with small tourism firms and their environmental behaviour, so it is difficult to determine just how much tourism enterprises follow the arguments outlined above. Middleton & Hawkins (1998) have suggested that small-scale tourism firms tend to adopt a green approach due to one or more of the following reasons: complying with laws or regulations; complying with procurement policies of other firms in the product supply chain; the desire to avoid negative public relations and to act as "good neighbours"; achieving a competitive advantage; reducing operating costs; conserving assets and resources; meeting association membership criteria; and/or meeting customer demands and expectations.

Their claims are supported by a number of other tourism researchers. For example, Carlsen *et al.* (2001) identified conserving assets and resources as one of the reasons that motivates small family firms to start up a tourism business. In their work into small tourism firms in Western Australia, they found that many people who had relocated to attractive rural areas to run such businesses also demonstrated a strong interest in nature and heritage conservation. In a similar vein, Getz (1994) found that "newcomers" to the Spey Valley in Scotland also held strong pro-conservation attitudes. More recently, Dewhurst & Thomas' (2003) study of tourism firms in the Yorkshire Dales showed that owners with a higher level of green concerns were also more likely to adopt environmental improvement practices in their internal operations. Denman (1994) examined some of the reasons why tourists visit particular sites and found that there was often a strong level of demand and expectation about appropriate environmental practices by such consumers. For example, many tourists who visited farms were specifically interested in wildlife or conservation issues. It would appear that tourism firms are subject to many of the same pressures that other small firms face to "go green."

Defining Environmental Best Practice in Small Tourism Firms

It is one thing to discuss, at a general level, the need for firms to be greener. It can be much more difficult to operationalise such goals. The implementation of good environmental practices within a small firm can be a difficult task. As Wehrmeyer (1995) has pointed out, there is a vast range of steps which can be undertaken to improve the environmental performance of a firm.

A number of researchers and writers have postulated an extensive set of practical measures which can be introduced into almost all business premises (Australian Greenhouse Office 1999; Durham University Business School 1997; Lord 1990). These measures include paper recycling and consumption reduction; packaging issues; energy audits; economising on water, lighting, electricity and gas consumption; the nature of motor vehicle and public transport usage; involvement with environmental lobby groups; equipment purchases and usage; staff training and participation (Australian Greenhouse Office 1999; Environment Protection Authority 1993; Prokop 1993; Ralston 1990; WA Department of Environmental Protection 1999). A number of the most common suggested measures is shown in Table 1.

Within the tourism sector, the recent movement towards sustainable tourism has given rise to an extensive body of environmental policies, programs and practices relevant to small firms. At the macro-level, the World Tourism Organisation (2003) has enunciated a set of environmental principles that are included within its Global Code of Ethics (see Table 2). Another set of desirable practices has been promulgated by the Green Globe 21 certification program, which aims to accredit and brand sustainable tourism businesses around the world based on their environmental, social and economic performance. This program is helping to deliver a range of environmental and social improvements through the firms that it certifies. Likewise, the Nature and Ecotourism Program (NEAP) developed by the industry body Ecotourism Australia is a certification scheme aimed at achieving best practice by ecotourism operators in Australia. Qualifying businesses must seek out new and cleaner technologies and apply these to ensure resources such as water, energy, fauna and flora are conserved and regenerated (Issaverdis 2000). Ways of achieving best practice include conducting impact assessments, providing interpretation and education, selective land use, minimising environmental degradation, conservation initiatives, natural

Table 1: Possible environmental practices in a small firm.

Transport
  Recycle motor vehicle oil
  Use public transport in lieu of private
  Car pooling

Packaging
  Recycle/reuse packaging
  Reduce packaging consumed
  Order and store in bulk

Water
  Water reuse/recycling
  Install water wise shower heads
  Install dual flush toilets
  Purchase biodegradable detergents

Energy, buildings and landscaping
  Use natural light (skylights, etc.)
  Solar passive buildings
  Solar heating
  Provide indoor plants
  Use recycled timber
  Install energy efficient light bulbs
  Walkways over sensitive native vegetation
  Stick to the path signs
  Plant local native vegetation
  Use timers for lighting
  Use timer controls for airconditioning
  Undertake an energy audit
  Use energy ratings when choosing new office equipment

Recycling
  Recycle linen to welfare groups
  Recycle bins (for paper, cans, glass)
  Recycle paper for office use

Waste
  Install worm farms for vegetable waste
  Recycle green (food, vegetation) waste

Business operations and process
  Use ozone-friendly cleaning products
  Develop a statement of environmental aims
  Communicate the statement to all stakeholders
  Staff training

Table 1: (*Continued*)

Include environmental issues in the firm's business plan
Safe storage of hazardous materials
Calculate the whole life cost of each product produced

External organisations
Discounts for environmental groups (when booking rooms, facilities, etc.)
Lobby politicians on environmental issues
Join an environmental group
Sponsor an animal in the zoo/conservation project

Sources: Lord (1990), Ralston (1990), Environment Protection Authority (1993), Australian Greenhouse Office (1999), Durham University Business School (1997), and Australian Bureau of Statistics (1997).

Table 2: World Tourism Organisation Global Code of Ethics — Article 3 Tourism, a factor of sustainable development.

1. All the stakeholders in tourism development should safeguard the natural environment with a view to achieving sound, continuous and sustainable economic growth geared to satisfying equitably the needs and aspirations of present and future generations;
2. All forms of tourism development that are conducive to saving rare and precious resources, in particular water and energy, as well as avoiding so far as possible waste production, should be given priority and encouraged by national, regional and local public authorities;
3. The staggering in time and space of tourist and visitor flows, particularly those resulting from paid leave and school holidays, and a more even distribution of holidays should be sought so as to reduce the pressure of tourism activity on the environment and enhance its beneficial impact on the tourism industry and the local economy;
4. Tourism infrastructure should be designed and tourism activities programmed in such a way as to protect the natural heritage composed of ecosystems and biodiversity and to preserve endangered species of wildlife; the stakeholders in tourism development, and especially professionals, should agree to the imposition of limitations or constraints on their activities when these are exercised in particularly sensitive areas: desert, polar or high mountain regions, coastal areas, tropical forests or wetlands, propitious to the creation of nature reserves or protected areas;
5. Nature tourism and ecotourism are recognized as being particularly conducive to enriching and enhancing the standing of tourism, provided they respect the natural heritage and local populations and are in keeping with the carrying capacity of the sites.

Source: World Tourism Organisation (2003).

Table 3: Environmental practices for sustainable tourism.

- Adoption of energy saving technology and programs
- Use of alternative energy sources
- Control of noise emissions
- Treatment, control and reuse of waste water and sewage
- Adoption environmentally friendly product purchasing policies
- "Hardening" of environments to withstand increased usage without deterioration
- Employment of construction practices intended to result in minimal site disruption
- Development of environmental guidelines for construction firms
- Use of fines to ensure builders adhere to practices designed to minimise disruption to the natural environment and construction site
- Use of building design principles and materials to reduce energy consumption
- Development of cooperative arrangements with natural area management bodies
- Employment of interpretive services (including information centres) to enhance visitor/guest understanding of the physical and cultural environment
- Use of environmentally friendly construction materials, such as plantation timber
- Selection of environmentally friendly service suppliers and products
- Employment of regular environmental audits
- Use of above ground construction for buildings and paths
- Use of biodegradable chemicals
- Employment of recycling programs
- Use of endemic plants for landscaping purposes
- Employee education regarding environmental practices & issues
- Establishment of carrying capacity limits
- Establishment of voluntary community committees to assist in controlling environmental impacts stemming from visitation
- Zoning areas for specific uses
- Issuance of permits to control site/area usage
- Establishment of user charges
- Provision of financial support for environmental groups
- Rehabilitation of degraded environments
- Education of guests/visitors regarding "green" living principles
- Supervision of interaction between tourists and physical and/or cultural environments
- Economic contributions to communities via employments and the local sourcing of products and services
- Development and use of impact monitoring and evaluation systems
- Commissioning or directly undertaking research regarding environmental impacts stemming from tourist activities
- Commissioning or directly undertaking research relating to the resource base on which tourism depends
- Employment of environmental impact assessments prior to construction
- Incorporation of issues associated with environmental management into the strategic planning process
- Community consultation

Source: Harris & Leiper (1995).

area management and working with local communities. At the individual firm level, Harris & Leiper (1995) case studied a range of tourism organisations in Australia and identified a number of industry practices leading to sustainable tourism (see Table 3).

A wide range of measures are possible, and different owner/managers and their firms may choose to display environmentally-conscious activities in a number of different ways. This makes it somewhat difficult to compare and objectively evaluate the performance of small firms, since responses can take so many different forms.

The Current Environmental Performance of Small Firms

In recent years, a number of studies into the environmental responses of small firms in various countries, including Australia, Denmark, the United Kingdom and the USA, have identified several trends that seem common to most enterprises (Barnes 1994; Hillary 1997; Hutchinson & Chaston 1994; Hutchinson & Gerrans 1997; Merritt 1998; Petts *et al.* 1998, 1999; Tanner *et al.* 1996; Tilley 1998).

In general, most small business owner/managers believe that the environment is an important issue, and support protection of the environment per se. Response in favour of these propositions is overwhelmingly clear, and usually in the vicinity of 80–90%. However, awareness of formal environmental management systems, specific environmental laws and/or remediation processes is generally very poor and quite limited. Small firms are generally much less likely to embark on environmental improvement programmes than large firms, to have adopted a written environmental policy, to utilise a formal environmental management standard, or to have undertaken an environmental audit.

Moreover, there is a significant discrepancy between personal viewpoints and business activity (Tilley 1998). The generally positive attitudes towards the environment do not appear to be reflected in owner/managers' knowledge base or their actual business practices. Merritt has called this paradox "... the so-called SME problem in environmental management" (1998: 91).

Even where environmental programs are undertaken, they tend to be largely reactive in nature, one-off, and focus on emission reduction ("end-of-pipe treatments") rather than on pro-active pollution prevention measures. Most small firms appear unwilling to embark on substantial changes in materials, production processes or operations management, and prefer to focus on ad-hoc solutions, such as a greater use of materials recycling (Hillary 2000).

Barriers to the Adoption of Good Environmental Practices

Why does this gap between environmental goals and performance occur? There are numerous reasons why small firms often fail to adopt best practice environmental performance, or even to simply improve their performance beyond current levels.

In the first place, it may be that there are no direct causal links between attitudes and action: an owner/managers' concern for the environment does not necessarily translate into changes in business behaviour, either at the firm-wide or individual level (Petts *et al.*

1999). Petts *et al.* (1998) have suggested that the link between environmental attitudes and managerial behaviour is often weak because it lacks "immediacy": poor environmental impact often does not have a direct impact on the firm.

Secondly, most small firms report having difficulty in identifying the benefits of improved environmental performance, such as potential financial gains (in the form of cost savings arising from wastage reductions or reduced resource consumption), marketing advantages, or other benefits which can accrue from environmental pro-activity (Hillary 1997; Hutchinson & Gerrans 1997; Murphy *et al.* 1995; Tanner *et al.* 1996). This makes it harder for them to justify adopting an environmentally responsible stance (Palmer 1998).

Another problem may arise from a lack of pressure from suppliers or consumers for greater environmental performance. Most small firms in the cited studies did not report any pressure from stakeholders to improve their performance, which runs contrary to the argument put forward by the proponents of market-based environmentalism that market forces will inevitably produce greater environmental change (Merritt 1998).

A further problem may be methodological. To date, the bulk of research conducted into the environmental activities of small firms has been conducted through an examination of the impact of formal environmental management systems (EMS), such as ISO 14000, British environmental quality standards BS 5750 and 7750, or the European Union's Environmental Management and Audit Scheme (Barnes 1994; Hillary 1997; Hutchinson & Chaston 1994). Whilst useful, such studies are limited in their scope, and are focused on only one particular aspect of business procedures.

Finally, the dichotomy may be due to the fact that the wrong types of analytical tools for measuring environmental performance are being used. Small firms appear to have some fundamental differences compared to large firms, and many of the traditional types of ways of "going green" are simply inappropriate for small enterprises, since they fail to recognise the very different context such firms operate in compared to a large corporation. If such is the case, then perhaps different ways of measuring environmental responsiveness need to be used, so that a more accurate and comprehensive picture of SME behaviour may be developed (Hutchinson & Chaston 1994; Merritt 1998). This should include a mixture of different measuring tools, and should also aim to measure environmental performance over a number of different criteria, not just based on one or two issues.

There also appear to be a number of barriers that are specific to small firms in the tourism sector. As has been mentioned before, many small operators establish tourism ventures to support their lifestyle goals, such as the opportunity to live in a rural or regional setting. However, where there is a conflict between the two, then it appears that maintenance of lifestyle will usually win out over conservation goals (Carlsen *et al.* 2001). Indeed, Buhalis & Fletcher (1995) have also noted that small tourism firm operators are often willing to accept some environmental damage in order to increase their personal income. Other managers do nothing because they are unwilling to be seen as "preaching" to guests about the need for improved conservation (Dewhurst & Thomas 2003). Finally, the increasing trend towards linking the licensing of nature-based tourism operations to environmental accreditation has been perceived as a threat by some tourism operators (Issaverdis 2001), thus reducing the likelihood that they will cooperate with efforts to produce better environmental outcomes. Some small operators believe that the cost of achieving environmental accreditation or certification may outweigh the marketing or environmental benefits that they eventually receive (Issaverdis 2001).

An Example: Small Tourism Firms in Western Australia

A recent survey of almost two hundred small family businesses in Western Australian tourism (Carlsen *et al.* 2001) provides an insight into the current environmental practices and perspectives of small tourism firms.

The study sought to examine a number of different aspects about the environmental activities of the firms and their owner/managers. One hundred and ninety-eight small tourism businesses throughout Western Australia were surveyed about a number of environmental performance indicators.

Respondents were first asked if they included a number of specific environmental improvement practices in the operations of their businesses (see Table 4). Although this list is by no means exhaustive, it does provide a barometer that measures current business practices. Some activities were very widely undertaken; others had a much lower uptake. Water conservation was practiced by 79.5% of tourism firms, which reflects the dry conditions prevalent in Western Australia. Recycling of materials was done by 58.5% of the respondents, and educating guests on conservation matters by 51%. The lowest participation rate was in alternative, non-polluting energy sources (39.2%). Overall, a minimum of 40% of the businesses indicated they were undertaking the various practices listed.

In addition to these practical activities, the environmental perspective of the owner/managers was evaluated by asking them if they belonged to any conservation-oriented groups. Thirty-one percent indicated they did, and forty-eight groups were named (many respondents were members of more than just one group). The largest group was that of a farm improvement and landcare groups (thirty mentions), which covered conservation matters related to agricultural practices. Seventeen specific conservation groups were mentioned, including local organisations such as the regional Leeuwin Conservation Group (6),

Table 4: Environmental practices of family businesses in rural tourism and hospitality, Western Australia ($n = 198$).

Practices	Yes (Number)	%
Follow water conservation procedures	149	79.3
Follow a recycling program for materials	110	58.5
Educate your guests on conservation matters	96	51.3
Eliminate non-organic chemicals	91	49.5
Specific targets for waste reduction	91	49.2
Specific targets for energy conservation	84	44.2
Use alternative, non-polluting energy sources	73	39.2

Source: Carlsen *et al.* (2001).

the national Australian Conservation Foundation (5), Greenpeace (3), Wildernesss Society (2), the Conservation Council of Australia (1), and the World Wildlife Fund (1).

Clearly, these results indicate that there is still considerable scope for greater "green" practices amongst small tourism firms. It also appears to lend weight to the argument that the simplest environmental improvement programs, and those with the greatest obvious financial return, are more likely to be undertaken than more complex measures whose benefits are hard to quantify. For example, water conservation can be implemented through a number of relatively simple steps, and, since water rates are based on usage levels in Western Australia, also has a clear financial return. At the same time, the results also indicate that many tourism firm owner/managers have enough personal "green" interest to warrant joining a specific environmental group, thus lending support to the argument that there is a high level of inherent interest and support for environmental improvement amongst the small tourism sector — even if subsequent performance does not match this.

Building Greener Firms in Future

In general, recent research into SMEs and the environment has argued that greater environmental performance will come about through one of two options. The conventional approach argues that that regulatory and commercial considerations are the main driving force towards environmental improvement, and should be the focus of effort to improve the greening of SMEs (Palmer 2000; Townsend 1998). The alternative school of thought has been to argue that changes would largely take place due to the attitudes and values of the business owner, and that a focus should be placed on identifying "green" businesses which could spearhead the movement for changes in business practices (Tilley 1998).

There are many small firms who fall into the second category. These enterprises "go green" because their owners attach a personal significance to environmental responsibility and sustainable business practices. For example, Carlsen *et al.* (2001) cite several case studies of "green" tourism businesses which lead the way in Australia and New Zealand. In another example, Ryan (1997: 180) documented one family that developed and operated a river rafting business in New Zealand. He noted their positive attitude toward conservation: ". . . for the Megaws compliance with regulations designed to protect a natural environment are not perceived as an imposition, but rather a means of supporting what they, themselves, perceive as being essential for the place within which they live and work." In another case, Sofield & Getz (1997) examined the commitment to nature conservation amongst a small firm operated by one family, who had created Undara Lava Lodge in Queensland, Australia. They found that the family had devoted sufficient financial and land resources, as well as the personal commitment, to successfully establish a national park and tourist resort which incorporated many sustainability principles in its design and operations.

However, relying on the "green" attitudes and perspectives of owners is clearly not enough. As the above discussion has shown, many small firms run by owner/managers with pro-environmental perspectives do not produce eco-friendly results. The existence of this discrepancy between behavioural intentions and practices is not new. Research in many different disciplines has shown that a substantial gap often exists between attitudes and practices. Argyris & Schön (1974) noted that many managers suffered from conflicting modes of behaviour between "espoused theory" (how an individual wishes to believe he or she has behaved) and "theory in use" (how an individual actually behaves when under pressure). Indeed, Freire (quoted in Hunter *et al.* 1999: 102–103) has claimed that "... one of the major struggles in every individual is to diminish the difference between what one says and does, between the discourse and the practice."

Attitudes are not, after all, always effective predictors of behaviour. Thirty years ago, one of the major researchers working in the field of attitude study suggested that perhaps the most appropriate definition of an attitude was as a marker of "... what people *think* about, *feel* about, and how they *would like to behave* ..." (Triandis 1971: 14), rather than as an indicator of what they actually do. Whilst small firm owner/managers tend to have quite "green" attitudes on the whole, the performance of their firms does not reflect this set of values.

As the above discussion suggests, if greener changes are to take place within the tourism sector, then it will probably not be driven by "eco-friendly" small business operators, but by pragmatic considerations. There are several steps that could be undertaken to achieve this.

Providing Green Business Advice

Several studies, such as Schaper (2002a, b) and Tilley (1998), have found that eco-literacy and information are one of the key determinants of environmental performance. Many SME owner/managers report that they are unable to obtain information and advice about how to make their businesses greener. As Palmer (2000) has suggested, the most important consideration for SMEs is that environmental information be practical, easy to access, and in a form which can be applied quickly to their own firm. It is preferable if it has a direct, obvious impact on environmental performance.

In many parts of the world, government and non-government agencies exist to provide advice, support, information, training and other services to the small business sector. These organisations include the Business Enterprise Centre network in Australia, the Small Business Administration in the USA, the Small Business Enterprise Centre system in New Zealand, and Business Link in the United Kingdom. The opportunity currently exists for government and non-government agencies alike to boost environmental performance through the provision of practical, easy-to-understand knowledge for small businesses (Friedman & Miles 2002). However, to date most of these support agencies have often overlooked the environment, or given it only minor attention. Likewise, the various departments of environmental protection (or equivalent) in such countries have tended to focus on working with large corporations, rather than on small firms, to improve the environmental performance of industry.

Dispensing environmental advice through business support agencies will also require small business advisers themselves to be fully briefed on such issues. In the community-based small firm support sector, there has been an intensive debate as to whether consultants should actively encourage firms to embrace a particular course of action, or merely provide assistance when owners come seeking help on a specific issue (Sirolli 1995). Since environmental matters are rarely seen as a first-order business issue in most firms, the former course of action is preferable.

Working with Industry Associations and the Professions

It will also be important to disseminate information to other types of business advisers. Most small firms do not actually utilise these free services; indeed, most still rely on their traditional sources of support (especially accountants) for advice, and only a minority ever use government-sponsored agencies (Schaper & Jay 2003). To this end, it may be necessary to work with professional bodies to give their members the skills and opportunity to help small clients go greener. A recent example of this has been the activities of CPA Australia, one of the professional bodies representing accountants: their work has included prominent articles on "how to work with your clients to green their business," sponsorship of research into the field, and advice for practising accountants.

Picking the Low-Hanging Fruit

A common approach in many environmental improvement programs is to first target the areas of most obvious return. By focusing the firm's activities on goals that produce an immediate financial return or other obvious payoff, the interest of the owner/manager and staff can be maintained, and build some internal impetus in tackling other improvements that may be more complex, difficult to implement, and produce lower returns for the firm. For example, advice on green practices for rural tourism can be found in Agenda 21 and its ten priority action areas for the private sector: waste minimization; energy conservation and management; management of fresh water resources; waste water management; hazardous substances; transport; land use planning and management; involving staff, customers and communities in environmental issues; design for sustainability and partnerships for sustainability (Carlsen *et al.* 2001; World Tourism Organisation n.d.). Each of these represent areas in which relatively simple, yet still significant, changes can be quickly and easily effected.

Reforming the Curriculum: The Role of Tourism and Business Educators

The role of universities, technical and further education (TAFE) colleges, professional institutes and other trainers may also be a critical future determinant in improving the environmental performance of small firms. These bodies provide a range of educational services for existing and prospective tourism firms, including programs of study in such fields as business planning, operations management, new venture startups, human resources, legal issues, marketing, financial skills and growth management.

The inclusion of environmental information within such courses can help develop a greater sense of environmental awareness amongst students, and so encourage them to apply this knowledge to improving processes within their own firm. The imprimatur of an external institution can also improve the legitimacy of environmental management as an issue for small business owners. Moreover, such information is largely seen as without cost for the small firm owner, since it is already included in the curriculum, rather than being made additional to it. A number of specific educational publications about green tourism practices already exist (see, for example, Harris & Leiper 1995; McKercher 1998; Middleton & Hawkins 1998), as well as periodicals such as the *Journal of Sustainable Tourism*.

Building Internal Networks

Small business owners often learn best, and are more interested in hearing from, their peers than from external sources. Whilst a professional adviser may sound daunting and remote, the experiences of other business operators are usually of direct interest. Hearing the case studies of other small tourism firms, and building informal support networks where small business owner/operators can swap ideas, share problems and work together can be an important ingredient in encouraging the adoption of greener business practices.

Recognising Best Practice

It is also important to reward those firms who do make the effort to go greener. Friedman & Miles (2002) found that awards for best practice were important for small firms, and that such schemes can be used to effectively recognise, reward and promote improved environmental practices. Both the Green Globe 21 and NEAP programs include annual awards, although eligibility to enter is reserved for certified and accredited tourism businesses only. Small business awards, celebratory stories, free publicity, formal and informal recognition all provide a means by which the efforts of tourism businesses can be acknowledged and made public. These measures help maintain interest amongst the small enterprise community; they also provide a tangible reward for effort, which is especially important since many environmental improvements tend to take a long time to be realised, or may not have an obvious internal benefit.

A Future Research Agenda

As the above discussion has suggested, there are a number of key questions regarding small firms and the environment that are yet to be fully investigated. This holds true for most small enterprises, and is especially valid within the tourism sector. The environmental impact, performance and improvement of small tourism businesses is an area in which much more research needs to be conducted. These questions revolve around the policies, programs and practices that will enable small firms to overcome the "green gap" between current and best environmental practices.

In terms of macro-level policies, critical questions include:

(1) How effective are the various global tourism organisations (such as the World Tourism Organisation and Green Globe) in facilitating the greening of small tourism firms?
(2) How can government most effectively encourage small tourism operators to adopt enhanced environmental practices?
(3) How effective is legislation and licensing in forcing small businesses to comply with environmental standards?

(4) How effective is self-regulation for small enterprises in protecting environmental resources?

(5) What other policy incentives should be instituted to encourage small tourism firms to go green?

Further research into the value of current environmental programs for small tourism firms is also required. Some of the more pertinent issues worthy of investigation are:

(1) How effective are accreditation and certification programs in achieving environmental best practice in small tourism firms?

(2) What are the most appropriate channels for disseminating environmental information for SMEs in tourism?

(3) What are the most effective triggers that facilitate small firms adopting environmental improvement programs?

(4) What are the barriers to the uptake of environmental improvement programs amongst small tourism firms?

(5) How effectively do environmental awards encourage good environmental practice?

Finally, research into the actual current environmental practices of small businesses would be helpful in establishing baseline data. This could examine the following questions:

(1) What are the common practices of sustainable tourism firms?

(2) How important is heritage and nature conservation when establishing small tourism businesses?

(3) What are the sectoral differences within small tourism firms in relation to environmental performance?

(4) Are there any demographic differences between green tourism firms and less-environmentally responsible ones? Do owner/operators from particular age, gender, educational or cultural backgrounds operate "greener" firms than others?

(5) What are the geographic differences (rural vs. urban) between the environmental performance of small tourism firms?

The answers to these questions will go some way to addressing the green gap and ensuring that both the individual and cumulative impacts of tourism are minimised through improved environmental activities by small tourism firms.

Conclusion

Creating greener tourism enterprises is a complex activity. It requires attention to a number of different, but important, issues: choosing the right mix of environmental improvement activities; understanding the factors which motivate the behaviour of the owner/manager; and introducing practical steps which can be easily implemented within firms.

Encouraging small firms to become more environmentally responsible is not just the sole province of the owner/manager. It also requires a contribution from staff, industry agencies, government and the active support of the community that such firms exist within. As Hodge (1995: 27) has pointed out ". . . with respect to nearly all environmental problems, we know how to find a solution technically . . . the question is whether we choose to prevent it." The effort and cost of such change will be substantial — but ultimately the cost of not doing so may be even greater.

References

Australian Bureau of Statistics (1997). *Australian transport and the environment*. (Cat. No. 4605.0) Canberra: Australian Bureau of Statistics.
Australian Bureau of Statistics (2002). *Small business in Australia 2001*. Canberra: Australian Bureau of Statistics.
Australian Greenhouse Office (1999). *Working with small business to increase profits, improve competitiveness and reduce environmental impact*. Canberra: Australian Greenhouse Office, Commonwealth Department of the Environment.
Barnes, P. (1994). A new approach to protecting the environment: The European Union's environmental management and audit regulation. *Environmental Management and Health*, 5(3), 8–12.
Bolin, R., & Greenwood, T. (2003). *Tourism businesses in Australia*. Occasional Paper No. 34, Bureau of Tourism Research, Canberra.
Buhalis, D., & Fletcher, J. (1995). Environmental impacts on tourist destinations: An economic analysis. In: H. Cocossis, & P. Nijkamp (Eds), *Sustainable tourism development* (pp. 3–24). Aldershot: Avebury.
Burke, T., & Hill, J. (1990). *Ethics, environment and the company*. London: Institute of Business Ethics.
Carlsen, J., Getz, D., & Ali-Knight, J. (2001). The environmental attitudes and practices of family businesses in rural tourism and hospitality sectors. *Journal of Sustainable Tourism*, 9(4), 281–297.
Charter, M., & Polonsky, M. J. (1999). *Greener marketing: A global perspective on greening marketing practice*. London: Greenleaf.
Day, R. M., & Arnold, M. B. (1998). The business case for sustainable development. *Greener Management International* (23), 69–92.
Denman, R. (1994). Green tourism and farming. In: J. Fladmark (Ed.), *Cultural tourism* (pp. 215–222). Papers presented at the Robert Gordon University Heritage Convention.
Dewhurst, H., & Thomas, R. (2003). Encouraging sustainable business practices in a non-regulatory environment: A case study of small tourism firms in a U.K. National Park. *Journal of Sustainable Tourism*, 8 (in press).
Durham University Business School (1997). *The business adviser and the environment*. Durham: Durham University Business School.
Environment Protection Authority (1993). *Greenhouse saving office equipment*. Melbourne: Environment Protection Authority, Government of Victoria.
Fineman, S. (1997). Constructing the green manager. *British Journal of Management* (8), 31–38.
Friedman, A. L., & Miles, S. (2002). SMEs and the environment: Evaluating dissemination routes and handholding levels. *Business Strategy and the Environment*, 11, 324–341.
Gallarotti, G. M. (1995). It pays to be green: The managerial incentive structure and environmentally sound strategies. *Columbia Journal of World Business*, 30(4), 38–57.
Getz, D. (1994). Residents' attitudes towards tourism: A longitudinal study in Spey Valley, Scotland. *Tourism Management*, 15(4), 247–257.

Harris, R., & Leiper, N. (1995). *Sustainable tourism: An Australian perspective*. Australia: Butterworth-Heinemann.

Hill, J., Marshall, I., & Priddey, C. (1994). *Benefiting business and the environment*. London: Institute of Business Ethics.

Hillary, R. (Ed.) (2000). *Small and medium-sized enterprises and the environment*. Sheffield: Greenleaf.

Hodge, I. (1995). *Environmental economics*. London: Macmillan.

Hunter, D., Bailey, A., & Taylor, B. (1999). *The essence of facilitation*. Auckland: Tandem Press.

Hutchinson, A., & Chaston, I. (1994). Environmental management in Devon and Cornwall's small and medium sized enterprise sector. *Business Strategy and the Environment, 3*(1), 15–22.

Hutchinson, W. E., & Gerrans, P. A. (1997). *Awareness and perceptions of small to medium enterprise of environmental management processes and standards in Western Australia*. Perth: Faculty of Business, Edith Cowan University.

Hutchinson, A., & Hutchinson, F. (1997). *Environmental business management*. London: McGraw-Hill.

Issaverdis, J.-P. (2000). Best practice ecotourism. In: M. Newson (Ed.), *Australian ecotourism guide 2000* (pp. 14–15). Brisbane: Ecotourism Association of Australia.

Issaverdis, J.-P. (2001). The pursuit of excellence: Benchmarking, accreditation, best practice and auditing. In: D. Weaver (Ed.), *The encyclopedia of ecotourism* (pp. 579–594). Oxon: CAB International.

Lord, B. (1990). *The green workplace: A practical guide to an environmentally safe workplace*. Melbourne: Information Australia.

McKercher, R. (1998). *The business of nature-based tourism*. Melbourne: Hospitality Press.

Merritt, J. Q. (1998). EM into SME won't go? Attitudes, awareness and practices in the London Borough of Croydon. *Business Strategy and the Environment, 7*(2), 90–100.

Middleton, V., & Hawkins, R. (1998). *Sustainable tourism: A marketing perspective*. Oxford: Butterworth Heinemann.

Murphy, P. R., Poist, R. F., & Braunschweig, C. D. (1995). Role and relevance of logistics to corporate environmentalism — an empirical assessment. *International Journal of Physical Distribution and Logistics Management, 25*(2), 5–19.

Palmer, J. (1998). The economics of environmental improvement: Will SMEs grasp the nettle of environmental accounting? *Social and Environmental Accounting, 18*(2), 5–10.

Palmer, J. (2000). Helping SMEs improve environmental management. In: R. Hillary (Ed.), *Small and medium-sized enterprises and the environment* (pp. 325–342). Sheffield: Greenleaf.

Petts, J., Herd, A., Gerrard, S., & Horne, C. (1999). The climate and culture of environmental compliance within SMEs. *Business Strategy and the Environment, 8*(1), 14–30.

Petts, J., Herd, A., & O'hEocha, M. (1998). Environmental responsiveness, individuals and organisational learning: SME experience. *Journal of Environmental Planning and Management, 41*(6), 711–731.

Porter, M. E., & van der Linde, C. (1995). Green and competitive: Ending the stalemate. *Harvard Business Review, 73*(5), 120–134.

Prokop, M. K. (1993). *Managing to be green*. San Diego: Pfeiffer and Co.

Ralston, K. (1990). *Working greener: Strategies for sustainable work*. Melbourne: McCulloch Publishing.

Ryan, C. (1997). Rural tourism in New Zealand: Rafting at River Valley ventures in the Rangitikei. In: S. Page, & D. Getz (Eds), *The business of rural tourism: International perspectives* (pp. 162–187). London: Thomson International Business Press.

Sagoff, M. (1988). *The economy of the earth: Philosophy, law and the environment*. Cambridge, UK: Cambridge University Press.

Schaper, M. (2002a). Small firms and environmental management: Predictors of green purchasing in Western Australian pharmacies. *International Small Business Journal, 20*(3), 235–249.

Schaper, M. (2002b). The environmental performance of home-based businesses in Western Australia. *School of Management Working Paper Series*, No. 7. Perth: Curtin University.

Schaper, M., & Jay, L. (2003). Which advisers do micro-firms use? Some Australian evidence. *Journal of Small Business and Enterprise Development, 10*(2) (in press).

Schmidheiny, S. (1992). *Changing course: A global perspective on development and the environment.* Cambridge, MA: MIT Press.

Sirolli, E. (1995). *Ripples in the Zambezi: Passion, unpredictability and economic development.* Perth: Institute for Science and Technology Policy, Murdoch University.

Sofield, T., & Getz, D. (1997). Rural tourism in Australia: The Undara experience. In: S. Page, & D. Getz (Eds), *The business of rural tourism: International perspectives* (pp. 143–161). London: Thomson International Business Press.

Tanner, M. M., Twait, C. L., Rives, J. M., & Bollman, M. L. (1996). Barriers to waste reduction efforts: Small business response. *Journal of Environmental Systems, 24*(3), 299–310.

Tilley, F. J. (1998). The gap between the environmental attitudes and the environmental behaviour of small firms: With an investigation of mechanical engineering and business services in Leeds. Doctor of Philosophy (Ph.D.) thesis. Leeds Metropolitan University, UK.

Townsend, M. (1998). *Making things greener: Motivations and influences in the greening of manufacturing.* Aldershot: Ashgate Publishing.

Triandis, H. C. (1971). *Attitudes and attitude change.* New York: Wiley.

Wehrmeyer, W. (1995). *Measuring environmental business performance: A comprehensive guide.* Cheltenham: Stanley Thomas.

Western Australian Department of Environmental Protection (1999). *Eco-Office program.* Perth: Department of Environmental Protection, Government of Western Australia.

World Tourism Organization (n.d.). *Agenda 21 for the travel and tourism industry: Towards sustainable development.* Madrid: WTO.

World Tourism Organisation (2003). *Global code of ethics for tourism* [online]. http://www.world-tourism.org/frameset/frame_project_ethics.html (accessed 17 March).

Chapter 14

Small Firms and the Principles of Sustainable Tourism: The Case of Cycle Tourism

Nigel D. Morpeth

Introduction

The issue of the long term sustainability of resources for tourism places a responsibility on public sector organisations and associated agencies to apply legislative frameworks and planning acumen to develop, promote and manage tourism within particular locations. Arguably, whilst small tourism firms might play a vital role in servicing the needs of tourists within diverse locations, what is not certain is how receptive they are to business practices underpinned by the principles of sustainable tourism (see Bramwell *et al.* 1996; Countryside Commission 1995; FNNPE 1993) particularly if they are servicing the "needs" of car based tourists. Therefore increasingly within the context of U.K. national parks there is a challenge for policy-makers and managers to ameliorate the environmental impacts of mass car based tourism and create diversified forms of tourism which develop opportunities for environmental and economic gains for host communities. In this respect Tolley & Turton (1995: 370) note that "if genuine sustainability is to be achieved, the bicycle — or something very like it — has to occupy a much more central role than the car in future transport policy." Lumsdon (1995) argues that there are tangible sustainable tourism principles exemplified by cycle tourism, with associated small scale infrastructure development creating local and community based tourism opportunities. Moreover, it is an activity which is slow paced, has a low environmental impact and has the potential to attract high spending tourists (see also Cope *et al.* 1998; Sustrans 1995). However what is not certain is whether there is an emergence of small firms who are positively disposed to servicing the needs of cycle tourists as part of a wider commitment to promoting the principles of sustainable tourism.

This chapter initially provides an account of the significance of the development of recreation and tourist trails designed specifically for cycle tourists and their role in promoting principles of sustainability. It focuses in particular on the first section of the 140 mile Sustrans inspired C2C cycle route which traverses the Lake District National Park, within the North of England. The role of small tourism firms in servicing the accommodation needs of cycle tourists within the urban settlement of Keswick (a significant "first stop" accommodation centre on the first night of the route) is examined via a small-scale survey of accommodation providers. The same survey also provides insights into the receptiveness of the accommodation sector to provide for the hospitality requirements of cycle tourists, and explores whether accommodation providers are motivated to offer specific facilities for cycle tourists through a wider commitment to promoting the principles of sustainable tourism.

Is Small Beautiful?

Nearly thirty years ago the mantra of "small is beautiful" was sloganised by Schumacher (1974) as an alternative paradigm which challenged the traditional tenets of economic growth and organisation. Leiper (1995) countenanced caution in linking the "small is beautiful mantra" to tourism as a "failsafe" approach to ensuring that the conditions for sustainable tourism are achieved. He argued in part that small tourism businesses were not necessarily equipped to implement environmental "best practice" and that, in fact, it was larger tourism enterprises that had the resources to implement the principles of sustainability largely based on improvements to environmental management systems. Within a U.K. context a 1998 Groundwork Report highlighted that "larger companies have an important role to play as mentors in sharing and facilitating the improved environmental performance of their SME suppliers" (1998: 13).

Harris & Leiper (1995: xxi–xxii) highlighted that tourism businesses potentially respond to "push factors" and might derive four categories of benefits to adopting sustainable practices, ranging from *tangible benefits* that create measurable financial benefit to the business, to *intangible benefits* of customer and community support through demonstrating commitment to "environmental good practice." They argued that increasingly, tourism businesses might be operating in conservation locations where they had to meet environmental standards and meeting this commitment was tantamount to a *survival benefit. Catalytic benefits* are derived from periodic environmental reviews or audits which might determine how to respond to environmental wastage where cost savings might be implemented.

Whilst tourism enterprises per se might be motivated to respond to these "push factors" Tilley (1996), Horobin & Long (1996) and Dewhurst & Thomas (2003) note that there is a gap between the environmental awareness of small businesses and their actions, and that there are "resistant forces" (Tilley 1996: 242) which prevent small businesses from being more proactive in the application of environmental sustainability. Additionally, Jacobs (1997: 4) highlights that "sustainable development represents a 'historic compromise' between the ideology of capitalism and its environmental critique. It has enabled a single environmental discourse to develop, used by governments (of all political complexions) and business organisations as well as by environmental groups."

The Countryside Commission (1995) highlighted that "Tourism enterprises have a central role to play in fostering sustainable tourism. The way they conduct their business forms an important component of the impact of tourism on the environment. They are also very well placed to influence the behaviour of their guests, and may in turn benefit their growing market of visitors who are concerned about the environment" (1995: 43). They also emphasised that "success in increasing local benefit from tourism is partly dependent on the many scattered and small enterprises which make up the rural tourism product being helped to run profitable businesses, market themselves effectively and provide the visitor with a good experience" (1995: 36). This report linked the importance of farm diversification initiatives and training opportunities and "active local enterprise networks, such as farm holiday groups" (1995: 36). Arguably whilst such initiatives offer scope for the role of the small tourism firm in promoting the principles of sustainability they do not necessarily address the organisational constraints of small firms.

Tilley argues that there is dissonance between small firms' "environmental attitudes (aspirations) and their environmental behaviour (practices)" (1999: 238). She argues that generally larger firms have the capacity to employ "environmental problem solving" which might incorporate environmental management systems including reporting, auditing and accounting and environmental management standards (1999: 239). Furthermore, the inference from Tilley's work is that these techniques of environmental problem solving are by no means applicable to the organisational structure and owner-manager characteristics of small firms. Tilley's qualitative analysis of small firms revealed a "low standard of eco-literacy and poor environmental awareness" (1999: 241) and a myopic approach to their environmental impact, citing the primacy of economic imperatives. Tilley argues that these "resistant forces" to positive environmental action can be addressed partly by the incentives of an effective public regime of effective environmental policy manifested through education and training, and a regulatory framework and institutional reform but that ultimately small firms need to be motivated morally and ethically to adopt the principles of sustainable development to change the "internal regime" of their businesses. However central to Tilley's thesis is that as small firms constitute 99% of U.K. business their environmental impact should not be underestimated. Citing the work of Groundwork (1995) Tilley (1999) posits that "small firms cumulatively could contribute as much as 70% of all industrial pollution."

Tourism and the Operationalisation of Principles of Sustainability

Butler (1998: 31) notes the pitfalls of using a narrow sectoral focus to applying the principles of sustainable development to tourism when he states that "there is . . . a clear lack of consensus about the way in which this definition should be translated into the management of people, resources and environments in a manner that would achieve universal acceptance." Whilst authors have highlighted the dominant role of public sector organisations in policy making for sustainable tourism (Butler *et al.* 1998; Jackson & Morpeth 1999), there is also evidence of the receptiveness of the private sector to operationalising the principles of sustainability within sustainable tourism development (WTTC 1996). However, what deserves further consideration is the role of small businesses in promoting the principles of sustainable tourism.

Lifestyle Entrepreneurship and Tourism

This chapter acknowledges the work of Horobin & Long (1996) and Dewhurst & Thomas (2003) in positioning the role of the small firm in working towards sustainable tourism and in this sense explores further the role of lifestyle entrepreneurship in small tourism businesses (Ateljevic & Doorne 2000; Williams *et al.* 1989) and their empathy with the principles of sustainable tourism. More specifically this chapter follows the central theme of the work of Ritchie (1999) in investigating the role of cycle tourism in operationalising the principles of sustainability. Whilst Ritchie's (1999) advocates that it is important to understand the demand-led factors in the (re)-conceptualisation of sustainable tourism development, this study focuses on the supply-side factors in the development of infrastructure for sustainable tourism activities.

Research by Thomas (1998) into the management of small firms, highlights the characteristics of a taxonomy of ownership, which identifies that owners of tourism and hospitality businesses are motivated by both commercial and "lifestyle considerations." It is possible that the wider philosophy of business objectives for small firms related to cycle tourism might value principles of sustainable tourism, and combine these principles within commercial considerations.

There is evidence of small tourism firms catering for cycle tourism. The Alternative Travel Group, for example, was initially established on the principles of conservation and sustainable tourism and organised itineraries for cyclists and walkers in routes throughout Europe. Beioley (1995) identifies that within the U.K., there are approximately 350 cycle tourism businesses and perhaps typical of these businesses is Bicycle Beano, founded in the early 1980s, as a two-person business. The owners of the business were initially involved in "bicycle politics" lobbying for the development of an improved cycling infrastructure in the Midlands of the U.K. and then as "serious" participants (Stebbins 1979) in the activity of cycling, became lifestyle entrepreneurs creating a cycle tourism business.

Cycle Tourism Infrastructure Development

Lumsdon definition of cycle tourism which incorporates both tourists and excursionists, stating that; "cycle tourism recreational cycling activities ranging from a day or part-day casual outing to a long distance touring holiday. The fundamental ingredient is that cycling is perceived by the visitor as an integral part of an excursion or holiday, i.e. a positive way of enhancing leisure time" (1995: 1). Likewise, Beioley (1995) provides a detailed profile of the growing applications of cycle tourism within a U.K. context, with the East of England Tourist Board (1996) (see also Lumsdon 1995; Ritchie 1998) also emphasising that the cycle tourism market is very segmented ranging from the independent day cyclist, day cycle hirer, short break tourer, to the independent and group cycle tourer to solo and group mountain bikers.

Sustrans (1997) highlight how the work of Euro Velo on the development of a Pan European network of family friendly cycle trails has been supported by the European Community, and regional, national and local government. Typical of the quality infrastructure for cycle tourism in Europe envisaged by Euro Velo, is a network of cycle routes within Austria which, since 1987, has seen the creation of 30 long distance routes covering 4,000 km. Elsewhere, established routes within Europe are the 470 km Noordzeeroute from Den Helder in the Netherlands to Boulogne-sur-mer in France, which typifies cross-border cycle tourism routes in Europe and is listed as part of the Dutch National Cycle Network.

This route is part of the emerging North Sea Cycle Route which links Norway, Sweden, Denmark, Germany, the Netherlands and the U.K. in a developing 6,000 km route.

Within a U.K. context Sustrans, a sustainable transport charity, works on practical projects to encourage people to walk, cycle and use public transport to both reduce and mitigate the adverse effects of motor traffic. Sustrans, has been constructing traffic-free paths, catering for walkers, people with disabilities and cyclists since the early 1980s. Their initial aim in partnership with local authorities was to create a 2,000 mile national network of traffic free routes, which would link urban centres throughout the U.K. Routes combine traffic-calmed roads with traffic free-paths, utilise disused railway lines and river and canal paths. With the boost of £42.5 million of funding from the U.K. Millennium Commission in 1995, Sustrans working in conjunction with local authorities have accelerated the creation of a 10,000 mile National Cycle Network (NCN). The rationale for route development is to enable local communities of approximately 20 million households to be 10 minute cycle ride from the route. However, the use of this network for cycle tourism has become an increasing priority for route development.

Cycling in the U.K. is increasingly becoming a major policy issue at both national and local level. In 1996, the production of a National Cycling Strategy, signalled the growing national status of cycling and recognised it officially as an environmentally-friendly form of transport. In part, the purpose of the U.K. National Cycling Strategy was to create a focus for organisations and individuals, working towards creating a physical change in the transport infrastructure for cycling, through the setting of common objectives and targets for cycle use.

Case Study: C2C Cycle Route

A barometer of Lumsdon's (1995) predicted increased leisure and tourism use of a national network is the developing C2C route between Whitehaven and Sunderland in the North of England. When it opened in 1995 it was the first U.K. based long-distance cycle route to be popularised by the U.K. T.V travel programme, "Wish You Were Here." Route development emerged due to the commitment and financial input of 15 local authorities and the Lake District National Park.

The route was a significant "marker" in the evolution of the Sustrans inspired 10,000 mile, National Cycle Network and shifted the utilitarian cycling focus to a leisure and tourism potential of route development. The suppression of latent demand for cycle tourism was viewed by Sustrans as a symptom of a lack of appropriate infrastructure for cycle tourism.

In terms of the monitoring of the C2C, Cope *et al.* (1998) were initially responsible for route usage monitoring in 1996 and 1997 using a combination of automatic route counters and interview techniques. They calculated that between 12,000 and 15,000 cyclists used the route annually spending between £1.07 and £1.85 million, with 90% cyclists of male gender and 50% of cyclists aged between 26 and 40 years old. Forty-two percent of cyclists were from the North — East of England.

Sustrans (1996) note that the majority of companies involved in servicing the needs of cycle tourism are small and that these businesses play a vital role in providing accommodation opportunities for cycle tourists. They highlight the positive response of accommodation providers to the development of the 140 mile C2C route from Whitehaven in Cumbria to Sunderland in County Durham in the U.K. and provide evidence of the economic benefit to pubs, hotels and cafes en route with the suggestion that cycle tourism has boosted rural economies and employment.

Sustrans (1996) highlighted typical responses of small tourism businesses to the benefits of an expansion in cycle tourism activity on the C2C route: "The C2C from Whitehaven to Sunderland has led to a big expansion in the demand for our bed and breakfast accommodation. Fortunately or unfortunately we have been unable to meet demand, having to turn away many potential customers" (John Fisher, Homecroft B&B, Whitehaven, Cumbria, U.K. cited in Sustrans, Network News, Autumn 1996). Likewise another accommodation provider highlighted that: "Virtually all my visitors have arrived on a bicycle — no problems with parking and such friendly people" (Lorna Egan, Langley House, Langwathby, Penrith, U.K. cited in Sustrans, Network News, Autumn 1996).

In a summary of Sustrans monitoring of tourism on the C2C cycle route during 2000 they indicated that 55.8% of respondents stayed in Bed and Breakfast accommodation, estimating that accommodation expenditure on the C2C cycle route ranged between £630,067 and £755,618. In estimating the impact of the C2C on businesses in the route corridor a telephone survey of businesses and service providers "close to" the C2C cycle route revealed that 77% of Bed and Breakfast providers felt that their business "benefited directly" from the existence of the route. The summary of the report noted the "most commonly cited forms of benefits" related to an increased number of customers, higher turnover, and growth in room occupancies. Spending in Bed and Breakfast accommodation ranged from £15 to £30 with 88% of respondents indicating that they provided secure bicycle storage to encourage C2C users to use their accommodation.

A Profile of Bed and Breakfast Providers in Keswick-on-Derwentater

This section reports on the findings of a small-scale research project which investigates the response of Bed and Breakfast providers to serving the accommodation needs of cycle tourist within the town of Keswick-on-Derwentwater, within the Lake District National Park. This town is a significant first night accommodation centre for cycle tourists traversing the C2C route from west to east and this study explores if a commitment to the principles of sustainable tourism was a key consideration for Bed and Breakfast providers to promote special facilities for cycle tourists.

The Cumbria Tourist Board Guide (2002) was used to identify "cycle friendly" Bed and Breakfast accommodation providers. There were 95 Bed and Breakfast/ Guest Houses listed in the Cumbria Tourist Board Guide (2002) with 10 accommodation providers highlighting that they are "cycling friendly." These ten accommodation providers were sent a short questionnaire by e-mail and received a follow up phone call to determine the reasons why they had decided to positively promote their accommodation to cycle tourists, and to determine whether this initiative was based on an underlying commitment to supporting the principles of sustainable tourism. A 50% response rate was received.

The profile of respondents suggested that businesses can be classified as micro-firms (which had been in existence from 3 months to 10 years) operated largely by husband and wife "teams," not always on a full time basis, with one part of these husband and wife teams engaged in other forms of employment. Respondents estimated that between 1 and 40 cyclists stayed annually, staying a range of 1 to 7 nights, with estimates that on average approximately 50% of cycle tourists were doing the C2C route (no formal records were kept which differentiated between cyclists and other staying guests).

Whilst 10 Bed and Breakfast providers publicised "cycle friendly" facilities to attract cyclists (and activity tourists engaged in walking), contrary to the insights from Sustrans (2000) there was ambivalence towards the positive commercial benefits of attracting C2C cyclists. This was largely based on the limited accommodation capacity of the surveyed Bed and Breakfast providers (maximum of 6 bedrooms), and the expressed view that C2C cyclists are likely to want to stay for just one night; providers "were reluctant to take bookings for one night stays, especially on a Friday." However, respondents indicated that they were happy to "share" cyclists so that larger C2C cycle groups might stay in a number of Bed and Breakfast providers in the same street.

Whilst the summary of Sustrans Monitoring Report (2000) highlighted that 40% of Bed and Breakfast providers advertised in the Sustrans C2C "official guide" only one of the Bed and Breakfast providers surveyed in Keswick used this form of advertising. This has implications for how cycle tourists might become aware of "cycle friendly" Bed and Breakfast accommodation, particularly as one of the respondents is situated some 300 metres from the C2C route. Further, although they have a sign welcoming cyclists, "only one cyclist had visited them the previous year."

Dewhurst & Thomas' (2003: 9) recent work on the attitudes of small firms owners to sustainable tourism, suggests that small firms are largely influenced by "personal influences (which) affect individual decisions on environmental issues." The study of Bed and Breakfast providers in Keswick explored attitudes to sustainable tourism and whether these attitudes were a motivation to want to attract cycle tourists. Respondents provided disparate responses to the concept of sustainable tourism which included that "tourism has a growth potential and can respond to the challenges of war, weather and foot and mouth disease" to more commonly held views that "it is not something we consider," "we are too busy to think about it" and "it is not something which we have thought about as we are pleased to get anyone." The evidence from this very small sample of respondents is that commercial imperatives and the survival of their business was of paramount importance rather than a commitment to advance the wider principles of sustainable tourism in specifically attracting tourists who have a better capacity to engage in a non-motorcar based form of tourism.

Conclusions

Although there is evidence of a boost to business arising from the development of the C2C cycle route, Sustrans' "upbeat" assessment of the benefits to the Bed and Breakfast sector was not replicated within the small-scale research in Keswick. Ironically, out of a population of 95 Bed and Breakfast providers, the ten providers that promoted "cycle friendly" facilities were ambivalent about the benefit of the development of the C2C route with the suggestion that they did not necessarily have the capacity to accommodate larger groups of

C2C cyclists. In fact, they discouraged one night stays particularly at the start of weekend because of the prospect of attracting longer staying guests. There was an air of despondency about the parlous economic situation caused by the 2001 Foot and Mouth epidemic and its curtailing of tourist visitation in the Lake District, with the view that commercial survival overrode wider considerations about promoting the principles of sustainable tourism. The popularity of the C2C cycle route, and the generally positive feedback from Bed and Breakfast providers reported by Sustarans, however, suggests that interventions to maximise the benefits of C2C cycle tourism are likely to yield positive results. Such interventions are reliant upon collaboration and the co-operation of the key agencies that have a role to play in the management of tourism at a local level.

References

Ateljevic, I., & Doorne, S. (2000). Staying within the fence: lifestyle entrepreneurship in tourism. *Journal of Sustainable Tourism, 8*(5), 378–392.

Bramwell, B., Henry, I., Jackson, G., Goytia, P. A., Richards, G., & van der Straaten, J. (1996). *Sustainable tourism management: Principles and practice*. Tilburg: Tilburg University Press.

Beioley, S. (1995). On yer bike — Cycling and tourism. *Insights* (September), B17–31 NL.

Butler, R., Hall, C. M., & Jenkins, J. M. (1998). *Tourism and recreation in rural areas*. Chicester: Wiley.

Cope, A., Doxford, D., & Hill, T. (1998). Monitoring tourism on the U.K.'s first long-distance cycle route. *Journal of Sustainable Tourism, 6*(3), 210–223.

Dewhurst, H., & Thomas, R. (2003). Encouraging sustainable business practices in a non-regulatory environment: A case study of small tourism firms in a U.K. National Park. *Journal of Sustainable Tourism*.

East of England Tourist Board (1996). *England's cycling country: A cycling tourism strategy for the East of England 1996–1999* (pp. i–iv). Hadleigh, Suffolk: East of England Tourist Board.

Federation for Nature and National Parks in Europe (1993). *Loving them to death?: Sustainable tourism in Europe's Nature and National Parks*. Germany: FNNPE.

Horobin, H., & Long, J. (1996). Sustainable tourism: The role of the small firm. *International Journal of Contemporary Hospitality Management, 8*(5), 15–19.

Jackson, G., & Morpeth, N. (1999). Local agenda 21 and community participation in tourism in tourism policy and planning: Future or fallacy. *Current Issues in Tourism*.

Lumsdon, L. (1995). Cycle tourism a growth market. Conference for Cycle Tourism: A Growth Market. Staffordshire University (24 February).

Ritchie, B. (1998). Bicycle tourism in the South Island of New Zealand: Planning and management issues. *Tourism Management, 19*, 567–582.

Stebbins, R. A. (1979). *Amateurs: On the margin between work and leisure*. California, NL: Sage.

Sustrans (1995). The national cycle network: Update one (September).

Sustrans (1996). *Network news* (Autumn). Bristol, NL: Sustrans.

Sustrans (1997). *European cycle routes: A report on national and international developments*. Bristol, NL: Sustrans.

Sustrans (2000). *Monitoring tourism on the C2C cycle route during 2000 — a summary*. Newcastle: Sustrans.

Thomas, R. (1998). An to the study of small tourism and hospitality firms. In: R. Thomas (Ed.), *The management of small tourism and hospitality firms* (pp. 1–6). London: Cassell.

Tilley, F. (1999). The gap between the environmental attitudes and the environmental behaviour of small firms. *Business Strategy and Environment*, 238–248.

Williams, A. M., Shaw, G., & Greenwoood, J. (1989). From tourist to tourism entrepreneur, from consumption to production: Evidence from Cornwall, England. *Environment and Planning A, 21*, 1639–1653.

Chapter 15

Accommodating the Spiritual Tourist: The Case of Religious Retreat Houses

Myra Shackley

Introduction

The growth in importance of religious tourism in a time of increasing secularisation (at least in the Developed World) is one of the great paradoxes of contemporary cultural tourism. All the organisations involved in the commercial side of the religious tourism business are small firms. They vary in size, product, character and ownership from monastic religious communities operating accommodation businesses as charitable foundations to highly commercial private-sector retailers (souvenirs, bookshops, religious items) and specialist tour operators involved in organising pilgrimage itineraries. Even those people who travel independently for religious purposes are catered for by small firms operating catering and merchandising outlets or connected with the development of interpretative facilities such as audio-visual presentations, site museums and artefact displays. Although acting under the umbrella of larger organisations, individual churches, chapels, mosques, synagogues and shrines generally operate as quasi-autonomous small firms (Shackley 2002). Because the core attractions of the religious tourism business are generally managed by not-for-profit organisations the volume and value of these peripheral commercial activities may frequently be underestimated. Indeed, the accommodation and hospitality business associated with religious tourism has been the subject of very little sustained analysis (Shackley 2002). This chapter focuses upon one segment of the religious accommodation market, namely the Retreat House, taking an international perspective on the retreat business and its position in contemporary religious tourism, and then focusing in detail, by way of example, on an analysis of U.K. Retreat Houses.

Religious Tourism

Tourism to religious sites as a phenomenon is present in most countries and associated with all the world's major religious traditions. Moreover, religious sites not only attract the faithful but also act as visitor attractions for the cultural tourist, although the extent

Small Firms in Tourism: International Perspectives
Copyright © 2004 Published by Elsevier Ltd.
ISBN: 0-08-044132-7

of this varies between countries. In the USA, for example, levels of religious tourism are relatively low except for significant sites such as the Mormon buildings of Salt Lake City, Utah (Shackley 2001) and a few major buildings like the "Crystal Cathedral" in California (mainly visited for architectural reasons). America and Canada also have many visitor attractions associated with indigenous religions, including Native American sites such as the pueblos of New Mexico. Over the last two decades there has also been a great increase in the number of American Buddhist temples, monasteries and Retreat Houses, especially in California and the south west. There is also considerable interest in visiting religious communities such as the Amish, whose distinctive culture has made them a tourism attraction, and sites associated with the Shaker movement. South of the USA/Mexican border, there are innumerable local and regional Roman Catholic pilgrimage sites, mostly associated with veneration of the Virgin Mary.

In Europe, Christian religious sites form the single most important category of visitor attractions. Moreover, they are the repositories of nearly 2000 years of European cultural history, celebrated in architecture, art, liturgy and literature. Not surprisingly, Europe contains the largest number of Christian sacred sites in the world that provide facilities for worship, prayer and pilgrimage and also act as museums, visitor attractions and major elements in European cultural tourism (Vuconic 1996). As a basis for its religious tourism industry Europe contains the Vatican, the great Marian shrines such as Lourdes, Fatima, Knock and Medjugorje, the basilicas of Ravenna, Santa Sophia in Istanbul, the monasteries of Mount Athos plus innumerable churches and cathedrals. It is home to the origins of the great monastic traditions (Benedictine, Franciscan, Dominican, Jesuit) and still houses numerous working convents and monasteries, many of which offer contemporary hospitality as centres for retreats and conferences. Today, estimates suggest that there are 560 million Christians in Europe of a number of different denominations including members of the Anglican, Roman Catholic, Orthodox, Protestant and independent Christian churches. The changing political landscape of Europe has also opened up new religious tourism opportunities. In Eastern Europe and the former Soviet Union many Orthodox churches, once dormant under unfavourable political systems, are now being re-opened and revived, especially in eastern Europe and the former Soviet Union (Nolan & Nolan 1992).

Throughout the world more people, for whatever reason, are visiting religious sites. Spain has now re-opened the medieval pilgrim hostels on way to Santiago de Compostela, one of Europe's most important pilgrimage destinations, and it is estimated that 3.5 m pilgrims/year make a visit (Bywater 1994). This is only a small fraction of the 12 million visitors/year who come to the cathedral of Notre Dame in Paris, the most popular tourist attraction in Europe. Managing such huge volumes of visitors to these sacred sites presents immense challenges, not least in balancing the need to conserve the fabric of the site with the provision of a special experience for the visitor. Christian religious sites function for the visitor as witnesses to a message and value system as well as being places of encounter with the numinous and interesting artefacts.

In an earlier work (Shackley 2001), the writer suggested a simple classification for religious sites as visitor attractions:

(1) Nodal site that acts as a focus for surrounding urban ecclesiastical and secular buildings (e.g. Mormon Tabernacle, Chartres cathedral).

(2) Archaeological sites no longer important for worship but visited as tourist attractions (e.g. deserted monastic buildings such as Cistercian Abbeys of Yorkshire).

(3) Burial sites such as catacombs or cemeteries now mainly visited as tourist attractions (e.g. Catacombs of Rome, Père Lachaise cemetery in Paris).

(4) Shrines marking apparitions of the Virgin Mary that have become centres of pilgrimage and healing (e.g. Fatima, Lourdes, Medjugorje, Knock).

(5) Pilgrimage routes and centres (e.g. Compostela, Canterbury).

(6) Sacred islands often associated with Celtic Christianity or European monastic traditions (e.g. Mt San Michel, Iona, Lindisfarne).

(7) Working convents/monasteries that are often important providers of accommodation, retreats and spiritual direction.

(8) Festivals and events at scales from local to international (e.g. exhibition of Turin Shroud, Millennium events).

(9) Secular places with religious associations, especially Holocaust sites.

This chapter examines category (7), Retreat Houses, whose business is steadily increasing even at a time of decline in the numbers of people worshipping in Christian churches. Visitors to sacred sites may be divided into two basic groups; those whose primary purpose is to gain a religious experience (including pilgrims) and the potentially far larger group of those whose major motivation is visiting an element of the Europe's religious heritage. Visiting Christian sacred sites (particularly when there is a large concentration of such sites within an urban centre) is also a major motivation within the European short break market since a very high proportion of all visits to major religious centres lasts only for a single day or two-night stopover. In the U.K., spending on day trips has increased by 48% between 1994 and 1998 to a total of more than £65 bn (ETC 2001) with the short break market especially to cities increasing to 34.7 m trips in 1999. Domestic religious travel (often involving small, highly-specialised direct sell operators) is a growth market. Religious tourism also has merchandising implications — annual sales of religious souvenirs in Italy are estimated at US$255 m (Bywater 1994) and > 200 shops in Lourdes depend on sales of religious objects. The tourism industry of one European country (Vatican City) is entirely dependent on its religious sites, and in many others, including the U.K., religious sites are vital elements in the cultural tourism industry (Borg *et al.* 1996). Such tourism is relatively recession-resistant, but it is highly vulnerable to political uncertainties (Boniface 1995).

Defining Retreat Houses

All countries in the Developed World have some locations providing specific accommodation for people in search of peace, quiet and spiritual input. Such places may belong to any religious tradition, but the majority are either Christian or Buddhist. Within the Developing World there are few such Hindu sites (although *ashrams*, which perform a similar function, are common throughout India and the Far East). Islam encourages its followers to undertake the *haj* (pilgrimage) to Mecca at least once in their lives, which has resulted in an enormous *haj*-related industry in Saudi Arabia, though without the provision of much permanent accommodation, and there are a number of secondary locations significant for Muslim pilgrims including the Sinai region of Egypt (Shackley 1999) and tombs of famous *imams* in Syria and Uzbekistan (Airey & Shackley 1998; Shackley 1988). Especially in the USA, and to a certain extent in the U.K., many Retreat Houses have also been started based around "New Age" personal or traditional (indigenous) spiritualities, creating a modest degree of overlap in motivation with tourism to health spas and health resorts. However, in mainland Europe (especially France and Spain) Retreat Houses are almost exclusively associated with Roman Catholic monasteries or convents although in countries such as Switzerland they may be associated with any Christian tradition, as is the case in the U.K. For the purpose of this paper, the term "Retreat House" is being used to denote a small firm that provides catered accommodation and spiritual input for guests in search of peace and quiet, whether or not this is associated with a religious or monastic experience.

Throughout the Developed World, Retreat Houses are located in quiet, country settings. Most provide some kind of (optional) worship framework, all include space for people to do nothing (libraries and gardens) and some are famous for their simple but excellent food. Most Retreat Houses have high levels of repeat business, low marketing costs and somewhat idiosyncratic management methods. In the U.K. and Europe, the religious Retreat House is a small firm, to be considered as a subdivision of the hospitality industry, which provides accommodation for cultural tourists, usually residents of the host country, on a short break. However, many American houses make provision for much longer retreats, often by older retired people, supplementing motel-style accommodation with trailer hook-ups and long stay cabins. By contrast, U.K. and European houses often place a maximum stay limit to discourage this phenomenon. Unfortunately, there is no standard definition of what is meant by "retreat." For some people "making a retreat" can mean doing nothing in a vaguely religious atmosphere. For others, making a retreat is synonymous with taking educational or developmental courses (using either day or overnight accommodation), or attending workshops. For others, a retreat is a seriously religious affair sometimes carried out in silence, or else involving sermons, meditation and perhaps individual spiritual guidance. Some retreatants wish to be temporarily part of a religious community, others visit a Retreat House with friends or with a formally organised mixed group. But despite this diversity of provision and motivation, Retreat Houses do have certain features in common.

Retreat Houses in the U.K.

Retreat Houses offer (predominantly) short break holidays (1–3 nights), of which U.K. residents made 67.2 m short break trips and spent £7,858 m on them in 2000 (English Tourism Council, 2000). However, of the 129.9 million bednights spent in short break accommodation, probably less than 1.6 million were spent in Retreat Houses (ca. 1.2%). Unfortunately, U.K. domestic tourism statistics do not specifically include information retrieved for this sector, which is usually hidden within the category "hotel/motel/guest house." However, various not-for-profit organisations such as the Christian Research Organisation (Brierley 2002) and the Association for Promoting Retreats (APR 2002) collect data on Retreat Houses, which has been used in the compilation of this chapter. Their material has been supplemented and refined by the writer's own fieldwork, which involved visits to a large number of Retreat Houses during 2002–2003, and semi-structured interviews with the managers of twelve establishments. These interviews lasted 1–4 hours, with questions focused around general management, marketing strategy, financial control and programme organisation. Supplementary informal interviews were also held with other Retreat House staff at the selected establishments, and an archive of publicity and marketing material was accumulated which, when combined with financial data from the Charities Commission, provided a good overview of the sector.

The Retreat House product is complex. All Retreat Houses offer serviced accommodation, often combining relatively high standards of catering with quite simple rooms, generally located in a pleasant, rural setting. Retreat Houses in the U.K. are predominantly Christian (although there is a marked growth in Buddhist retreats) and generally incorporate a chapel or church. They may only cater for individual guests or small parties, may offer only residential or only day accommodation, be run by a religious community or by a profit-making foundation and vary immensely in size. Some may offer nothing except peace and quiet, others have complex programmes of courses and events, both organised by the house and organised by outside parties. There is a very considerable degree of overlap between a Retreat House and a Christian Conference Centre (see below).

It has been estimated that small firms, employing 1–10 people, made up about 91% of the hospitality business in the U.K. in 1997 (Morrison *et al.* 1999). All religious Retreat Houses qualify as small firms, some employing only a handful of staff. A small Retreat House with around 12–15 bedspaces might sell 2–3,000 bednights/year and turn over less than £60,000, often making a loss. A medium sized Diocesan Retreat House will typically turn over £150–200,000/year, but a large Christian-run conference centre can easily turnover £1.25 m, often making a substantial profit. The number of employees in a Retreat House can vary from 3 to 50, of which about 30% could be described as management. About 60% of Retreat Houses are registered with the Charity Commission and have part, or all, of their business VAT exempt. But although superficially the Retreat House fits well into the small hospitality firms sector, it presents some quite unusual features, including the lack of any entrepreneurial connections. Indeed, Retreat Houses are deeply conservative product-led organisations whose constricted operating environments mean that, unlike other small firms, they may have little potential for flexibility, adaptive or innovation. However, they share some characteristics with other small firms such as a particular type of service focus and being owner-managed (although the "owner" may be a religious community) in a holistic and (usually) in an environmentally responsible way. Retreat Houses are often only marginally profitable, operate against deficiencies in cash flow, funding and human resources — all features commonly seen in other hospitality small firms. But Retreat Houses are seldom aiming for growth. Indeed, they are likely to contract in size as a function of a reduction in room numbers resulting from conversion to en suite facilities. Some Retreat Houses go suddenly out of business, often the result of a particular religious community deciding to stop providing retreats, or even to stop existing. Many houses are run by religious communities at a substantial loss, and even more have a very flexible pricing structure, will offer free accommodation to the needy and are not motivated by the need to make a profit. On the other hand, some Retreat Houses have very healthy balance sheets, but these are usually medium-large in size and have diversified into the conference and training market, enabling them to maximise room occupancy.

Classifying the Sector

It is hard to calculate the exact number of U.K. Retreat Houses, since the sector has some grey edges making it difficult to distinguish, in some cases, between Retreat House, conference centre and private accommodation. Some "Retreat Houses" offer a product that only partially conforms to the criteria, such as accommodation being provided in a spare flat/cottage for people wanting a quiet break. At the other end of the spectrum the definition of a Retreat House overlaps with that of a professionally-run conference centre. Most, but not all, U.K. Retreat Houses are listed annually in the magazine "Retreat" (published by the Association for Promoting Retreats) and in the Good Retreat Guide (Whiteaker 2001) with a good USA listing in the publication "Sanctuaries" (Kelly & Kelly 1996). Other Retreat Houses not listed in these guides may only market themselves to a specific (often local) group or organisation, and even properties that are listed may have gone in/out of use during the year in which the listing is published (Silf 2002). One major source for information about this sector is the annual publication "UK Religious Trends" (Brierley 2002/2003), which differentiates Christian-run accommodation in conference centres and hotels (usually purpose-built or adapted), from that provided in Retreat Houses. Table 1 summarises data from this publication for the last two decades, which shows that there are nearly twice as many conference centres as Retreat Houses. No comparable statistics exist elsewhere. However, there is a considerable degree of overlap with some establishments featuring both classifications including major monastic foundations which both have purpose-built conference accommodation in addition to Retreat Houses and facilities for day visitors.

Many houses are unclear about exact bedspace numbers because they are extremely flexible — some will offer peripheral off-site accommodation such as beds in local houses, tents and caravans in busy periods. Others have dormitory accommodation that again can accommodate varying numbers of people. However, a "best guess" estimate is that there are around 500 Retreat Houses of different types in the U.K., offering anywhere between 5,000 and 6,000 bedspaces. Retreat Houses are not all open every day of the year, some close seasonally and some have a cleaning week over the winter. Overnight rates can vary from nothing to around £40; taking a median of £25 this suggests that the annual value of the residential business of the retreat sector exceeds £13 m. However, many Retreat Houses actually make more money from offering day accommodation for courses, meetings and

Table 1: Number of properties in sequential editions of the U.K. Christian Handbook (Brierley 2002/2003).

Date	1982	1984	1986	1988	1991	1993	1995	1997	1999	2001
Conference centres, guest houses and hotels	161	199	219	241	250	276	245	261	268	242
Retreat houses	81	111	130	112	114	114	110	128	123	111
Total	242	310	349	353	364	390	355	389	391	353

Source: Association for Promoting Retreats (2002).

groups than they do from overnight stays, and not all offer residential accommodation. It is suggested that the true annual value of the U.K. sector may be nearer to £25 million.

In 2001, U.K. Retreat Houses could accommodate (on average) 29 people, 49% in single rooms. Conference centres were nearly twice as large, accommodating 59 people, but with only 17% in single rooms. This difference reflects the difference in market; a Retreat House offers a product aimed at individuals who require quiet space, whereas a conference centre attracts groups and families, and encourages shared rooms since the emphasis is not on privacy, but on participation. Many Christian-run conference centres opened in the 1970s and 1980s, whereas 50% of Retreat Houses were opened before that period (some can trace their origins back to before the Reformation), and few new ones have appeared recently, with many closures. The number of Retreat Houses grew by 30% between 1983 and 1997, partly as a result of religious communities diversifying into the retreat market. The vast majority of conference centres (72%) are interdenominational, with 15% Anglican-run, 2% Roman Catholic and the remainder run by other Christian denominations. This is quite different from Retreat Houses, which are more likely (41%) to be Roman Catholic or Anglican (43%) with only 14% interdenominational, reflecting their evolution from (and management by) religious orders.

Accommodation and Bedspaces

In the U.K., a Retreat House is often located in a scenically attractive area and may be a quiet, rambling building of historical interest with lovely grounds and views. In the past, Retreat Houses were often poorly heated but most have improved substantially, although many still offer rather Spartan accommodation when compared with a traditional hotel/guesthouse. Rooms will often be rather small and simply furnished. En suite facilities are rare, and there are no mod cons such as in-room televisions, mini-bars, room service, hairdryers or trouser presses. Compensations include a cheap rate, a sense of separation from the world, an opportunity to spend quiet, unstructured time in a pleasant location and (usually) excellent homemade food. However, there will be little choice of menus (sometimes none at all). In most houses all guests eat together, sometimes with the host community, and may be required to assist with clearing tables. Few Retreat Houses are licensed, although some operate an "honour bar" system (which usually makes a profit), and few will provide in-room coffee trays, substituting coffee/tea making facilities in corridors and ample availability of homemade cakes and biscuits. Guests may also have to cope with fixed mealtimes, early starts and early finishes (often co-ordinating with monastic timetables) and be prepared to assist by stripping beds at the end of a stay. In smaller houses guests may be required to bring their own soap/towels.

In the USA, Retreat Houses may be far less Spartan. They are much more likely to include en suite rooms (or at the worst a bathroom shared between two rooms) and higher levels of in-room comfort. This is not unrelated to the fact that most USA Retreat Houses are relatively recently constructed and many are purpose built. By contrast, monastic houses in France and Spain may still preserve a gloomy, medieval cloistered atmosphere, which for some visitors just adds to their attraction.

Table 2 illustrates an approximate breakdown of the sector by bedspace availability.

Table 2:

Size of House, in Bedspaces	Number of Houses	Average	Total Bedspace	% of Sector
1–5	22	3	66	1.2
6–10	35	8	280	4.8
11–20	38	15	570	9.9
21–30	24	25	600	10.5
31–40	37	35	1295	22.5
41–50	13	45	585	10.1
51–60	3	55	165	2.9
61–70	10	65	650	11.3
71–80	6	75	450	7.8
81–90	1	85	85	1.5
91–100	1	95	95	1.7
101–200	6	150	900	15.7
Total	196	55	5741	99.9

Although, from Table 2, the "average" house seems to have 55 bedspaces the distribution is skewed by a few large (101–200 bedspace) houses that contribute nearly 16% of total bedspaces. In fact, over 43% of bedspaces occur in medium-sized houses with total bedspace availability varying between 21 and 50. Less than 6% may be found in very small houses (under 10 bedspaces). However, the above table utilises statistics from the Association for Promoting Retreats, which does not include non-Christian Retreat Houses, omits some larger conference centres and major pilgrimage destinations such as Walsingham (which sells an annual 10,000 bedspaces in its various accommodations). All houses include rooms with facilities for the disabled, often with twin-bedded rooms equipped for a disabled person and their carer. One characteristic of Retreat House accommodation is the low percentage of en suite rooms, easily the most difficult feature for Retreat Houses to address since they are competing in a marketplace where such facilities have become the norm. Some houses have upgraded (sometimes at the cost of bedspace availability as rooms have needed to be combined) but others have deliberately chosen to remain simple in order to distinguish their product from that of an hotel. Others would like to upgrade room facilities but lack the necessary capital; all complain of increasing weight of legislation relating to Health and Safety, Food Hygiene and Disability. Where houses do include en suite rooms, policies on their allocation vary. Some (but very few) make an additional charge but most allocate either on the basis of need (giving the en suite room to someone with a disability or small children) or allocating the room (as is done at Walsingham) to members of a group who come from a socio-economic background where en suite facilities are not the norm, simply to give them a treat. Accommodation in some houses is divided by gender, usually when the accommodation is intrinsically attached to a religious community that maintains a rule of enclosure. Thus some convents or monasteries will only allow guests of the same gender to stay in the main house, but generally have mixed accommodation in a separate guesthouse. Some houses offer extensive dormitory accommodation in addition to normal guest rooms, especially those near pilgrimage sites or houses which specialise in providing retreats for children and young people.

On average, Retreat Houses have about 30% bedspace occupancy because of seasonality and a strong bias towards weekend business. This compares with an average of 43% occupancy for serviced accommodation in general in the U.K. (English Tourism Council 2002). The greatest challenge for a Retreat House is to develop a programme that attracts the mid-week visitor. Most houses advertise a programme of formal courses as well as being open for individual and group visits, though these may be scheduled at different times since they may not mix. A small house may offer nothing except peace and quiet, with the possibility of attending services or talking to a counsellor. Medium-sized Retreat Houses usually offer a public programme for around 10% of the time. The larger the house the bigger the formal programme — a really large Retreat House such as Worth Abbey (Surrey) may offer formal courses for more than 200 days/year whereas a smaller house may have just one weekend course per month. Course lengths are variable, some just a single day, others lasting as long as a week.

Marketing is done at minimal cost, often just by a mention or a small display advert in the magazine "Retreats," or by listing on the houses' website. Popular events can get booked long ahead, but all houses report that they have had to cancel courses at short notice because of lack of interest. Most houses try to work out a diary that allows space for an open-access programme as well as time when use of the house is reserved for specific groups. In a Diocesan Retreat House, for example, the latter might include clergy selection conferences, ordination retreats, diocesan meetings and training courses as well as days or weekends for parish groups. Some houses have no accommodation and are merely open for day visits and courses. Typically, a house offers a combination of all these things but there are infinite variations.

Currently popular courses include anything to do with music and retreats based around music, located in places with strong musical tradition or attached to a house of religion where services are still sung (preferably in Gregorian chant, ideally in Latin) are booked solid years ahead. Other popular favourites include courses involved with painting, calligraphy and embroidery and events that involve gardens or gardening. More specifically religious courses might feature the life and works of a saint or major church figure, look at a religious trend (such as Celtic spirituality) or be concerned with specific types of prayer. All Retreat Houses report that there are discernible fashions in courses, and that specific retreat conductors attract a faithful audience, whatever they are talking about. Many houses have noted the presence of "groupies" who follow such individuals, as well as people who seem to have an addiction to attending retreats and will sign up no matter what the course or the subject.

Management and Staffing

Around 30% of Retreat Houses are associated with, and managed by, the major traditional religious orders, though the guest accommodation may be in separate premises. Of these houses, 50% belong to orders that own only a single house, comprising (in the U.K.) around 40 different Anglican and Roman Catholic communities, both male and female. Within the larger orders the Benedictine tradition dominates with 17% of religious houses, as might be expected from an order with a strong tradition of providing monastic hospitality. Franciscans run 10% of U.K. religious Retreat Houses, Carmelites 6% and Jesuits 4%.

Within any Retreat House, whether religious or lay run, around round one third of staff are management. The average retreat or conference centre employs 7–9 full time staff (although a small number have no full time staff at all) with a total of about 2,500 staff employed in conference centres and about half that number in Retreat Houses, figures which have doubled in the last 20 years because of a decline in the number of members of religious orders working in the hospitality business, and an increase in the number of lay staff. A substantial percentage of the labour market chooses to work in SME's (rather than large firms) for varied reasons (Burns 2001; Dewhurst & Burns 1993) and Retreat Houses provide highly favourable conditions of employment. However, wages are low (typically the national minimum wage for manual staff and the equivalent of a church stipend for managers) and sometimes non-existent for members of religious orders, but staff turnover is also extremely low. Hours and working conditions are flexible and often relaxed, informed by a strong Christian ethos that promotes care in the provision of hospitality as part of mission, not commerce. Staff go the extra mile to extend highly personal levels of service, tailored to the needs of groups and individuals. This can go to excessive lengths — one Retreat House provides for more than 50 different dietary variations if booked in advance. On the whole, Retreat Houses function with a relatively small permanent staff (many of whom live in), supplemented by seasonal and occasional staff bought in when needed. Such people have often worked for the house for many years, live locally and have an interest in the house and its activities. Their numbers may be supplemented by volunteers who work on specific projects in the house or gardens. In religious houses the "staff" might include senior religious such as the Abbot, Mother Superior or Prior plus designated community members with a vocation to manage guest accommodation and deal with outside world. However, in small communities finding such people can be a problem and there are several enclosed orders with high levels of demand for retreats and personal guidance where demand exceeds supply. Not all community members wish to be involved in this kind of activity, and declining community numbers may require downsizing or re-location of premises. Religious community members sometimes feel that guests unaccustomed to the retreat ethos may make unreasonable demands on their time, which is usually unpaid unless such staff are being "employed" by a course as a retreat conductor. This keeps costs low, but means that community members are working long, unpaid hours in the retreat business in houses which may be financially stretched, where their time and talents might be better employed in another direction. Because of the diminishing number of vocations to the religious life many Retreat Houses run by religious communities are forced to employ steadily-rising numbers of lay staff. In the case of conference centres these may include professional managers, but the employment of lay staff brings with it the complications of employment law and many other sets of bureaucratic regulations. The low staff turnover rates suggests that lay staff working in such organisations find considerable job satisfaction and good social relationships which partly compensates for poor pay. Retreat Houses located in very rural situations may experience problems recruiting staff, especially where they compete for workers with local residential homes and where staff need a car for transport.

Conclusions

It is suggested that some classification of U.K. retreat houses can be attempted by combining criteria of size, management and the nature of the activities and programme offered. The typology is suggested in Table 3.

There are, however, many variations on this basic theme. Retreat Houses can offer low-cost accommodation only because their facilities are simple, staffing costs and marketing budgets are low. Pricing retreats is most difficult — many houses operate a pricing system where rates are held below market level in order not to exclude those who could not afford to pay higher fees. The results are predictable, with the policy creating financial difficulties that houses may address by attempting to generate revenue from others sources including course and conference business. But although many Retreat Houses will refuse to raise their fees to market rates even when in dire need of cash, others take a more commercially pragmatic view and charge higher base rates but with substantial levels of concessions. Still others support their retreat business from more lucrative commercial ventures but a few small Retreat Houses still refuse to make any charge at all, although a voluntary donation is expected.

Because of their financial fragility Retreat Houses are vulnerable to environmental factors — many suffered badly from the 2000/2001 foot-and-mouth epidemic, for example. Increased levels of government legislation have forced some houses out of business. Rural locations may mean that heavy reliance on local transport. Great demands are placed on the members of religious communities who run Retreat Houses, who may find it difficult to meet visitor demands and still maintain religious routines. A small Category 3 monastic-run house run by a religious community, at a low cost to its customers may be fully booked many months ahead, with high levels of repeat business suggesting that guests are highly satisfied

Table 3: Typology of retreat houses — major categories.

Type	Description
1	Non-residential centre.
2	Single house, flat or cottage offering guest accommodation, usually privately run.
3	Small house (<20 rooms) offering up to 30 bedspaces, often in or attached to a house of religion or run by a charitable community. Offers a small formal programme, ca. <50/days per year.
4	Medium house (31–50 bedspaces) run by a Diocese, Charitable Trust or community, offering a formal programme 80–90 days/year.
5	Large house (100+ bedspaces), often purpose-built, with sports facilities and large gardens. Conference and course facilities with formal programme 200+ days/year.

with their experience. However, it can still have serious financial problems since it will not charge market rates. A reluctance to its increase room rates will mean that additional paid staff cannot be employed, placing a heavy burden both on the community and its volunteers. Exactly the opposite situation might be seen in a Category 5 Priory/Conference Centre whose turnover could exceed £1 m/year by providing facilities for day-visitors, deriving revenue from catering and marketing activities and running a successful conference business. Such places have high weekday room occupancy from conference business and are filled at weekend by private and group retreat business. Middle range Category 4 Retreat Houses typically allocate an annual average of 36 (mainly weekend) days allocated to formal courses, and extensive day bookings for courses and meetings filling midweek slots. Staffing levels are low enabling such houses, if efficiently-run, to make a substantial profit on only 30% bedspace occupancy, permitting upgrades and innovation.

Although the market for retreats in the U.K. is small it is growing, as the edges between making a retreat, taking a course or enjoying a quiet short break become increasingly blurred. However, although the annual value of the sector has been estimated (above) to exceed £25 m this still represents only a tiny percentage of the U.K. special interest short break market. At present, challenges for the smaller houses include the need to become commercial, to face up to the need to rationalise pricing structures and charge market rates, permitting the employment of lay staff and the generation of investment capital. Small Category 3 houses face additional problems as religious communities diminish in size and number, with their members becoming elderly. Many are either unable or unwilling to maintain unprofitable Retreat Houses when other financial strategies (which may include selling an expensive house and relocating, using the profits for pensions and healthcare) are more attractive. This issue is dealt with more fully elsewhere (Shackley in prep.). The success of larger Retreat Houses, irrespective of their management, seems to depend on professional attitudes to finance and the ability to fill midweek bedspaces while keeping marketing costs low. This specialised area of cultural tourism seems to be flourishing, but a successful house (of whatever size) needs to develop a product portfolio that maximises the distinctive character of the house and applies it to a series of different customer bases. Another facet of this project (Shackley in prep.) has extended this studying into an examination of the part played by Retreat Houses in the survival and diversification strategies of religious orders, considered from the perspectives of both strategic change and the sociology of religious hospitality.

References

Airey, D., & Shackley, M. (1998). Tourism development in Uzbekistan. *Tourism Management, 18*(4), 199–208.

Association for Promoting Retreats (2002). *Retreats 2002*. London: Association for Promoting Retreats.

Boniface, P. (1995). *Managing quality cultural tourism*. London: Routledge.

Brierley, P. (Ed.) (2002/2003). *U.K. Christian handbook: Religious Trends 3*. London: Christian Research.

Burns, P. (2001). *Small business and entrepreneurship*. London: Macmillan.

Bywater, M. (1994). Religious travel in Europe. *Economist Intelligence Unit Travel and Tourism Analyst, 2*, 39–52.

Dewhurst, J., & Burns, P. (1993). *Small business management* (3rd ed.). London: Macmillan.

English Tourism Council (2002). *U.K. tourism facts 2000*. London: English Tourism Council.

Morrison, A., Rimmington, M., & Williams, C. (1999). *Entrepreneurship in the hospitality, leisure and tourism industries*. Oxford: Butterworth Heineman.

Nolan, M. L., & Nolan, S. (1992). Religious sites as tourism attractions in Europe. *Annals of Tourism Research, 19*, 68–78.

Shackley, M. (Ed.) (1988). *Visitor management; case studies from world heritage sites*. Oxford: Butterworth-Heinemann.

Shackley, M. (1999). A golden calf in sacred space the future of St Katherine's Monastery, Mount Sinai (Egypt). *International Journal of Heritage Studies, 5*(2), 74–93.

Shackley, M. (2001). *Managing sacred sites; service provision and visitor experience*. London: Continuum Press.

Shackley, M. (2002). Space, sanctity and service the English cathedral as *heterotopia*. *International Journal of Tourism Research, 4*, 345–352.

Shackley, M. (in prep.). Guests and commerce in the future of religious orders; strategic change in the provision of religious hospitality.

Silf, M. (2002). *Soul space; making a retreat in the Christian tradition*. London: SPCK.

Whiteaker, S. (2001). *The good retreat guide*. London: Random House.

Vuconic, B. (1996). *Tourism and religion*. Oxford: Pergamon Press.

Chapter 16

Small Firm Performance in the Context of Agent and Structure: A Cross Cultural Comparison in the Tourist Accommodation Sector

Alison Morrison and Rivanda Meira Teixeira

Introduction

Factors influencing small firm performance can be classified under the three major headings of organisational development, functional management skills, and sectoral economics (Chaston & Mangles 2002). Furthermore, definitions of what constitutes "performance" will differ with perspective. For example, policy-makers may equate it to quantitative measures like return on investment or number of employees. Alternatively, owner-managers may assign qualitative measures, such as, defining performance against lifestyle benefits achieved. It would appear that the performance profile of small firms is a complex matter and multi-dimensional in scope and character (Scase & Goffee 1984). It embraces a convergence of: owner manager motivations, goals and capabilities; internal organisational factors; region specific resources and infrastructure; and external relationships (Mitra & Matlay 2000; Storey 1994; Shaw & Conway 2000). Thus, it is argued in this chapter that the constituent elements of which small firm performance is composed represent an intricate weaving of the internal and external, subjective and objective, and conventional economic rationality alongside what some might term as irrationality. As argued by Hill *et al.* (2002), this acknowledges that small firms have their own particular characteristics. They affect the way they operate and largely determine their internal preoccupations and concerns, which will not be immune to the external environment. Consequently, studies that polarise into the small firm owner-manager as the primary agent in an economic process on one hand, and objective structures influencing factors of production or service on the other provide only partial, "one piece of a jigsaw" type of knowledge. For as Gorton (2000: 277) proposes: "the formation and performance of small firms is inevitably embedded within the founder's social world, not just in terms of objective structures but also subjective configurations such as family background." This emphasises the importance of synthesising

Small Firms in Tourism: International Perspectives
Copyright © 2004 by Elsevier Ltd.
All rights of reproduction in any form reserved
ISBN: 0-08-044132-7

"agent" and "structure" into a duality of social relations (Southern 1999) in order to more fully comprehend what are the constituent elements of small firm performance, and how they combine to create the complete tableau as constructed by owner-managers in their respective social worlds.

Thus, this chapter and the empirical research reported therein seek to surface and relate the constituent elements associated with both agent and structure within the context of small firm performance in the tourism sector. For example, from an agency perspective, within this sector the vast majority of firms globally belong to the indigenous population, are family run, and the smallness of physical, employee and market size is consciously preserved by owner-managers (Lockyer & Morrison 1999; Main 2002; Morrison 2002). By definition such firms typically supply fewer than 50 rooms, employ less than 10 people, and operate in the lower reaches of the market (WTO 2000). While from the perspective of structure, the collective critical mass of these small tourism firms is of importance as they produce the bulk of the essentially local ambience and quality of visitor experiences at tourism destinations on which the future growth of overseas and domestic markets depend (Middleton & Clarke 2001). Thus, within a highly fragmented industry structure the small firms have the potential to contribute valuable tourist destination differentiators providing a complimentary contrast to the often homogenized and standardized corporate brands.

The chapter progresses this line of agent-structure enquiry through the integration of relevant academic literature with findings from a cross-cultural study involving Scotland and Brazil. The study was of a qualitative, exploratory and interpretative nature into the complex relationships between the owner-managers, their internal organization, external environment, and consequences for firm performance. The samples were drawn from the small urban tourism firm sector located in the cities of Glasgow, Scotland and Aracaju, Brazil. A sampling frame was constructed from the respective directories of tourist accommodation, identifying those that conformed to the sample selection criteria of size of operation (4–50 bedrooms), independently owned and not part of a corporate group. For Glasgow a sample of 22 firms was secured representing 33% of the total population, and was composed of 50% hotels, 45% guesthouses, and 5% bed and breakfasts. In Aracaju, the sample contained 21 firms representing 33% of the total population, and was composed of 53% hotels and 47% guesthouses. Semi-structured in-depth interviews involving closed and open-ended questions were administered to each small firm in the samples by the same researcher to ensure consistency. In the majority of these firms there was either one owner-manager or a dominant owner-manager and this was the person interviewed. Questions pertained to their individual, social and economic contexts, within which they were encouraged to formulate their own responses. Data collection and analysis worked from an interpretative approach, involving induction of research categories and frameworks from the interview transcripts, and subsequent refinement until an informative comparative theory about small urban tourism firm performance emerged from the data.

The content of the chapter is presented within a framework that firstly investigates structural dimensions as presented in the form of industry and locale. Relative to the significance for performance, the industry context is investigated, and the countries in which the small firms are embedded compared and contrasted. Discussion then moves to the organisational setting of the small firms and critical exploration of the key constituent elements of structure, behaviour and resources impacting on agent's actions. Where appropriate, quotations from owner-managers are incorporated to illustrate key issues. Where these appear either "A" for Aracaju and "G" for Glasgow is inserted in brackets to refer to its city source. Finally, findings pertaining to both structure and agent are synthesised to provide a foundation of understanding relative to small urban tourism firm performance that incorporates international dimensions.

Structural Dimensions

The structural dimensions refer to the conditions in which the small firms exist. It is important to take these into account for as Southern (1999: 83) argues: "they operate in and around the small firm in such a way that they enable certain things to take place, but at the same time they impose some form of constraint on what can actually take place." Structural dimensions of relevance are now discussed within the contexts of the tourism industry sector and the locale of the cities of Glasgow and Aracaju.

Industry

The industry context of the study is that of urban tourism, which represents a complex of activities that are interlinked in a particular milieu and enables cities to attract tourists (Law 2000). Within developed countries this is seen as one way to revive the fortunes of places that have lost their heavy industries, bringing new jobs, many of which are based on cultural attractions, and generally improving the environment (Richards 1996; Yale 1997). Within developing countries urban tourism has often been used as a means to economically and socially revitalise poor areas, where a rich architectural heritage is seen as an economic asset and currency generator. At the same time, there is recognition that tourism itself may be degrading socially and do little to benefit the poorest, other than the provision of low-wage jobs in the service industry (http://www.american.edu). Nevertheless, within both developed and developing countries tourism has become an important and significant component of the economy of many cities, representing an export industry. Although the scale will vary, there is usually recognition by private and public agents that it is a sector with growth potential and should be encouraged (Law 2000, 2002).

Furthermore, the tourism industry presents itself as a potentially attractive site for investors to enter with relative low legal or professional barriers provided that the necessary finance is in place (Morrison 1998; Morrison *et al.* 1999). What is significant about this sector is that it has held consistently solid appeal to those individuals seeking to combine domestic and commercial activity. Furthermore, as Blackburn (1999) notes, although the family has ceased to be a productive unit in the market economy, it remains one in the domestic economy, such as represented by the tourist accommodation sector. This strong lifestyle business entry motivation is reflected in the traditional image presented of small tourism firms (Andrew *et al.* 2001). Findings from this study indicated that in both countries the only apparent barrier to entry into the industry sector was finance, and this was facilitated in a number of instances through family ownership of real estate in a tourist area, capital gained during a previous career, family inheritance, or redundancy money from former employers. For example: "... *I came here from Rio de Janeiro because my new wife had a project to turn her house into a guesthouse — in a city like Aracaju that can give a couple a good quality of life"*(A). For those owner-managers with young families a primary attraction of the industry sector was the ability to combine child-care with commercial income earning activities within their domestic environment. This attraction is further augmented by the location of these firms within quality urban environments within which to socialize and educate offspring and to attain a certain aspired lifestyle. One owner-manager said that: *"We like the Glasgow area, the children have their school and we are making a good living out of the guesthouse . . . the main concern is our children's education and we will stay here until it is finished"* (G).

These findings help in part to explain the reasons why small firms continue to dominate the tourism industry internationally, however, the continuity of this positioning is dependent on a number of structural features at work in the sector. For example, Table 1 summarises the factors that Morrison (2002: 8) identified to explain the reasons why some small tourism firms endure, while some may be endangered.

Within the context of the urban structural environment such as experienced in Glasgow, it is proposed that the small firm may be more vulnerable to the activities of corporate groups and operation within a relatively mature and sophisticated market place. However, the owner-managers recognize this situation and believe that they provide a sound quality of tourist accommodation that has distinctive local character, augmented by the personalized service of family-run firms. Specific reference was made, confirming Middleton and Clarke's (2000) earlier assertion, that the small firms represented an antithesis to the anonymous, standardized branded large hotel in the form of a more "authentic" tourist

Table 1: Enduring and endangering factors.

Enduring	Endangering
Located in sectors and peripheral geographic and/or economic locations that are unattractive to corporate investment	Located in sites of corporate activity, financial investment and new product development
Providing an "authentic" tourism and hospitality experience, with clearly differentiated, quality products and services to niche markets	Floating product and service within the market place that is undifferentiated and vulnerable to the competitive practices of corporate groups
Lifestyle attraction, low barriers to entry and sustenance of operation despite human and financial resource poverty	Economic climate and general external forces severe, discouraging lifestyle indulgence and unmasking resource deficiencies
Contribution to sustainable regional development and adding value to the economy, society and the environment	Policy makers lack awareness of potential contributions, and neglect to provide appropriate support infrastructure

accommodation: "*. . . we concentrate on getting to know our clients and helping them with their stay in Glasgow. We don't just sell rooms, we are offering hospitality for our guests, providing them with local knowledge and guidance is part of our service*"(G). A distinct contrast in responses was found in Aracaju where there is as yet limited corporate activity and investment. Hence, as one owner-manager said: "*. . . there is plenty of scope for entrepreneurs with limited capital. I feel that Aracaju has a lot of potential to grow tourism as it is still very much in the early stages*" (A). In addition, there appears to be a relatively unsophisticated approach by owner-managers to the market place, for example, this is evidenced in the form of parochial concerns about the activities of the small guesthouses that charge less because they operate below the taxation threshold, and there is a preoccupation with only the domestic market. Thus, within the emerging tourism market of the Aracaju context the endangering factors outlined in Table 1 may not be as intense as within the mature tourism market of Glasgow, which is restructuring to favour the economics of larger corporations. This could suggest that the industry structure may be more benign and receptive to small tourism firm entry within Aracaju than in the more mature and developed urban environment of Glasgow. On the other hand, it may be that the intensity of the presence of the standardized brand of the corporate in Glasgow presents small firms with a potentially lucrative niche market opportunity to provide a more customized and "human" product and service as a distinctly differentiated alternative.

Locale

Attempts to develop urban tourism cannot be understood without reference to the economic, social and physical structures of the host city (Law 2000, 2002), thus Table 2 provides such a statistical profile of the cities of Glasgow and Aracaju. From this and findings of the study it is apparent that both cities are comparable in terms of offering a wide range of natural, built and cultural attractions with tourism potential. However, thereafter the respective contextual locales reflect contrast and difference as opposed to criteria of likeness and similarity. More specifically, comparative analysis generates four sets of specific structural dimensions that impact on small tourism firm existence and performance relative to: the stage of economic development; the tourism and policy infrastructure that is in place; variables influencing the quantity and quality of human resource; and market forces. These are now discussed.

Clearly, the Scottish and Brazilian country contexts of Glasgow and Aracaju respectively are very dissimilar. Glasgow is located in the central-belt of Scotland, a developed country, and it has historically been regarded as the industrial capital. The City is now the third most popular city for overseas visitors and U.K. short breaks behind London and Edinburgh, and has the fastest rate of growth of all major U.K. tourist destinations. Whereas Brazil is classed as a developing country and Aracaju is at the preliminary stages of tourism development. Aracaju is located on the coast in the State of Sergipe, which is the smallest state in the North East region; it has the smallest population, and the highest GDP per capita in the region.

The factors above have implications for the degree of sophistication of the tourism and policy infrastructure. For example, emerging from a post-industrial era, over the period 1985–2003, Glasgow has become a major centre for tourism, recreation, culture and

Table 2: Local contexts: Statistical profile.

Characteristics	Aracaju, Brazil	Glasgow, Scotland
Status	Capital city of the State of Sergipe	Historically the industrial capital of Scotland
Population (1999)	462,534	611,440
Area (km)	181.8	113.3
People per km	2,544	5,397
Jobs in service sector	53,568 (12%)	287,784 (84%)
Employees in tourism	4,424 (1%)	21,000 (3.4%)
Average gross weekly earnings (2000)	£60.00	£391.80
Unemployment rate (2001)	4%	4.9%
Serviced accommodation (rooms) (2000)	2,026	5,226
Average room size accommodation	87.5% < 50	90% <50
Average annual occupancy	50%	70%
Increase in bedroom stock	400% (1980–2000)	20% (2000–02)
Tourism expenditure domestic per night (1999)	£29	£38
Domestic market	98% (Neighbouring State of Bahia, Northeast region 85%)	70%
Overseas market	2%	30% (Europe 50%, North America 33%)

Sources: Greater Glasgow and Clyde Valley Tourism Board (2002), http://scottish-enterprise.com; http://www.ibge.gov.br, PRODETUR (2002).

conference business. For more than a decade, the City Council, in partnership with other public and private sector bodies, has been vigorously implementing a strategy aimed at improving and enhancing Glasgow's attractiveness as a place to live, work and visit and as a centre for investment. Aracaju is home to the biggest polo arena of the state and is a main gateway to the State. However, its airport only services national/domestic flights. The main attraction of the city is the tranquil quality of life, scenic beaches, an average temperature of 27°C all year round, and many cultural festivals. In contrast to Glasgow, the public sector in Aracaju is not considered by owner-managers to have been effective in establishing policies to attract tourists, nor have they controlled the quality of the building in the popular beach area, which detracts from the appeal of the resort. Furthermore, there is a contrast in the size of the firms investigated with 9% of businesses in Glasgow having 50 rooms as opposed to 14% in Aracaju. Reasons to explain this include: variations in the cost of land and real estate with the cost in the popular beach area in Aracaju still relatively low while in Glasgow costs are high as physical space in an intensively built environment is at a premium; planning and building authorities encouragement of tourism development in Aracaju is somewhat *laissez-faire*, but in Glasgow there are many restrictions; and the density of population per kilometre in Glasgow is 62% more than in Aracaju.

Human resource management appears consistently as an aspect that significantly challenges small tourism firms (Baum 1999) and was confirmed in this study particularly with reference to the labour markets. The majority of the population in Glasgow is educated to at least secondary education level. Traditionally, the complement of primarily family employees has been augmented by part-time employment of students drawn from the three universities in the city. However, the industry structure is dominated by the service sector and competition for such employees has intensified with the establishment of Glasgow as a preferred location for telesales call centres. As one owner-manager said:"... *a lot of the young people who normally came into this line [hospitality] of work are going there because it pays more*" (G). Within Aracaju the human resource challenge is quite different and the low social status and wages associated with working in tourist accommodation means that students very rarely select it as an income generation opportunity. Furthermore, more than half of all people in employment are illiterate or have less than one year at primary school level, with a significant proportion having received little schooling and remaining illiterate. For owner-managers, this can result in severe problems in terms of, for example, oral and written communication, lack of hygiene, uncultured behaviour and limited social skills with guests. Weekly earnings are at a bare subsistence level in Aracaju facilitating the employment of members of staff. This is not the case in Glasgow where staff other than family is kept minimal in order to control costs. For example, only 20% of firms in Aracaju fall into the brackets no employees 1–5, and 67% into the brackets 6–10/11–20. The corresponding figure for Glasgow is 50% and 18%.

Clearly, the locale of small firms will influence their competitive position (Bennett & Smith 2002). Both locales have seen a rapid investment and increase in bedroom stock. While this has been more dramatic in Aracaju it has been lead by small firms, and there are no hotel chains although there are plans for an IBIS hotel in 2003. In contrast, it is the hotel groups, such as Holiday Inn, Marriott, Thistle, Hilton and Radisson that have dominated investment in Glasgow. In addition, many of the established corporate owned hotels have undergone substantial refurbishment and upgrading. Aracaju is dependent on the domestic market of which 70% is composed of salesmen, company representatives, and public servants, and the remainder leisure tourists in the high season. Glasgow offsets domestic demand with a balance from overseas markets. Leisure tourism dominates in May to September and business demand out with these months. The split between leisure and business is 70 and 30% respectively. Aracaju's occupancy rate is highly seasonal swinging from 90 to 100% in the high season to 10% in the low. This leads operators to adopt what may be considered to be somewhat extreme survival strategies from a business ethics perspective, such as, renting bedrooms by the hour to couples in the low season to improve yield management performance. In comparison, in Glasgow occupancy rates are less volatile ranging from 60 to 80% throughout the year, achieving 100% in the high season. Furthermore, competitive advantage is also highly specific to the locale (Bennett & Smith 2002). Within both, perceived competitive advantages are common with the most dominant being personal service and customer care, followed by location, and small size that facilitates flexible, customised service.

Agent Dimensions

This section explores the organizational setting of the small tourism firms relative to structure, behaviour and resources serves to provide insight into the internal workings of the enterprises and how key elements influence the actions of the owner-managers. These are now discussed.

Structure

It is logical to argue that every small business starts somewhere, usually with the founding owner-manager who has not only a business idea, but also the determination to turn it into a reality (Kets de Vries 1996). As such owner-managers could be regarded as critical human capital (Edelman *et al.* 2002), with their role representing a distinct managerial position (Reid *et al.* 2002). In Glasgow 82% of the firms were officially founded by males of which 36% were represented by couples, within Aracaju comparable statistics are 67 and 30% respectively. It would appear that these statistics may mask the more dominant role of females in the management of the small tourism firms, certainly when roles were investigated they were found to be highly gendered with, for example, males responsible for financial control and maintenance, and females concerned with the likes of catering, cleaning and decoration. Furthermore, the organisational structure of the majority (c. 70%) of the firms in the samples was that of family businesses with partnership shared among spouses, immediate and extended family members, reflecting findings from previous studies (Blackburn 1999; Carter *et al.* 2002). Family members are active in the owner-managed businesses, taking on roles such as general management, supervision, and accounting, however, this is much more pronounced in Aracaju with 93% having at least one working relative in the firm as oppose to 42% in Glasgow.

The majority of small firms reach maturity at a very modest level of sales. Consequently, simple, informal organizational structure that was adequate to support the firm at start-up may well be retained throughout its lifecycle (Dewhurst & Burns 1989; Morrison & Teixeira 2002). This was reflected in the small firms in both locales, with organizational structures being relatively flat hierarchies composed of the two levels of owner-manager and employees as would be expected as a consequence of their smallness. However, a contrast was noted in the form of number and levels of employees. In particular, in Glasgow the common form of structure was that of a husband and wife team taking on all major responsibilities and decisions aided by very few staff, most of who were part-time employees. Based in a quite different labour market where there is an excess of relatively cheap labour, it is understandable that the number of employees within the firms in Aracaju was considerably higher. This indicates the manner in which the external business environment tends to determine recruitment activities (Gray 2002). Nevertheless, the role of the owner-managers remains pivotal within both locales, and although the complexity of human resource management may be higher in Aracaju, they assign menial tasks such as cleaning and cooking to employees.

Other than ownership, organisational structure also manifests itself through the characteristic of "smallness," which can be regarded as either an asset or a constraint dependent on perspective. The question why is it that the majority of the small tourism businesses remain micro in size has vexed academics and policy makers over the decades. For example, Edelman *et al.* (2002) suggest that organizational constraints in less glamorous industries may inhibit small firms from successfully pursuing strategies for innovation and growth. While Gorton (2002) points out that firms supply goods that are not easily tradable over space may serve a restricted, local market that will have bearing on business performance. Both of these explanations could well be equally related to the tourism sector. Findings from this study indicated the following reasons for retention of smallness working from a number of different physical, human and financially derived angles, which in combination stunt growth and protect the status quo of smallness as follows:

- emotional attachment associated with the physical space, in that it is often also the family home, constrains business growth;
- concern about market potential and any resultant loss of the distinctive differentiating features associated with "smallness";
- managerial capacity is sufficient to cope with existing size, but growth would bring with it the need to employ from out with the family circle which is not perceived as desirable;
- financial poverty in that while it is relatively easy to raise additional funds for expansion securing an adequate return on investment to pay back loans was problematic; and
- the impact of external effects such as economic, policy and social trends on operation that serve to constrain small firm growth.

Illustrations of Glasgow owner-managers' perspectives on size are as follows: *"We would like to expand, but we would have to be sure that we could fill extra rooms . . . there is always the danger if we expand too much, we will no longer be able to keep the coziness of the hotel . . . we would become like a Days Inn"*(G). From a managerial perspective size protection is related to human and financial resource poverty as it was said that: *"It's big enough for us to handle and anyway we couldn't afford to finance expansion . . . these things restrict us"* (G). However, the Aracaju sample was more articulate as regards constraints at a basic business level that impacted on the owner-managers' potential to grow the firm. The key significant factors being: volatile tourist market demand; the fiscal environment that results in high taxes; an economy in recession; and general government bureaucracy. For example, one owner-manager said: *"The biggest problem is the lack of tourism policy and infrastructure in the state . . . there is no professionalism in this area. Tourist come to Aracaju and don't know what they can do . . . there is not even a map of the city"* (A).

Behaviour

To give a context in which to understand the behaviour of the owner-managers an overview of profile is now provided. This is significant for as Gray (2002:64) states: "The most important constraint on SME growth lies in these non-growth career motivations and personal expectations of individual small firm owner-managers . . . Furthermore, if the mode of earning a living is also bound up with a certain lifestyle many decisions will be based on non-business criteria." This is particularly relevant within the context of the tourism sector where for many small firms maintenance and protection of a certain lifestyle will be prioritized over commercial focus on profit maximization (Sherwood *et al.* 2000; Thomas *et al.* 2001). As such, Goffee (1996) cautions against assuming that all small businesses will exhibit similar behavioural characteristics, and it is also argued that analysis requires to be sensitive to sectoral differences (Edelman *et al.* 2002; Reid *et al.* 2002). Thus variations in behaviour may be a consequence of, for example, demographics, approaches to the organisation of economic and professional activities, business entry motivations, management of personal and business goals, and industry sector characteristics as is now discussed.

Owner-managers falling into the middle-aged bracket of 41–60 years represented 46% in Aracaju and 68% in Glasgow, and the majority of them were indigenous to their local communities. In terms of educational background, 80% of owner-managers in Aracaju had higher education qualifications, and 10% to primary education level. Only 3% of those with higher education had a tourism degree as tourism has only been recently introduced into higher education in the State and there are currently no hospitality degrees. In Glasgow, 40% of owner-managers had higher education qualifications, 33% of which were in hospitality or tourism. A significant number (53–58%) of owner-managers in both locales were involved in other business activities out with the provision of tourist accommodation. Within Glasgow these were in hospitality related fields, such as, restaurants and student accommodation, and others like real estate and property renovation, and stabling and livery of horses. Some owner-managers split their time between the small firm and part-time employment in, for example, nursing and insurance. In Aracaju the relationship to tourism of other business activities was not as pronounced and took the form of ownership in the likes of car rental, pharmacy, and petrol station enterprises. Employment external to the small firm favoured the professions, for example, doctor, lawyer, and government official. Those who had previous experience of the tourism industry prior to business start-up were 20% in Aracaju and 32% in Glasgow. In both countries, respondents perceived tourism as a sector where practical experience is more relevant than formal education. As one stated: *"the basic business is pretty straightforward. We don't do evening meals, we only do B&B, so it is very simple."* Another said that: *"you don't need to know many things, it is very simple running a pousada[guesthouse] and you can learn by doing"* (A). Thus, although Gray (2002) suggests that entrepreneurship, as evidenced in this context in starting a small firm, implies a large degree of relevant practical, technical and business experience, as Szivas (2001) confirmed, this does not seem to be a feature within the tourism sector.

Furthermore, traditionally in tourism, many investors have been motivated by the appeal of, often romanticized, notions of the quality lifestyle that may be experienced. For example, Andrews, Baum & Morrison (2001) summarize the following range of lifestyle entrepreneur business entry motivations:

- meet people and act in a host capacity while still maintaining a relatively unencumbered lifestyle;
- inhabit in an accommodation and/or location that might be outside of the comfortable envelope of the proprietors income however;
- move away from perceived "rat race" of modern corporate living; and/or

- operate a commercial concern, which does not demand 12-month attention but benefits from the effects of seasonality with six to eight month annual closed season.

Findings from this study indicated that common to both locales is that business entry motivations reflect a mix of similar personal and business considerations and circumstances. However, in Aracaju it is business motivations that dominate relative to identifying a market gap in terms of the shortage of tourist accommodation alongside the potential for tourism growth and availability of land for development. For example, "... *after an informal survey I realized that Aracaju had hotels but not guesthouses. I don't know much about the sector but I believed that something simple, comfortable where I could give personal attention to guests would work*" (A). In Glasgow, it was family circumstances that were the dominant motivation to start a business in the tourism sector. A typical response was: "*I had a young family. I needed to make money and not leave home. My husband was too old to get employment, so I started the B&B*" (G). Business opportunity came second as a business entry motivation, taking the form of identification of niche markets: "... *the market is there in Glasgow for not a high class but an above average B&B that is affordable*" (G); and "*we saw a demand for something in between a guesthouse and a more expensive hotel — that is were we are positioned*" (G). Thus, motivations between the two locales differ perhaps because the different stages of the destinations development lifecycles, however, business entry motivations that reflect sensitivity to market conditions share similarities.

This close relationship between the commercial and domestic domains was reflected in both locales, with the majority of owner-managers finding it difficult to separate personal from business goals. In particular, this was due to the long hours associated with operating a service operation, with high levels of customer contact and interaction that deals in the immediacy of real time (Lovelock 1991). Concern was expressed as to how this may lead to tensions and conflicts that could be injurious to both the firm and family relationships, and was particularly relevant for the owner-managers living on the business premises. For example: "*They [personal and business goals] are absolutely together ... the hotel is a 24-hour business and I am a slave to it*" (A); and "*It has been a problem for me. It brought about my divorce*" (G). Others view the achievement of business goals as a means to the satisfaction and sustenance of those of a personal and family nature: "*It is a dream come true. I had always wanted to have my own horses and to own a hotel — now I have both. I've worked hard for it, long hours, extra days but it's worth it when you see what you can provide for your children and how nice our lifestyle is with the horses*" (G); and "... *as long as I am well organized, I can be flexible with my time and spend more time with my children than if I was an employee*" (A). There was a small group of owner-managers that attempted to keep their business and personal lives separate due to prior negative experiences, for example, one said that: "*too much personal involvement in your business brings worries and pressures. I went through that in my previous career — now I am not interested and make sure I have the freedom to enjoy my personal life*" (G). Primary small firm performance indicators employed by owner-managers are fairly standard in the form of bedroom occupancy rate, annual revenue, break-even point, and guest satisfaction. In addition, an insight into applied economic indicators of such businesses is reflected in the following discourse: "*We would probably need to operate at 25% occupancy to cover our costs. It depends on how you look at that, my wife doesn't take a wage, neither do I ... when we make a profit at the end of the year we take that — its our reward for all the hard work*" (G). As Deakins *et al.* (2002) argue this indicates a management of cash flow to achieve survivalist objectives rather than growth, grounded in the particular contextual environment in which they operate. Within this given context industry structure dimensions are distinctive in that they enable and support the foregoing behaviours provided the economics of operation allow their indulgence.

Resources

As previously stated the majority of small firms in the samples operate a family business model. Reid *et al.* (2002) caution that such organizations may suffer from an introverted nature arising from their limited capabilities and lag behind current policies and practices being content to follow looped, established routines. However, Habbershon & Williams (1999) suggest that the model can represent a unique bundle of resources because of the interaction between the family, its individual members and the business. Such an approach has advantages in that it may focus attention on the largely hidden contribution of family members, and in particular female entrepreneurs, in small firm management and development (Carter *et al.* 2001). In addition, the family firms in the study expressed less human resource management problems than those relying on paid employees. Habbershon & Williams (1999) summarise elements of such a resource base as follows:

- a unique working environment which fosters a family oriented workplace and inspires greater employee care and loyalty;
- more flexible work practices;
- family members are more productive than non-family employees;
- a shared "family language" allows more effective communication;
- family relationships generate unusual motivation, cement loyalties, and increase trust;
- transaction costs are lowered; and
- decision-making is informal and efficient.

This positive perspective on the advantages of family labour as an organizational resource is significant given that both in Aracaju and Glasgow the dominant challenge facing the small firms was that of human resources. The uneducated and uncultured profile of the tourist accommodation labour market proved particularly difficult for owner-managers in Aracaju as employees are deficient in communication and social skills, interpersonal relationships between members of staff tend to be volatile, and attitudes to service and customer care are limited. One owner-manager said that: "*The biggest problem to deal with is employees. The legislation is very paternalistic and that makes the employer/employee relationship even more difficult. It is necessary to teach even the most basic of social skills . . . I spend most of my day explaining and teaching them*" (A). The key issues that confront human resource management in Glasgow are reliability, frequent turnover, communication and training. Explanations included: "*Because the hospitality industry is so competitive labour costs are forced right down. I'd love to be able to pay staff more but I just can't afford it*" (G); and "*More than anything else staff turnover is because there are so many new hotels arriving on the scene, the quality and quantity of staff are not here in Glasgow at the moment*" (G);

and *"They don't care, there is no pride in their work . . . it is not seen as a career"* (G). Thus, locational differences can be observed in terms of the characteristics of the labour markets from which Aracaju and Glasgow small firms derive their employees. However, within both locales human resource management represents the dominant challenge within these service businesses.

This is exacerbated by the managerial capabilities that are dependent on the focal owner-manager and are challenged due to difficulties and pressures arising out of the 24-hour nature of the work. For example: *"You don't really have a personal life because you are here the whole time. My husband and I don't get out together, one of us has to be here to answer the door, the phone or the guest if they need something"* (G); and *"Holidays? I use occasional business trips as holidays. It is difficult to be far from the business"* (A). Furthermore, this managerial resource constraint influences attitudes towards enterprise development, as illustrated by these quotes: *"I think we are operating at the limit of our time and abilities. To have more rooms, more customers, it would mean more staff, more facilities laundry etc.."* (A); and *"10 rooms are fine. I don't have the ambition anymore. I did 10 or 20 years ago but not now . . . growing bigger gives you more worries and I don't want that. I am quite happy as it is"* (G).

Discussion and Conclusions

The foregoing has provided a foundation on which to build understanding relative to small urban tourism firm performance derived from the duality of relations between structure and agent. In addition, by adopting an approach that compares and contrasts two distinctively different geographic locations an international dimension has been introduced. This serves to illuminate factors that are generic to agents within the tourism industry structure, and those that are a dependent on the locale in which they are located. Table 3 provides a summary of these factors, which frames the following discussion and conclusions.

Firstly, relative to the structural dimensions common industry characteristics were found in terms of: contemporary consumption patterns indicate that the urban tourism sector has significant market potential; barriers to entry limited to that of a financial nature with an ease of asset or capital conversion into the economics of small firm operation; the nature of the service activity facilitates a marriage of domestic and commercial domains which support family business models and sustains lifestyle aspirations particularly relative to parenting; with the growth of the globalised corporate tourist accommodation offer small firms can position themselves in the market place to offer a significantly differentiated niche market experience.

Secondly, the owner-manager, or agent, represents a distinct managerial position within the organization, structures the small firm. While the gender of this agent remains hazy due to differences between formal and informal business "ownership" dimensions, within the domestic/commercial environment of tourism accommodation provision roles appear to be highly gendered. They are organized to incorporate family members in a simple structure, with recruitment practices being significantly influenced by the characteristics of the host labour market. The agent makes conscious decisions to retain the "smallness" of operation based on internal criteria of an emotional, market positioning, managerial capabilities,

Table 3: Generic and local dependent factors.

	Generic
Structure: Industry	• Barriers to entry other than finance low • Market demand exists for differentiated niche market offering • Supports a domestic/commercial business model • Market potential of the urban tourism sector
Agent	• Owner-manager as key decision-maker with variable management capabilities pressurized by demands of service operation • Domestic/commercial compromises of motivations and objectives • Lifestyle, hobbyist and/or family "charity" priorities over those of business • Gendered and family roles may act as vital human asset or business development impediment • Human resource management challenges a consequence of the characteristics of the labour market • Constrained financial resources and domestic/commercial nature of capital investment • Retention of "smallness" of physical, employee and market size
	Locale Dependent
Structure: Locale	• Culture, social and educational systems that dominate • Economic stage of development • Fiscal environment degree of encouragement of small firms • Labour market composition and characteristics • Tourism market evolution stage and competitive forces • Tourism policy and infrastructure existence and extent

and/or financial resources nature. Criteria of significance from the external environment include volatile market demand, fiscal disincentives, economic recession, and government bureaucracy. Within this small firm structure, it can be expected that the agents' behaviours will be a product of the socialization and educational system to which they have been subjected in their host societies, and reflect values consistent with their middle-aged status. Owner-managers engagement in business activities out with the tourist accommodation may be explained relative to the need to cross-subsidise and the possibility that the small firm may operate sub-optimally; it represents a hobby pursuit or indulgence that is consciously supported from other economic earning streams; or it is a "charitable" means to provide employment and economic outlets to support family members. This feature, along with business entry motivations and objectives that combine personal, family and domestic with business, commercial and market is likely to impact on small firm performance as compromises and tradeoffs are inevitable. That said, the family aspect can contribute critical human capital to the small firm, particularly relative to serving to neutralize some of the human resource recruitment and management challenges faced in both countries. It is important to emphasise that this aspect dominates the concerns of owner-managers of the small firms both in Glasgow and Aracaju, and although the issue is competition for service employees, and lack of educated and socially skilled, respectively the low pay and social status associated with this type of employment exists in both societies. This management aspect is exacerbated by the 24 hour service nature of operation, and the limited and constrained managerial capabilities within the simple organizational structure of the small firm. Finally, Table 3 summarises the local structural factors that differentiate Glasgow from Aracaju along social, economic, and political dimensions, all of which interact with the components of production or service required to fuel the internal operations of the agent within the structure of the tourism industry.

This chapter has presented the findings from literature and a cross-cultural comparative study. In conclusion, one of the most remarkable observations is the extent of industry and agent similarities surfaced relative to small firms within distinctly different locales. Furthermore, continuous and intricate interweaving of the constituent elements of which small firm performance is composed as embodied in industry sector economics and characteristics, with locale conditions, as they interacted within the social work of the agent validates the synthesized, dual structure-agent approach to the investigation of small firm performance.

References

Andrew, R., Baum, T., & Morrison, A. (2001). The lifestyle economics of small tourism businesses. *Journal of Travel and Tourism Research, 1*(6), 16–25. http://www.stad.adu.edu.tr

Baum, T. (1999). Human resource management in tourism's small business sector: Policy dimensions. In: D. Lee-Ross (Ed.), *HRM in tourism and hospitality* (pp. 3–16). London: Cassell.

Bennett, R., & Smith, C. (2002). Competitive conditions, competitive advantage and the location of SMEs. *Journal Small Business and Enterprise Development, 9*(1), 73–86.

Blackburn, R. M. (1999). Is housework unpaid work? *International Journal of Sociology and Social Policy, 19*(7/8), 1–20.

Carter, S., Anderson, S., & Shaw, E. (2001). *Women's business ownership: A review of the academic, popular and Internet literature*. London: Small Business Service, Department of Trade and Industry.

Carter, S., Tagg, S., Ennis, S., & Webb, J. (2002). *Lifting the barriers to growth in U.K. Small businesses*. London: Federation of Small Business.

Chaston, I., & Mangles, T. (2002). *Small business marketing management*. Basingstoke: Palgrave.

Deakins, D., Morrison, A., & Galloway, L. (2002). Evolution, financial management and learning in the small firm. *Journal of Small Business and Enterprise Development, 9*(1), 7–16.

Dewhurst, J., & Burns, P. (1989). *Small business planning, finance and control*. London: MacMillan Education.

Edelman, L., Brush, C., & Manolova, T. (2002). The impact of human and organizational resources on small firm strategy. *Journal of Small Business and Enterprise Development, 9*(3), 236–244.

Goffee, R. (1996). Understanding family businesses: Issues for further research. *International Journal of Entrepreneurial Behaviour and Research, 2*(1), 36–48.

Gorton, M. (2000). Overcoming the structure-agency divide in small business research. *International Journal of Entrepreneurial Behaviour and Research, 6*(5), 276–293.

Gray, C. (2002). Entrepreneurship, resistance to change and growth in small firms. *Journal of Small Business and Enterprise Development, 9*(1), 61–72.

Greater Glasgow and Clyde Valley Tourism Board (2002). *Value and volume of tourism to greater Glasgow and Clyde Valley.* http://media.seeglasgow.com [29/09/2002].

Habbershon, T., & Williams, M. (1999). *A resource based framework for assessing the strategic advantages of family firms.* Working Paper Series No. 101, The Wharton School, University of Pennsylvania.

Hill, J., Nancarrow, C., & Wright, L. T. (2002). Lifecycles and crisis points in SMEs: A case study approach. *Marketing Intelligence and Planning, 20*(6), 361–369.

Kets de Vries, M. (1996). *Family business: Human dilemmas in the family firm.* London: Thomson International Business Press.

Law, C. (2000). *Urban tourism: Attracting visitors to large cities.* London: Mansell.

Law, C. (2002). *Urban tourism: The visitor economy and the growth of large cities.* London: Continuum.

Lockyer, C., & Morrison, A. (1999). *Scottish tourism market: Structure, characteristics and performance.* Glasgow: Scottish Tourism Research Unit/Fraser of Allander Institute, University of Strathclyde.

Lovelock, C. (1991). *Services marketing.* Englewood Cliffs: Prentice-Hall.

Main, H. (2002). The expansion of technology in small and medium hospitality enterprises with a focus on net technology. *Information Technology and Tourism, 4,* 167–174.

Middleton, V., & Clarke, J. (2001). *Marketing in travel and tourism.* Oxford: Butterworth-Heinemann.

Mitra, J., & Matlay, H. (2000). Towards the new millennium: The growth potential of innovative SMEs. Paper presented at *ICSB World Conference,* Brisbane.

Morrison, A. (1998). Small firm statistics: A hotel sector focus. *The Service Industries Journal, 18*(1), 132–142.

Morrison, A. (2002). Small hospitality business: Enduring or endangered? *Journal of Hospitality and Tourism Management, 9*(1), 1–11.

Morrison, A., Rimmington, M., & Williams, C. (1999). *Entrepreneurship in the hospitality, tourism and leisure industries.* Oxford: Butterworth-Heinemann.

Morrison, A., & Teixeira, R. (2002). Small hospitality firms: Business performance obstacles. Paper presented International Small Hospitality and Tourism Firm Conference, Leeds Metropolitan University, Leeds (September).

PRODETUR (2002). Plano Estategico do Turismo de Sergipe, SEPLANTEC-SE/PRODETUR-NE II Secretaria de Planejamento de Estado, Aracaju.

Reid, R., Morrow, T., Kelly, B., & McCartan, P. (2002). People management in SMEs: An analysis of human resource strategies in family and non-family businesses. *Journal of Small Business and Enterprise Development, 9*(3), 245–259.

Richards, G. (1996). *Cultural tourism in Europe.* London: CAB International.

Scase, R., & Goffee, R. (1984). *The real world of the small business owner.* London: Routledge.

Sherwood, A.-M., Parrott, N., Jenkins, T., Gillmor, D., Gaffey, S., & Cawley, M. (2000). Craft producers on the Celtic fringe: Marginal lifestyles in marginal regions? Paper presented at *15th International Society for the Study of Marginal Regions Seminar,* Newfoundland.

Southern, A. (1999). The social and cultural world of enterprise. In: S. Carter, & D. Jones-Evans (Eds), *Enterprise and small business: Principles, practice and policy* (pp. 78–96). London: Financial Times/Prentice-Hall.

Szivas, E. (2001). Entrance into tourism entrepreneurship: As U.K. case study. *Tourism and Hospitality Research, 3*(2), 163–172.

Storey, D. (1994). *Understanding the small business sector.* London: Routledge.

Thomas, R., Lashley, C., Rowson, B., Xie, G., Jameson, S., Eaglen, A., Lincoln, G., & Parsons, D. (2001). *The national survey of small tourism and hospitality firms: 2001*. Leeds: Centre for the Study of Small Tourism and Hospitality Firms, Leeds Metropolitan University.

World Tourism Organisation (2000, September). *Marketing tourism destinations on-line*. WTO Business Council.

Yale, P. (1997). *From tourism attractions to heritage tourism*. Huntington, ELM Publications. http://www.scottish-enterprise.com/about/lecs/glasgow/local/statistics [29/09/2002]. http://www.ibge.gov.br [13/01/03]. http://www.american.edu/TED/urbtour.htm [13/01/2003].

Chapter 17

Coping with Resource Scarcity: The Experience of U.K. Tourism SMEs

Marcjanna M. Augustyn

Introduction

Contrary to the commonly held view that resource abundance is a prerequisite for business success, Hamel & Prahalad (1993) argue that firms characterised by relatively high levels of resource scarcity often attain higher growth rates and enjoy greater competitive advantage than firms characterised by a relatively high level of resource abundance. Indeed, these influential commentators argue that it is the resource scarcity, combined with a high level of a firm's aspirations, which drives the firm's creativity. This view seems to be of utmost importance and relevance to tourism small and medium-sized enterprises (SMEs)[1] which face the problem of resource scarcity and which perceive resource scarcity as the major barrier to growth.

Drawing upon the relevant theoretical frameworks and the practice of successful resource-scarce U.K. tourism SMEs, this chapter discusses strategic approaches towards overcoming the problem of resource scarcity and embarking on a growth trajectory. Further research implications are also specified.

How Do Resource-Scarce Firms Achieve High Performance Levels?

The question of the ways in which firms cope with resource scarcity and attain high performance levels directs our attention to the resource-based view of the firm (hereafter RBV). Central to this approach is viewing the firm as a pool of resources and capabilities, which are the primary determinants of the firm's sustainable competitive strategy (Barney 1991; Peteraf 1993; Rangone 1999; Wernerfelt 1984). There are two critical notions associated with the RBV approach: resources and organisational capabilities.

Resources include the tangible and intangible assets owned or controlled by a firm (Amit & Schoemaker 1993). Organisational capabilities are the long-lasting bundles of integrated resources that form a unique set of organisational abilities and that enable a

Small Firms in Tourism: International Perspectives
Copyright © 2004 by Elsevier Ltd.
All rights of reproduction in any form reserved
ISBN: 0-08-044132-7

company to undertake a particular productive activity and provide a particular benefit to customers (Grant 2002; Hamel & Prahalad 1994; Ulrich & Lake 1990). According to Besanko *et al.* (1996), organisational capabilities should be valuable across multiple products or markets, embedded in organisational routines and unique in relation to other firms.

The RBV contrasts and complements a more traditional Porterian approach to strategy formulation, which assumes that it is the industry external environment and the firm's competitive positioning that should determine the firm's strategy. While the RBV does not reject the validity of Michael Porter's (1980, 1985) approach to strategy formulation, it stresses that the focus on external environment alone is insufficient in formulating the firm's competitive strategy, as the external environment analysis may lead several firms to adopting similar strategies. Instead, the RBV's focus on the internal environment of the firm (i.e. organisational resources and capabilities) provides a greater opportunity for a firm to formulate unique strategies that lead to the achievement of high performance levels (Grant 2002). The uniqueness of such strategies results from the fact that while firms may possess similar resources, their experiences, knowledge, skills and organisational culture as well as the ways in which those resources are integrated into distinct capabilities differ from firm to firm.

According to Grant (1991), the importance of the resource-based view of strategy is also associated with the fact that the external environment, and particularly customer preferences and the technologies for serving customers, is continuously changing. Therefore, defining a business in traditional terms of the market that the firm serves may not provide sufficient stability and constancy of direction. Instead, defining a firm in terms of its bundle of resources and capabilities (i.e. in terms of what the firm is capable of doing) may provide the firm with a much more stable basis on which to build its competitive position.

The RBV scholars observe that an effective exploitation of a company's resources and capabilities is crucial to a firm's success and is the primary factor influencing the firm's performance (e.g. Barney 1991; Collins & Montgomery 1995; Hamel & Prahalad 1994; Jones & Tilley 2003; Man *et al.* 2002; Peteraf 1993; Rumelt 1991). Outcomes of recently conducted empirical research across various economic sectors confirm this thesis (e.g. Afuah 2002; Lerner & Almor 2002; Schroeder *et al.* 2002; Spanos & Lioukas 2001). What are the major mechanisms that enable firms to effectively exploit their resources and capabilities?

The RBV identifies two major avenues for the effective resource exploitation that lead to high performance levels: resource leverage and building organisational capability platforms. Understanding the firm's resources and capabilities provides the basis for exploiting the firm's strengths and developing further the firm's resources and capabilities. The RBV does not assume, however, that the firm needs to possess abundant resources to be successful. On the contrary, Hamel & Prahalad (1993) stress that resource scarcity is the driving force for a firm's creativity in utilising their resources and developing capabilities. The subsequent parts of the chapter discuss the two strategic routes towards overcoming the problem of resource scarcity and embarking on a growth trajectory, i.e. resource leverage and building capability platforms. Examples are drawn from the practice of U.K. tourism SMEs.

Approach One: Resource Leverage

The development of the concept and subsequently the practice of resource leverage is attributed to G. Hamel and C. K. Prahalad who in the early 1990s published a number of highly influential articles and elaborated their principal ideas within the volume *Competing for the Future*, published in 1994. They argue that resource leverage is about the continual search for new, less resource-intensive means of achieving strategic objectives; it is about enlarging the firm's resource base and multiplying its impact (Hamel & Prahalad 1994).

Resource leverage significantly differs from traditional resource allocation practice. Contrary to resource allocation, that attempts to assign the right resources to the most promising opportunities through the techniques of portfolio planning and capital budgeting, resource leverage focuses on accumulating tangible and intangible resources and multiplying their impact (Hamel & Prahalad 1994). As Hamel & Prahalad (1993) argue, resource allocation can at best yield productivity gains in the short term, while in the long term, continuous economising will compromise the firm's ability to grow. On the contrary, resource leverage is a more creative response to scarcity and provides a more stable approach to attaining long-term growth.

Hamel & Prahalad (1994) argue that resource scarcity drives firm's tactical creativity, leading to stretch and providing a motive for resource leverage. Hence, creating a misfit between resources and aspirations (where aspirations outstrip existing resources) and strategic stretch (i.e. finding out more resource-efficient ways of matching the existing advantages of competitors) are the prerequisites for effective resource leverage (Mintzberg *et al.* 1998).

Hamel & Prahalad (1993, 1994) suggest five distinct ways to achieving resource leverage. They include concentrating, accumulating, complementing, conserving and recovering resources.

Concentrating resources prevents divergence of resources and involves converging resources on a few priority goals, focusing resources on those goals in a sequential manner and targeting those activities that will make the biggest impact in terms of customer perceived value (Hamel & Prahalad 1994).

Accumulating resources aims at extending the existing resource base in the shortest possible time and involves extracting the firm's experiences (learning) and accessing resources and capabilities of other firms (borrowing) (Hamel & Prahalad 1993).

Complementing resources increases the effectiveness and efficiency of existing resources through linking them with complementary resources and capabilities. It involves integrating and harmonising all resources in such a way as to represent a more efficient use and better product performance (blending) and ensuring that the firm controls the resources that multiply the value of the firm's unique capabilities (balancing) (Hamel & Prahalad 1994).

The purpose of conserving resources is to ensure that the firm's existing resources and capabilities are fully utilised. It can be achieved by reusing resources and capabilities through different products or markets (recycling), making collaborative arrangements with other firms (co-opting) and ensuring that the resources are not exposed to unnecessary risks (protecting) (Hamel & Prahalad 1994).

Recovering resources from the marketplace aims at minimising the time between investment and the return on investment and doing it faster than competitors with a similar resource commitment (expediting success) (Hamel & Prahalad 1994).

One of the advantages of Hamel & Prahalad's stretch and resource leverage theory is its intended applicability to both large and small businesses. As the authors stress:

> There is no honour in being small. Just as bigness without stretch and leverage is an obesity, smallness without stretch and leverage is impotence. Thus, anyone running a small company should be enormously encouraged by the fact that there are so many examples of companies that overcame seemingly insuperable resource handicaps and build positions of global leadership (Hamel & Prahalad 1994: 273).

Resource Leverage: The Experience of U.K. Tourism SMEs

An exploratory case study aimed at identifying the type of and assessing the level of resource leverage practices among U.K. tourism SMEs was conducted in 2002 (Augustyn 2002). Criterion-based sampling was employed for the selection of the case study subjects. In particular, the tourism SMEs had to be growth oriented and had to sufficiently differ in terms of their general profiles. Three case study subjects were selected (labelled Firm A, Firm B and Firm C), one representing the sector of incoming tour operators, one representing the sector of travel agents and one representing the sector of visitor attractions (Table 1).

A specifically designed questionnaire, based on Hamel & Prahalad's (1993, 1994) theory of resource leverage, was piloted and distributed to the case study subjects. The instrument contained a mixture of closed multiple, open-ended and closed scaled questions. The scaled questions contained 79 statements assessed by the respondents on a 7-point scale. The interpretation of the scale varied depending on the nature of the questions, but in most cases ranged from 1 (very strongly disagree) to 7 (very strongly agree). It also included a value 0 for non-applicable statements or statements about which a respondent had no opinion. The data was organised, categorised and analysed with the support of the Sphinx Survey software.

Table 1: General profile of the case study subjects.

Attribute	Firm		
	A	B	C
Age of the firm (years)	1	17	32
Type of business	Incoming tour operator	Travel agent	Visitor attraction
Location (county)	Hampshire	Bedfordshire	Northumberland
Employees (No.)[a]	6	15	25
Departments (No.)	1	5	2
Managers (No.)	1	4	2
Position of the respondent	Owner	Partner	Director

[a] Equivalent of full-time jobs.

Pre-requisites for resource leverage In order to establish whether the firms' aspirations outstrip their existing resources, the level of the firms' resources relative to their competitors and the level of the firms' aspirations were assessed. The resources subject to this assessment included physical resources, human resources, financial resources, and intangible resources (e.g. image, reputation, culture, ideas, technology). The level of the firms' resources differed, with Firm A characterised by the scarcest resources (Table 2). The level of the firms' aspirations was very high in the case of Firm A and Firm C and high in the case of Firm B. Thus the biggest misfit between resources and aspirations occurred in Firm A (a 6-point difference, the highest possible), slightly smaller in Firm C (a 5-point difference) and the smallest in Firm B (a 3-point difference).

In order to identify the level of the firms' stretch approach, three dimensions of stretch were assessed (Table 2):

(1) The firm's *intent*, i.e. the level of consistency of the firm's strategic intent with the stretch approach;
(2) The firm's *activities*, i.e. the level of consistency of the firm's activities with the stretch approach;
(3) The firm's *outcomes*, i.e. the level of attainment of the expected stretch outcomes.

Table 2: The level of consistency of the case study subjects' practices and approaches with the resource leverage theory.

Dimension	Firm		
	A	B	C
1. Resource level	1	3	2
2. Aspirations level	7	6	7
3. Stretch level	5	5	5
3.1. *Stretch: Intent*	6	5	5
3.2. *Stretch: Activities*	5	5	4
3.3. *Stretch: Outcomes*	5	6	6
4. Leverage level	6	5	6
4.1. *Potential for leverage*	6	5	6
4.2. *Leverage practices*	6	5	6
5. Performance level	3	4	4

Note: The scale ranges from 1 to 7, where 1 indicates the lowest level and 7 indicates the highest level. The scale values (1–7) are in some cases translated into seven non-numerical levels corresponding with the following values: 1 = Very Low; 2 = Low; 3 = Lower-Medium; 4 = Medium; 5 = Upper-Medium; 6 = High; 7 = Very High.

While all three firms were characterised by an equal, upper-medium level of the stretch approach (Table 2), the firms displayed differences in terms of scores for individual stretch dimensions and in terms of scores for individual indicators associated with each stretch dimension.

The results indicate that all firms subject to this study possessed several characteristics highly consistent with the stretch approach. These included:

- possessing shared aspirations that stretch beyond the available resources and capabilities of the firms and which are identified on the basis of a careful study of the business environment;
- viewing every employee as a contributor to success;
- designing programmes of employee involvement;
- accelerating the acquisition of market and industry knowledge;
- searching for niche markets; and
- avoiding downsizing their aspirations.

All firms studied also revealed a number of characteristics inconsistent with the stretch approach. These included:

- lack of constancy of effort and purpose;
- impatience, which affects their firms' long-term strategic intent; and
- attempting to match the market rivals strengths, which affects their firms' ability to exploit differences.

The firms displayed a significant difference in relation to one indicator of the stretch approach, i.e. emphasising the need for doing more with less. While Firm A and Firm C placed a very high emphasis on attaining more with less resource commitment (value 7), Firm B placed little emphasis on this practice (value 3). This may be associated with the higher level of resource abundance in the case of Firm C as compared with the other two firms.

The above results indicate that all firms in this study possessed the pre-requisites for effective resource leverage. First, their aspirations outstripped existing resources to a greater or lesser extent. Second, all three firms were characterised by an equal, upper-medium level of stretch approach, which means that although the firms took a mixed strategic approach, which combined the characteristics of stretch and characteristics of other strategic approaches, the stretch approach was dominant in their strategic thinking. Following Hamel & Prahalad's (1993, 1994) theory, it could therefore be expected that all firms would creatively manage their resources and that the highest level of creativity would occur in the case of Firm A which displayed the biggest misfit between resources and aspirations. Did the results of the study aimed at assessing the level of resource leverage confirm this thesis?

The level of resource leverage   In order to establish the level of resource leverage, the firms were assessed against two dimensions (Table 2):

Table 3: Potential for resource leverage: The case study subjects' strengths and weaknesses.

Indicator	Firm					
	Strengths			Weaknesses		
	A	B	C	A	B	C
Sharing improvement ideas across departments		6	7			
Seeking consensus among all employees on long-term goals			7			
Determining strategy against the firm's capabilities			7			
Studying business environment to find opportunities	7		7			
Avoiding downsizing to attain resource productivity	7		7		3	
Avoiding investment cuts to attain resource productivity	7				3	
Integrating resources in ways that multiply the value of each	7					
Sharing resources among various departments		6		4		
Focusing investments on a small number of activities that the firm docs better than other firms		6		4		
Searching for ways to grow output on a static resource base		6				1
Possessing well developed organisational capabilities						

Note: The numbers in columns 2–7 indicate respective values (scale range. 1–7).

(1) *Potential for Leverage*, i.e. the firm's capacity for resource leverage; and
(2) *Leverage Practices*, i.e. the level of consistency of the firm's practices with the desired resource leverage practices.

In relation to the firms' potential for resource leverage, 11 indicators were assessed. Table 3 presents the firms' strengths and weaknesses within this area. The indicators that received the highest values (i.e. 7 or 6) represent the strengths of the firms while the indicators that received the lowest values (i.e. 1, or the lowest available within the range of 2–4) represent the weaknesses of the firms.

Table 3 clearly indicates that the firms differed greatly in terms of the number and the nature of the strengths and weaknesses they possessed in relation to their potential for resource leverage. The only two similarities within the area of strengths occurred in the case of Firm A and Firm C, i.e.:

- undertaking a careful study of the internal and external environment in the search for unexplored opportunities before committing resources on a particular project;
- finding other than downsizing ways to generate greater resource productivity.

One strength, i.e. sharing of ideas for improvement across departments, was common to Firm B and Firm C.

The weaknesses were not particularly prominent and they varied form firm to firm. It should be noted, however, that Firm B displayed relatively strong signs of focusing on downsizing and investment cuts to attain resource productivity (Table 3). These practices are typical of resource allocation rather than resource leverage.

Table 4 presents the strengths and weaknesses of the case study subjects in relation to the dimension of leverage practices. Based on Hamel & Prahalad's (1993, 1994) theory, the practices are grouped into 5 ways that lead to the attainment of resource leverage. Within each group, specific means of attaining resource leverage were assessed using a number of indicators, which are not presented in this table. For the purpose of this analysis, the dimensions that received the highest values (i.e. 7 or 6) represent the strengths of the firms while the dimensions that received the lowest values (i.e. 1, or the lowest available within the range of 2–4) represent the weaknesses of the firms.

The only two resource leverage approaches common to all firms included learning from experience and recycling resources, both within the area of the firms' strengths (Table 4). The common practices within the learning dimension included seeing each success or failure as an opportunity to learn, employing well developed techniques for generating ideas by employees, and applying lessons learnt by the customer-contact employees. Recycling resources and capabilities included such common practices as using employees' skills to perform diverse functions, using the same tangible resources as a basis for producing different products, and using the outcomes of market research for diverse purposes.

The results presented in Table 4 also indicate that Firm A and Firm C possessed many strengths and very limited weaknesses in terms of pursuing the practices that lead to resource leverage, with targeting constituting the strongest approach to resource leverage common to those two firms.

Blending was the strongest approach common to Firm B and Firm C and involved technological integration, functional integration and new product imagination.

While certain approaches to resource leverage constituted strong points in the case of Firm A and Firm C, they were rather weak in the case of Firm B. These included accumulating resources through borrowing, complementing resources through balancing and recovering resources (Table 4). Firms A and C were therefore characterised by:

- their strong ability to access and internalise their partners' resources that are needed for the development of unique organisational capabilities (borrowing);
- exerting a high level of control over the resources that multiply the value of the firms' unique capabilities (balancing); and
- increasing the speed with which invested resources yield returns, which leads to resource multiplication and an ability of these firms to pre-empt their competitors (resource recovery).

Firm B did not develop these qualities to a high degree.

Despite the differences that the firms displayed within both dimensions of resource leverage, the results indicate that Firm A and Firm C attained an equal, high level of resource leverage while Firm B reached the upper-medium level (Table 2).

Table 4: Resource leverage practices: The case study subjects' strengths and weaknesses.

Way	Means	Firm					
		Strength			Weakness		
		A	B	C	A	B	C
Concentrating resources	Converging resources on a few long-term goals						
	Focusing resources on a few precise improvement goals	6					4
	Targeting the high-value activities	7		7			
Accumulating resources	Learning through mining internal experience	6	6	7			
	Borrowing, i.e. accessing & internalising resources of partners	6		7		3	
Complementing resources	Blending disparate skills to create new capabilities		6	6			
	Balancing, i.e. gaining control over complementary resources	6		6		3	
Conserving resources	Recycling, i.e. reusing skills and resources	6	6	7			
	Co-opting resources via the pursuit of common objectives			6		4	
	Protecting resources from unnecessary external risks	6				4	
Recovering resources	Expediting, i.e. increasing the speed of resource recovery	6		6		4	

Note: The numbers in columns 3–8 indicate respective values (scale range: 1–7).

Discussion and implications for future research   The results of this study are generally consistent with Hamel & Prahalad's (1993, 1994) theory of resource leverage which assumes that creating a misfit between resources and aspirations and the strategy of stretch lead to developing more creative approaches to resource management and greater levels of resource leverage. However, while the highest level of resource leverage did occur in the case of Firm A, which displayed the largest misfit between resources and aspirations, the same level of resource leverage characterised Firm C, which had a slightly lower level of misfit between resources and aspirations. This minor anomaly may be explained by the fact that Firm A had been operating for one year only, while Firm C for 32 years. The younger age of Firm A may imply that their resource level is generally lower resulting in a greater resource-aspiration gap. However, further studies aimed at investigating the relation between the firm's age and the extent of the resource-aspiration gap has to be undertaken in order to substantiate this explanation.

Despite the relatively high level of resource leverage (ranging from upper-medium to high) that the three firms displayed, the level of the firms' performance ranges from lower-medium to medium (Table 2). This may be due to the fact that the firms did not fully adopt the stretch approach. It may also be explained by the nature of the tourism industry and general characteristics of small firms within the tourism sector. However, further studies aimed at identifying factors that influence the performance of tourism SMEs, and studies aimed at investigating the relationship between a firm's level of resource leverage and its performance level have to be undertaken in order to substantiate this explanation.

Finally, as resource leverage is about the continual search for new, less resource-intensive means of achieving strategic objectives, the five generic approaches to resource leverage identified by Hamel & Prahalad (1993, 1994) and the list of practices associated with each approach may not be exhaustive. Therefore, an in-depth qualitative study into the means of achieving resource leverage within the sector of tourism SMEs could uncover new and unique routes to resource leverage within this sector.

Approach Two: Building Capability Platforms

The second approach to effective resource exploitation that leads to high performance levels focuses on building organisational capability platforms. Many scholars agree that resources rarely create value on their own and the existing resources must work together in order to create unique organisational capabilities if they are to be fully productive (Grant 2002; Hamel & Prahalad 1994; Mintzberg *et al.* 1998). These unique organisational capabilities constitute an essential source of competitive advantage, as they represent the hidden or invisible assets of an organisation that cannot be easily imitated by a competitor (Mintzberg *et al.* 1998; Prahalad & Hamel 1990; Teece *et al.* 1997). As organisational capabilities are not product specific but contribute to the competitiveness of a range of products offered by a firm in the process of reusing these capabilities (Itami 1987; Makadok 2001), their development contributes significantly to resource economy.

According to Hamel & Prahalad (1994), to be considered an organisational capability (also known as a core competence), a particular ability must pass three tests. First, the test of customer value, i.e. the capability must make a disproportionate contribution to customer perceived value. Second, the test of competitor differentiation i.e. the capability must be unique within a particular industry. Third, the test of extendibility, i.e. the capability must form the basis for the development of more than one product and/or entering more than one market.

In view of those three tests, the value of organisational capability changes over time as the business environment changes (Turner & Crawford 1994). Consequently, as

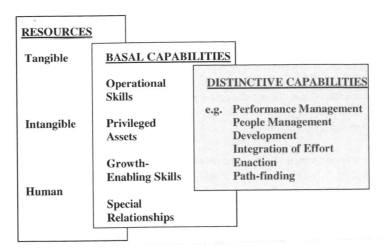

Figure 1: The process of building capability platforms. *Source:* Author, based on Baghai *et al.* (1999) and Turner & Crawford (1994).

Teece *et al.* (1997) stress, organisations must take a dynamic approach to capability development, which assumes that once capabilities have been built they need to be occasionally reconfigured to address the changing internal and external environments.

An important aspect in building dynamic capability platforms is the hierarchical nature of capabilities, where more general, broadly defined capabilities are formed from the integration of more specialised resources and capabilities (Grant 2002). According to Turner & Crawford (1994), there are two major stages in developing the firm's capability platforms. First, a unique combination of firm's resources leads to the development of basal capabilities, i.e. those capabilities that the firm commands for its competitive performance. Second, a unique combination of basal capabilities leads to the development of distinctive capabilities, i.e. capabilities that give the firm competitive advantage (Figure 1). Turner & Crawford (1994) stress that due to the dynamic nature of the business environment, what once constituted distinctive capability may become a basal capability.

A useful framework for classifying basal capabilities for growth is offered by McKinsey Consultants (Baghai *et al.* 1999) who identify four groups of capabilities:

- *operational skills* (i.e. how well the company operates management information systems, research and development, product and service design);
- *privileged assets* (i.e. assets that are unique to the organisation, difficult to imitate and confer a competitive advantage on their owner);
- *growth-enabling skills* (i.e. acquisitions skills, risk management skills, and capital management skills); and
- *special relationships* (e.g. with existing customers and suppliers, powerful individuals, businesses and governments) that can unlock growth opportunities that would otherwise not be available (Baghai *et al.* 1999).

While the above classification of capabilities is useful in identifying basal capabilities, the changing nature of distinctive capabilities makes it difficult to provide a full list of such capabilities. Nevertheless, some classifications that the literature provides may assist firms and researchers in identifying distinctive capabilities. The classification developed by Turner & Crawford (1994) is discussed here, as it proved useful in interpreting the primary study results discussed later in the chapter.

Turner & Crawford's (1994) typology consists of 11 categories of management capabilities, including:

- *performance management*, i.e. the ability of a firm to monitor performance against clearly set goals within a strategic framework and to reinforce or adjust activities in response to current outcomes and circumstances with a view to improving current performance and initiate positive incremental change;
- *resource application*, i.e. the ability of a firm to ensure that suitable resources work together to best support the organisation's strategic intent and to maximise the benefit gained from the assets available;
- *people management*, i.e. the ability of a firm to motivate staff to achieve willingness and the intent to work in ways consistent with the firm's objectives;
- *integration of effort*, i.e. the ability of a firm to co-ordinate the actions of the firm's members and to ensure coherence among the firm's practices, systems and policies so that the firm's efforts are focused on achieving its objectives and counter-productive or wasted effort is prevented;
- *enaction*, i.e. the ability of a firm to carry decisions into action in a timely and effective way;
- *pathfinding*, i.e. the ability of a firm to identify, crystallise and articulate achievable new directions for the firm to find new avenues for survival and profit;
- *development*, i.e. the ability of a firm to change the firm's assets in order to enhance their relevance to the firm's activities and directions over time with a view to increasing the firm's capability to perform effectively in the future through the creation of assets well suited to its future circumstances (Turner & Crawford 1994).

Turner & Crawford (1994) argue that in order to adapt quickly to the changing business environment and pre-empt its rivals, a firm should possess a portfolio of distinctive capabilities and continuously develop new ones. Within this context, McKinsey's Consultants' analytical framework for studying dynamic capability platforms (Baghai *et al.* 1999) proves to be particularly useful in gaining an insight into the type of capability platform that facilitates launching the firm onto the next step of its incremental growth staircase.

Building Capability Platforms: The Experience of U.K. Tourism SMEs

A study aimed at investigating the nature of capability platforms for growth within the sector of U.K. tourism SMEs was conducted in 2002. One of the essential issues examined was the way in which organisations convert their scarce resource base into capability platforms that enable them to grow over different time horizons.

Given the detail necessary to consider such issues a comparative case study approach was adopted. Criterion-based sampling was employed in the process of selecting the case study subjects from the population of U.K. private tourism SMEs.[2] In particular, the enterprises should have been operating for at least 5 years and should have enjoyed sustained growth over that period. Furthermore, the firms should have employed less then 50 people at the beginning of their operation.[3] Finally, the data necessary for the attainment of the aim of the study needed to be accessible and comparable. Three case study subjects were selected (labelled Firm 1, Firm 2 and Firm 3), one representing the sector of tourist accommodation, one representing the sector of travel services and one representing the sector of event organisers (Table 5). Semi-structured in-depth telephone interviews with the senior management of these firms were conducted. The data was analysed against McKinsey Consultants' analytical framework for studying dynamic capability platforms

Table 5: Profile of the case study subjects.

Attribute	Firm		
	Firm 1	Firm 2	Firm 3
Age of the firm (years)	102	46	8
Employees (No.)	80	135	68
Type of business	Private Limited (family)	Private Limited (family)	Private Limited
Location (county)	Powys	Northamptonshire	West Yorkshire
Trade description	Hotel with restaurant	Coach and bus services	Organisation of events & training
1992 SIC U.K. code	5511	6023	7484
Main services	Accommodation Catering Special events Health treatment Other	Supplier of transport to the travel trade, Local Authorities, schools Tailored tours Holidays Excursions Coach Hire Corporate transport	Events management Incentive programmes Business travel Team-building sessions Other
Key growth indicators[a]			
Employee growth	0	-9^b	+48
Net sales growth	+15	-2^b	+39
Net sales per employee growth	+15	$+7^b$	−6
Operating income growth	+14	+175	+23
Net income growth	+85	+36	+23
Total assets growth	−24	+14	+29
Remuneration per employee growth	+6	$+11^b$	+23
Profit before tax growth	+141	+25	+30
Profit after tax growth	+84	+30	+23

[a] Percentage growth (+)/Decline (−) over 3 years (base: 1999).
[b] Over 2 years (base: 2000).

Table 6: Key resources of the case study subjects.

Firm Resources	Firm 1	Firm 2	Firm 3
Tangible	Grand building	Travel shop	2 offices in the UK
	Location	Variety of coaches	1 office in the USA
	Diverse facilities		
Human	Professionalism		
	Experience		
	Employee Commitment		
	Management Continuity		
		IT manager	Expertise
Intangible	High Standard of Service		
	Membership of Professional Bodies		
	External Recognition		
	Established Customer Base		
			Organisational culture

(Baghai *et al.* 1999). The terminology used in describing the distinctive capabilities adopted for the purpose of this study originates mostly, but not exclusively, from Turner & Crawford's (1994) classification of capabilities.

The first stage of this investigation involved the assessment of key resources of the case study subjects that the managers of these companies perceived as assets within three categories: tangible, human and intangible resources. As indicated in Table 6, the three firms possessed a number of similar resources, particularly within the area of human and intangible resources (the nature of business that each firm is involved in explains the differences in the types of tangible resources). Each firm identified professionalism, experience and employee commitment as the most valuable human resources. The majority of intangible resources were also common to all firms, including a high standard of service, membership of professional bodies (e.g. trade associations), established customer base and external recognition (awards, accreditation).

What basal capabilities did the firms develop using the resources that they possessed? Despite a very high level of similarity in the type of resources that each firm possessed, the types of basal capabilities developed by each firm differed to a greater extend than their resources did (Table 7). The greatest level of similarity occurred within the group of privileged assets, where all three firms possessed the same type of basal capabilities, i.e. flexibility of infrastructure or service, reputation, customer loyalty, and value distribution network. Within the group of operational skills, all firms developed the capability of responding to trends and within the group of growth enabling skills, the capability of leadership. The capability of developing special relationships with customers and access conveying bodies was also developed by all firms studied.

The results of the study indicate that some capabilities were developed only by two of the three firms studied (Table 7). The firms also possessed unique basal capabilities that other firms studied did not. For example, within the category of operational skills,

Table 7: Key basal capabilities of the case study subjects.

Firm Capabilities	Firm 1	Firm 2	Firm 3
Operational skills	Responding to trends		
	Product enhancement		
		Discovering new competitive arenas	
	Attracting quality staff		Attracting quality staff
	Motivating & enthusing		Motivating & enthusing
	Creating a 'wow' factor		
	Effective customer service		
		Cost reduction	
			Attention to detail
Privileged assets	Infrastructure/service flexibility		
	Reputation		
	Customer loyalty		
	Value distribution network		
Growth-enabling skills	Leadership		
		Geographic expansion	
	Staff development		Staff development
		Acquisition-based expansion	
			Merger-based expansion
Special relationships with:	Customers		
	Access conveying bodies		
	Suppliers		Suppliers
	Powerful individuals		Powerful individuals
	Overseas labour markets		

Firm 1 possessed the capability of creating a "wow" factor and an effective customer service, Firm 2 possessed the capability of cost reduction and Firm 3 possessed the capability of attention to detail. While the similarities between the three firms indicate that the same basal capabilities contributed to the firms' competitiveness regardless of the sector they represented, the differences indicate that the firms converted similar resource base into unique basal capabilities that enabled those firms to compete within those specific sectors.

The resources converted into basal capabilities constituted the basis for the development of distinctive capabilities for growth, i.e. the capabilities that lie behind the growth of each firm at each stage of their growth history. Table 8 presents a summary of findings within this area.

The types of distinctive capabilities enabling the growth of these firms differed in terms of either the nature of those capabilities or the step on the firms' growth staircase for which they were crucial. While similar resources constituted the basis for the development of the basal capabilities and subsequently the distinctive capabilities, the different priorities of these firms (Table 8) and the different industry environments within which those firms operated, may explain the differences in the type of distinctive capabilities developed by each firm. The only distinctive capability common to all firms was resource application.

Table 8: Growth staircase and distinctive capabilities of the case study subjects.

Firms' Variables	Growth Staircase				
	Prior to 1960s	1970s	1980s	1990s	Current/Future
Distinctive capabilities					
Firm 1	Product innovation	Development; resource application	Performance management	People management	Crisis management development
Firm 2	Market niche dominance	Development; resource application	Post-acquisition management	Development; capital management	Path-finding
Firm 3	NA	Resource application[a]	Post-merger management[b]	Enaction, integration of effort; people management[c]	Performance management; path-finding
Priorities					
Firm 1			Guest comfort and enjoyment		
Firm 2			Highest standard of service and reliability		
Firm 3			Delivering creative, experimental solutions that inspire improved performance and knowledge in teams and individuals		
Growth-enabling factor					
Firm 1			Management continuity		
Firm 2			Management continuity		
Firm 3			Corporate culture		
Barrier to growth					
Firm 1			Raising finance		
Firm 2			Competitive labour market		
Firm 3			None		

[a] Refers to 1987–1997.
[b] Refers to 1998–1999.
[c] Refers to 2000–2001.

The study indicates that despite resource scarcity, the firms had been enjoying continuous growth. An analysis of the firms' recent growth indicators (Table 5) confirms this thesis. The growth of those firms can be attributed to the firms' ability to build capability platforms that launched them onto the next stage in their growth history. However, the study also revealed that apart from the firms' ability to build capability platforms, the growth of each firm was strongly attributed to the presence of one growth factor that was constant throughout the firms' history. In the case of Firm 1 and Firm 2, management continuity constituted such a growth factor while in the case of Firm 3, corporate culture. It can therefore be argued that while the growth of a firm is dependant on the firm's ability to build capability platforms, it is also dependant on the presence of the key growth-enabling factor that is constant regardless of the stage of the firm's growth history. To substantiate this statement, further studies into the factors that enable growth of tourism SMEs need to be conducted.

Conclusions

The theoretical and empirical considerations presented in this chapter indicate two strategic approaches open to tourism SMEs that attempt to overcome the problem of resource scarcity and embark on a growth trajectory: resource leverage and building capability platforms. Both approaches are grounded in the resource-based view of the firm, which focuses attention on the effective and efficient exploitation of organisational resources and capabilities to the advantage of the firm. While resource leverage concerns searching for new, less resource-intensive means of achieving strategic objectives and multiplying the impact of the existing resource base, building capability platforms focuses on the process of a creative integration of organisational resources into unique and long-lasting clusters of organisational abilities that lie behind the firm's products. In view of the dynamic nature of the business environment, the value of organisational capabilities changes over time. Therefore, the process of building capability platforms that have a potential for launching the firm onto the next growth stage is a never-ending cycle.

These two approaches to coping with resource scarcity are not, however, mutually exclusive. On the contrary, resource leverage incorporates the focus on capability development, while the process of building capability platforms requires employing some of the resource leverage means, such as borrowing, blending and reusing resources. The complementary nature of these two strategic approaches is also underpinned by a principle that is common to both approaches, i.e. viewing resource scarcity as an opportunity for creativity rather than as a barrier to growth. Such creativity, as confirmed by a number of empirical studies, leads to the attainment of higher performance levels.

The potential usefulness of both approaches to tourism SMEs in their attempts to cope with resource scarcity has been confirmed through two primary case studies undertaken in 2002. The results of both studies indicate that U.K. tourism SMEs not only utilise these two approaches but also, more importantly, achieve relatively high performance levels. This is particularly true in the case of building capability platforms. However, as both studies were of an exploratory nature, each investigating three subjects only, generalisations should be avoided at this stage. Instead, more extensive quantitative studies and more in-depth qualitative studies aimed at identifying the ways in which tourism SMEs cope with resource scarcity and the effect of the approaches taken on firms' performance are required. Nevertheless, the theoretical and empirical considerations presented in this chapter provide sufficient argument for encouraging tourism SMEs to rethink their view of and responses to resource scarcity.

Notes

1. The sector of tourism SMEs (i.e. tourism-related enterprises which employ up to 250 people, where enterprises which employ up to 50 people are classified as small firms) is highly diverse in terms of their long-term aspirations and goals, ranging from lifestyle firms, i.e. firms whose owners-managers are not interested in developing their businesses but are content with the steady income that their businesses generate (Deakins 1999), to growth oriented firms, i.e. firms that aim to confer their competitive advantage on and gain superiority over their rivals. While the chapter focuses on growth oriented tourism SMEs, some approaches discussed are relevant to all tourism SMEs, regardless of their primary aspiration.

2. An online directory of UK Registered Companies "FAME" constituted the sample frame.

3. The current number of people employed could exceed the limit of 50 as the firm's growth could have resulted in the increase in the number of people employed.

References

Afuah, A. (2002). Mapping technological capabilities into product markets and competitive advantage: The case of cholesterol drugs. *Strategic Management Journal, 23*, 171–179.

Amit, R., & Schoemaker, P. J. H. (1993). Strategic assets and organisational rent. *Strategic Management Journal, 14*, 33–46.

Augustyn, M. M. (2002). Leveraging resources into capabilities: The practice of three U.K. small tourism enterprises. In: R. Thomas (Ed.), *Small firms in the tourism and hospitality sector. Conference proceedings* (CD-ROM). Leeds: Leeds Metropolitan University.

Baghai, M., Coley, S., & White, D. (1999). *The alchemy of growth. Kickstarting and sustaining growth in your company*. London: TEXERE Publishing.

Barney, J. B. (1991). Firm resources and sustained competitive advantage. *Journal of Management, 17*, 99–120.

Besanko, D., Dranove, D., & Shanley, M. (1996). *Economics of strategy*. New York: Wiley.

Collins, D. J., & Montgomery, C. A. (1995). Competing on resource strategy in the 1990s. *Harvard Business Review* (July–August), 118–128.

Deakins, D. (1999). *Entrepreneurship and small firms* (2nd ed.). London: McGraw-Hill.

Grant, R. M. (1991). The resource-based theory of competitive advantage: Implications for strategy formulation. *California Management Review* (Spring), 114–135.

Grant, R. M. (2002). *Contemporary strategy analysis. Concepts, techniques, applications* (4th ed.). Malden, MA: Blackwell.

Hamel, G., & Prahalad, C. K. (1993). Strategy as stretch and leverage. *Harvard Business Review* (March–April), 75–84.

Hamel, G., & Prahalad, C. K. (1994). *Competing for the future. Breakthrough strategies for seizing control of your industry and creating the markets of tomorrow*. Boston: Harvard Business School Press.

Itami, H., with Roehl, T. W. (1987). *Mobilizing invisible assets*. Cambridge, MA: Harvard University Press.

Jones, O., & Tilley, F. (2003). *Competitive advantage in SMEs. Organising for innovation and change*. Chichester: Wiley.

Lerner, M., & Almor, T. (2002). Relationships among strategic capabilities and the performance of women-owned small ventures. *Journal of Small Business Management, 40*, 109–125.

Makadok, R. (2001). Toward a synthesis of the resource-based and dynamic capability views of rent creation. *Strategic Management Journal, 22*, 387–401.

Man, T. W. Y., Lau, T., & Chan, K. F. (2002). The competitiveness of small and medium enterprises. A conceptualisation with focus on entrepreneurial competencies. *Journal of Business Venturing, 17*, 123–142.

Mintzberg, H., Ahlstrand, B., & Lampel, J. (1998). *Strategy Safari. A guided tour through the wilds of strategic management*. Hemel Hempstead: Prentice-Hall Europe.

Peteraf, M. (1993). The cornerstones of competitive advantage: A resource-based view. *Strategic Management Journal, 14*, 179–191.

Porter, M. (1980). *Competitive strategy. Techniques for analysing industries and competitors*. New York: Free Press.

Porter, M. (1985). *Competitive advantage. Creating and sustaining superior performance*. New York: Free Press.

Prahalad, C. K., & Hamel, G. (1990). The core competence of the corporation. *Harvard Business Review* (May–June), 79–91.

Rangone, A. (1999). A resource-based approach to strategy analysis in small and medium-sized enterprises. *Small Business Economics, 12*, 233–248.

Rumelt, R. (1991). How much does industry matter? *Strategic Management Journal, 12*, 167–185.

Schroeder, R. G., Bates, K. A., & Junttila, M. A. (2002). A resource-based view of manufacturing strategy and the relationship to manufacturing performance. *Strategic Management Journal, 23*, 105–117.

Spanos, Y. E., & Lioukas, S. (2001). An examination into the causal logic of rent generation: Contrasting Porter's competitive strategy framework and the resource-based perspective. *Strategic Management Journal, 22*, 907–934.

Teece, D. J., Pisano, G., & Shuen, A. (1997). Dynamic capabilities and strategic management. *Strategic Management Journal, 18*, 509–533.

Turner, D., & Crawford, M. (1994). Managing current and future competitive performance: The role of competence. In: G. Hamel, & A. Heene (Eds), *Competence-based competition* (pp. 241–263), Chichester: Wiley.

Ulrich, D., & Lake, D. (1990). *Organisational capability. Competing from the inside out*. New York: Wiley.

Wernerfelt, B. (1984). A resource-based view of the firm. *Strategic Management Journal, 5*, 171–180.

Chapter 18

Strategic and Structural Variables in Internationalization: The Case of Swiss Tourism SMEs

Andrew Mungall and Colin Johnson

Introduction

Following a review of internationalization literature, this chapter presents the findings of a questionnaire survey among small and medium-sized Swiss tourism enterprises, and examines the process of their internationalization. It deals in particular with the major structural and strategic variables which affect the degree of internationalization of tourism establishments.

In generic terms, there are many schools of thought on internationalization, and the literature is rich and complex. Space does not permit a full discussion, and the following is intended to provide only a necessary outline. The establishment chain model was one of the first major attempts to conceptualize the way in which firms internationalize. According to this model, internationalization is a process that follows an orderly sequence of growth in incremental stages (Johanson & Wiedersheim-Paul 1975, later modified by Johanson & Vahlne 1979). Two of the major elements of the model are knowledge and commitment. *Knowledge* of the foreign markets is crucial in determining the *commitment* of the company to entry into them. As the company learns more about the new markets, more resources are committed. Although influential for many years, it has been argued that the model stays at a general, deterministic level, and has no explanatory power concerning the reasons *why* internationalization occurs, or the conditions that would encourage it (Turnbull 1993). Other major criticisms of the model are that the theory does not take into account the operating environments of the respective companies, or the managerial strategies of the companies, which have been shown to be crucial in the internationalization process. Finally, with the "born global" outlook of contemporary companies, it is clear that companies do not nowadays follow the sequential process. Among service companies, too, the "instantly international" outlook is becoming increasingly prevalent today (McAuley 1999). In addition, transnational hotel corporations pursue a mixture of expansion strategies combining both equity and non-equity concurrently (Contractor & Kundu 1998).

Economists have been extremely influential with the internalization, foreign direct investment and eclectic paradigm models. The internalization paradigm has been in existence from the late 1970s with Buckley & Casson as its chief proponents (Buckley & Casson 1998). Central to the paradigm is the avoidance of transaction costs by companies "internalising" the intermediate product market. Growth in companies continues until the benefits of further internalization are outweighed by the costs. Whilst the paradigm has remained one of the major schools of thought in internationalization theory and has been tested in several different domains (Buckley & Casson 1993; Oviatt & McDougall 1994), it is unable to explain the level, structure or location of international production (Kundu 1994).

Foreign direct investment postulates that, in addition to the internalization advantages proposed by the previous school, there must also be some unique firm specific advantages (FSA) that must be exploited before competitors copy them, with the inevitable erosion that follows. When FSAs are combined with advantages derived from international locations and by internal exploitation, international companies then gain an edge over indigenous operators.

In the hotel industry, examples of firm specific advantages are global reservation systems and brand equity which allow international operators economies of scale and scope in their offer to guests when traveling abroad. However, critics of generic FDI theory state that while it explains patterns of investment, it does not elucidate a long-term process of international expansion. Furthermore, the majority of research has been undertaken on TNCs, with FDI theory not being applicable to small- and medium-sized enterprises.

FDI theory has been developed and extended by Dunning (1993), who for the past 30 years has been developing and refining the "eclectic paradigm." The eclectic paradigm is the most all-encompassing version of FDI, and has been advocated and rigorously tested in a number of different industry sectors, in both manufacturing and services. The eclectic paradigm considers internationalization within the framework of three types of interrelated advantages defined by Dunning as ownership, location and internalization (OLI). Ownership advantages are, as the name implies, competitive advantages that the firm owns vis-à-vis its competitors. Location advantages consist of political, economic and natural factors that firms consider when deciding to locate abroad. Internalization advantages derive from a firm deciding to integrate various assets and skills within the framework of the company rather than trading them in the marketplace. Criticisms of the eclectic paradigm mostly concerned the static nature of the model, and the need to integrate the strategic intent of companies into it. Dunning (2001) acknowledged these shortcomings and proposed improvements.

A fourth school of thought, network theory, states that firms engaged in distribution and production form systems of relationships developed between, in particular, customers, suppliers, competitors and governments (Johanson & Mattsson 1988). Networks may take many forms and include strategic alliances, joint ventures, licensing agreements, subcontracting, joint research and development and joint marketing activities (Ireland *et al.* 2001). The networks that develop are the result of a *cumulative process* with relationships being made, extended and terminated. As firms internalize, the number and strength of the relationships between different parts of the network increase. As internationalization is based upon the organization's set of network relationships rather than company-specific advantages, externalization rather than internalization takes place (Coviello & McAuley 1999).

An important point is that the long-term survival of the firm is dependent upon resources controlled by others. A firm's success in entering new international markets may be more dependent on its relationships within current markets than it is on the cultural and other characteristics of the chosen market. One of the advantages of network theory is that it can be adapted to smaller enterprises, and has been tested on SMEs in differing industry sectors and geographical locations (Chetty & Blankenburg Hom 2000; McAuley 1999). Furthermore, networks allow firms to overcome typical industry weaknesses, and have been seen as important in accelerating access or entry into new markets (Coviello & Munro 1995). As network theory is newer than the stages, internalization and FDI models, there are fewer academic studies, especially of an empirical nature. Some criticisms of the model, however, may be levelled at the possible overlaps between the four, rather blurred categories (i.e. it is possible to be both in the "early starter" or "international among others"). Nor, as with the FDI model and the eclectic paradigm, does the concept take account of the decision-making and strategic intent of the company. Finally, the model does not include exogenous variables that often result in internalization, such as the level of domestic competition and government policies towards FDI (Chetty & Blankenburg Hom 2000).

Fifthly, one of the latest schools of thought is represented by Segal-Horn (1998). Segal-Horn suggests that, owing to fundamental changes in the nature of services, these developments have led to increased concentration, with service industries moving away from highly fragmented markets towards greater concentration, with clear market leaders. In many sectors (including the international hotel industry) they resemble oligopolies. Additionally, many services are seen to comprise "hard," tangible elements that may now be industrialized, and separated from the point of service delivery (McLaughlin & Fitzsimmons 1996). It is also possible to codify, and therefore transfer internationally, the all-important core competencies and information-specific assets of service enterprises (together with, for example, consumer franchises relating to strongly branded services). The end result is a greater similarity between manufacturing and service firms.

The final school of thought, specifically in relation to hotel industry internationalization has been proposed by Contractor & Kundu (1998) who combined elements from several disciplines, including transaction cost and agency theory, corporate knowledge and organizational capability theories in the production of their syncretic model which addresses some of the key decisions behind the choice of methods of expansion.

More recent research has embraced alternative methodologies, stressing the importance of learning and internal resources of the firm (Tallman & Fladmoe-Lindquist 2002) within the organization, and the pivotal role of the owner in the international development of SMEs (Lloyd-Reason & Mughan 2002). This draws on the marketing and entrepreneurial literature, with the suggestion that current models do not have many of the answers regarding small firm internationalization (Fillis 2001). Many of the existing models are unable to account for the fact that the "born global" companies may exist in opposite ends of industry spectrums (for example, in both the craft company and the high-tech firm). Management competencies include adopting a global vision and using technology to exploit advantages in the marketplace are seen as key attributes in the internationalization process (Fillis 2001).

There are also specific behavioral attributes that would advance or retard internationalization on the part of the owner, especially in relation to cultural orientation. This may be influenced by a number of factors including language capabilities, and degree of inter-cultural awareness (Lloyd-Reason & Mughan 2002). Recent literature also maintains that internationalization is not in the main export-driven (considered from an "external" viewpoint) but also, owing to the increasing use of strategic alliances, countertrade and joint manufacturing, is increasingly a linked or integrated phenomenon (Fletcher 2001).

Internationalization of Swiss Tourism SMEs: The Study

The study reported here had 4 main objectives:

(a) to analyze the various forms of internationalization in the sector;
(b) to assess the degree of internationalization of establishments;
(c) to identify the most important variables that are likely to impact upon the behavior of firms with respect to internationalization;
(d) to highlight factors considered important in encouraging or impeding internationalization.

As mentioned above, many studies on the internationalization of the tourism and hotel industries have focused on it from the perspective of large multinational chains, with their choice of where, when and how to expand internationally. Clearly, this is not a useful model for studying tourism SMEs which are limited in terms of their resources, especially financial. It was decided, therefore, to examine internationalization from 3 different perspectives:

(a) Importance of foreign customers in share of sales turnover;
(b) Importance of foreign goods and services suppliers;
(c) Importance of foreign partnerships in marketing activities.

On the basis of the various forms of internationalization defined above, the following internationalization indicators were determined:

(a) Internationalization indicators based on the number of types of goods and services supplied from abroad;
(b) Internationalization indicators based on the number of activities linked to the acquisition of foreign clientele attributed to a foreign partnership;
(c) Internationalization indicators based on the significance of foreign customers in relation to the turnover.

An aggregate internationalization indicator was developed on the basis of those mentioned above. In order to do so, a weighted average was calculated on the basis of these indicators. The allocation of a weighting coefficient was based on the intensity of the internationalization effort involved. The conclusion was that, in relation to the number of goods and services supplied from abroad and the number of activities linked to the acquisition of a foreign clientele covered by a foreign partnership, the effort made is significant. This is not necessarily the case, however, as regards the proportion of the turnover derived from the foreign clientele.

With these different indicators of internationalization, the responding firms had to choose between the following four possible levels: very weak, weak, moderate and strong. On that basis, two groups of establishments were defined: on one side weakly internationalized firms which indicated either a very weak or weak level of internationalization and on the other side significantly internationalized firms which chose either a moderate or strong level.

Research Design and Methods

The study is based on a questionnaire undertaken by the Ecole hotelière de Lausanne and the Ecole Suisse de tourisme from Sierre. The study was based upon an earlier generic study of Swiss PMEs (Dembinski & Bologna 2000). Questionnaires were sent to all hotel (6,589 hotels) and tourism establishments (3,855 firms) in Switzerland. Indeed, nearly all the existing firms active in the sector could be considered as SMEs, according to the definition of the European Commission (Commission Recommendation, 96/280/EC). In this context, an SME is an enterprise which:

(a) has fewer than 250 employees;
(b) has either an annual turnover not exceeding 40 M Euro or an annual balance-sheet not exceeding 27 M Euro;
(c) conforms to the criteria of independence. An independent SME is an SME that is not owned for 25% or more of the capital or the voting rights by one enterprise or jointly by several enterprises falling outside the definition of an SME.

According to the Swiss Federal Ministry for Economic Affairs, on average 87% of the Swiss tourism establishments had fewer than 9 employees in 1998, and 99% less than 50 employees. Moreover, only one in 1,000 enterprises employed more than 250 people. In addition, according to the Swiss Hotel Association the yearly turnover of Swiss hotels amounted in 1998 to 103,900 trs. per employee. Based on the distribution of the Swiss tourism establishments according to their respective number of employees, the annual turnover of 87% of Swiss hotels was lower than 625,000 Euro (1 million Swiss Francs), and 99% less than 3 millions Euro (5 millions Swiss francs).

Given the close link between the results of hotels located in urban areas and the international nature of both Geneva and Zurich, the hotel industry was divided into three categories: hotels located outside cities, i.e. in rural areas, hotels located in cities, or urban areas (except Geneva and Zurich), and hotels located in the cantons (states) of Geneva and Zurich. Moreover, other tourist sectors were divided into four groups: tourist offices, transportation of passengers, travel organization/sales, and other tourist activities. The passenger transportation is divided between air transport, cable transport, rail transport, road transport and water transport, while the sub-branch "other tourist activities" is composed of firms dealing with the following activities: (a) organization of sporting events, excursions, courses; (b) organization of congresses and seminars; (c) organization of cultural events; (d) use of other leisure infrastructures; and (e) leasing activities.

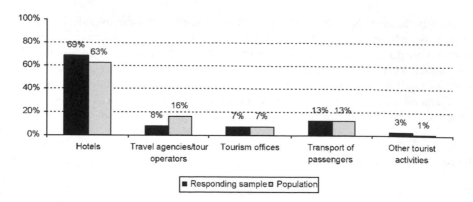

Figure 1: Distribution of the responding establishments according to the different sub-sectors. *Source:* Swiss Tourism Federation (population); questionnaire (responding sample).

In total, 10,444 establishments were contacted for the survey. Seven hundred and fifty-five of them returned questionnaires, which constitutes a general response rate of 7%. Among the different tourism sub-branches, the rate of response was 7% for hotels, 11% for tourism offices, 8% for transportation of passengers, 3% for travel agencies and tour operators and 1% for the other tourist activities.

In terms of the distribution of the responding establishments according to the different sub-branches, as shown in Figure 1, hotels are over-represented in the sample, with a share of nearly three quarters compared to two thirds for the sector. On the other hand, travel agencies as well as tour operators are under-represented with only 8% of the sample, compared to twice that in the sector. The other branches in tourism are representative, with 13% from the transport of persons, 7% from the tourism offices and only 1% from the other tourism activities.

Among establishments active in the transport of persons, cable transport is over-represented with 55% compared to 36%, as well as water transport with 5% compared to 1%. Conversely road transport and air transport are under-represented with 28 and 7%, respectively, instead of 41 and 20%, respectively.

Generally speaking, the responding hotels are over-represented by large and of upper-class segment firms located in cities, which are mostly significantly internationalized. At the same time, the responding sample of hotels is under-represented by small and of lower category hotels located in the countryside, which are on average weakly internationalized. Thus, the empirical results found about the degree of internationalization of tourism establishments were overestimating the share of significantly internationalized firms and underestimating the share of weakly internationalized ones.

Internationalization in the Swiss Tourism Sector

In general terms, more than 80% of the answering sample is weakly internationalized. Only 13% are moderately internationalized and 6% strongly internationalized. The perception

Table 1: Degree of internationalization: Distribution of the responding sample according to the different indicators of internationalization.

	Very Weak (%)	Weak (%)	Moderate (%)	Strong (%)	Total[a]
Indicator based on the number of goods and services supplied by foreign firms	83	13	2	2	629
Indicator based on the number of marketing activities covered by foreign partners	25	44	25	6	282
Indicator based on the share of turnover realized with foreign clients	41	36	13	10	594
General indicator	51	30	13	6	234

[a] Total number of responses.

by the sector of its degree of internationalization does not contradict these results. 60.5% of establishments consider themselves either local or national, while 39.5% either European or global.

The picture is not so clear when considering different forms of internationalization. While around 20% of the sector is significantly internationalized in general terms, the sector is less internationalized in terms of goods and services supplied by foreign suppliers (4%) than for marketing activities covered by foreign partners (31%) or the share of turnover realized with foreign clients (23%) as shown in Table 1.

Within each form of internationalization, significant differences in the degree of internationalization may be found according to the different components of the indicators of internationalization.

Table 2: Indicators of internationalization based on the number of goods supplied by foreign firms: Distribution of the responding sample according to the type of goods.

	Very Weak (%)	Weak (%)	Moderate (%)	Strong (%)	Total
Perishable goods	75	16.5	3.5	5	527
Durable goods	58.5	19	8.5	14	583
Other goods	30.5	13		56.5	23
Total	75	8		17	12

Table 3: Indicators of internationalization based on the number of services supplied by foreign firm: Distribution of the responding sample according to the type of services.

	Very Weak	Weak (%)	Moderate (%)	Strong (%)	Total
Management services		61.5	15.5	23	13
Accountancy services		25	25	50	8
Marketing services		79	16	5	76
Consultancy services		47	41	12	17
Other services		89	11		9
Total		84	12	4	102

Indicators of Internationalization Based on the Different Types of Goods and Services

Firstly, in the case of numerous goods supplied by foreign firms, the sector is less internationalized considering perishable goods than durable goods. Reflecting the nature of the product, in terms of perishable goods, only 8% of establishments are either moderately or strongly internationalized compared to 23% for durable goods as seen in Table 2. Perishable goods are normally purchased in the surrounding region, among local suppliers.

Secondly, looking at the range of services supplied by foreign firms, some of them appear to be significantly more internationalized, perhaps representing the influence of the major companies such as Pricewaterhousecoopers and Anderson, in for example, accountancy or consultancy. These areas appear moderately to strongly internationalized (respectively 75 and 53% of the establishments), while this share falls to 40% for management services and to 21% for marketing services, for additional details, please see Table 3.

Table 4: Indicators of internationalization based on the number of marketing activities covered by foreign partnerships: Distribution of the responding sample according to the type of marketing activity.

	Very Weak	Weak (%)	Moderate (%)	Strong (%)	Total
Communication activities		30.5	50	19.5	82
Distribution and sales activities		48.5	41.5	10	149
Affiliation to a global reservation system		29	52	19	73
Other marketing activities		50	25	25	12
Total		58.5	34	7.5	212

Table 5: Indicators of internationalization based on the share of turnover realized with foreign clients: Distribution of the responding sample according to their region of origin.

	Very Weak (%)	Weak (%)	Moderate (%)	Strong (%)	Total
European clients	35.5	30		34.5	482
North American clients	51	20	14.5	14.5	603
Asian clients	59	20	11	10	600
Clients form the rest of the world	58	22	12	8	600
Foreign clients	41	36	13	10	594

Indicators of Internationalization Based on the Number of Types of Marketing Activities Covered by Foreign Partners

Based on marketing activities covered by foreign partners, internationalization is more significant for communication as well as for global reservation systems where 70% of establishments are either moderately or strongly internationalized, compared to distribution and sales (which represents only 50%). For additional details, please refer to Table 4.

Indicators of Internationalization Based on the Share of Turnover Realized with Foreign Clients

Finally, based on the share of turnover realized with foreign clients, internationalization is stronger with European clients, and to a less extent with those from North America, than with the clients from the rest of the world. Thirty-five percent of establishments are strongly internationalized with European clients, while this share is 29% with North American clients and 20% with the clients from the rest of the world (see Table 5 for details). This is due to the higher share of these clients among foreign tourists, as well as to their higher average purchasing power.

This general picture of internationalization among firms active in the Swiss tourism sector differs according to their respective characteristics.

Internationalization and the Structural Characteristics of Tourism Establishments

The section deals with the five major structural characteristics of tourism establishments that have been considered by the study as potentially influencing their respective degree of internationalization. Namely, these structural variables are composed first of all by the location as well as the sub-sector they belong to. Then, when considering the main tourism sub-sector, hotels, their size, category and form of management are taken into account.

Distribution of the Sample According to the Structural Characteristics of Tourism Establishments

Among tourism establishments:

(i) Tourism sub-branches

The sample is mainly composed of hotels. This activity concerns more than two-thirds of the responding sample. To a lesser extent, transport of persons is also a significative tourism sub-sector, as mentioned above, for 13% of the sample. This sub-branch is divided into five parts, according to their respective frequencies: ski lifts, road transport, air transport, rail transport and water transport. Besides, tourism offices as well as the sub-sector of travel organization & sales represent each 8% of the responding sample.

(ii) Location

Among the different locations of the establishments, there is a significant predominance of mountain areas (mentioned by half of the sample) and to a less extent, the countryside (location quoted by a third of the sample). Urban locations are cited by a quarter of the sample.
   Among hotels:

(iii) Size

The sample is characterized by a majority of small establishments. On average, 75% of the sample have less than 20 employees (full-time equivalent), and the share of those having less than 10 employees is 55%. On the other end of the scale, more than 50 employees are mentioned by less than 9% of the sample. A similar distribution is found in terms of room capacity among hotels. Nearly, 60% of them mention a number of rooms lower than 25, while only 4% have more than 100 rooms.

(iv) Category

More than half of the sample belongs to the medium category. To a lesser extent, the share of the simple class (22%) is significant as well. The share of upper segments is lower, with the first class segment representing 17% of the sample and the luxury establishments 5%.

(v) Form of management

Nearly 90% of the sample has an independent management form. Only some 10% are affiliated.

Importance of Structural Factors to the Level of Internationalization

Let us consider firstly the level of internationalization of establishments active in the Swiss tourism sector according to two of their structural characteristics: tourism sub-sectors and location.

Table 6: Aggregate indicator of internationalization according to the tourism sub-sectors.

	Very Weak (%)	Weak (%)	Moderate (%)	Strong (%)	Total
Hotels	29	57	12	2	179
Tourism offices	16.5	83.5			12
Transport of passengers	60	40			25
Travel organization and sales	33	56	11		9
Other tourism activities	25	75			4
Total	51	30	13	6	234

(i) Tourism sub-sectors

As shown in Table 6, the general degree of internationalization is significantly weaker for tourism offices and transport of passengers. This is particularly true when considering internationalization based on the number of marketing activities covered by foreign partnerships. This result puts forward the national strategic vision characterizing many firms active in these two tourism sub-sectors.

However, when considering only the hotel sub-sector, the hotels located in Geneva and Zürich (the two most international cities in Switzerland) are significantly internationalized.

(ii) Location of establishments

As seen in Table 7, the general degree of internationalization does not significantly differ according to the location of the establishments. Locations in the countryside, however, are significantly very weak. This result is clearly shown for internationalization based on the number of marketing activities covered by foreign partnership. This reflects the fact that tourism actors located in the countryside only collaborate with their local tourism offices for their marketing activities. On the basis of turnover realized with foreign clients, internationalization is significant for urban locations, however. The strong business tourism in the two main cities in Switzerland, Geneva and Zürich, is highly international. Geneva is

Table 7: Aggregated indicator of internationalization according to the location of establishments.

	Very Weak (%)	Weak (%)	Moderate (%)	Strong (%)	Total
Cities	32	51	13	4	69
Countryside	56	37	7		43
Mountains	30	60	10		122
Total	33	56	9.5	1.5	234

Table 8: Aggregate indicator of internationalization according to the number of rooms.

	Very Weak (%)	Weak (%)	Moderate (%)	Strong (%)	Total
Less than 10 rooms	62.5	37.5			16
Between 11 and 25 rooms	45	52.5	2.5		40
Between 26 and 50 rooms	12.5	69.5	18		56
Between 51 and 100 rooms	16.5	71.5	9.5	2.5	42
More than 100 rooms	15.5	30.5	38.5	15.5	13
Total	26	60	12	2	167

known for its international governmental organizations such as the European headquarters of the United Nations, and Zürich for its international financial centre.

When considering the different tourism sub-sectors in the different locations, hotels represent the mostly internationalized tourism sub-sector in cities. Moreover, on a strategic level (foreign clients and foreign partners) travel agencies and tour operators located in the mountain areas appear to be also significantly internationalized.

Now let us consider the degree of internationalization of hotels according to three of their characteristics: size, category and form of management.

(iii) Size of establishments

As illustrated in Table 8, the general degree of internationalization of hotels is significantly different according to their room capacity. It is significantly higher for hotels with more than 100 rooms, and significantly lower for small properties with less than 10 rooms. This result is also clearly shown with each of the three indicators of internationalization; i.e. at the operational level (foreign suppliers of goods and services) and strategic level, as well as at the level of the targeted clients.

(iv) Category of establishments

The general degree of internationalization of establishments is significantly different according to their respective category, as shown in Table 9, being significantly higher for luxury establishments and weaker for all establishments at the lower end of the scale. This is especially true with internationalization based on the number of marketing activities covered by foreign partners, confirming the international strategy followed by luxury hotels, as well as the internationalization based on the share of turnover realized with foreign clients (especially targeted at international business tourism and rich foreign travelers).

(v) Form of management

The general degree of internationalization is significant only for affiliated establishments, as illustrated in Table 10. In the sub-sector of hotels, affiliations are mainly to international groups. Moreover, many independent establishments tend to be individualistic in their respective business approaches. This result can be found with each of the three indicators

Table 9: Aggregate indicator of internationalization by category of hotel.

	Very Weak (%)	Weak (%)	Moderate (%)	Strong (%)	Total
Luxury		23	54	23	13
First class	22	64	14		42
Medium class	24	69	7		84
Simple category	63	37			27
Total	33	56	9.5	1.5	234

of internationalization. At an operational level, regarding foreign suppliers of goods and services, internationalization is significant for establishments which are members of a chain, as they often work with groups from the country of origin of the chain for operational tasks. At the strategic level, regarding the number of marketing activities covered by foreign partners, internationalization is significant for affiliated establishments, as they often benefit from the marketing services of either the chain or a partner of the chain. Finally, at the level of the targeted public, regarding the share of turnover realized with foreign clients, establishments with chain contracts are significantly internationalized, benefiting from the marketing policies of the chain.

The responding sample can be divided into two groups according to the importance of structural characteristics of firms regarding their level of internationalization. On one side, the group of weakly internationalized establishments is composed of tourism offices and firms active in the transport of passengers, as well as hotels, travel agencies and tour operators and firms active in other forms of tourism activity located in the countryside. On the other side, the group of significantly internationalized establishments is mainly composed of hotels located in Geneva and Zürich, as well as travel agencies and tour operators located in the mountain areas.

Table 10: Aggregate indicator of internationalization by form of management.

	Very Weak (%)	Weak (%)	Moderate (%)	Strong (%)	Total
Independent management	26	66	7	1	129
Management contract	43	38	14	5	21
Contract of franchise		50		50	2
Contract of voluntary chain	12.5	62.5	25		24
Contract of other chain		40	60		5
Total	33	56	9.5	1.5	234

Concerning the responding hotels, two groups can also be identified: on one side, weakly internationalized hotels which are mostly independent properties with less than 10 rooms and of lower category; on the other side, significantly internationalized hotels, characterized by being affiliated properties with more than 100 rooms and in the luxury category.

Internationalization and Strategic Variables

As well as in the case of structural factors previously discussed, the degree of internationalization measured by the share of turnover realized with foreign clients is significantly different according to certain strategic factors. This section briefly discusses some of the issues raised in response to various marketing activities that were believed to be significant in the internationalization process, and included the relative importance which companies gave to activities independently undertaken such as advertising, direct mail (both by traditional post, fax and e-mail), sales marketing, public relations and sponsoring. Issues were also raised in connection with activities undertaken with partners, e.g. joining a network of sales and distribution abroad (such as for tour operators), affiliation to a global reservation system, and the development of a web site, either with partners or independently.

Distribution of the Sample According to the Strategic Variables

(i) Recourse to the different forms of marketing activities

While nearly all (97%) the responding establishments mention having recourse to some forms of marketing, marketing activities undertaken independently are much more commonly used (84%) than those covered by a partnership (46%). Urban hotels, especially those in Geneva and Zürich, represent the only tourism sub-sector where marketing with a partner-organization is significant. It is another sign of the individualistic business approach followed by many establishments in the Swiss tourism sector. Also, more than three-quarters of the sample mentioned the use of the Website as a marketing tool, as do a significant number of establishments working in other tourism activities.

(ii) Distribution of the sample according to the different marketing activities undertaken independently

Two thirds of establishments mentioned having undertaken less than three independent marketing activities. Among them, a quarter does not undertake any, especially hotels located in Geneva and Zürich, and travel agencies and tour operators. Only a few undertake five or six such activities, especially tourism offices.

Among the different independent activities of marketing, advertisement is the one mostly used by the establishments in the tourism sector. More than half (61%) mentioned it. This share is significantly higher for tourism offices as well as firms active in the transport of passengers. To a lesser extent, the use of direct-mailing by mail or fax is also significant, as nearly half of the sample mentioned it. At the other end of the scale, sponsoring only concerns 15% of the sample. Besides, this share is around 32% for direct-mailing by e-mail as well as sales promotion and public relations.

(iii) Distribution of the sample according to the different marketing activities undertaken with partners

Three-quarters of the sample undertook either one or two marketing activities through partnership. This share is significantly higher for actors in the other tourism activities. Three such activities were mentioned only by 18.5% of the responding sample. However, this share is significantly higher for hotels situated in Geneva and Zürich, as well as for tourism offices.

Among the different activities of marketing through partnership, distribution and sales represent the one mostly used by establishments in the tourism sector. Nearly, three quarters (69%) mentioned it. This share is significantly higher among firms active in the transport of passengers. Communication activities were mentioned by more than half of establishments (56%). This share is significantly higher for tourism offices, firms active in the transport of passengers as well as those in the other tourism activities. In addition, affiliation to global reservation system was mentioned by nearly half of the sample (45%). This share is significantly higher among hotels located in cities, especially in Geneva and Zürich.

(iv) Distribution of the sample according to the existence of a Web site

More than three quarters (78%) of the sample have a web site. This share is significantly higher in the sub-sector of other tourism activities.

(v) Distribution of the sample according to the services offered by the Web site

(a) *Languages*

Around two thirds (61%) of the responding sample use less than four languages on the Web site. Two languages are significantly used by the Web sites of hotels in Geneva and Zürich, as well as by those of firms active in the other tourism activities. One language is used by the Web site of a significant number of firms active in the transport of passengers as well as of travel agencies and tour operators.

German is used by 90% of the sample — not surprisingly, as it is the mother tongue of most of these establishments. Moreover, foreign tourists in Switzerland are in majority Germans and Austrians. In addition, English is used by nearly two-thirds of the sample confirming its importance when international marketing is concerned. It is significantly used by hotels in Geneva and Zürich as well as by firms active in the other tourism activities. Then follow finally the two other national languages, French (39%) and Italian (11%).

(b) *Online services*

To date online services are not widely offered in the Swiss tourism sector. Three quarters of the sample do not offer more than one online service, and as much as a third does not provide any. There is a lack of interactivity in many of the sites. Among the different tourism establishments, only hotels as well as firms active in the other tourism activities significantly offer two online services on their Web sites.

Direct reservation is the mostly offered online service, as more than half of the sample mentioned it. It is significantly used by hotels in Geneva and Zürich. At the other end of the scale, online payment was put forward by only 17% of the sample. It is significantly used by hotels in Geneva and Zürich, as well as firms active in the sub-sector of other tourism activities.

Concerning the share of online reservations, the sample is divided into two parts. On one side, more than half mention a share lower than 4%, while on the other a quarter mentioned a share higher than 9%. The latter was significantly mentioned by firms active in the sub-sector of other tourism activities.

Importance of Strategic Factors to the Share of Turnover Realized with Foreign Clients

As strategic factors cover activities designed to reach foreign clients, their importance to the level of internationalization is analyzed on the basis of the indicator of internationalization based on the share of turnover realized with foreign clients.

(i) Marketing activities undertaken independently

Establishments having undertaken such activities are significantly internationalized only if five or six of such activities are concerned. It is especially the case for hotels located in Geneva and Zürich which do not significantly use so many of these activities. However, it is also the case for tourism offices (especially when considering European clients) who significantly make use of this number of activities, and travel agencies and tour operators (especially when considering clients from North America and Asia). At the same time, the share of weakly internationalized establishments is significant among firms having not undertaken any independent marketing. This is especially the case for tourism offices as well as establishments active in the other tourism activities.

Finally, the share of turnover realized with foreign clients does not significantly differ according to the type of marketing activity undertaken independently.

(ii) Marketing activities covered by partnerships

Establishments having undertaken partnerships to cover marketing activities are significantly internationalized only if three such activities are covered. It is especially true for hotels situated in Geneva and Zürich as well as for clients from North America and Asia.

As illustrated in Table 11, among the different types of marketing activities covered by partnership, only affiliation to global reservation systems is associated with a significant share of turnover realized with foreign clients. This relation is especially true for hotels situated in Geneva and Zürich and travel agencies and tour operators, as well as for foreign clients coming from North America and Asia.

(iii) Existence of a Web site

The indicator of internationalization is significantly weak for establishments which do not have any website. It is especially true when considering hotels in Geneva and Zürich as well as travel agencies and tour operators.

Table 11: Internationalization based on the share of turnover realized with foreign clients according to the types of marketing activities covered by partnerships.

	Very Weak (%)	Weak (%)	Moderate (%)	Strong (%)	Total
Recourse to partnership covering communication	33	36	16	15	136
Recourse to partnership covering distribution and sales	29	41.5	14	15.5	174
Recourse to partnership covering global reservation system	20	38	26	16	114
Recourse to partnership covering other activities of promotion	17.5	53	17.5	12	17
Recourse to partnership	28.5	41.5	16.5	13.5	248

(iv) Services offered on the Web site

(a) *Languages*

The share of turnover realized with foreign clients is significant only when five languages are used on the Web site. It is especially true for hotels in cities (especially when considering European clients) and outside cities (especially when taking into account clients from North America and Asia), as well as travel agencies and tour operators (especially with clients from North America).

Among the languages used by the web site English and Dutch are most used by significantly internationalized establishments. It is especially the case for hotels situated in Geneva and Zürich when considering English, while Dutch is more the case for hotels located outside cities.

(b) *Online services*

The indicator of internationalization is significantly weak for establishments not offering any online service. It is especially true for hotels located in Geneva and Zürich. Moreover, only establishments offering online payment are significantly internationalized. It is especially true for hotels located in Geneva and Zürich as well as travel agencies and tour operators, especially when considering clients from North America and Asia. Finally, the share of turnover realized with foreign clients is not significantly influenced by the share of online reservations. This is due to the low average share of online reservations.

The responding sample can be divided into main two groups according to the importance of strategic variables in the degree of internationalization, as measured by the share of turnover realized with foreign clients. On one side, significantly internationalized firms are composed of: (a) hotels in Geneva and Zürich independently undertaking five or six marketing activities, as well as three marketing activities through partnerships, and offering online payment on their web sites; (b) hotels not situated in Geneva and Zürich using five languages on their web sites; (c) travel agencies and tour operators independently undertaking five or six marketing activities (especially to target clients from North America and Asia), using five languages (especially English) and offering online payment (especially with clients from North America and Asia) on their Web sites; (d) tourism offices independently undertaking five or six marketing activities (especially to target clients from Europe).

On the other side, there are weakly internationalized establishments composed of: (a) hotels in Geneva and Zürich without any Web site, and those not offering any online service on their Web sites; (b) tourism offices who have not undertaken any marketing activity independently; and (c) firms active in the other tourism activities, who similarly have not undertaken any independent marketing.

Conclusions

One of the main findings from the study is that only 20% of the sample is significantly internationalized. The picture is similar but with slight differences when the different forms of internationalization are considered. On a strategic level, with internationalization based on the number of marketing activities covered by foreign partners, this significantly internationalized share of the sample is 31%. This share is 23% on the level of targeted public, with an internationalization based on the share of turnover realized with foreign clients, and only 4% on an operational level with internationalization based on the number of goods and services supplied by foreign suppliers.

The analysis of the impact of structural and strategic variables on internationalization identifies two groups of establishments. The first one covers weakly internationalized establishments, which represent the large majority of the sector. These firms have a domestic focus, reflected in terms of the clients targeted, the partners selected to work on marketing activities, as well as the suppliers of their goods and services. This group is mainly composed of most tourism offices and companies active in the transport of persons as well as travel agencies and tour operators and firms engaged in the other tourism activities located in the countryside, and hotels characterized by small size, by their lower categories, most importantly, by being independent in their management and behavior. Partnerships to advance marketing activities are not considered very important, with a preference for traditional, independent, marketing activities. A large number of these enterprises do not have a Web site, perhaps owing to limited financial resources.

Secondly, there is a minority of establishments mainly composed of large hotels, mostly urban (especially in Geneva and Zürich), located in the upper-market segment and which are members of hotel chains. They have already tried to exploit the potential from increasing internationalization: e.g. through partnerships covering such areas as marketing activities (for example, affiliation to global reservation systems, which are very effective, especially with clients from North America and Asia). They have also developed Web sites and have a growing share of online reservations. To a lesser extent, this group also includes some companies active in travel organization and sales with an international focus and located in the mountain areas.

Thus, the importance of the development of the internationalization process is different between these two groups of firms. For those which are significantly internationalized, the process of internationalization is a component of their general strategy. They already consider themselves as actors of the international tourism market. So, in this context, the development of the internationalization process is necessary to improve their competitiveness. At the other end of the scale, a majority of the weakly internationalized tourism companies act only within the national tourism market. In this context, the development of the internationalization process is not a priority. However, a growing proportion of these firms face financial difficulties. The number of bankruptcies in this sector has significantly increased. This evolution has pushed many financial institutions and the various State credit agencies to be more restrictive in their respective credit policies. Thus, many of these nationally-focused tourism establishments are increasingly led to become more active with respect to the growing international tourism market. International competition might push these firms to cooperate between themelves in order to increase their respective chances of benefitting from the international dimension. In the short run, this cooperation seems easier to achieve for the development of operational internationalization (e.g. the use of foreign suppliers of goods and services for a group of tourism companies) than for the development of strategic internationalization. However, for many of these firms, it becomes a question of financial survival. The State might intervene to lend some of these establishments financial support of some kind. For that, however, a picture of the different potential factors working either in favor or against internationalization would be needed.

References

Buckley, P. J., & Casson, M. (1993). A theory of international operations. In: P. J. Buckley, & P. Ghauri (Eds), *The internationalization of the firm*. London, UK: Academic Press.

Buckley, P. J., & Casson, M. C. (1998). Analysing foreign market entry strategies: Extending the internalization approach. *Journal of International Business Studies, 29*(3), 539–562.

Chetty, S., & Blankenburg Hom, D. (2000). Internationalisation of small- to medium-sized manufacturing firms: A network approach. *International Business Review, 9,* 77–93.

Contractor, F. J., & Kundu, S. K. (1998). Franchising vs. company-run operations: Modal choice in the global hotel sector. *Journal of International Marketing, 6*(2), 28–53.

Coviello, N. E., & McAuley, A. (1999). Internationalization and the smaller firm: Review of contemporary empirical research. *Management International Review*. Wiesbaden, Third quarter.

Coviello, N. E., & Munro, H. J. (1995). Growing the entrepreneurial firm. *European Journal of Marketing, 29*(7), 49–61.

Dembinski, P. H., & Bologna, M. C. (2000). *Internationalization des PME suisses*. Ecodiagnostic, Geneva, Switzerland.

Dunning, J. H. (1993). *Multinational enterprises and the global economy*. Wokingham, UK: Addision-Wesley.

Dunning, J. H. (2001). The eclectic (OLI) paradigm of international production: Past, present and future. *International Journal of the Economics of Business, 8*(2), 173–190.

Fletcher, R. (2001). A holistic approach to internationalization. *International Business Review, 10,* 25–49.

Fillis, I. (2001). Small firm internationalization: An investigative survey and future research directions. *Management Decisions, 39*(9), 767–783.

Ireland, R. D., Hitt, M. A., Camp, M., & Sexton, D. L. (2001). Integrating entrepreneurship and strategic management actions to create firm wealth. *The Academy of Management Executive, 15*(1), 49–63.

Johanson, J., & Mattsson, L. G. (1988). Internationalization in industrial systems — a network approach. In: P. J. Buckley, & P. Ghauri (Eds), *The internationalization of the firm*. London, UK: Academic Press.

Johanson, J., & Vahlne, J. E. (1979). The internationalization process of the firm — a model of knowledge development and increasing foreign market commitments. In: P. J. Buckley, & P. Ghauri (Eds), *The internationalization of the firm*. London, UK: Academic Press.

Johanson, J., & Wiedersheim-Paul, F. (1975). The internationalization of the firm — four Swedish cases. In: P. J. Buckley, & P. Ghauri (Eds), *The internationalization of the firm*. London, UK: Academic Press.

Kundu, S. (1994). *Explaining the globalisation of service industries: The case of multinational hotels.* Ph.D. thesis, Rutgers, The State University of New Jersey, USA.

Lloyd-Reason, L., & Mughan, T. (2002). Strategies for internationalization within SMEs: The key role of the owner-manager. *Journal of Small Business and Enterprise Development, 9*(2), 120–129.

McAuley, A. (1999). Entrepreneurial instant exporters in the Scottish arts and crafts sector. *Journal of International Marketing, 7*(4), 67–82.

McLaughlin, C. P., & Fitzsimmons, J. A. (1996). Strategies for globalizing service operations. *International Journal of Service Industry Management, 7*(4), www edition, emerald-library.com/brev/08507dcl.htm

Oviatt, B. M., & McDougall, P. P. (1994). Toward a theory of international new ventures. *Journal of International Business Studies* (First Quarter 199), 45–64.

Segal-Horn, S. (1998). The internationalization of services. *The Strategy Reader.* Blackwell Business/The Open University, Oxford, UK.

Tallman, S., & Fladmoe-Lindquist, K. (2002). Internationalization, globalization and capability-based strategy. *California Management Review, 45*(1).

Turnbull, P. W. (1993). A challenge to the stages theory of the internationalization process. In: P. Buckley, & P. Ghauri (Eds), *The internationalization of the firm*. London, UK: Academic Press.

Chapter 19

Small Tourism Firms in e-Europe: Definitional, Conceptual and Contextual Considerations

Harry Matlay

Introduction

Traditionally, small firms have played an important and stabilising role in the socio-economic and political development of Great Britain and that of most Western European nations (Storey 1994). In recent times, governments in Western Europe have actively promoted a more enterprising society, in an attempt to solve a diversity of economic problems. Increasingly, a healthy and expanding small business sector has come to be perceived as the panacea to a host of problems associated with relative economic decline, persistently high inflation and long-term youth and adult unemployment (Matlay 2000). The drive to promote the development of small firms in Western Europe in general and in the European Union in particular has ensured a political topicality that manifested itself in an influx of both general and specific support measures and training initiatives (Thomas 1996). Designated funds for research into various aspects of small firm finance, management and development were also made available from a growing number of regional, national and EC-wide sources (Thomas 1998). Although the focus, consistency and impact of official support that relates specifically to small tourism firms can vary from country to country, the importance afforded by Western European governments to the ongoing development and sustainability of the "fastest growing industry" remains generally high (Matlay 1998a). It is not difficult to see why: international cross-country comparisons have shown that the contribution of the tourism industry in terms of employment, Gross Domestic Product (GDP) and Balance of Payments throughout Western Europe is consistently greater than that of most other sectors of an economy (Matlay 1998b). Furthermore, it is generally agreed that Western Europe is characterised by mature and well-developed industrial economies, inhabited by an aging and comparatively affluent population (Litteljohn 1995). It would not be unreasonable, therefore, to predict that tourism would continue to represent one the largest economic activities in the region and that in terms of demand there is still potential for further and widespread growth (Middleton 1998).

Since the 1989 collapse of Communism in the former Soviet bloc, most countries in Central and Eastern Europe have undergone a prolonged transition period from a centrally planned, command system to a more or less liberalised, Western-style market economy. In common with contemporary Western beliefs and attitudes, much of the public and private strategy adopted in relation to economic regeneration in the region appears to be centred upon the interrelated concepts of entrepreneurship and small business development (Matlay 2001). Typically, the dominant "entrepreneurial culture" paradigm — based upon market-led demand, innovation and opportunistic risk — contrasts radically with the traditional, Soviet inspired "bureaucratic administrative" system that was dominated entirely by centralised decision-making and control processes (Bateman 1997). Interestingly, however, soon after socio-economic and political liberalisation, most of the countries of Central and Eastern Europe began experiencing the combined pressures of rapidly falling demand for goods/services, accelerating inflation and rising unemployment (Agh 1998). Invariably, such difficult economic conditions propelled entrepreneurship and small business development issues into the forefront of political agendas as the newly elected governments struggled to continue the privatisation and restructuring of their economies (Batt 1991). Geographically, Central and Eastern Europe extends across roughly the same land mass as Western Europe. From the end of the Second World War in 1945 and until the "democratic revolutions" of 1989, the region was more or less cut off from Western Europe and the rest of the world by Soviet domination and the isolationist policies of native communist dictatorships (Aslund 1992). Before the radical changes that occurred in the region beginning with 1989, much of the tourism flow involved exclusively visitors to and from other Eastern bloc countries. With very few exceptions, tourism flows to the West and the rest of the world were banned and outside visitors were only allowed entry in small numbers, mostly as part of strictly controlled and highly organised trade delegations (Lockwood 1995). During the early 1990s, the initial development of tourism in these countries depended largely upon the existing infrastructure, which was relatively weak and underdeveloped and driven mostly by a need to attract hard currency from foreign business travellers (Middleton 1998). In recent years, however, the overall development of tourism in Central and Eastern Europe appears to have accelerated, partly due to external investment in both medium-sized and large ventures but also owing to private-public collaborations that increasingly benefited smaller firms in the region (Matlay 2003).

During recent decades, the rapid evolution of computers and related Information Technology (IT) has enabled businesses of various sizes, location and economic activity to design and adopt new and innovative business strategies (Negroponte 1995). Importantly, the mass production of IT equipment and the ready availability of quality support services have led to the creation of new firms and even entire industries (Moulton 2002). From the mid 1990s onwards, Information and Communication Technologies (ICTs) and the Internet began impacting significantly upon organisational growth, development and competitiveness — at both micro- and macro-economic levels (Martin & Matlay 2001). Increasingly, as more individuals and firms became connected electronically, the speed, direction and emphasis of strategic change and competitive drive have shifted away from traditional trade towards online business transactions taking place in a fast growing Digital Economy (Magretta 1999). As a generic term, the "Digital Economy" (often used interchangeably with "e-Economy," "New Economy" or "Internet Economy") is based on digital technologies and communication networks that provide a global platform upon which businesses can interact, communicate, collaborate and sell/purchase a vast variety of products and services (King *et al.* 2002). The transition from the "old" or "traditional" to the e-Economy has been described as a disruptive and highly volatile process, fuelled mainly by international competition and reasonably priced and readily available ICTs (EC 2001). Crucially, however, King *et al.* (2002), identifies entrepreneurial drive and behaviour as the main factor that determines whether a firm, industry or region will succeed in exploiting these technologies. As the vast majority of tourism firms are Small or Medium-Sized Enterprises (SMEs) it was inevitable that this industry would also be affected by the ongoing digital revolution (see, Buhalis 1998; Matlay 1998a). On the supply side, tourism firms increasingly adopt innovative methods and the Internet in order to ensure sustainable competitive advantage. On the demand side, a sophisticated, knowledgeable and demanding breed of customers increasingly use the Internet in search of flexible, specialised and realistically priced destinations. In this context, smaller tourism firms need to redress their inherent disadvantage of scale and maximise their advantage in terms of niche market specialisation and managerial reactive speed (O'Connor & O'Keefe 1997).

The purpose of this chapter is to provide the reader with an introduction to definitional, conceptual and contextual issues associated with the emergence of e-Businesses and Internet trading in e-Europe and the effect that these developments could have on small tourism firms operating in Western, Central and Eastern Europe. The chapter is organised in six parts. The first section provides a brief introduction to the salient issues associated with the emergence of electronic trading in Europe. In the second part, the reader is familiarised with the research sample and methodological considerations related to the pan-European research study upon which the chapter is based. The next section contains a critical overview of the main SME indicators in Western, Central and Eastern Europe, as evaluated in the research study. The forth section outlines the main SME indicators relating specifically to small tourism firms in e-Europe. In the fifth section, the reader is provided with a succinct overview of the impact that e-Business and Internet trading could have on small tourism firms operating in e-Europe. The concluding section summarises the findings of the research study and outlines the main approaches that small tourism firms in e-Europe should adopt in order to sustain or enhance their competitive strategies.

SMEs in Europe: Research Sample and Methodological Considerations

It is generally accepted that SMEs make a considerable contribution to the socio-economic infrastructure of European economies (Storey 1994). Until recently, however, there was no standard, uniformly acceptable definition of what exactly constitutes an SME. A number of definitions, mostly based on "objective" measures of size — such as employee numbers, turnover, profitability and net worth — were used in an attempt to quantify this vast and diverse sector of an economy. Apart from size measures, "economic" and "statistical" definitions were also employed for the purpose of quantifying the contribution of national or European SME sectors (Matlay 1998a). Unfortunately, none of these definitions proved successful in accurately quantifying either the size of an SME sector or any quantitative changes occurring within it over given periods of time (Bridge *et al.* 1998). Furthermore, definitional incompatibility rendered cross-country and pan-European comparisons difficult to achieve:

complicated standardisation and harmonisation formulae were needed in order to render at least some of the data acceptable for empirical and/or comparative research. Typically, to overcome low compatibility or unacceptably high standardisation errors, most researchers tended to use the definition that best suited their immediate purpose (Matlay 1998b). In the case of official publications and reports, cross-sectoral analyses were mostly limited to those countries where data were collected and/or published in a more compatible form (see, for example, ENSR 1997). To overcome such measurement and compatibility problems, the EC took the lead and suggested a standardised, formal SME definition (EC 1996). Further efforts were made to improve the quality of statistical data affecting Member States, as published and/or used within the EC, the European Central Bank (ECB) and the European Statistical System (ESS). The EC is currently progressing towards the improvement of infra-annual macro-economic statistics, in respect to the timeliness, frequency and coverage of data, the differentiation between Eurozone and non-Eurozone, the standardisation of relevant methodologies and accessibility of statistical information (EC 2002a). Arguably, better quality and statistically compatible pan-European data are collected by commercial firms that specialise in the provision of business intelligence — by country, industry and region as well as a number of other statistically useful criteria (GIR 1998). These data, however, are for limited distribution only and can prove prohibitive in terms of the overall cost of cross-border comparisons.

In view of the rapid and radical changes taking place in Europe and elsewhere in the developed and developing world it is becoming increasingly important to quantify and specify the diverse and heterogeneous mass of SMEs at all levels of economic activity. Based on longitudinal analysis of commercial databases at local, regional and national levels, it has become possible to accurately estimate the number, economic activity and contribution of SMEs across Europe (GIR 2000a, b). For the purpose of this chapter, SMEs are defined as non-primary (i.e. excluding agriculture, hunting, forestry and fishing) private firms that employ fewer than 250 individuals or full time equivalent (FTE). By convention, within the standardised EC SME definition, the following size bands can be distinguished (EC 1996):

(1) Micro-Firms: firms that employ fewer than 10 individuals (including the self-employed).
(2) Small Firms: firms with a payroll of between 10 and 49 employees
(3) Medium-Sized Enterprises: firms employing 50 to 249 individuals.

Those firms that employ in excess of 250 employees are classified as Large Organisations (LOs) and are beyond the scope of this chapter. Since its publication in 1996, the EC SME definition has been widely adopted and used throughout the academic, research and practitioner communities and it has contributed significantly to the standardisation of comparative data across the world. This definition is used in this chapter in relation to all the quantitative data presented for Western, Central and Eastern Europe.

SMEs in Europe: Main Indicators

The importance of SMEs in Europe can be usefully gauged by analysing the most recent cumulative quantitative indicators available (Table 1), including the number of

Table 1: SMEs in Europe: Main indicators[a] (2000).

Main Indicators	Geographical Location	Total SMEs	Micro Firms	Small Firms	Medium-Sized Enterprises
Number of businesses (000s)	Western Europe	20,793	19,709	986	98
	Central/Eastern Europe	11,645	10,965	611	69
Average business size (employee no.)	Western Europe	4	3	19	184
	Central/Eastern Europe	5	4	21	185
Total employment (000s)	Western Europe	95,893	59,127	18,734	18,032
	Central/Eastern Europe	69,456	43,860	12,831	12,765

[a] *Source:* GIR (2002).

economically active firms, average size and employment Figures. There are, however, considerable differences between the SME sectors of Western Europe and those of Central and Eastern Europe. The origins of the modern, Western European SME sectors can be traced back to the Industrial Revolution that began in Britain and spread across the world during the 18th and the 19th Century. Following the end of the Second World War, most countries in Western Europe began rebuilding and modernised their economies along the principles of free market competition. Due to political and socio-economic reasons, their SME sectors were actively supported and nurtured. In contrast, however, The Soviet inspired and controlled economies of Central and Eastern Europe were slow to modernise and gradually fell behind their Western Europe counterparts. Furthermore, while entrepreneurship and small businesses flourished in the "Free Europe," socialist doctrine actively discouraged, and made it prohibitively expensive or even illegal to own private businesses. Total State monopoly on resources, production and decision making processes had a retarding effect upon national SME sectors in Central and Eastern Europe. Since the 1989 dramatic upheavals in the region, the privatisation and breakdown of the mainly large, state-owned firms has been both slow and uneven. Furthermore, few of the newly democratised governments possessed the knowledge or the means to support their budding SME sectors. Risk aversion and the effects of political uncertainty in the region meant that foreign investment was slow to boost economic growth in the majority of the former communist countries. Private and corporate reluctance to invest in Central and Eastern Europe still affects economic development in the region, and is most acutely felt in those in those countries that are perceived to lag behind with their democratic reforms.

The most recent statistics (GIR 2002) estimated that by 2000 the total number of SMEs in Europe had increased to 32,438,000 economically active business units. Numerically, micro-firms dominate the European SME sector: at 30,674,000 they represented 94.56% of all the firms that operated in this sector of the economy. In comparison, small firms only accounted for 1,597,000 firms or 4.92% of the economically active units and medium-sized enterprises were represented by 167,000 businesses or 0.52% of the total. Similarly, the total number of employees or full time equivalent (FTE) attributable to the European SME sector was estimated at 165,349,000 individuals. The micro-firm proportion of employment, which included the self-employed category, accounted for 102,987,000 employees or 62.28% of the SME employment in Europe. Small and medium-sized enterprises contributed, respectively, a further 31,565,000 (19.09%) and 30,797,000 (18.63%) employees to the European economy.

Estimated at 20,793,000 firms, the SME sector of Western Europe is almost twice as large as that of Central and Eastern Europe. By 2000 the Western European SME sector has expanded to approximatively 11,645,000 economically active units. In relation to the total SME population, micro-firms dominate the structure of this sector in both regions: 19,709,000 or 94.79% in Western Europe and 10,965,000 or 94,16% in Central and Eastern Europe. Similarly, it is estimated that there were 986,000 (4.74%) small firms and 98,000 (0.47%) medium-sized enterprises in Western Europe as compared to 611,000 (5.25%) and 69,000 (0.59%) in Central and Eastern Europe. When comparing total employment in SMEs across Europe it is important to note that the average business size is higher in Central and Eastern Europe. Thus, in Western Europe, micro-firms accounted for 59,127,000 individuals or 61.66% of the total SME workforce contribution in the region. Small firms and medium-sized enterprises contributed a further 18,734,000 (19.54%) and 18,032,000 (18.80%) employees. In Central and Eastern Europe micro-firms provided jobs for 43,860,000 individuals or 63.15% of the total employment attributable to the SME sector, while small firms and medium-sized enterprises added a further 12,831,000 (18.47%) and 12,765,000 (18.38%) employees. It is suggested that, due to the current restructuring and downsizing in Western Europe and the ongoing privatisation and modernisation of Central and Eastern European economies, the contribution of SMEs to the European economy is likely to increase further during the next few decades.

Tourism SMEs in Europe: Main Indicators

It is now widely accepted that tourism represents the largest economic activity in Europe, with potential for further and sustainable growth. Estimates relating to the tourism industry's direct contribution as well as its indirect effect upon other sectors of an economy can vary considerably across Europe. This is partly due to the inherent socio-economic and cultural diversity of the continent, which incorporates a wide variety of national and regional identities. In addition, local business, demographic and geographic variations can impact significantly upon tourism related demand and supply. In simplistic terms, it is sometimes claimed that the tourism industry in Western Europe is mature while its counterpart in Central and Eastern Europe is described as emergent. There are, however, a number of important similarities between the tourism industries in these two regions of Europe. The continent as a whole offers a tremendous variety of interesting and popular destinations for leisure as well as business tourism. In both regions tourism is continually changing and adapting, in line with market demands for improvements in the stock of long-haul, word class destinations (in terms of quality as well as value for money). A vast proportion of the tourism industry in Europe operates in the private sector and it is subject to the business turbulence caused, amongst other factors, by prevailing regional and international economic conditions. Conversely, the industry is dependent, to a large extent, upon public sector collaboration and support to mitigate the adverse circumstances caused by successive, boom and bust economic cycles. Importantly, however, although the main developments in the tourism industry tend to be dominated by large firms, the vast proportion of related business activities involve SMEs operating in local and regional markets. The importance of tourism SMEs is amply illustrated by the latest available GIR (2002) quantitative data presented in Table 2.

In 2000, the total number of tourism SMEs in Europe was estimated at 2,763,000 firms, of which 1,501,000 or 54.33% operated in Western Europe and the balance of 1,262,000 or 45.67% were located in Central and Eastern Europe. Tourism micro-firms dominated the industry with 1,422,000 (94.74%) economically active units in Western Europe and 1,197,000 (94.85%) in Central and Eastern Europe. In Western Europe, small tourist firms were represented by 74,000 (4.93%) economically active units and 5,000 (0.33%) medium-sized enterprises. Similarly, in Central and Eastern Europe, there were 61,000 (4.83%) small tourist firms and 4,000 (0.32%) medium-sized enterprises. The average business size of tourism firms is larger than that of SMEs in general, and, as a consequence of labour intensiveness, the total employment contribution of the industry is proportionally higher. Thus, in total, tourism SMEs accounted for 19,778,000 jobs in Europe. In Western Europe, tourism

Table 2: Tourism SMEs in Europe: Main indicators[a] (2000).

Main Indicators	Geographical Location	Total SMEs	Micro Firms	Small Firms	Medium-Sized Enterprises
Number of businesses (000s)	Western Europe	1,501	1,422	74	5
	Central/Eastern Europe	1,262	1,197	61	4
Average business size (employee no.)	Western Europe	6	5	26	197
	Central/Eastern Europe	7	6	29	202
Total employment (000s)	Western Europe	10,019	7,110	1,924	985
	Central/Eastern Europe	9,759	7,182	1,769	808

[a] *Source:* GIR (2002).

SMEs contributed 10,019,000 jobs to the regions labour force. Proportionally, the largest contribution was made by tourist micro-firms at 7,110,000 (70.97%) followed by 1,924,000 (19.20%) jobs in small firms and 985,000 (9.83%) in medium-sized enterprises. Similarly, tourism SMEs in Central and Eastern Europe accounted for 9,759,000 jobs, of which 7,182,000 (73.59%) were employed in micro-firms, 1,769,000 (18.13%) in small firms and the balance of 808,000 (8.28%) in medium-sized enterprises. Despite difficult economic circumstances and ongoing restructuring in Europe and elsewhere, the tourism industry in the region has grown steadily over the last decade. Forecasts are generally optimistic in relation to the future of tourism and related industries in Europe. The Internet and Electronic Commerce, in particular, are hailed as great opportunities (as well as threats) to the future of tourism in the region.

The Impact of e-Business on Small Tourism Firms

The recent and widespread adoption of Intranets, Extranets and the Internet as business platforms have radically transformed the global economy and, in the process, have promoted the rapid growth and expansion of e-Business across the world. As a result, in the accelerating pace of inter- and cross-border transactions "doing business electronically" encompasses most, if not all, the components of "traditional" trade, including marketing, ordering, payment and support for the delivery of a vast portfolio of products. Furthermore, e-Business also includes the electronic provision of a variety of services, together with after-sales support, online legal advice and sales-related feedback from and to (dis)satisfied customers (Timmers 2000). Increasingly, in strategic management terms, e-Business is perceived to represent either a complementary aspect of traditional trade or a completely new way of doing business. Whole sectors of the national and international economy have been transformed and new industries have emerged in the wake of the ongoing ICT revolution (Martin & Matlay 2001). Both at macro- and micro-economic levels, the use of Internet has facilitated innovation, knowledge management and learning at an unprecedented speed and scale (Martin & Matlay 2003). In terms of ICT adoption and development, operational change is no longer viewed as an option but a strategic necessity that businesses of all sizes, economic activity and geographic location, must undertake in order to survive and prosper in the "new economy" (King *et al.* 2002).

Historically, various forms of electronic commerce (e-Commerce) have existed for over 30 years, mainly in the form of electronic data interchanges (EDIs) that have been developed for defence or heavy manufacturing purposes. Even allowing for conceptual and definitional variations within generic terms such as Telecommunications, IT and ICT, the competitive advantage potential of information "networks" or "highways" have been recognised or acknowledged as far back as the 1970s (Dertouzos 1997; Earl 1988; Runge & Earl 1988). Until recently, however, integrated information systems or CALS, (such as Computer Assisted Lifecycle Support or Computer Aided Logistics Support) have been fairly limited in their diffusion, usage and uptake (Kalacota & Whinstone (1996). Their limitations in terms of adoption were mainly due to the very high levels of investment that CALS required in terms of research and development (R&D) and related expenditure. Nevertheless, the competitive edge that it conferred upon the corporations involved in this type of R&D both justified and necessitated the magnitude of associated investments.

Timmers (2000: 4) argues that "... recently, however, we have seen explosive development in electronic commerce ... the causes of that are, of course, the Internet and the World Wide Web (WWW), which are making electronic commerce much more accessible." There is still a great deal of speculation about the direction and potential of e-Commerce (Matlay 2002a). Importantly, however, as more individuals and firms become connected electronically, a noticeable change in competitive drive has taken place (Magretta 1999). Increasingly, strategic management of change appears to favour "online business transactions" to the detriment of the more "traditional trade" routes. However, the most lucrative aspect of e-Commerce is still business-to-business (B2B) trading, although the volume of Business-to-Consumer (B2C) and Business-to-Government (B2G) transactions has also increased considerably in recent years (Barnes & Hunt 2001).

The economic turbulence associated with the SME sector (see Bridge *et al.* 1998; Storey 1994) appears to be even more pronounced in those industries where strategic change has been associated with the emergence of e-Business (Matlay 2002a). Furthermore, in most sectors of economic activity, the transition from "traditional" to e-Commerce has been described as a disruptive and highly volatile process, fuelled mainly by international competition and reasonably priced as well as readily available ICTs (EC 2001). As a common denominator of strategic change, entrepreneurship has been identified as the main factor to determine whether a firm, industry or region will succeed in exploiting the opportunities inherent in e-Commerce (King *et al.* 2002). Interestingly, however, e-Entrepreneurship is evident not only in firms but increasingly noticeable at local, regional and national levels (Matlay 2001). Furthermore, as national economic activities converge into strategic trade associations and/or communities, e-Entrepreneurship is developing beyond its generic or traditional boundary.

Perhaps the best example of e-Entrepreneurship at European level is provided by the strategies adopted by EC Member States in order to facilitate the benchmarking of national and regional e-Business policies for their SME sectors (EC 2002b). At the March 2000 Lisbon summit, the European Union has formally set itself the target of becoming — by 2010 — one of the most competitive knowledge-based economy in the world (EC 2000). It is obvious that the achievement of such an ambitious target will depend largely upon e-Entrepreneurship and the commitment of its estimated 19 million SMEs to using ICTs and the Internet as a leading edge "business tool" (Matlay 2002a). The 2002 benchmarking report has identified a number of support initiatives, both at national and EC level, to assist SMEs in their efforts to adopt e-Business. These ranged from basic awareness raising events to more specific support measures and incentives designed to facilitate the business use of the Internet. Importantly, however, in 2003 a "European e-Business Support Network" will be established in order to strengthen and co-ordinate national and regional initiatives in support of the increasing adoption of e-Business in SMEs. Its stated prime objective would be "... to agree on common principles for the support of SMEs in the field of e-Business and to identify specific goals for e-Business policies" in e-Europe (EC 2002b: 38). Other European countries that expect or aim to join the EC are also encouraged to follow in the footsteps of Member States in order to identify specific goals for SME related e-Business strategies and to share best practice in this important area of economic activity (Matlay 2003).

Whichever definition or measurement criterion is chosen, the vast majority of tourism firms in Europe can be categorised as SMEs (GIR 2002; Matlay 1998a; Middleton 1998). In view of the considerable impact that e-Business appears to have on SMEs in general, it is perhaps inevitable that the tourism industry would also be significantly affected by the ongoing digital revolution (Buhalis 2003). Accordingly, Matlay (1998a) notes that on the supply side, tourism SMEs increasingly adopt innovative e-Marketing tools and use the Internet in their drive to secure their competitive advantage. Conversely, on the demand side, a sophisticated, knowledgeable and demanding breed of customers progressively use the Internet in their search for flexible, specialised and/or realistically priced leisure destinations. Thus, smaller tourism firms need to redress their inherent disadvantage of scale and maximise their advantage in terms of scope, niche market specialisation and reactive speed to macro- as well as micro-economic changes (O'Connor & O'Keefe 1997). Furthermore, Duff (2002) argues that the tourism industry, in common with other sectors of the economy, needs to adapt to the opportunities offered by the Internet and the emerging Digital Economy. Thus, the use of the Internet as a marketing platform offers small specialist firms considerable prospects to both reach and to cover traditional and emerging tourism markets. According to the Office of National Statistics, by December 2001, more than 9.8 million household in the U.K. were connected to the Internet — which represents a four-fold increase since 1999 (ONS 2002). Such tremendous growth is perhaps indicative of the potential expansion of the tourism market, stimulated by Internet connection of desktop, portable and hand-held computers, mobile phones and digital interactive televisions. Furthermore, the availability and increased take-up of domestic broadband services adds not only speed but also scope to the search spectrum that discerning Internet shoppers can enjoy from the comfort of their homes. It is still unclear, however, at which point in time and under what circumstances is the e-Tourism market likely to reach maturity or saturation (Goeldner *et al.* 2000).

Tourism SMEs, in common with most commercial organisations in this size category, rely considerably upon "value-chain analysis." The analysis of the relevant "chain" of activities that add value to a tourism firm's products and/or services can provide its management with valuable strategic and marketing data. Furthermore, a broader supply chain that might include suppliers, distributors and strategic partners, would necessitate supply chain management on a holistic or multi-layered basis (Matlay 2003). The rapid development of e-Commerce has intensified and added further value to supply chain management and, through on-line trading, is gradually transforming the tourism into an "electronic" or "virtual" market — often referred to as "Cyber Tourism" (Adamson & Tool 1995; Barnes & Hunt 2001). An in-depth analysis of recent developments in the e-Tourism market by Buhalis (2002) has shown that the use of ICTs by small tourism firms can provide cost effective tools with which to target and develop the most appropriate market segments. For example, relatively inexpensive combinations of mass-produced hardware and customised software could be used for inventory control as well as for strategic and tactical purposes. Similarly, Intranets and Extranets allow employees and authorised partners full access to a wide variety of relevant company, sector and industry data. Thus, strategic management of knowledge can enable small tourist firms to collect information about competencies, functions, partners, and niche markets, which could be utilised to resolve or pre-empt existing, emerging and/or contentious issues.

Traditionally, the use of IT in the tourism industry often emerged as a compromise solution arrived to by an organisation while attempting to balance the supply and demand curves relevant to its chosen strategy (Matlay 1998a). Mostly, however, small tourism firms lack the in-depth knowledge and the skills that are needed in order to accurately identify and measure existing demand (Matlay 1998b). Thus, in most cases, marketing strategies are based on perceived rather than actual supply and demand curves. In the emergent e-Tourism market, it is more often the size and the complexity of demand that drives the extent and the direction of ICT strategy. As Buhalis (2002:2) argues "... on the one hand ICTs facilitate the expansion of the industry and the enlargement of the market, and on the other the growing volume of demand require advanced ICTs for the management of tourism organisations." As the industry relies considerably upon information- and knowledge-based collaboration it is widely predicted that the dependence of small tourism firms upon developments in e-Business will increase substantially in the near future (O'Connor 1999; O'Connor & Horan 1999; WTO 2001).

Standing & Vasudavan (2001) point out that there are significant barriers to the adoption of e-Business in small tourism firms. Specifically, these appear to relate to the relatively high costs associated with the implementation and operation of Internet trading. There are, however, a number of more general difficulties associated with smaller firms, including lack of strategic planning, endemic shortages of skills and expertise, and the fact that a great proportion of smaller firms are family businesses managed by their owners (Matlay 2002b). In Standing & Vasudavan's (2001: 131) ranking of the barriers to internet adoption, the four most important factors involved start-up costs, lack of staff expertise, operating costs and the difficulty of providing adequate training. In contrast, the most important factors associated with successful implementation of e-Business in small tourism firms reflected the dedicated support of, and the dependence on, customers, top management, suppliers, consultants and employees. In sustainable competitive terms, however, small tourism firms operating in e-Europe might have limited choices in relation to e-Business implementation. Increasingly, it appears that it is mainly a question of "when" rather than "whether" small tourism firms would adopt e-Business strategies alongside or instead of their "bread and butter" business strategies (Matlay 2002a). Most industry observers agree that ICTs can offer small tourism firms considerable benefits in terms of business efficiency, product and service differentiation, cost reductions and speed of operational response. Furthermore, the proliferation of new technologies throughout the tourism industry is changing both the image of these small firms and the modes of their product and service delivery. Justifiably, Buhalis (2003: 337) concludes his seminal book by suggesting that tourism small firms "... need to understand, incorporate and utilise ICTs, in order to be able to serve their target markets, improve their efficiency, maximise profitability, enhance services and maintain long-term prosperity for both themselves and destinations."

Concluding Remarks

The widespread adoption of Intranets, Extranets and the Internet as business platforms have transformed the global economy and promoted the growth and expansion of e-Business across the world. There are a number of important reasons why e-Business is radically restructuring the European economy. First, the recent developments in the Internet and the World Wide Web have ensured that more individuals and firms become connected electronically, resulting in a dramatic change in competitive drive, from traditional trade towards e-Business. Second, the transition from traditional to e-Business is often a disruptive and highly volatile process, fuelled mainly by international competition and reasonably priced as well as readily available ICTs. Third, entrepreneurship has been identified as the main factor that determines whether a firm, industry or region will succeed in exploiting the opportunities inherent in e-Business. Fourth, official support for e-Business is evident not only at firm level, but increasingly promoted at local, regional and national levels. Finally, the rapid growth associated with e-Business is more obvious in those industries where strategic change is closely related to the drive for sustainable competitive advantage. In this context, the tourism industry in Europe is well positioned to take advantage of the ongoing advances in ICTs.

Recent research has established that the tourism industry in Europe is currently undergoing a rapid and radical change from more traditional means of trading towards an increasing volume of e-Business. The majority of business units active in this sector of the European economy are small firms and it is amongst these that the potential of e-Business is likely to have the most profound impact. The quest for sustainable competitive advantage amongst small tourism firms is driven by important demand and supply factors. On the supply side, tourism SMEs increasingly rely on innovative e-Marketing tools and use the Internet in their drive to secure sustainable competitive advantage. Conversely, on the demand side, a sophisticated, knowledgeable and demanding class of customers progressively use the Internet in their search for flexible, specialised and/or realistically priced leisure destinations. Interestingly, in the context of ongoing developments in e-Business, traditional differences between small tourism firms operating in Eastern, Central and Western Europe are gradually being eroded. However, despite the availability of reasonably priced ICTs and related hardware, much remains to be done in Eastern and Central Europe to bring up to Western European standards an industry that is still in its free market infancy. Help is increasingly available from a variety of public and private sources, including chambers of commerce, trade organisations, entrepreneurial networks and cross border trade exchanges.

In recent times, industry observers have acknowledged that ICTs offer small tourism firms considerable benefits in terms of business efficiency, product and service differentiation, cost reductions and speed of operational response. There are, however, considerable barriers that could affect the rate of e-Business adoption in small tourism firms. These include difficulties related to the perceived costs associated with the implementation and operation of e-Business as well as a lack of medium- to long-term strategic planning. Small tourism firms also suffer from endemic skill shortages and deficiencies in ICT related expertise. Importantly, however, in terms of sustainable competitive strategy, small tourism firms in e-Europe might have limited choices in relation to e-Business implementation. It emerges that it is mainly a question of "when" rather than "whether" small tourism firms would adopt e-Business strategies alongside or instead of their more traditional business strategies. It is increasingly obvious that to survive and prosper in a rapidly changing and highly volatile global economy, small tourism firms in e-Europe need to adopt and utilise

ICTs, in order to improve their efficiency, enhance their products and services and to better serve their chosen target markets.

References

Adamson, M., & Tool, D. (1995). *Multimedia in the home: The battle for the living room*. Financial Times Report, London: Telecoms and Media Publishing.

Agh, A. (1998). *The politics of central Europe*. London: Sage.

Aslund, A. (1992). *Market socialism or the restoration of capitalism?* Cambridge: Cambridge University Press.

Barnes, S., & Hunt, B. (2001). *E-Commerce and V-Business: Business models for global success*. Oxford: Butterworth-Heinemann.

Bateman, M. (Ed.) (1997). *Business cultures in central and eastern Europe*. Oxford: Butterworth-Heinemann.

Batt, J. (1991). *East central Europe from reform to transformation*. London: Pinter Publishers.

Bridge, S., O'Neill, K., & Cromie, S. (1998). *Understanding enterprise, entrepreneurship and small business*. Basingstoke: MacMillan.

Buhalis, D. (1998). Strategic use of information technologies in the tourism industry. *Tourism Management, 19*(5), 409–421.

Buhalis, D. (2002). eTourism: Strategic and tactical impacts of information communication technologies for tourism. MI-CG Online Conference [www.tourism-2002.com].

Buhalis, D. (2003). e*Tourism: Information technology for strategic tourism management*. Harlow: Pearson Education Limited.

Dertouzos, M. (1997). *What will be: How the new world of information will change our lives*. London: Piatkus Books.

Duff, A. (2002). *E-Tourism for England: Context, vision and strategy for the EnglandNet programme*. MI-CG Online Conference [www.tourism-2002.com].

Earl, M. (Ed.) (1988). *Information management: The strategic dimension*. Oxford: Clarendon Press.

ENSR (1997). *The European observatory for SMEs*. Fifth Annual Report, Zoetermeer, The Netherlands.

EC (1996). SMEs: Recommendation of the commission. *Official Journal of the European Communities, L107/6*, 1–4

EC (2000). Lisbon summit.

EC (2001). *The e-Economy in Europe: Its potential impact on EU enterprises and policies*. Report of the e-Economy Conference, Brussels (March).

EC (2002a). *Towards improved methodologies for Eurozone statistics and indicators*. Brussels, COM (2002) 661 (November).

EC (2002b). *Benchmarking national and regional e-Business policies for SMEs*. Final report of the e-Business Policy Group, Brussels (June).

GIR (1998). *The tourism industry in the new Europe*. Coventry: Global Independent Research.

GIR (2000a). *The tourism industry in the new Europe: Conceptual considerations*. Coventry: Global Independent Research.

GIR (2000b). *The tourism industry in the new Europe: Contextual considerations*. Coventry: Global Independent Research.

GIR (2002). *Understanding the tourism industry in Eastern, Central and Western Europe*. Coventry: Global Independent Research.

Goeldner, C. Ritchie, B., & McIntosh, R. (2000). *Tourism: Principles, practices and philosophies.* New York: Wiley.

Kalacota, R., & Whinstone, A. (1996). *Frontiers of electronic commerce.* Reading, MA: Addison-Wesley.

King, D., Lee, J., Warkentin, M., & Chung, H. (2002). *Electronic commerce: A managerial perspective.* New Jersey: Pearson Education International.

Litteljohn, D. (1995). Western Europe. In: P. Jones, & A. Pizam (Eds), *The international hospitality industry* (pp. 3–24). London: Pitman Publishing.

Lockwood, A. (1995). Eastern Europe and the former Soviet States. In: P. Jones, & A. Pizam (Eds), *The international hospitality industry* (pp. 25–37). London: Pitman Publishing.

Magretta, J. (1999). *Managing in the new economy.* Boston, MA: Harvard Business School Publishing.

Martin, L., & Matlay, H. (2001). "Blanket" approaches to promoting ICT in small firms: Some lessons from the DTI ladder adoption model in the U.K. *Journal of Internet Research, 11*(5), 399–410.

Martin, L., & Matlay, H. (2003). Innovative use of the Internet in established small firms: The impact of knowledge management and organisational learning in accessing new opportunities. *Qualitative Market Research, 6*(1), 18–26.

Matlay, H. (1998a). *Small and medium-sized enterprises: Tourism focus.* Report to the Welsh Tourist Board, Cardiff (February).

Matlay, H. (1998b). *Small tourism firms in Eastern, Central and Western Europe: An empirical overview.* Paper presented at the International Tourism Conference, Llandudno (May).

Matlay, H. (2000). Training in the small business sector of the British economy. In: S. Carter, & D. Jones (Eds), *Enterprise and small business: Principles, policy and practice* (pp. 323–336). Harlow: Pearson Education Limited.

Matlay, H. (2001). Entrepreneurial and vocational education and training in central and eastern Europe. *Education and Training, 43*(8/9), 395–415.

Matlay, H. (2002a). *E-this, e-that and e-the other: Towards a theory of e-everything.* Paper presented at IBM eBusiness Conference, Warwick (June).

Matlay, H. (2002b). Training and HRD strategies in family and non-family owned small businesses: A comparative approach. *Education and Training* (8/9), 357–369.

Matlay, H. (2003). *E-Babel: In search for a theory of e-everything.* Paper presented at the UCE Business School Research Seminar, Birmingham (March).

Middleton, V. (1998). *Sustainable tourism: A marketing perspective.* Oxford: Butterworth-Heinemann.

Moulton, B. (2002). GDP and the digital economy: Keeping up with the changes. In: E. Brynjolfsson, & B. Kahin (Eds), *Understanding the digital economy: Data, tools and research.* Cambridge, MA: MIT Press.

Negroponte, N. (1995). *Being digital.* London: Hodder and Stoughton.

O'Connor, G., & O'Keefe, B. (1997). Viewing the web as a marketplace: The case of small companies. *Decision Support Systems, 21,* 67–83.

O'Connor, P. (1999). *Tourism and hospitality electronic distribution and information technology.* Oxford: CAB.

O'Connor, P., & Horan, P. (1999). An analysis of web reservation facilities in the top 50 international hotel chains. *International Journal of Hospitality Information Technology, 1*(1), 77–87.

ONS (2002). *Internet access: Households and individuals.* Office for National Statistics, April [www.statistics.gov.uk].

Runge, D., & Earl, M. (1988). Getting competitive advantage from telecommunications. In: M. Earl (Ed.), *Information management: The strategic dimension.* Oxford: Clarendon Press.

Storey, D. (1994). *Understanding the small business sector.* London: Routledge.

Thomas, R. (1996). Enterprise policy. In: R. Thomas (Ed.), *The hospitality industry, tourism and Europe: Perspectives on policies* (pp. 117–134). London: Cassell.

Thomas, R. (1998). Small firms and the state. In: R. Thomas (Ed.), *The management of small tourism and hospitality firms* (pp. 78–97). London: Cassell.

Timmers, P. (2000). *Electronic commerce: Strategies and models for business-to-business trading.* Chichester: Wiley.

WTO (2001). *eBusiness for tourism: Practical guidelines for destinations and businesses.* Madrid: World Tourism Organisation.

Author Index

Subject Index